T0301354

THE ROLE OF CANADIAN CITY MANAGERS

In Their Own Words

Edited by Michael Fenn, Gordon McIntosh, and David Siegel

Local government has rapidly become both more important and more complex and the quality of municipal management is becoming more significant every day as local governments deal with a vast array of organizational and community challenges.

The Role of Canadian City Managers brings together experienced city managers and municipal chief administrative officers (CAOs) across Canada to analyse the daily issues that they face. Each chapter deals with a particular issue or challenge, such as council/staff relations, collaborative initiatives, and crisis readiness. The book contributes to the literature on local government and public administration by providing insights from the "real time" lived experiences of city managers, spoken in their own words. The book also speculates about the contemporary leadership role of the city manager and the future of the city management profession.

The Role of Canadian City Managers is a useful resource for scholars and students of local government and public administration, as well as public servants who work with or aspire to leadership roles within local government.

MICHAEL FENN has been an Ontario deputy minister, municipal CAO of Hamilton and Burlington in Ontario, and founding CEO of Toronto-area transportation and health authorities.

GORDON MCINTOSH is adjunct faculty at the University of Victoria, a sessional instructor in the School of Business at the University of British Columbia, and a sessional instructor in the School of Leadership at Royal Roads University.

DAVID SIEGEL is a professor emeritus of political science at Brock University.

The Role of Canadian City Managers

In Their Own Words

EDITED BY MICHAEL FENN,
GORDON MCINTOSH,
AND DAVID SIEGEL

UNIVERSITY OF TORONTO PRESS
Toronto Buffalo London

Toronto Buffalo London
utorontopress.com

ISBN 978-1-4875-4886-5 (cloth) ISBN 978-1-4875-5743-0 (EPUB)
ISBN 978-1-4875-5232-9 (paper) ISBN 978-1-4875-5538-2 (PDF)

Library and Archives Canada Cataloguing in Publication

Title: The role of Canadian city managers : in their own words / edited by Michael Fenn, Gordon McIntosh, and David Siegel.
Names: Fenn, Michael, editor. | McIntosh, Gordon A., 1955– editor. | Siegel, David (David Timothy), editor.
Description: Includes bibliographical references and index.
Identifiers: Canadiana (print) 20230155510 | Canadiana (ebook) 20230155561 | ISBN 9781487548865 (cloth) | ISBN 9781487552329 (paper) | ISBN 9781487555382 (PDF) | ISBN 9781487557430 (EPUB)
Subjects: LCSH: Municipal government by city manager – Canada. | LCSH: City managers – Canada. | LCSH: Municipal government – Canada.
Classification: LCC JS1710 .R65 2023 | DDC 320.8/54 – dc23

Cover design: Val Cooke
Cover image: S-BELOV/Shutterstock.com

We wish to acknowledge the land on which the University of Toronto Press operates. This land is the traditional territory of the Wendat, the Anishnaabeg, the Haudenosaunee, the Métis, and the Mississaugas of the Credit First Nation.

University of Toronto Press acknowledges the support of the Ontario Municipal Administrators' Association (OMAA) for funding in aid of this publication.

University of Toronto Press acknowledges the financial support of the Government of Canada, the Canada Council for the Arts, and the Ontario Arts Council, an agency of the Government of Ontario, for its publishing activities.

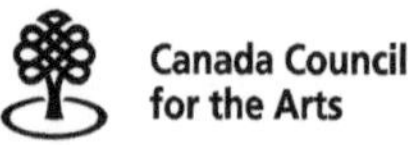

Funded by the Government of Canada
Financé par le gouvernement du Canada

Contents

Acknowledgments

A book like this is truly a cooperative effort. We had considerable support throughout the creative process, but as editors we take responsibility for any errors or omissions.

Our greatest gratitude goes to the thirty-one authors who contributed chapters to the book. They are all highly experienced experts in their fields and people of action who have learned to express themselves in as few words as possible, but we asked them to do something that was outside their comfort zone: to step back and take a long, detached view of how they did their jobs and to provide a detailed discussion of how they operated. Several of them initially demurred on the grounds that they were not capable of shifting gears in this way. Ultimately, we found them too modest. In fact, we are very pleased and indebted to them for the thoughtful analytical chapters they have produced.

In the course of developing this book, we had the wonderful experience of working with Linda Rapp, who, despite illness, crafted the distinctive chapter now titled "Nurturing the Community's Soul Source." We were all saddened by Linda's untimely passing. We believe that her imaginative and community-focused chapter is part of her legacy as a great city manager.

We were given valuable encouragement along the way. Zack Spicer, then of the Institute of Public Administration of Canada, encouraged our efforts and suggested that we approach the University of Toronto Press. Daniel Quinlan of the Press was enthusiastic and supportive from our first contact, even though this book does not fit the traditional mould of what an academic press would publish.

The Ontario Municipal Administrators' Association provided valuable financial support to the project, and Maureen McCauley of OMAA provided moral support in a variety of ways.

The three anonymous reviewers of the manuscript played a major role in the final quality of the book. We thank them for understanding the innovative aspect of this endeavour and for helping us to build on an innovative concept while developing a credible academic book.

Finally, Barry Norris, our freelance copy editor, played a valuable role in polishing our manuscript into a clear and highly readable book.

With the cooperation of this broad group of people, we feel we have produced a volume that will be a valuable source of information for both current and aspiring city managers and possibly even for the elected officials and other community members who work with these important civic leaders.

Michael Fenn
Gordon McIntosh
David Siegel
October 2022

THE ROLE OF CANADIAN CITY MANAGERS

Introduction

The quality of municipal management is becoming more important every day as local governments deal with a vast array of organizational and community challenges. This does not seem like a radical statement, but municipal management has not attracted a great deal of attention. Local government traditionally has been seen as the "nuts and bolts" level of government: it's about pipes and roads, and how difficult can it be to manage that?

The truth is that local government has rapidly become both more important and more complex. Elected officials and managers are the front-line place shapers. Both directly and through those they regulate, municipal governments determine the environment in which we live our daily lives and on which our local economies rely. They are at the grass roots of dealing with important and complex issues such as climate change and poverty reduction. The days of "nuts and bolts" management have been replaced by strategic leadership. Municipal managers are now responsible for managing thousands of employees and billions of dollars worth of assets to provide essential services while responding to emerging community needs.

Unfortunately, the serious study of municipal management has lagged the real world. This book aims to help close that knowledge gap in a unique way. In twenty-three chapters written by experienced city managers (and municipal chief administrative officers, or CAOs), we analyse the daily issues they face. In the concluding chapter, the book's editors pull these individual contributions together to speculate about the contemporary leadership role of the city manager and the future of the city management profession. As the challenges facing our communities grow, the search for solutions can lead to impatience with the capacity of executive leadership in the face of often cautious and parochial municipal councils. The lure of US-style "strong mayor" solutions is appearing in some parts of Canada, potentially eroding the role of the non-political, general management professional – the chief administrative officer – which Ontario Associate Chief Justice Frank Marrocco has called a "key pillar in the structure of the municipality."

This book is directed at two audiences. One audience is current and aspiring city managers and other senior municipal managers who value the experience-informed advice of respected peers in guiding their careers. The other audience is academic – both scholars and students – and other interested observers of the municipal scene. This audience will get a seldom-seen insight into how senior municipal managers make decisions and carry out their day-to-day responsibilities, and how their "fishbowl" environment influences those decisions.

There are other books by academics or commentators telling city managers what they should do (Nalbandian, 1991; Plunkett, 1992; Siegel, 2015; Svara, 2003; Tindal & Tindal, 2019). There are autobiographical or biographical books by or about individual city managers that recount the person's accomplishments and provide some lessons to others (Diehl, 2016; Gilbert, 1978; Harlow, 1977; Ridge, 2020). Other efforts attempt to explore the adaptive leadership imperatives of contemporary city managers to real-time situations (Fenn & Siegel, 2017; McIntosh, 2009). To our knowledge, however, this is the first book that deals with current municipal management issues by focusing on the lived experiences of practising managers.

During Canada's often difficult re-examination of its relationship with Indigenous peoples, one of the positive dividends has been a better appreciation of the value of the wisdom of those with mature experience, such as Elders. We have also learned the role that "story telling" can play in helping us understand our world and how to deal with challenges. It provides the kind of narrative that Sandford Borins is writing about when he says that it provides "a distinctive means of ordering experience; a particular mode of perceiving, representing, and communicating events; a way of structuring meaning in time" (Borins, 2011, p. xi). This book aims to benefit from that lived experience and reflections on it.

This is not the usual how-to book on management. There are already many books on how to do financial management, or human resource management, or strategic planning. Aspiring and active city managers should read those books because they need to be familiar with those foundational aspects of their job. Rather, this book speaks directly to decision-making and management issues that city managers face, and the authors draw on their personal experience to discuss how they have handled those issues.

The terms city manager and chief administrative officer – in French, directeur(trice)-général(e) – are commonly used in Canada to refer to the general manager of the municipal corporation: the most senior appointed official who manages all other municipal staff. In practice, there seems to be no difference in the duties assigned to the people bearing these different titles – in this book, authors use the titles interchangeably. As editors, we have come to believe that a title such as "city manager" or "town manager" does a better job of conveying the nature, importance, and expectations of the position to communities and their elected officials. Intuitively, being a manager seems to carry more weight than being an administrative officer. "City manager" also aligns with the term in use in the United States for over one hundred years. However, the titles CAO and city manager are both still widely used in Canada, so we follow that convention in this book.

We were fortunate to be able to attract a very strong group of contributors. We began by choosing the topics we wanted to cover, then we brainstormed to identify ideal candidates throughout Canada to contribute on each of the topics. We wanted someone who had a rich experience of dealing with the topic and who could write the kind of chapter we wanted. To ensure a balance of perspectives on debated subjects, we often sought two chapters on an individual topic. In seeking authors, we aimed for a balanced roster of women and men from small towns and large cities and from all the regions of Canada.

We were aware that we were asking quite a bit of these people. Like busy, successful people everywhere, they often feel they don't have much time to reflect or to share what they have learned along the way – the occasional conference presentation or Rotary Club speech has to suffice. Likewise, when committing their insights to "paper," municipal professionals rarely stray beyond the relentless cycle of writing and editing reports to council.

We asked contributors to be candid and to provide examples of the successes and failures they have experienced. They went some distance in providing that kind of information, but for those working in a political arena where job security is a realistic concern, there might be practical limits to what they may say publicly on some subjects. Sometimes the reader might need to read between the lines.

Some had undergraduate memories that caused them to recoil at meeting the standards of academic writing, and some simply doubted their experience and perspectives would be of interest to a broad audience. It speaks well of the professional pride of these people that virtually everyone we asked gamely agreed to contribute. In the chapters that follow, the great results speak for themselves "in their own words." We are confident that their unique contributions will be welcomed by municipal professionals and local government observers and scholars across Canada.

This is not a typical academic book that begins by being grounded in a theory and then develops that theory in orderly steps through successive chapters. We wanted to produce a book that reflected the real-time lived experiences of highly respected practitioners, along with some references to academic literature. But this is not meant to be an academic tome: in the words of one anonymous reviewer, it should be seen more as providing "valuable 'primary source materials' than as a set of discrete works of academic research." Given the current state of the field, we feel that this practical focus will provide more value and perhaps be an agenda for further, relevant scholarship.

Each of the twenty-three chapters is self-standing; they do not build on one another and can be read in any order. The book can be treated as a reference book to be pulled off the shelf as needed to see what experts have to say about emergency management or working with other governments. To assist the reader, table 0.1 identifies the major topics covered in the chapters. Each chapter also begins with a short introduction by the editors to the author(s) and the topic of the chapter.

Table 0.1 Topics Covered in Chapters

Topic	Relevant Chapters
Career management	*1* – City Management: More than a Job *4* – Using Your First 100 Days Strategically *21* – From Dreams of Being a Rock-and-Roll Drummer to City Manager *22* – A City Manager's Career Journey
Community development	*19* – Nurturing the Community's Soul Source *20* – Community Development: Navigating the Rocky Shoals of Community Change
Council-staff relations	*2* – Aspirational Incrementalism: Developing a Vision *3* – Building Support for Strategic Planning and Priorities *5* – The Challenge of Leading Up: Strategic Alignment with Council *6* – Council-Staff Relations: Forward Motion or Spinning Wheels? *7* – The Most Important Relationship in Local Government: Mayor and City Manager *8* – City Manager and Mayor: Independent or Partners?
Crisis management	*16* – More than Resilience: Towards an "Antifragile" Organization – The Case of Gatineau *17* – Managing during a Crisis: Lessons from Fort McMurray
Dealing with community organizations	*2* – Aspirational Incrementalism: Developing a Vision *3* – Building Support for Strategic Planning and Priorities *11* – Indigenous and Municipal Relationships: The Art of Collaboration *18* – Building Partnerships: Hard Work, Patience, Commitment, Adaptation, and Opportunities *19* – Nurturing the Community's Soul Source *20* – Community Development: Navigating the Rocky Shoals of Community Change

Topic	Relevant Chapters
Dealing with Indigenous communities	*10* – Diversity from Bottom to Top: The City Manager and Workforce Diversity *11* – Indigenous and Municipal Relationships: The Art of Collaboration *19* – Nurturing the Community's Soul Source
Dealing with other governments	*14* – Five Strategies for Successful Municipal Intergovernmental Relations *15* – Leading Beyond: Building Relationships for Intergovernmental Collaboration
Diversity and inclusion	*9* – What Does Diversity-Inclusion Look Like in Action? *10* – Diversity from Bottom to Top: The City Manager and Workforce Diversity *11* – Indigenous and Municipal Relationships: The Art of Collaboration
Partnerships	*10* – Diversity from Bottom to Top: The City Manager and Workforce Diversity *11* – Indigenous and Municipal Relationships: The Art of Collaboration *18* – Building Partnerships: Hard Work, Patience, Commitment, Adaptation, and Opportunities *19* – Nurturing the Community's Soul Source
Personal mastery and mentoring	*21* – From Dreams of Being a Rock-and-Roll Drummer to City Manager *22* – A City Manager's Career Journey *23* – Mentoring: Building the Next Generation of Municipal Professionals
Profession of city management	*1* – City Management: More than a Job *21* – From Dreams of Being a Rock-and-Roll Drummer to City Manager *22* – A City Manager's Career Journey
Strategic directions	*2* – Aspirational Incrementalism: Developing a Vision *3* – Building Support for Strategic Planning and Priorities *4* – Using Your First 100 Days Strategically *20* – Community Development: Navigating the Rocky Shoals of Community Change
Team building	*9* – What Does Diversity-Inclusion Look Like in Action? *10* – Diversity from Bottom to Top: The City Manager and Workforce Diversity *11* – Indigenous and Municipal Relationships: The Art of Collaboration *12* – The Gift of Clarity and the Freedom to Innovate *13* – Rowers, Coasters, and Drillers: How Team Building Can Improve Your Crew

Of course, this list entails an element of "rough justice," as many chapters look at a variety of issues or have differing "takes" on both perennial and contemporary issues. We hope you will find this tour of the municipal management world an enlightening journey.

REFERENCES

Borins, S. (2011). *Governing fables*. Information Age Publishing.

Diehl, R. (2016). *Serving with pride in the public eye*. Friesen Press.

Fenn, M., & Siegel, D. (2017). *The evolving role of city managers and chief administrative officers*. Institute on Municipal Finance and Governance, University of Toronto.

Gilbert, B. (1978). *This city, this man: The Cookingham era in Kansas City*. International City/County Management Association.

Harlow, L. F. (1977). *Without fear or favor: Odyssey of a city manager*. Brigham Young University Press.

McIntosh, G. (2009). *Defining situational leadership for the local government CAO*. University of Victoria.

Nalbandian, J. (1991). *Professionalism in local government: Transformations in the roles, responsibilities, and values of city managers*. Jossey-Bass Publishers.

Plunkett, T. J. (1992). *City management in Canada: The role of the chief administrative officer*. Toronto: Institute of Public Administration of Canada.

Ridge, T. (2020). *Welcome to the hall: A practical guide for municipal leaders*. Municipal World.

Siegel, D. (2015). *Leaders in the shadows: The leadership qualities of municipal chief administrative officers*. University of Toronto Press.

Svara, J. H. (2003). *Dichotomy and duality: The relationship between policy and administration in council-manager cities*. M.E. Sharpe.

Tindal, C. R., & Tindal, S. N. (2019). *Guide to good municipal governance* (2nd ed.). Municipal World.

1 City Management: More than a Job

JANICE BAKER

Now CAO of the fast-growing Regional Municipality of Peel, west of Toronto, for much of her career Janice Baker was city manager of Mississauga, Canada's sixth-largest city, working with the long-serving and formidable Mayor Hazel McCallion. A recent Vanier Award winner for leadership in city management in Canada, Baker also draws on her experience as a professional accountant and with the Canadian Association of Municipal Administrators (CAMA). Using scholarship and practical experience, Baker discusses what it means to be a professional in a field without the bulwark of being a regulated profession; she then challenges city managers to embrace professionalism in its various aspects.

The purpose of this chapter is to assess the current status of the city management profession in Canada and to identify the challenges and opportunities that lie ahead for the profession.

There have been long-standing debates and discussions about the status and role of city/town manager or chief administrative officer (CAO) – the terms are often used interchangeably:

- whether councils should be obligated to have such a position;
- whether it should be created by statute and given clear roles and responsibilities; and,
- most critically, whether it should have statutory independence from the role of elected officials.

A number of municipal associations have advocated for legislated status and protection for the position. Some provinces have taken steps in this direction, but it is inconsistent across the country. In Ontario, for example, while positions such as clerk, chief building official, fire chief, and medical officer of health are statutory in nature and have obligations and protections under statute, the city manager/CAO position does not have the same status in the Municipal Act. The debate has recently been brought to the forefront again by the Collingwood Judicial Inquiry report issued in November 2020. In the report, titled *Transparency and the Public Trust*, Ontario Associate Chief Justice Frank N. Marrocco states: "The CAO is a full-time position that comes with significant responsibility. Someone with the education and experience required to maintain a culture of integrity and to provide the best information and advice to Council should always fill the CAO role. The CAO must operate independently, advising Council and carrying out Council's direction while remaining unaffected by political influence" (Marrocco, 2020, p. 36). He goes on to make recommendations, among which are: "The Province of Ontario should amend section 229 of the Municipal Act to mandate that municipalities the size of the Town of Collingwood appoint a chief administrative officer" and "The Province of Ontario should amend the Municipal Act to describe fully the role and responsibilities of the chief administrative officer."

Why is there hesitation to take this step for the CAO role? One reason might be that the public is unfamiliar with the role. I was often asked: "What does a city manager do?" I usually answered by drawing an analogy to the private sector equivalent – i.e., "I am like the CEO of a company, and council is the board of directors."

Even the title is somewhat confusing to the public. In most communities, the mayor, as the head of council and the spokesperson for the organization, is well known, and the perception is that the mayor "runs" the city. Residents and businesses occasionally will contact their local councillor, usually if they have a problem, but they might not even know who the city manager is or the critical role the city manager plays in building their community, delivering services, and providing good governance.

Another reason might be that no clear academic or professional credential defines a city manager. City managers come from a wide range of recognized professions, backgrounds, experiences, and sectors, many of which are themselves regulated and have professional codes of conduct (e.g., lawyers, engineers, accountants). The notion of the city manager position being a profession in and of itself has been a hard one to cement in people's minds, since job advertisements for the role almost always require many years of experience but can vary widely on academic or professional credentials. In Ontario, several post-secondary institutions have tried to develop a Master of Public Administration program rooted in local government, but have struggled to make this a job requirement when hiring a CAO. There have been discussions by provincial and national associations about some form of accreditation, and in the United States the International City/County Management Association has a credentialing program, but it is voluntary. The reality is that most city managers are judged only by their council and ultimately are accountable only to their council, which sets the bar for what is acceptable. Most councils want to define their city manager's competencies and performance indicators for themselves, and would feel free to ignore relatively toothless recommendations from an outsider. This is why the recommendations from Justice Marrocco's inquiry resonated with those doing this challenging job in Ontario.

In my experience, city managers are viewed as the chief problem solver by the council they serve. On the most practical level, councils want their city manager to prevent problems from emerging that will be difficult for the council to deal with and to make problems that have emerged go away. Because the type and nature of problems can vary greatly, the role requires a bit of a "Jack of all trades" approach with heavy reliance on the technical experts on your team and their experience. Once you sit in the seat, you are no longer the required expert on whatever your chosen "profession" might have been. In my case, even though I was a Chartered Professional Accountant, council went to our finance director when it wanted financial advice, which is as it should be, but when things were going badly on an issue in any part of the community or organization, councillors came to me.

I believe that much of the desire for a statutory framework for the role is rooted in attempts to answer the question: "How do we protect people from being unfairly terminated?" I have been told (anecdotally) that the average tenure of a CAO is five to seven years. I seem to be an exception to that rule, having served as city manager in Mississauga, Ontario, for fifteen years. A neighbouring municipality, in contrast, went through five appointed and four acting CAOs during the same time. All the appointments but one were from outside the organization. City manager positions turn over, sometimes frequently and often involuntarily. In other words, many of us get fired. I think this might also compromise the perception of city manager as a profession: if it is a profession, why are so many members told to "move on," especially after an election?

There is currently no widely recognized and accepted national designation or degree associated with being a city manager. If those in the job have been unable to make it a profession by way of credentialing, what do they need to do to show the professionalism of their work? Most critically, how do we groom and attract the top-notch talent required to carry on this important work? Growing the next generation of leaders in the sector is work that must be shared among academic institutions, national and provincial local government associations, and successful individuals in the role who have figured it out. But it also requires the input and engagement of elected officials. Their perspective and the processes and criteria they use to fill the top job are material factors in shaping perceptions of the role.

The debate seems to come down to whether the role rises to the level of a profession in its own right or is simply an important job usually done by professionals. If the latter is the case, how do we advance the idea of its being a profession? Over a hundred years ago, Abraham Flexner provided a definition of a profession that is still widely used today: "[P]rofessions involve essentially intellectual operations with large individual responsibility; they derive their raw material from science and learning; this material they work up to a practical and definite end; they possess an educationally communicable technique; they tend to self-organization; they are becoming increasingly altruistic in motivation" (Flexner, [1915] 2001, p. 156). City managers certainly meet these criteria. The scale of their responsibility is both organization-wide and community-wide. Advice and recommendations to council must be grounded in research. Decisions must be translated into action, and communicated to staff and the public. In general, most who work in the profession enjoy the sense of building something greater than themselves: a community. So, while I think we can easily tick the boxes of Flexner's definition, it might be worth digging deeper into the analysis, using Flexner's "headings."

"[I]ntellectual operations with large individual responsibility"

The scale, scope, and complexity of municipal operations are significant. Municipalities deliver a wide range of services, and the competencies needed to operate in such a complex environment are broad. In Mississauga, for example, our competencies include requirements to be strategic, to develop culture and people, to demonstrate business acumen, and to drive innovative change.

One of the critical roles of the city manager is to build corporate culture. The statement "culture eats strategy for breakfast" – a phrase originated by Peter Drucker and made famous by Ford president Mark Fields – is true. Building culture within the organization must be led by the city manager, who must "walk the talk" without exception. The best piece of advice I ever received was, "Janice, you cast a long shadow." I needed to understand as a leader that what I did and said would be always under scrutiny. Inconsistencies between words and actions, putting my interest ahead of those of the corporation and the team, or taking privileges for myself that were not available to others would be a sure-fire way to lose the trust of the team

The city manager's job is to build a workforce that can produce the desired results, and to do that you need robust leadership skills at every leadership level. You must be able to rely on your whole team. They need to know what you expect and what the goals are. Having great leaders is critical for staff retention, and I made it a priority for us to learn and practice those skills together. Our flagship event was an annual Leadership Conference comprised of two days of learning based on a theme. Themes were selected from leadership attributes and competencies where we needed to build muscle. This was all about ensuring managers knew and understood their role in shaping culture and driving employee engagement and productivity. While city managers can come from a variety of different disciplines, all must have a certain skill set that is passed along through both the corporate culture and professional development.

"[T]hey derive their raw material from science and learning;
this material they work up to a practical and definite end"

Operationalizing strategy is one of the most critical roles of a city manager. In the end, you are judged on what you deliver. "Intellectual operations" and "science and learning" come together to deliver services. Beyond that, there are many strategic, policy and resource decisions that the CAO must understand and be able to defend at a council meeting. As the leader of a staff made up of technical experts in many disciplines, the city manager plays a lead role in setting priorities for the organization and for meeting the expectations of council and the public. Translating the technical into recommendations and decisions that are easy to understand and receive the support of elected officials is the very essence of a practical and definite end.

"[T]hey possess an educationally communicable technique"

The engagement and development of staff is a critical success factor for municipalities. In most organizations, labour costs are the highest expenditure, so if you are not creating an environment where people can succeed and be productive, you are failing your team. Unfortunately, in the municipal sector, we do not do succession and succession planning well. For some it is simply a matter of numbers. Very small communities have small teams, which makes succession planning challenging. In medium-to-large settings, however, not having a succession plan can force council to look outside for talent because it has not had a conversation about the internal talent pool.

Often, councils are not engaged in the discussion of who comes next and what kind of bench strength exists at the second-in-command level. Municipalities that do not have a robust succession plan in place for their senior team are missing an opportunity, not only to make their organization a great place to work where people can advance their careers, but also to promote continuity, stability, and consistent values in leadership. This also creates an opportunity to reflect on the diversity of the workforce, especially at the leadership level.

Mississauga is a community built on immigration throughout its history. Its demographics show the city is truly a quilt, with no one community dominating, and in my opinion stands as a very successful example of Canadian multiculturalism. As would be expected, the corporation's workforce is routinely scrutinized and compared to the community's demographics. Gender diversity is an area where we were successful: during my tenure, around 50 per cent of our positions at director level and above were occupied by women. Despite having a robust succession planning program, however, we were less successful in other aspects of diversity, with only a small number of our leaders coming from the BIPOC community. During the last years of my tenure, we were actively implementing a diversity and inclusion strategy that was still a work in process when I left.

In the Regional Municipality of Peel, we have placed a strong emphasis on creating an inclusive workplace and community, starting with a workforce census and a series of courageous conversations to understand the lived experiences of our employees. There is an ongoing need for strong leadership in this area from current and future city managers.

How do you set the context for these succession planning discussions with council? First, it needs to be made clear that having these discussions is not about giving up your authority to hire and fire or manage the team – which is clearly the role of the city manager. It is a dialogue to understand what needs to be done to get those with potential ready, in the eyes of council, to compete for the top job. Education of council members and dialogue with them about issues of governance are a priority and the responsibility of the city manager. These should be formal discussions and part of an *in camera* council agenda. The need for confidentiality should be stressed at every session. The sessions need to be done in a serious and mature way that engages council in discussion of expectations, deliverables, strategy, performance of self and others, and conversations about values, integrity, roles, and responsibilities.

I did this annually with council. I started out having one-on-one discussions, but learned it was better to have those discussions as a group. This weeded out the pet peeves of individual councillors, and built more of a consensus view of the corporation's talent. I held the discussions during the *in camera* portion of a council meeting, which gave the discussions some official weight. It is important to have the support of the mayor and a shared understanding of goals. In my experience, sessions like these are best facilitated with specific questions. If it is helpful, a third party can be brought in who is experienced in this process. Just asking "give me feedback" often leads to a laundry list of local issues and problems, or a rehash of old grievances that sets a negative tone. Leadership of a session like this is critical. Councillors should do most of the talking, but they need to be talking about the right things.

I always wrapped this discussion around my own annual performance appraisal. These reviews are daunting, but they are an opportunity to have a heart-to-heart discussion with council about how things are going and to hear their opinions first-hand. Using a model like the *CAMA Performance Evaluation Toolkit* (CAMA, n.d.a), I scheduled two *in camera* sessions. The first was to talk about the performance of the individual commissioners on our leadership team and the state of our succession plan. The second was to review my own performance against an annual agreement approved by council. By including not just deliverables but also competencies, including values-based competencies, issues can be aired and, if not resolved, at least better understood.

It is important to engage councillors so they can learn and understand their role in the succession planning process. Council and the mayor were invited to conference sessions. We did panels featuring the mayor talking about what was important to council and expressing appreciation to the team. I was fortunate to have had two mayors who understood and supported this kind of investment and who appreciated the role and value of the professionals who worked hard every day to deliver. This was all done with a goal of keeping council involved and knowledgeable.

At the same time, it is important to make it clear that this is your turf and they are being invited in. These are also opportunities to show staff the politics that can influence decision making so they are better prepared to work in that zone. And when staff question decisions, it gives you a context to explain decisions and the factors, including any political factors, that entered into the decision-making process. These are opportunities to hone political acumen across the corporation.

Having these discussions in the open and not in the back room drives a better understanding of roles and responsibilities and allows for conversations about where the lines are at a time of calm, rather than trying to draw them in times of crisis. Communication with council is key and critical, and if council is briefed on culture and what you are trying to create, it is far more likely to support and champion what you are doing, and might even help you do it. In summary, the current generation of professionals has an obligation to develop the next generation, which it does through professional development and supporting their professional associations.

"[T]hey tend to self-organization; they are becoming increasingly altruistic in motivation"

Professional associations define the profession, transmit knowledge and professional values from one generation to the next, and have codes of ethics that hold the individual professional accountable.

Fully developed professions, like accounting, law, or medicine, are self-regulating in that current members of the profession define the body of knowledge and experience needed for admission to the profession. There are also standards of practice and codes of conduct that practising professionals must meet. And if they do not meet those standards and comply with those codes, they can be disciplined by the professional association, including being barred from practising the profession.

The city management profession does not go as far as other professions in these aspects of self-regulation and perhaps never will, which could be a good thing. It has no ability to screen new entrants – city councils hire whom they want as city managers. While professional associations have codes of conduct, there is some question about whether they are enforceable. And even if they are enforceable, a professional association cannot prevent someone from being appointed as a city manager or continuing in that role if found guilty of some serious misconduct.

City managers come from a variety of different backgrounds that serve the needs of their municipalities. Many are members of a recognized profession such as accounting or engineering. A municipality might need someone with a particular background to meet its current needs, even if the person does not fit the usual mould of a city manager.

There might be a time when professional associations can put some sort of stamp of approval on a person who aspires to become a city manager, which might have an impact on how a municipality views the applicant for the manager's job. Professional associations could discipline or expel members for violation of the code of conduct, which would also send a valuable signal to municipalities.

I sat on the boards of both the Canadian Association of Municipal Administrators (CAMA) and the Ontario Municipal Administrators' Association (OMAA). There was often dialogue around the table on the state of the job of city manager and those who serve in it. Provincial and national municipal associations understand that responsibility, and they deliver programs and services to support those of us in the role. There is nothing more valuable than a network in the local government sector, and conferences and other gatherings of colleagues can help build a robust one. These associations have resources, learning opportunities, conferences, and codes of conduct. CAMA has developed toolkits such as *Performance Evaluation*, and *Political Acumen* (CAMA, n.d.a) that have been designed by experts specifically for those in the role, with input from those who practise it.

We are also joined by the common issues, challenges, and opportunities that we all face. In my experience, whenever I faced a difficult issue, there was always someone I could call on who had dealt with it before. Having a network meant that help was a phone call away. That network was fostered by joining and being active in the associations. Sharing knowledge, plans, and advice is a way of life in the sector. These are the altruistic actions that knit together the professionals who do the job, and that is the true spirit that defines the profession of city manager.

The real challenge and calling of the role, however, is maintaining the highest ethical standards. This is where the true test of altruism needs to be met. Earlier I referenced the city manager as the chief problem solver. Quite often, these problems can turn into conflicts – a disagreement with approved policy, a criticism of a decision from a key constituency, or a mistake made by staff. Whatever the root cause, problem solving in this scenario will sorely test your leadership skills. Honesty is always the best policy in this job, but to navigate what can sometimes be choppy waters brutal honesty might be needed. In times of difficulty, you often must tell people things they do not want to hear. Then it is good to remember that you work for all of council, not for individual councillors (I put those words right in my performance agreement). If I faced an issue where it was unclear that I had the authority to act, I took it back to council, the elected body with the ultimate authority to decide.

Of course, not every hill is one to die on. You have to pick the battles that matter. Judgment is a job requirement and good judgment an invaluable asset. You must work in the uncomfortable zone, sometimes with a camera on you.

Do you have to be prepared to lose the job to do it well in tough times? I always said yes to this question. Your ethics and integrity can be sorely tested, but they should never be compromised. I thought about walking away a couple of times when things were really tough with a council. Fortunately for me, I also learned that the adage "this too shall pass" is also true after those issues resolved themselves through elections.

Conclusion

How does this all tie back to the discussion we started with: is the job of city manager a profession? I hope I have made a convincing argument that it meets the test, at least as defined by Flexner. But it is the final standard, altruism, that speaks to the ethical challenges that must be navigated that is the most critical. The job exists in a political environment and context. It is a public role, but those who do it are not always well known to the public they serve. How the city manager position is perceived is more heavily affected by the conduct, performance, and outputs of those who practise it than it will ever be by factors such as credentials. There is a knowledge gap between the professional and those the profession serves, and without an ethical standard of service, those we serve could be exploited. Each of us is a standard bearer, and the standard we must meet is and should be high. As professionals, we have a service-oriented obligation to the broader society.

The public needs to have confidence and trust in the people they elect, as well as in the independent bureaucracy that supports and advises elected officials. In most of Canada, that municipal bureaucracy is headed by a person with the title of city manager or chief administrative officer. Everyone who becomes a city manager has a responsibility to build and keep that trust and confidence. We must take that responsibility seriously. That is the key element of the profession that makes it more than just a job.

REFERENCES

CAMA (Canadian Association of Municipal Administrators). (n.d.a). *CAO performance evaluation toolkit*. Retrieved from http://www.camacam.ca/about/resources/cao-performance

CAMA. (n.d.b). *Political acumentoolkit*. Retrieved from http://www.camacam.ca/about/resources/political-acumen-toolkit

Flexner, A. ([1915] 2001). Is social work a profession? *Research on Social Work Practice*, 11(2), 152–65. Retrieved from https://pgdsw.files.wordpress.com/2010/07/is-social-work-a-profession-a-flexner.pdf

Marrocco, F. A. (2020, 2 November). *Transparency and the public trust: Report of the Collingwood Judicial Inquiry*. Retrieved from http://www.collingwoodinquiry.ca/report/index.html

2 Aspirational Incrementalism: Developing a Vision

BRUCE MACGREGOR AND DAVID SZWARC

Municipalities are functionally and operationally very diverse and fragmented organizations. How do you go about unifying an organization and instilling a vision that allows you to rise above incrementalism and to focus on the big issues? In this chapter, Bruce Macgregor and David Szwarc coin the phrase "aspirational incrementalism" to explain how they dealt with the inevitable pull towards incrementalism, while still moving their organizations in the direction of their vision. They have had similar careers as chief administrative officers (CAOs) of very large regional municipalities in the Greater Toronto Area – Macgregor in York Region, north of Toronto, and Szwarc in Peel Region, west of Toronto. As CAOs of two of the largest municipal governments in Canada, they had to confront the inevitable "centrifugal forces" in any large and multifaceted municipal organization and figure out how to implement a vision that moved the organization forward.

Introduction

The authors of this chapter are both veteran CAOs, serving regional municipalities in the Greater Toronto Area. David Szwarc served as Peel Region's CAO for fifteen years and Bruce Macgregor is in his fifteenth year as York Region's CAO. The two municipalities abut the City of Toronto and each has a population over one million. Both CAOs come from operational roles in the municipal sector, David from social services in two regional municipalities and the provincial government, and Bruce from public works, where he served senior roles at the regional and local municipal levels.

One major challenge that both of us have faced as municipal CAOs has been developing for council approval a vision and a strategic plan for the municipality. This is a challenging exercise in any organization, but particularly so for a municipality, because municipalities are responsible for delivering a diverse range of services through a traditionally fragmented or "composite" organization. In this chapter, we coin the term "aspirational incrementalism" to describe a means for setting an inspired direction for local government decision making that is successful when applied incrementally. Throughout the chapter, we draw upon examples from our combined thirty years of experience as municipal CAOs to illustrate this approach to municipal administrative leadership.

In the first section, we describe the fragmentation of local governance and the implications for managing the organization. The second section describes two approaches to managing: composite and strategic management. The final section analyses how aspirational incrementalism allowed us as CAOs to work with council and the community to balance the aspirational desires of the community with its willingness to (and tolerance for) change.

The Composite Municipal Organization

Municipalities in Canada are composite organizations, traditionally fragmented because of the broad mix of service responsibilities and the equally broad mix of service delivery arrangements. The composite structure is furthered through the political process for electing the municipal council members who provide governance.

The fragmented structure begins with the status of municipalities as "creatures of the province," a reference to the fact that the Canadian Constitution gives the provinces exclusive control over creating and setting out responsibilities of municipalities. Local governments can only exercise powers that have been delegated to them by their provincial governments, and this delegation frequently comes with significant conditions. This is even more apparent in Ontario, where municipalities deliver services, such as public health and social services, otherwise provided by provinces elsewhere in Canada; these services are delegated to municipalities under tightly defined and partially funded mandates.

Traditionally, municipal services are often clustered in departments that align with provincial legislation that governs those services, such as water, waste management, human services, housing, roads, public health, and land-use planning. This influence over organizational structure reinforces a composite structure that can align departments with external factors rather than broader community objectives.

Unlike many businesses in the private sector, where employees are encouraged to gain experience across the corporation before rising to the executive ranks, the composite nature of municipal responsibilities rarely affords that opportunity to its aspiring leaders during their career development. Traditionally, leaders in municipal departments have extensive experience in the services delivered by that department and are expected by their councils to be experts in their particular field.

Fragmentation of the composite structure can be exacerbated by the electoral system. In most municipalities, candidates run for office based on individually formed mandates, not on an overt affiliation with a political party. Most Canadian municipal governments are "non-partisan" or without local political party representation. When a non-partisan municipal council is formed after an election, it rarely comes into office with a predetermined, agreed-upon policy agenda that is shared by all or even a majority of members of council. Over time, decision making can be further complicated, as the composition and tenor of council can change substantially every few years. A newly formed or reconstituted council might not have a mutually agreed reference upon which to base policy, program, or financial decisions. Leaders in federal and provincial governments are accustomed to party discipline, so they can become confused when they see coalitions shift in local governments on different issues. They are also surprised when a local government supports one decision made by a government, but opposes the next decision.

Osborne and Gaebler (1993) note that politicians are bombarded with problems an individual or interest group wants solved on a relatively short-term basis and, by their choices in the allocation of resources, identify priorities. Savoie (2015, p. 113) recognizes that, "ultimately politicians have to arbitrate between sectional interests." In balancing the priorities of council, an effective administration should be mindful of the need for programs and services to evolve in response to the changing needs of the municipalities' residents and businesses.

The natural orientation towards a composite organization can present challenges to managing local government. One CAO likened his role to the head of a holding company with diverse lines of business (Siegel, 2015). Even that understates the problem because the municipal CAO must work with a council, which seldom speaks with one voice, to coordinate the activities of municipally funded organizations such as transit authorities, a police service board, utilities, and irrigation districts. These quasi-external influences that are not directly within the municipality's organizational structure nevertheless can impose a burden on limited financial resources.

York Region, for example, manages a 600-bus transit fleet – one of eight in the Greater Toronto Area. In 2017, the Region created a smartphone pay app – one of the first in the country. The app was a cost-effective solution to the desires of transit patrons with one very significant limitation: although riders immediately embraced the app with trips beginning and ending in York Region communities, approximately 65 per cent of transit riders also used Toronto Transit Commission and provincial (GO/Metrolinx) transit systems for their daily commute. Those transit users had to rely on the more dated PRESTO card – an obligatory provincial fare-payment system that costs the Region's transit system more to maintain.

Composite organizational structures also tend to favour ad hoc decision making, focusing on service- or sector-specific objectives. This structure relies on the CAO to serve as a referee, mediating areas where departmental or service objectives are in conflict or could be better aligned. In this circumstance, it can be challenging for the CAO to create a cohesive public service with a shared organizational culture

The composite approach to service delivery and decision making discussed above was also evident in Peel Region. The regional municipality had a well-established and successful municipal housing department that provided affordable rental housing through various forms of subsidies. Council encouraged its ability to operate like a private sector landlord, with short vacancy periods and very low rental arrears rates. The municipality also had a well-respected social services department that, among other responsibilities, operated homeless shelters for people who were temporarily without a home. It was not unusual, when the housing department evicted tenants who had developed rent arrears or other tenancy-related issues, to refer them to the social services department for shelter or income assistance upon eviction. The monthly cost to the municipality for providing rent subsidy through the housing department was considerably less than the cost of providing a bed in a homeless shelter through the social services department. Each department, however, focused on its own mandate and budget requirements and operated in relative silos to resolve a community challenge they actually held in common.

Two Alternative Management Models

Although not specifically set out in statute, the CAO's role could be described succinctly as striving to establish and maintain an organizational culture of engagement, purposefully driven and inspired to deliver vital community services. The traditional inclination towards separate and distinct programs, often reinforced by political perspectives, gives CAOs a choice between two options in carrying out their role.

Managing the Composite Organization

One option is to manage sectors individually, focusing on issues related to each service as they arise, and each is managed through a council direction that is often similarly focused. Peel's experience with the housing situation is a simple example of this. This approach involves the development of service plans for individual programs, informed by both internal and external resources that anticipate the environment in which the services are to be delivered, including aspects such as demand, funding, legislation, and community acceptance. Council then approves these service plans either directly or implicitly through its budget priority decisions.

In this manage-the-sectors-separately model, senior service managers and the CAO come together to resolve common management issues, including annual municipal budgets and issues related to any shared services in the municipality. This approach to managing municipal services treats each service as a discrete entity, sometimes with a contingent of its own internal support services such as human resources, information technology, and accounting processes, akin to the holding company example previously cited.

Charles Lindblom, in his seminal article "The Science of 'Muddling Through'" (Lindblom, 1959), argued that most decisions are made on the basis of what he called successive limited comparisons or incrementalism. Decision-making processes begin with some dissatisfaction with the status quo and seek an alternative that will improve, not necessarily optimize, the status quo. Herbert Simon referred to this as "satisficing" – that is, searching for alternatives close to the status quo that are satisfactory, rather than investing in the resources needed to find the perfect solution (Simon, 1997).

Lindblom felt that this was not only a good description of how most organizations operated, but also a desirable way of making decisions, because incremental decisions are relatively easy to sell to stakeholders, easy to implement because of this general support, and relatively easy to reverse if the result turns out to be undesirable.

A composite organization requires issues related to programs and services to be compartmentalized, typically aligning departments with the services each delivers, such as environment, social services, transit, public libraries, and so forth. Each department and its service responsibilities is separate from the other departments and their services. Decision making, both administrative and political, tends to follow Lindblom's model and in municipalities it is often aligned through standing committees of council that direct decision making in each service area, coming together, at least annually, in the context of budgeting for distribution of comparatively scarce resources.

This approach often implicitly makes financial considerations the primary basis for decisions about service integration or program synergies. Budget discussions focus on inputs for each service, with priority given to resources that are required to meet or resolve immediate service-level issues that might accompany population growth or resident service demands. It often requires difficult decisions about competing departments' priorities. It is not unusual in this situation for the support services required to sustain service growth to be given a lower priority than the "resident-facing" service, ultimately resulting in internal system bottlenecks. For example, in a municipality that is experiencing rapid residential growth, the demand for additional building inspectors can be seen by the CAO and council as a reasonable budget request, whereas the need for additional support staff to manage the "backroom" application and licensing processes and to keep mapping and other system information current is not met with the same enthusiasm.

A composite organizational model is often the default option for a CAO, particularly where it is favoured by councils. It can, however, overlook opportunities that might exist, as many municipal services no longer fit neatly into separate disciplines. In this model, the CAO's role and focus is to ensure that each discrete department functions efficiently with support from some organization-wide internal services. The efficacy of service delivery remains the responsibility of the service departments as, for example, does the role of a particular airline in passenger satisfaction. In this analogy, the CAO serves as air traffic controller, ensuring the safe, orderly, and accurate allocation and expenditure of resources, and resolves emergency issues as they arise.

Aligning Services Strategically

The other option that a municipal CAO can choose is to develop for council consideration and approval a vision and/or strategic plan for the municipality that looks for commonalities between services outcomes and that lays out an overarching plan for the municipality. This overarching plan does not replace discrete service delivery plans, but rather lays out a common set of community-based outcomes that can be achieved only if the goals in each service plan are achieved. It also takes into account the growing interdependence of services and policies that requires the coordination of services delivered through several departments. Encouraging economic development or reducing poverty cannot be successfully resolved if compartmentalized in one department.

This approach serves to better align elected members with the role played in the private sector by a board of directors, focusing on performance in advancing desired community outcomes through defined and measurable activities. The approach also adds an additional layer of complexity to the CAO's role over that faced in managing the elements of a composite organization. The first challenge for a municipal CAO who decides on this approach is to create a vision and corresponding overarching plan for the organization with the endorsement of council. The CAO is uniquely positioned to influence a municipal organization's vision. The challenges of engaging members of a municipal council in establishing such a vision and the overarching plan, often expressed as a strategic plan, have been documented elsewhere (Fenn, 1989), but it is worth mentioning the important components and challenges of such an approach.

Engaging a new or established council to develop a strategic plan can be undertaken in several ways. Including a description of the role of the plan and the process to establish or renew it in council orientation sessions and associated materials will lay the foundation for the work. It is important that council sees its input in the document. As most councillors are well positioned to understand the aspirations and needs of their constituents, those aspirations and needs should be evident in both the vision and plan. It should be made clear to council that establishing a comprehensive plan can act as a guide to decision making on all aspects of the organization and give both council and staff a reference point against which to measure the success of the entire organization's efforts.

A critical component of developing a comprehensive municipal vision and strategic plan is ensuring that council sees that it is informed by input from the multiple constituencies that make up a municipality. The composition and interests of these constituencies will vary and change over time. They could include residents' or ratepayers' associations, labour groups, business interest associations, organizations providing service in the municipality, and special interest groups. The groups or individuals representing these constituencies could be aligned with provincial or national groups or formed in reaction to a localized issue. Because they are organized and have a particular view on issues of interest to them, they are often enthusiastic in offering their perspective on the elements that should be considered in the municipal vision and strategic plan.

In early attempts to develop a strategic plan for the Region of Peel, council held consultation sessions in chambers and invited participation. The vast majority of the participants were representatives of special interest constituencies. Although their input was important, their perspective was not necessarily representative of the broader community's views. In an attempt to include as broad a community representative view as possible, the most recent process for obtaining input for the strategic plan in Peel included outreach to the broader community using tactics such as staffed booths at places where the general public could be engaged, such as shopping malls, community events, and fairs, and special exhibits at municipal service locations, including art galleries and museums. These outreach activities used a common format to ensure that all the engagement activities offered participants the same opportunities for providing input. In addition, engagement opportunities using digital media and devices were offered.

In crafting its vision of "strong, caring, safe communities," York Region engaged the public through multiple opportunities and media formats in association with periodic Official Plan updates. Targeted groups included, as in Peel, chambers of commerce and boards of trade, residents' associations, and community groups – including religious and cultural groups representing specific ethnicities. The results of these engagements were reinforced with statistically representative polling to confirm broader community sentiments and priorities. Through a practice of annual polling, York Region collects objective feedback from residents and businesses to continually inform directions taken by council. These types of broad and targeted community engagement cannot be rushed, and need to be part of a continual feedback loop informing council with an understanding of the issues and interests from a broad representation of their constituents.

After an election, a strategic plan is a meaningful way to align new council members with a common direction. Although engaging council in the development of a strategic plan is important, it is even more important that ownership of the plan remains with council to avoid its becoming simply another administrative "nice to have" or just an internal staff document. Following an election, council members are understandably eager to get on with governing the day-to-day operations of the municipality, especially those operations that affect issues that are important to each of them. Reluctance to set aside time to create a longer-term plan for the municipality can be an obstacle. There are several ways to allow these operational priorities to be addressed alongside the development of a strategic plan, including setting aside a portion of council meetings for discussion of the plan and recommending a subgroup of councillors form a task group to provide council input into the development of the plan. Ultimately, the plan will need to be approved by council; however, council's oversight of the ongoing operation of the municipality cannot be put on hold while the plan is being developed.

These approaches can demonstrate that supporting a strategic plan does not have the effect of transferring important decisions from elected representatives to municipal managers, or predetermining future policy and program decisions facing elected leaders. Ultimately, they demonstrate that the investment of time in developing a plan is an important component of the municipality's success in delivering services and managing many issues that arise during council's term.

A fundamental difference between this approach and managing the composite-organization approach is that, once established, a vision and strategic plan contain consistent, community-oriented themes that influence the various departments' individual service plans. For example, all the plans should align with a series of fundamental goals such as promoting economic vitality, healthy and resilient communities, environmental sustainability, and good governance (Region of Peel, n.d.a.; York Region, n.d.). The desired objectives or priorities with a council-supported vision help align the resources required to implement them. This vision for the municipality can also serve as an impetus to bring together or find commonalities among the various programs and the systems that support their delivery.

This joining up of government has been a growing expectation of the public for some time (Kernaghan, 2009; Osborne & Gaebler, 1993), and the development of an integrated vision, and its implementation, can be the solution to the otherwise siloed nature of municipal government and the inherent vagaries of ad hoc decision making playing out on the council floor.

The experience with the municipal housing and social services departments provided earlier in this chapter is a good example of how a strategic plan can guide the evolution of the municipality in line with the needs of the community. After Peel's council approved a plan with an emphasis on ending homelessness and reducing poverty, the two departments started several initiatives to support the residents with tenancy issues with a goal to avoid evictions. Over time the two departments merged into a single unit with a mandate that included providing supports for the full continuum of services to residents at risk of being homeless or in precarious housing situations.

In a similar effort, York Region combined two separate departments – health and social services – into one in an effort to better focus on outcomes influenced by the social determinants of health. This rearranging of structural priorities can renew the vigour with which staff teams focus on underlying causes and make inroads into better service delivery, particularly to vulnerable sectors.

Once a long-term, idealistic vision has been established, the CAO's challenge is to ensure that this vision drives day-to-day decision making throughout the organization. A strategic plan, linked to council's term, can focus on the community's identified needs and the shape and size of the programs and services to be delivered within the financial tolerance of council and resources available to the municipality. The CAO's job is to ensure that every subsequent decision aligns with and supports the implementation of the strategic plan or long-term vision. In this model, decisions that clearly support the implementation of the plan (or vision) will drive staff recommendations to council. The decisions are rationally informed, in that they are logically required to implement the vision, and are comprehensive, as they are made after evaluating reasonable alternatives required to achieve the desired outcomes.

The "rational-comprehensive" approach to decision making can be challenging to implement and sustain in a traditionally fragmented organization such as a municipality. As Tindal and Tindal (2019, p. 5) observe: "A well-governed municipality focuses on the big picture … It is future-oriented and sensitive to changes and challenges that await it. It has a clear sense of priorities and ensures scarce resources are wisely allocated accordingly. Those scarce resources include the time and energy of members of council and municipal staff, which need to be focused on important matters not pre-occupied with 'the crisis of the week.'" Despite this advice, it is not unheard of for strategic plans, once established, to gather dust rather than momentum. Commitment to strategic planning provides the opportunity to deal with day-to-day issues while also making incremental progress on longer-term necessities.

Many people would agree that Lindblom's thinking, noted earlier in relation to managing a composite organization, describes reality, but not everyone is comfortable with that reality. The idea of the "incrementalism trap" cautions that an acceptance of incrementalism makes people too comfortable with the status quo, stifles innovation, minimizes the initiative to look for connections between issues, and fails to recognize basic societal changes. Amitai Etzioni argued that "incremental decision-making amounts to drifting; action without direction" (Etzioni, 1967, p. 388).

The pitfalls of incrementalism described by Etzioni can be mitigated by a vision that drives consistent decisions across the organization through "aspirational incrementalism" – incrementalism within a vision, inspired with meaningful purpose.

Strategic planning has long been hailed as an organizational necessity (Bryson, 2018). Like the alignment of organizational values, it is an opportunity to "right-size" the aspirational goals set out in a community vision into measurable, achievable actions. It is the platform for setting realistic expectations. It is the foil to Simon's observed tendency to "satisficing." The organizational potential that can be delivered through the relentless pursuit of incremental improvement directed towards specific goals should not be underestimated (Graser, 2016; Graser & Leanage, 2017).

Once the vision is established and ordained by council, it should be seen as setting the direction, but not the precise path, to be followed by the organization. In other words, the aspirations established in the vision and enabled by the strategic plan provide the impetus to pursue a series of actions to achieve outcomes that look beyond day-to-day incremental decisions that are made in every municipality. The strategic plan is intended to align resources and efforts over the longer term to achieve the identified community-based outcomes. It is not intended to anticipate every decision that needs to be made on a daily basis. York Region's strategic plan sets out a number of specific actions framed under four fundamental pillars: Economic Vitality, Healthy Communities, Environmental Sustainability, and Good Government. Similarly, Peel Region's strategic plan has three pillars: Living, Thriving, and Leading. These pillars serve as frameworks that provide a context to support any community-focused activity, from the innovative to the routine.

Aspirational Incrementalism: Combining Two Seemingly Contradictory Decision-Making Approaches

The "aspirational-incrementalism" approach to municipal management starts with establishing the vision and developing a comprehensive corporate strategic planning framework to unify and clearly articulate actions. A growing cohort of municipalities has chosen to align strategic planning and multiyear budgeting with council terms. This drives consistency in the efforts of elected officials and staff. The budget connections keep strategic planning firmly rooted in what the municipality can afford, and they avoid the downside of aspirational planning that otherwise can result in "overpromising and under-delivering" (Howlett & Migone, 2018). The CAO can work with council continually to ensure that the plan is adapted to shorter-term priorities that might require program flexibility. The annual budget, and the priorities set therein, is best informed by the strategic plan, master plans, and related policies.

Aspirational incrementalism is related to, but somewhat different from, the concept of transformative incrementalism developed by Robert Buchan elsewhere in this book. Aspirational incrementalism is tied to the strategic plan that encompasses the entire unified organization, whereas transformative incrementalism focuses on community development, which is typically one part of the broader strategic plan. Transformative incrementalism is also a recipe for public service activism, whereas aspirational incrementalism begins with the council-led strategic planning process.

Aspirational incrementalism involves integrating the various parts of the planning process. For example, Peel Region's "Living" pillar included the aspirational goal of improving people's lives in their time of need (Region of Peel, n.d.a). Council set four shorter-term priorities under that goal, one of which was to "advance community wellbeing." The municipality undertook three major initiatives in response to this direction. One was to work with the community and police in providing public services to reduce human sex trafficking, which the police had advised was a serious and growing concern because of the municipality's location along major provincial highways. The second initiative was to eliminate traffic fatalities in the municipality. The third was to be an active partner with local police in developing and implementing a broad plan to improve community safety.

In the example cited above, if the municipality had taken the purely incremental approach, without an overall vision, it is quite possible that the roads department could have recommended to council as part of its operational plan the implementation of a strategy to eliminate traffic fatalities. It is less likely, however, that the health or human services departments would have become involved in reducing human sex trafficking or developing a community safety plan, as those two initiatives are not within the mandate of the legislation and policy direction that guides the services of municipal public health or human services departments in Ontario. The establishment of the strategic imperative of advancing community well-being to guide the work of the municipality provided the impetus for the municipality to recommend to council that the municipality work with other community agencies on these projects. Council's acceptance of these recommendations also influenced its budget allocations for service delivery over its term of office.

The implementation of the vision through a strategic plan can also attract partners such as other governments, the local health system, faith-based or business groups, and recreation associations. In York Region, a Human Services Planning Board brings together municipalities, school boards, police, health providers, and community support agencies to work on common priorities – an exercise focused on the better community outcomes articulated in the municipality's vision of addressing the social determinants of health. In recent years the board has focused its attention on mental health, homelessness, and affordable housing – some of the most persistent and chronic challenges facing urban communities.

An unexpected benefit of York Region's strategic plan resulted from the targeted completion of Business Continuity Plans for critical services. Continuity plans normally address interruptions resulting from natural hazards and disasters or labour disruptions. These plans also proved to be instrumental in the region's response to the COVID-19 pandemic. The plans helped identify services that could be suspended in favour of a substantial build-up of case and contact-tracing resources – a level of effort that needed to increase by an order of magnitude. The work and agency coordination facilitated over the years through the Human Service Planning Board helped sustain a productive and functional response to protecting the most vulnerable in our communities from the perils of the pandemic in the timely provision of shelter and supports.

Accountability Measures Give Credibility to Strategic Planning

Another challenge facing the CAO who adopts this approach is to work with senior administrative staff to review the strategic plan. They must provide annual updates to council about the progress towards achieving the goals set in the plan, with recommendations related to recalibrating any element of the plan to reflect significant changes in circumstances. This review needs to occur in time to inform the annual budget and work planning for the next year. This requires the CAO to ensure that there is a system to implement and track, from a corporate perspective, progress in implementing the plan. One approach to ensuring this occurs is to embed in the plan some key performance indicators to be monitored and reported. This has proven to us to be one of the most difficult aspects of the strategic-management approach.

Managers are often hard pressed to identify outcome-based key performance indicators; more often than not they will identify process indicators – indicators that show how busy the staff are in performing their duties. Connecting performance indicators to population or community-based indicators is helpful in monitoring meaningful progress towards an outcome. (Friedman, 2015). Considerable care is also required in the selection and development of department heads to ensure collaborative organizational and personal behaviours are strong characteristics. Public reporting on progress, at least annually, maintains accountability and helps overcome the notion of incrementalism set out by Etzioni as "action without direction."

Both municipalities mentioned above provide annual reports to council and community that indicate progress (or lack thereof) in implementing established priorities (Region of Peel, n.d.b.; York Region, 2021). York Region reports on thirty-one specific measures across all four priority areas. The results show trends, and are often expressed in per capita terms to reflect true progress (or lack thereof). Measures that are not trending in the desired direction are flagged and subject to variance reporting to describe the circumstances and any mitigating or corrective measures.

On its own, a reliance on arbitrarily established incremental progress is not a dependable way to achieve meaningful outcomes in delivering municipal services, but there are a few ways this can be encouraged. Internally, as departments update their service plans, clear alignment with council's strategic plan must be visible: there can be a tendency to align service plans with the overarching provincial legislation and policy framework, not with council's strategic plan. Service plans and annual budget recommendations to council should show how they support both immediate service requirements and the longer-term aspirations of council.

Another method of ensuring that accountability for strategic plan outcomes permeates the organization is to embed them in the performance measures used to evaluate individual managers. These individual performance measures, complemented by departmental service plans aligned to the strategic plan, can drive incremental progress towards achieving the aspirations of the strategic plan. Individual decisions throughout the year should be made with an understanding of how they will affect the implementation of that vision and plan. These should also form part of the performance reviews of the key leadership roles in the organization. Management workplans should include the expectation that work performed in their divisions is both aligned with and drives implementation of the strategic plan's goals.

In addition, having a strategic vision for the municipality can assist in overcoming the natural tendency for siloed departments. As part of a concerted effort to foster a community-focused culture in York Region and address the potential pitfalls of fragmented decision making, leaders in both the regional administration and the police service participate in joint leadership skills development. As opposed to sending individuals off to executive programs, comparable training is brought in-house through progressive stages of behavioural and skills development involving cohorts selected from across both organizations.

The strategic plan must be seen actually to drive the actions of the organization, both internally by staff and externally by the public.

Reports to council should indicate how recommendations are aligned; if there are delays or unexpected challenges in implementing parts of the plan, regular reporting should also include simple and credible reasons why the delays have occurred (Siegel & Szwarc, 2020). When decisions are made for reasons that seem contrary to the direction set in the plans, and there will be times when this occurs, the CAO must be able to articulate why a deviation from the plan is warranted.

If decisions of council are made that are contrary to the direction of the council-approved plan, an aspirational-incremental approach provides the CAO with the opportunity to inform the council of the apparent deviation. These situations should be handled with sensitivity, as it is not the role of the CAO to criticize council decisions. The CAO might need to suggest politely that, while council's decision helped to resolve an immediate issue, it might delay the implementation of the longer-term aspirations of the plan.

An aspirational-incremental approach to management also can have a positive effect on the organizational culture within the municipality. While aspirational goals are often politically desirable (for example, zero carbon, zero waste, zero traffic fatalities) and fitting goals of a long-range vision, their achievement requires a long series of incremental decisions and, as Lindblom points out, some of these will be successful and some will not. Employing only the rational-comprehensive approach to decision making, without tolerance for the occasional short-term failure, is not conducive to maintaining a motivated workforce: there is no better way to demotivate than to set out impossible tasks. Successive failures are bad for both careers and political aspirations, no matter how well they might be explained. Focused incrementalism allows for short-term corrections when necessary, which lead to the development of a productive and responsive public service aligned to a long-term council vision.

A municipal CAO faces the problem of leading an organization that provides a broad range of services. This makes it particularly important to lead by aligning the individual and collective talents and capabilities within the organization with the overall direction of the municipality. In addition to that council-driven direction, a CAO must also provide leadership to the employees of the organization by developing a corporate culture and resulting behaviours that greatly influence how the public experiences those programs and services (Mouritzen & Svara, 2002; Siegel, 2015).

In Peel Region, the CAO promoted a culture that championed a unified approach to service delivery across all programs, emphasizing the links between employee engagement, client satisfaction, and trust and confidence (Erin Research Inc., n.d.). York Region prioritizes "customer experience" across the entire organization, employing multichannel access and customer journey mapping constantly to address and improve customer experiences. In both municipalities, employee engagement levels are gauged through regular comprehensive employee surveys. A customer focus also extends to recruitment efforts through testing for desired behavioural traits (Erin Research Inc., n.d.).

Although there is a slight difference in the approaches of the two leaders, both reflect what James MacGregor Burns described as transformative leadership. Burns normally associated incrementalism with transactional leadership (Burns, 1978, p. 409), but the emphasis on aspiration provides an example of transformative leadership. Aspirational incrementalism is clearly geared to combining the interests of leaders and followers so that they are mutually supportive (p. 20).

Aspirational incrementalism can be a tool for CAOs to build dynamic workplaces by including senior managers in decision making outside their immediate service responsibility. The questions that leadership groups ask of each other, as well as the processes for making informed decisions, cascade down from those senior leaders to managers and supervisors, helping to ensure decisions are made consistently within the longer-term context of the organization (Bourke, 2017, p. xiii). Although setting direction through comprehensive planning is a key component of making measurable progress, establishing and maintaining a supportive culture is equally important.

Conclusion

Municipal organizations have evolved over time from providing very basic services such as a "house of refuge" or maintaining farm-to-market roads to managing complex, highly regulated services that span several governmental and non-governmental agencies. They must do this within the framework of a democratic process that ensures appropriate oversight by elected representatives by bringing together a disparate group of individuals, usually without the party platform more commonly associated with provincial and federal elections. Municipal organizations have also grown to include a broad range of multidisciplinary, professional skills.

Municipal organizational structures have evolved traditionally as a composite of otherwise fragmented services. Left untended, the consequence is a cost-reduction- and regulatory-compliance-driven organization that might not be structured optimally to deliver consistent, community-focused improvements. A key role for the municipal CAO or city manager is to establish and maintain an organizational culture of engagement, purposefully driven and inspired to provide vital community services effectively and efficiently.

At the beginning of this chapter, we coined the term "aspirational incrementalism" to describe a way of combining a long-term perspective with the recognition that the local government system has a strong natural bias towards incrementalism. Aspirational incrementalism can create a common, meaningful purpose to decision making, facilitate incremental progress towards longer-term ideals, and, most important, bring about alignment between municipal staff and elected officials. Although not a complete substitute for the need to react and respond to emerging concerns and challenges, strategic planning driven by longer-term, visionary outlooks – aspirational incrementalism – provides a proven and measurable way to deliver results.

REFERENCES

Bourke, J. (2017). *Which two heads are better than one? How diverse teams create breakthrough ideas and make smarter decisions*. Australian Institute of Company Directors.

Bryson, J. M. (2018). *Strategic planning for public and non-profit organizations: A guide to strengthening and sustaining organizational achievement* (5th ed.). John Wiley & Sons.

Burns, J. M. (1978). *Leadership*. Harper Torchbooks.

Erin Research Inc. (n.d.). *Client satisfaction and confidence in government*. Retrieved 29 October 2020 from https://www.peelregion.ca/reports/PDF/client-satisfaction-report.pdf

Etzioni, A. (1967). Mixed-scanning: A "third" approach to decision-making. *Public Administration Review*, 27(5), 385–92. https://doi.org/10.2307/973394

Fenn, W. M. (1989). Future focus: Burlington's strategic planning success. *Canadian Public Administration*, 32(2), 304–10. https://doi.org/10.1111/j.1754-7121.1989.tb01358.x

Friedman, M. (2015). *Trying hard is not enough*. BookSurge Publishing.

Graser, D. (2016, May). *Community benefits and tower renewal*. Retrieved from https://www.evergreen.ca/downloads/pdfs/HousingActionLab/TowerRenewal_Report_FINAL.pdf

Graser, D., & Leanage, N. (2017, May). *Realizing social and economic objectives through infrastructure planning and investment*. Retrieved from https://futurecitiescanada.ca/downloads/2018/FCC_CommunityBenefits_201808.pdf

Howlett, M., & Migone, A. (2018). Over-promising and under-delivering policy styles and policy-making: Exploring the linkages. In M. Howlett &

J. Tosun (Eds.), *Policy styles and policy-making: Exploring the linkages* (pp. 137–56). Routledge.

Kernaghan, K. (2009). Moving towards integrated public governance: Improving service delivery through community engagement. *International Review of Administrative Sciences*, 75(2), 239–54. https://doi.org/10.1177/0020852309104174

Lindblom, C. E. (1959). The science of "muddling through" *Public Administration Review*, 19(2), 79–88. https://doi.org/10.2307/973677

Mouritzen, P. E., & Svara, J. H. (2002). *Leadership at the apex*. University of Pittsburgh Press.

Osborne, D., & Gaebler, T. (1993). *Reinventing government: How the entrepreneurial spirit is transforming government*. Plume.

Region of Peel. (n.d.a). *2015–2035 strategic plan*. Retrieved from https://peelregion.ca/strategicplan

Region of Peel. (n.d.b). *Community for life*. Retrieved 29 October 2020 from https://peelregion.ca/strategicplan/dashboard/

Savoie, D. J. (2015). *What is government good at? A Canadian answer*. McGill-Queen's University Press.

Siegel, D. (2015). *Leaders in the shadows: The leadership qualities of municipal chief administrative officers*. University of Toronto Press.

Siegel, D., & Szwarc, D. (2020, June). Creating and maintaining the resilient organization – Part 3: Developing resilient employees. *Municipal World*, pp. 29–30, 40.

Simon, H. (1997). *Administrative behavior* (4th ed.). Free Press.

Tindal, C. R., & Tindal, S. N. (2019). *Guide to good municipal governance* (2nd ed.). Municipal World.

York Region. (2021, May). Retrieved from https://yorkpublishing.escribemeetings.com/filestream.ashx?DocumentId=22757

York Region. (n.d.). *York Region*. Retrieved 29 October 2020 from https://www.york.ca/wps/wcm/connect/yorkpublic/e9612765-7323-40bf-904c-715cd0c21d6b/18453_CorporateStrategicPlan-Approved.pdf?MOD=AJPERES

3 Building Support for Strategic Planning and Priorities

CHRIS MACPHERSON

One of the most important and difficult tasks facing a city manager is the need to develop a broad vision for the municipality and motivate the stakeholders in the municipality to become involved in developing and implementing that vision. Chris MacPherson has spent most of his career in Fredericton, the past ten years as CAO. When he was attending an Executive Leadership Program at Harvard he was exposed to the idea of the Power Wheel. In this chapter, he explains how he has used the Power Wheel to work with stakeholders to develop and implement the city's strategic plan.

I have had the good fortune to work for over forty-five years in what I feel is the most satisfying level of government: local government. Much has changed over that time in how local governments determine what services to provide, how they interact with citizens, and how they govern. In my early days, much of what a municipality did was heavily influenced by the mayor and/or a group of powerful city councillors without much of a formal system. The role of staff was to implement the vision given to them by the elected officials.

As time has gone on, local governments have evolved. They have become more sophisticated with policies, by-laws, and rules of engagement. Of course, the mayor and council still control policy making, but it happens in a structured way that generally maintains the distinction between council's policy role and the administrative responsibilities of the CAO and staff. In addition, public expectations have changed: citizens now anticipate the opportunity to provide input into the vision of the community.

With time, the role of the city manager or chief administrative officer has grown in importance. The CAO is not only the administrative head of the organization, but also a key leader in the organization, and can have tremendous influence on the strategic direction of the organization. The leadership role of the CAO is affected both positively and negatively by council. Councillors bring their beliefs, perspectives, biases, and style of engagement, while the collective group, like any team, is very much a living entity, where the addition or removal of any one player can create a shift in the dynamic. It can be stressful for the CAO after an election to see how the new council takes shape.

Lastly, the role of social media and citizen engagement is changing almost daily. Mayors and councillors can be heavily influenced by what they read and see on social media, and many regularly interact with those who comment on city activities. A few individuals can have a disproportionate influence on a city council.

So, how does the CAO navigate through the expectations of city council and the growing influence of social media and the public, and build upon the strength of municipal employees to foster a successful community? Before I begin sharing what I have learned over my career in terms of developing a strategic plan and vision for an organization, I want to re-emphasize the importance of the CAO. The hiring of the CAO is the most important decision a city council will make. The CAO is not only the head of the municipal bureaucracy, providing a consistent link between staff and council, but also a key advisor to the mayor and council. Although the overall vision and direction of the municipality ultimately are the purview of council, the influence of the CAO in shaping that vision should not be underestimated.

In private sector companies, board members realize that, to be successful, they need to have a high-performing chief executive officer (CEO), so they are willing to spend a great deal of time and money recruiting and retaining such a person. They understand that it is critical to find someone who has the aptitude, capacity, and values that are the right fit for the organization. While most city councils realize this, I expect some still believe the CAO simply looks after the operations and has little influence on the bigger policies and direction of the municipality.

Municipalities have a multitude of plans. There is the Municipal Plan (known as the Community Plan or Official Plan in some provinces), which is the land-use plan adopted by city council; this is often a legislative requirement. There is also an operational plan, which contains staff's strategies for how they will implement the Municipal Plan, and then there are the CAO's techniques for keeping the organization focused to deliver on the plans. This section of the chapter looks at the latter role of the CAO.

To keep the organization focused on delivering council's mandate, the CAO must engage with the key stakeholders in the community to gauge reaction and acceptance of council's plan. To assist this approach, the CAO needs a tool that is versatile and adjustable to the changing needs of the community for relationship building and ongoing consultation.

The Strategic Plan

Before describing the tool I use to make sure the organization stays focused on its plans, I want to outline briefly the key components of developing a strategic plan. I need not go into detail, as many others have described how to build a strategic plan and most methods have similar components (see, for example, Bryson, 2018; Fenn, 1988; Gordon, 2005; Kabir, 2007; Poister & Streib, 2005).

A strategic plan has upwards of nine components. The first step is to evaluate the organization's mission. What is the municipal mandate? Which level of government has jurisdiction over programs (municipal versus regional versus provincial)? Which program areas are currently being provided and which are not? Every province and territory differs in terms of legislative requirements placed on municipalities with regard to service provision. All municipalities are required to provide certain services specified in legislation, but beyond this list they can provide almost any service they wish unless explicitly forbidden by provincial legislation. As part of the mission evaluation, therefore, it is important to have an inventory of current programs to determine if there are gaps in service provision.

The second step is to articulate the current vision. This should be a joint exercise involving city council, the community, and senior staff. This often involves facilitated workshops, community gatherings, and joint stakeholder sessions. A basic question is what kind of community do we want to be: industrial, arts and culture, knowledge-based, tourism, retail, retirement, and so on? To understand what kind of community is wanted, you need to determine the community's major economic drivers: are they government services, medical, information technology, regional retail, or others? This allows you to see the strengths of the community and if they align with the kind of community residents want.

The third step involves the multitude of stakeholders who will want to help shape the plan's strategic direction. Today's dynamic environment limits the old practice whereby council would get in a room together with a facilitator and brainstorm a direction for the municipality. Obviously, the key players will be the mayor and council, with input from the CAO and senior management. There must also be an opportunity for key stakeholders in the community to have input into the plan; I address this later in the chapter.

After you have evaluated the mission, articulated a vision, and defined all the stakeholder preferences, the fourth step is to assess where you are currently. To do this, you need to consider a number of important elements. One is financial constraints and capacity: what are your current debt and debt capacity? what are your current capital plans? what are your community's long-term financial projections? what trends are associated with labour costs? what is the community's financial capacity? what is the projected growth or decline in the tax base and tax burden for residents and businesses? what are the effects on asset management and the infrastructure deficit?

The fifth step is to assess organizational constraints: what business issues and risks do you currently face? You will need to assess the culture, leadership, and management of the organization: what does the organization do well and how does it need to improve?

The sixth step relates the review of organizational constraints to an environmental scan. You will need to conduct a SWOT (strengths, weaknesses, opportunities, threats) analysis in addition to a PESTLE (political, economic, social, technology, legal, environmental) analysis.

The seventh step involves the development of strategic options and priorities. At this point, you will need to review plans and strategies that council has adopted. These might include a community or municipal plan, an economic development plan, a transportation plan, police and fire strategies, and other operational plans. Working with your senior leadership team, you should seek to develop four to six options for strategic long-term priorities, and consider the pros and cons of each option. Do you have the financial capacity to carry out the various options? Do you have the organizational capacity to deliver them? How do the various options relate to your environmental scan findings?

At this point you need to make a recommendation on which long-term strategic options should move forward and why. This should be accompanied by recommendations for any needed organizational changes, along with an assessment of the financial impact of those changes. You should note which strategic options are not recommended and the reasons for that.

The eighth step is to create a new vision statement based on your recommendations and input you received from stakeholders. This is an important step because the vision statement will be the future face of your municipality and a significant motivating factor for the municipal workforce.

The final step is the implementation plan, which outlines who will do what and when. This should include an updated, long-term financial plan that considers financial projections and incorporates funding required for strategic recommendations and core elements of various master plans. You should now have a good plan that allows your municipality to progress. A plan does not mean much, however, unless you also have a way of implementing it. This is the next stage in the planning process.

The Power Wheel

After a new vision and strategic direction have been created, the CAO needs to ensure that the plans are implemented, communicated to and accepted by community stakeholders, and adjusted as conditions change in the community. The technique I have used for more than a decade to stay abreast of changes in our community and organization, and to ensure that our community plans are implemented effectively, is an adaptation of the concept of the Power Wheel, which comes from the Harvard Kennedy School of Government's Executive Leadership program (Heifetz & Linsky, 2002). The general premise of the Power Wheel is to map out the necessary coalition for a specific program's development, implementation, and sustainment, using a central node as an anchor point. The model allows targeted attention to each individual stakeholder within the network. By isolating each node, specific concerns or interests can be addressed in the development, implementation, and sustainment plan while maintaining consideration for the network as a whole.

Although the tool is not specific to municipal government, it does work well when adapted for the work of the CAO. In its simplest terms, the Power Wheel defines your key stakeholders, both inside and outside your organization and community. This helps you to develop an engagement strategy, which is key to building support for council's plan. It is necessary to identify and address issues early. The stakeholders that are on the Power Wheel and their location on the Wheel can vary depending on how much value you place on each.

To define and build your Power Wheel, you begin by mapping community institutions, identifying key people in your community, and then reaching out and making contact. This is a very deliberate action, and the process should be repeated regularly. In effect, you are creating an environment where all stakeholders on the Power Wheel feel valued and heard, and know they can come to you if they have a concern, a fear, or a need to ensure their perspective is being represented. My own personal Power Wheel is illustrated in figure 3.1.

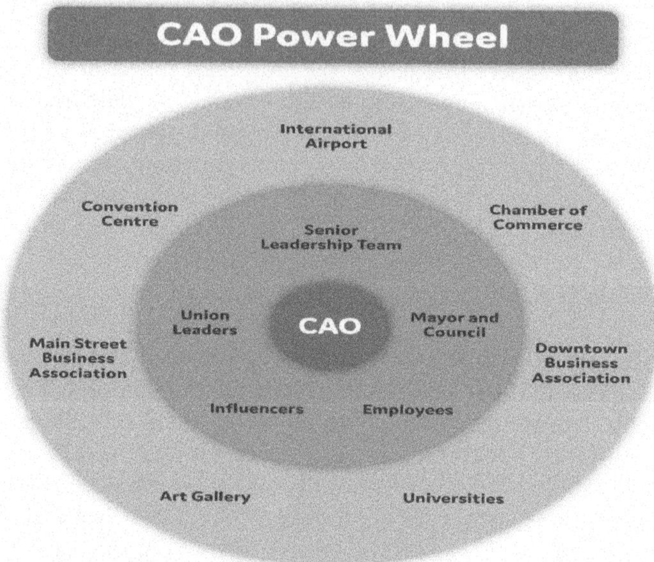

Figure 3.1 Chris MacPherson's Power Wheel

When I became the CAO in my community, I built my Power Wheel by first identifying all the key stakeholders:

- mayor and council as the key decision makers;
- staff (management and key staff influencers, along with union representatives);
- CEOs of separate civic operating agencies (airport, convention centre);
- important players from businesses and business associations (Chamber of Commerce);
- strategic connections in other levels of government (elected and staff);
- key contacts in other locally based public services (schools, universities, health); and
- significant leaders from civil society (community groups, volunteers).

After identifying the key community stakeholders in my Power Wheel stakeholders, I reached out to each one and asked for a meeting. In these initial meetings, I tried to understand the issues the stakeholders were dealing with, what their priorities were, and how they felt about the local government and its staff. I asked for suggestions they had for improvement and advice on how we could work together more effectively. I shared plans, priorities, and goals for the city, and got reactions to them.

This generated significant interest in the process. For example, internal stakeholders, such as city councillors, would often ask when it was their turn to come in to see me. In every case, my Power Wheel stakeholders wanted to maintain regular communication, and to this day I still work hard on my Power Wheel interactions – they have proven invaluable.

The Power Wheel Is Your Circle of Influence

Your Power Wheel should have an inner circle and an outer circle. The inner circle represents your scope of authority, your discretionary space in which to act. The boundaries of this inner circle are your frontier of leadership. The outer circle is populated by stakeholders who are beyond your authority, but with whom you must interact to accomplish your goals. We could spend our careers simply working within our inner circle. Real leadership, however, comes from moving beyond this inner circle and practising leadership in the outer circle. For example, sometimes you need to take a stand on a controversial community initiative because you believe it is for the greater good; it is too easy to stay in our safe zones.

You cannot practise leadership without meeting resistance. The challenge for all of us in leadership positions is to dance on the edge of our authority in a way that maximizes our chance of success and reduces the risks to the community and ourselves. We all know someone who lost their job because they stood up for what they believed, even though those beliefs did not align with those of their stakeholders. Therefore, building alliances that support you and your purpose can help you when you decide to step out of your inner circle.

Keys to Building and Maintaining Your Power Wheel

You should build your Power Wheel before you need it. The Power Wheel is a proactive approach to building and adapting your strategic direction and to building important relationships. It is important to understand the organizational structures of the entities you are dealing with so that you have some sense of how people in each organization function. In mapping out your personal Power Wheel, you should take note of the small "p" politics; this includes identifying people who share your values, and who will likely be loyal to you. Everyone on your Power Wheel will have their own agenda and perspective; to be successful, you must understand what those are.

The Power Wheel can be a great way to build your network and gain support for your initiatives. One of my great successes was building a relationship with one of my key stakeholders, the president of the Fredericton Fire Fighters' Association. As part of my efforts to build important relationships, I extended an invitation to all the presidents of the union locals represented within the city to meet with me monthly. Not all presidents took me up on my offer, but the president of the Fredericton Fire Fighters' Association did. Once a month he would come to my office and we would discuss the position of the International Association of Fire Fighters on issues. In response, I would identify municipal positions on finances, personnel, and so forth. Often, we would disagree on points, but in more than two years of meetings we built a relationship and mutual respect and trust. I understood very clearly the Fire Fighters' positions on issues, and they understood mine and the municipality's.

This relationship helped to eliminate the rhetoric that was often discussed publicly, which saw the municipality and the bargaining group seemingly on opposite sides of a manufactured line. Through our communication and understanding, we experienced a significant reduction in grievances and labour-management issues. This carried through to a better relationship in the station houses when I would visit.

Another example is related to a recent provincial election. The party that won the election ran its campaign partly on the platform of municipal reform. This included changes to labour arbitration (as it relates to police and fire collective agreements), regional cost sharing of local government services, and property tax reforms. As soon as the new government took power, the local Chamber of Commerce contacted me to see if municipal staff could give a presentation to its members on what municipal reforms were all about, and how they would impact our city and the Chamber's members. I truly believe the personal relationship I developed over the years through the Power Wheel led the staff of the Chamber of Commerce to contact me first instead of commenting publicly and perhaps saying something that would hurt the municipality or themselves.

As you build your Power Wheel, take a step back and ask yourself: are there any blind spots? are any key stakeholders missing? One common blind spot at the upper-management level is the connection to the influencers in your organization. These are the key front-line staff members, throughout the organization, who have a good understanding of the pulse at the operational level. You need to build a relationship with these individuals, build trust with them, and seek out their insight. Operating at the top of the organization, you receive information that likely has been filtered through the various levels, each with its own lens, creating a very narrowed focus of communications.

By having influencers as part of your Power Wheel, you can hear raw, unfiltered, and timely information that you would not obtain through normal channels. This can help you understand how, at the operational level, policies are being received, if employees are engaged in their work, and if any work groups need assistance to succeed. A key advantage of having regular contact with influencers is that many issues can be addressed before they escalate through those previously mentioned filters and become serious problems.

I place great importance on my connections with influencers because of the impact this group of stakeholders can have on the performance of the organization. This group also can have significant influence on public sentiment towards the city's plans and priorities. In my case, I have 700 employees who have families, friends, and colleagues across the region. They also are likely part of wide social media networks (Facebook, Instagram, and others) that can assist in correcting misinformation or sharing accurate information. If done correctly, you can take advantage of this captive audience to gain support for your plans and priorities.

My first step in connecting with this valuable group of stakeholders was to establish annual corporate CAO goals that my office would publish. These would be posted on every office wall, every hallway, and every lunch room across all municipal buildings in the form of the eye-catching poster shown in figure 3.2. I felt it was important that all staff knew where we were headed in the coming year.

These goals would also operationalize the adopted plan and priorities of the city. I made sure they were formally adopted by city council at the start of each year. CAOs are aware that (at least in most cases) it can be a challenge to keep city council on task and not move from one thing to the next; I believe formally adopting annual goals can assist.

Second, I embarked on an annual CAO road show. Beginning in January each year and running through to the end of February, I have conducted over thirty information sessions in every city building, speaking to every employee group. At these meetings, I would report on the CAO goals from the previous year and go over in detail the goals for the coming year. I would speak about council's priorities and address any misinformation out in the community. Then I would open it up to a Q&A session in which individual staff members could ask me questions

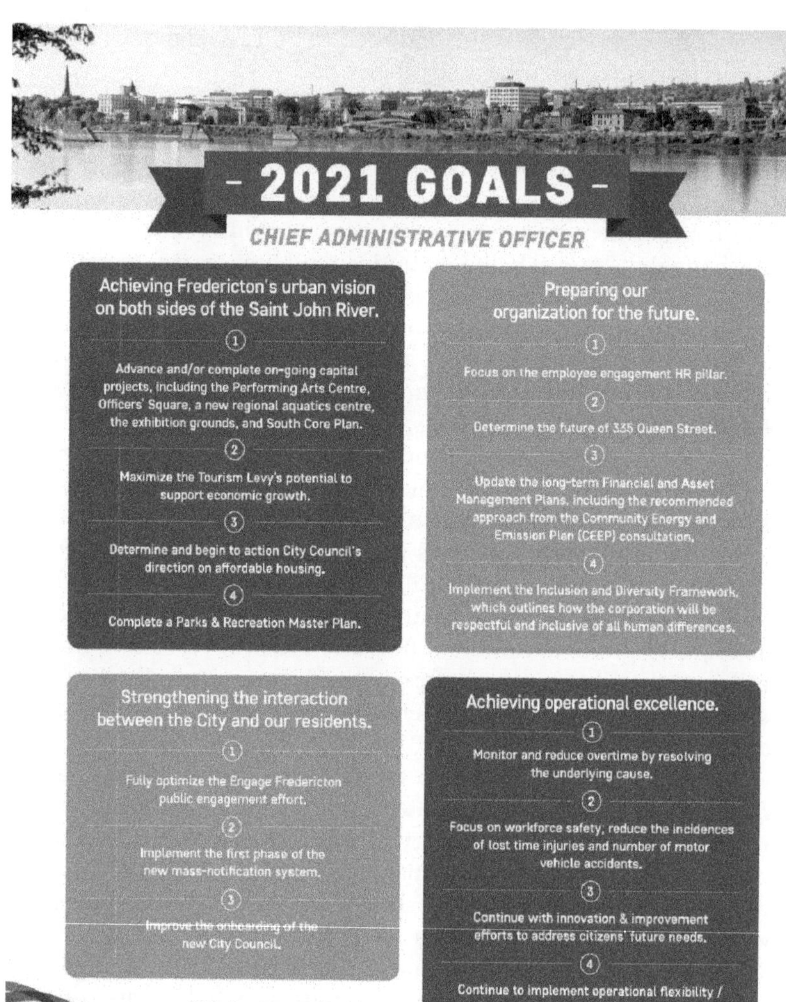

Figure 3.2 The CAO for Fredericton's 2021 Goals

directly. These sessions could be in a fire hall, speaking to a platoon, at an early morning police briefing, at a transit garage, at a 911 centre, or community arena. It is important in my view to go and see them in their workplace. I always go alone and, in most cases, have no other management in the meetings. In the ten years that I have been doing the road shows, there has been a marked difference in the comfort level of staff asking questions and engaging in conversations with me. It has provided me the opportunity to gain support for the plans and priorities of the city.

Establishing corporate goals and engaging in conversations with front-line staff are important because they are effective in gaining support from this large, influential network. However, I have also employed other tactics to engage our front-line employees. These have included a significant continuous improvement in the use of employee engagement surveys, Lean 6 Sigma methodology, which resulted in cross-departmental project teams, waste walks, visual management, and daily management (daily huddles using Plan, Do, Check, Act analyses).

Conclusion

It is important to engage the mayor and council in the building of plans, priorities, and goals that are in sync with adopted plans (such as the community plan). Once this has been completed, the CAO can use a Power Wheel to keep stakeholders (both internal and external) informed, connected, and supportive of the direction in which the city is headed.

The Power Wheel is a great way to identify key stakeholder priorities as you build your strategic direction beyond mayor, council, and senior staff. But it takes dedication, time, and commitment to execute properly. There are several key relationships to build into your Power Wheel:

- You need partners and allies; you cannot be successful on your own.
- You need to know who might oppose and challenge your views. You should meet with them regularly and understand their fears and the pressures you might be putting upon them.
- Know how your mayor and council are faring with the pressures they face.
- Identify those in your Power Wheel who might be negatively affected by your decisions, and stay connected to them. Make sure they know they can reach out to you; it alleviates fears.
- Have partners and confidants. They might not care about the issue, but they will care about you.

The Power Wheel is but one tool a CAO can use to ensure the best-laid plans are successfully implemented and not just sit on a shelf and collect dust. Considering the time and effort that goes into planning for your municipality, you should consider investing some time and effort in techniques such as the Power Wheel to help you meet your goals.

REFERENCES

Bryson, J. M. (2018). *Strategic planning for public andnon-profit organizations* (5th ed.). John Wiley & Sons.

Fenn, W. M. (1988). Future focus: Burlington's strategic planning success. *Canadian Public Administration, 32*(2), 304–10. https://doi.org/10.1111/j.1754-7121.1989.tb01358.x

Gordon, G. L. (2005). *Strategic planning in local government* (2nd ed.). International City/County Management Association.

Heifetz, R. A., & Linsky, M. (2002). *Leadership on the line: Staying alive through the dangers of leadership*. Harvard Business School Press.

Kabir, S. H. (2007). Strategic planning in municipal government: The case of City of Ottawa. *Canadian Social Science, 3*(5), 5–14. http://doi.org/10.3968/j.css.1923669720070305.002

Poister, T. H., & Streib, G. (2005). Elements of strategic planning and management in municipal government: Status after two decades. *Public Administration Review, 65*(1), 45–56. http://doi.org/10.1111/j.1540-6210.2005.00429.x

4 Using Your First 100 Days Strategically

PATRICK MOYLE AND HASSAAN BASIT

You never get a second chance to make a first impression. The way a new manager uses the first 100 days on the job can have a significant impact on how well the rest of the manager's tenure will go. Patrick Moyle has had experience in seven different municipalities over a three-decade career as a civic administrator. In this chapter, he shares that first-hand experience with us. Hassaan Basit is President and CEO of Conservation Halton, one of Ontario's network of municipally funded regional environmental and stormwater management authorities. He supplements Moyle's story with his experience in leading a public sector organization through a significant transformation and his knowledge of management issues, public sector innovation, and navigating relationships to help serve the public and stakeholders.

Introduction

The first 100 days on the job for a new chief administrative officer likely will be the most important time in the CAO's career with the municipality. It will be a time when first impressions take on considerable importance as council and staff assess what they really have in their new leader. Once the announcement has been made, employment agreement signed, and press release issued, everyone will have questions: Is the new CAO an agent of change? Will there be a reorganization? What does it mean for senior officials who might have competed for the position? What is the CAO's management style? Can I work with this person? Why did the person leave his or her former organization and come here? If the new CAO was appointed internally, how will he or she adapt to the new role? Can I relate to this person? How will this appointment affect my career progression? Answers to these and other questions will be revealed during the initial 100 days of the CAO's tenure.

Although some of these questions are common to both elected officials and the civic administration, some are unique to each area. In his book, *Leaders in the Shadows: The Leadership Qualities of Municipal Chief Administrative Officers*, David Siegel (2015) uses the analogy of an hourglass to describe the relationship between the two groups. The top portion of the hourglass consists of council, which makes policy, while the bottom portion represents the appointed officials who implement council's policies. The CAO occupies the pinch point of the hourglass, ensuring that the wishes and policies of elected officials are successfully implemented by the public servants he or she leads, while, at the same time, as sole direct employee of council, being the representative and the voice of municipal staff.

The questions of a newly appointed CAO therefore will be unique to each part of the hourglass. Staff will be interested in knowing how to relate to the new leader, the person's style, approach, temperament, and perhaps most important, the impact the new leader might have on their work. Council likely will want to know if the new CAO can lead staff to implement its policies successfully. Other council questions might include how to ensure that the CAO leads staff but is not perceived to be the community's leader. As Siegel notes, is the CAO truly a *leader in the shadows* or an outspoken civic expert who might be too political in his or her role? Will the new CAO serve the entire council, or pay too much attention to the head of council or to leading members of council?

Many more questions will be in the minds of those who occupy that space in the hourglass. The community will also have many questions as well. Given such levels of interest, it is therefore crucial that the new CAO have a solid plan for the first 100 days on the job. This chapter can serve as a practical guide for this crucial phase of a leader's career. As the adage goes, you don't have a second chance to make a first impression. It is better to be well prepared and to present the most positive impression possible based on a thoughtful plan.

Before You Arrive

The development of a successful on-boarding plan actually begins well before you are appointed to the position. A typical final interview question is, "If you were successful in becoming our new CAO, tell us about your plan for the first thirty, sixty, and ninety days."

This question is asked for several reasons. It is meant to see if you are a take-charge leader with a proactive plan to optimize the implementation of policy and municipal services. Or are you a more reserved leader who will listen to all stakeholders and move cautiously? Your answer will also give the interview panel a sense of what you might have learned about the community and the organization. If you are an internal candidate, there might be an expectation that you have some specific actions to take, given your tenure at the municipality. Your answer also provides the interview panel the opportunity to establish how you would organize yourself to manage an activity that has a beginning, middle, and end. It is therefore important to give this potential interview question considerable thought beforehand, since you, the successful candidate, will be expected to back up your answer with consistent actions.

Although it is important to prepare for this interview question, it is equally important to research the organization, including the community, elected officials, senior staff leadership team, and structure. Previous budget documents are easily accessed online and often provide clues about priorities as well as the financial health of the organization. You should review the municipal strategic plan and the progress in achieving the plan's goals and objectives. It is also helpful to review archived meeting webcasts and the minutes and agendas of council and standing committees. Social media and any available mainstream materials can also help you gain an understanding of the issues you might confront during the first 100 days.

If possible, contact the previous CAO and ask about his or her experience in the role – although, depending on the circumstances of the CAO's departure, you might want to absorb such feedback through a more objective lens. If your predecessor left to "pursue other interests," try tactfully to get a sense of the reason for the departure: was it a matter of fit, inability to inspire the team, or related to performance? The CAO who left on good terms likely will be quite forthcoming about what to expect, in terms of both on-boarding and beyond.

Once you have collected and assessed all the data and narratives, you should be able to use this information not only to answer the 30/60/90-day interview question, but also to begin the process of entering into a new and exciting chapter of your career.

Arrival

Following what one hopes was a restful holiday, it is now time to make your entrance. On day one, you might be greeted by the head of council and brought to your office, followed by a tour of the city hall, along with introductions to councillors and staff and their numerous names and titles, many of which you are likely to forget by the end of the day. The one person you must remember is your executive assistant! That individual usually knows the inner workings of the office and commands real power and influence within the organization. Over time, you might wish to rotate that position by secondment, to give you insight into various parts of the organization and to provide a career development opportunity for promising employees. The balance of the first day will be filled with more introductions, tours, draft reports for committees and council, human resources paperwork, and a calendar already populated with meetings and meeting requests. Before you know it, the day will be over and you will leave the office with your new laptop, city-issued phone, and a briefcase full of files. With the first of your first 100 days behind you, you can begin to think about how best to implement the rest of that interview question, asked weeks earlier.

Entering a new organization is very much a learning experience. In some ways, it is similar to learning how to drive on a congested freeway for the first time. As a young driver, you might have been tested at the driver registration centre in a small car provided by the instructor, and your test usually occurred on the side streets near the test centre office. After carefully navigating the residential streets and more or less successfully parallel parking, you are issued a driver's licence. You spend the next 100 days or so driving those same familiar roads and improving your confidence daily. Finally, you plan a trip to the big city, which means you now must learn how to enter and exit freeway ramps and navigate eight lanes of traffic, often surrounded by massive transport trucks. It is a nerve-racking experience as you tightly grip the steering wheel, staying in your lane, and then panicking as you see your exit quickly approaching, requiring you to move four lanes to the right somehow. At that moment you recall the words of your driving instructor: "When you find yourself in unfamiliar territory, "DON'T MAKE ANY SUDDEN MOVES!" Instead, take a deep breath, focus and check your mirrors, look for blind spots, and move cautiously and safely. You can always exit safely at the next intersection rather than drive recklessly on a busy freeway.

This is precisely the advice that you, as the new CAO, should heed as you become acquainted with your organization. Be deliberate and listen, do not jump to conclusions, and ensure you have all of the information before making decisions about change. Making erratic or sudden moves will often create chaos and confusion, cost the taxpayer hundreds of thousands of dollars in severance payments, and likely shorten your time with the organization. Like the novice driver, proceed with caution, but continue to move forward while being very conscious of the surroundings.

The biggest mistake and the most sudden move that some new CAOs make is to implement the dreaded reorganization without taking the time to understand relationships and dependencies within and across departments. Council might tolerate and even encourage such actions as the new arrival is in the "honeymoon phase," but a reorganization is the sudden move that might define your time with the organization, instead of taking time to articulate a vision and develop a strategic roadmap. Some new leaders fail to recognize that managing a public sector enterprise is very different from managing a private one.

To be clear, changes to structure and the people within that structure might need to occur, but you must do this correctly and prudently. The first three to six months is simply not sufficient time to understand the culture, within both the civic administration and the elected official spheres of the "hourglass."

It is also important to realize that so-called successful change agents from the private sector rarely succeed in the municipal world. The primary reason for this lack of success is that the public and private sectors have some fundamental differences. In their excellent book, *The First 90 Days in Government*, Peter Daly and Michael Watkins reference an observation made by Roy Ash, former company CEO and one-time director in the US federal government. Ash noted that going from the business world to the public sector was like going from the minor to the major leagues in professional sports (Daly & Watkins, 2006, p. 4). Daly and Watkins suggest that, while all sports have rule books, "in public sector leadership, the book is thicker and its relevance to what is happening on the playing field is not always as clear as it is in the private sector" (p. 4). They also observe that the spectators of government actions and decisions are often noisier than those who follow the competitive battles between firms in the marketplace.

Municipalities are also required by legislation to be much more open and transparent than the private sector or even other orders of government. All decisions are made in public, often recorded through webcasts, and decisions are carefully documented for the public record. The "rules of engagement" that apply to Canadian municipalities are highly prescriptive, and their authority and power are set out in provincial legislation. The sheer number of those affected by municipal decisions exceeds the number of those affected by most private sector organizations, and it can be argued that the services municipalities provide are much more important – i.e., safe drinking water, public health, emergency services including fire, ambulance, and police, building controls, and so forth.

All these services have a direct impact on the quality of life, personal finances, liveability, and personal long-term planning for residents. It is natural then for residents not only to take an interest in the services the municipality provides, but also to have an emotional reaction to the adequacy of services provided. Any new municipal leader, especially someone new to the public sector, must understand this difference. The voice of the public cannot, and likely will not, be ignored by council. Perceptions of decisions will be as important as the effects of those decisions: head versus heart in decision making. Unlike in the private sector, where consumers may choose to take their business elsewhere, residents of a municipality cannot choose to have their roads or recreation centres built by other municipalities. Similarly, businesses may decide that some customers are not worth trying to satisfy or serve; in government, all residents must be served.

Finally, there is the issue of access to the decision makers. A member of the public can address a council meeting and speak about services, but rarely has the opportunity to appear before the board of directors of a Fortune 500 company. A dissatisfied consumer would never call a board director of their cable company or phone company; a dissatisfied municipal ratepayer will routinely call a council member directly.

It is therefore not surprising that some private sector leaders have difficulty adjusting to the municipal sector, especially those who think they can identify the structural and personnel weaknesses after being on the job for less than a year. It is interesting to note that none of the five very successful and respected CAOs profiled in Siegel's book deployed "gunslinger" approaches to change management. These successful CAOs knew how to manage change successfully by understanding and respecting the local culture and by thinking rationally and deliberately. They were not prone to making sudden moves.

During my municipal career, I served as CAO in four municipalities with annual budgets ranging from a few million to a billion dollars, as well as serving in an interim capacity as the city manager/CAO for three additional communities. During all these assignments, I resisted calls for a wholesale reorganization. Problems with the structure that first appeared to be obvious upon my arrival turned out not to be serious at all. A major reorganization would have only added to the confusion, while taking the time to solve the real problems ensured that the civic administration was ultimately successful, and it didn't take massive disruption to achieve that success.

I was also fortunate to work in the private sector during the midpoint in my career. My responsibilities were similar, at least on paper, as I led an organization that reported to one person: the owner of the business. The decision-making process was not much of a process at all, and the top portion of the hourglass was occupied by a single grain of sand (the owner), while the bottom portion contained several hundred employees. Occupying *that* pinch point was very different from my municipal experience. For example, I never discovered that "[d]irect access to critical resources ... [was] ... impeded by opaque, remote, and onerous bureaucratic systems with long lead times" (Daly & Watkins, 2006, p. 5).

The business imperative was very different, in that our primary objective was to earn a profit and ensure that the money borrowed from the bank was returned promptly and with interest. It was fast paced: decisions required only one sign off and Darwinism was the management philosophy. Change was constant, hard-and-fast rules were treated more like guidelines, and the successes were spectacular as were the failures.

Public sector organizations cannot paper over spectacular failures. They simply cannot sell off unprofitable divisions, terminate noisy or underperforming products, pick and choose which services to offer, or decide which consumers or clients they will serve. This level of risk avoidance often fuels the perception that municipal leadership is therefore limited to a playbook that avoids risk, pays lip service to true innovation, and is a career defined by staying in the middle lane, firmly and at all times. We will come back to this later, because while innovation might look different, municipalities can in fact be at the forefront of innovation within the public sector.

Build Networks

The first 100 days should involve the building of three networks, two external and one internal to the organization. It is often said that it is lonely at the top, and that is especially true for a new CAO. Whether you have been promoted from within or joined the organization as a department head from another municipality, your support network of peers suddenly might disappear. A department head can seek advice from peers within the same municipality, as they occupy the same position within the organizational hierarchy. All of this evaporates when you reach the apex of the organization. In some cases, members of your senior management team might have competed for your position.

You should establish two external networks during the on-boarding period. One should include professional development organizations such as the International City/County Management Association, Canadian Association of Municipal Administrators, and the provincial or state equivalents, which provide opportunities to learn and use the best practices from other CAOs. Several regional and annual association conferences provide training and networking opportunities that simply are not available anywhere else, given the uniqueness of municipal leadership. The executive directors of these associations generally are very helpful and can connect new CAOs with a peer who can provide advice and guidance. It also might be useful to retain the services of an executive coach or mentor if this is your first entry into the world of CAOs. In addition to providing technical advice, a mentor or coach can help you to work within and understand the relationships that come from managing in Siegel's hourglass.

The second external network that you should develop quickly consists of community leaders, such as successful businesspeople in the community, academics, and leaders from the not-for-profit sector, including organized community groups. When I first joined a municipality as the incoming CAO, I asked the economic development department to provide contact information for a handful of the largest employers in the community. During the first meeting with the CEO of a well-respected manufacturing business, I was surprised to learn that I was the first municipal employee who had asked to tour the plant and what the municipality could do to assist his business. He quickly contacted several other business leaders, and the network blossomed from there. These leaders employ taxpayers and provide significant revenue, and should be treated with respect. Many are also very adept at managing people – an essential skill for a CAO – and they can be a tremendous resource during the first 100 days and beyond. Business leaders also communicate with council members and their views are influential.

The third network to build is internal. Essentially, it is part of the discovery phase of the on-boarding process. Contrary to what some might think, all forms of intelligent life are not confined to the senior leadership team of your municipality. It is imperative that, during the first 100 days, you, as the new CAO, get out of your corner office and meet the employees who deliver the services. The interface between the taxpayer and the municipality is not the CAO, but the civic employee who collects the taxes at the counter, issues the building permit, works in the local arena, ploughs and maintains the roads, drives the transit bus, and so on. Many of these employees will progress through the organization and eventually assume leadership positions. By taking the time to get to know your employees, a network of what I referred to as our "spark plugs" was developed in each community where I worked. Although they all came from different backgrounds and disciplines, they had much in common. They were bright, committed to public service, and wanted to be part of something bigger. This network was formalized into an advisory panel that provided a sounding board and source of new ideas and much energy. A "walk-about" management style during the first 100 days will introduce you to potential candidates to populate the network that eventually will become the organization's leaders.

I was also pleasantly surprised that the department heads were secure enough not to feel threatened or undermined by their staffs' participation in the program. Before selecting a candidate, it was important to receive the blessing of the department head, who in most instances saw the value of supporting the employee's career development opportunity.

Find a Coach or Mentor

Once you have established these networks, it is also useful to find an experienced coach or mentor. There are very few new problems in civic administration, and chances are good that the immediate problem or issue you might be facing has been managed by someone else previously. There are essentially two ways to learn: either from your mistakes or from others who possess significant leadership experience. The former method might be inevitable, but the latter tends to be more effective in terms of both cost and efficiency.

A mentorship relationship can take several forms. Many current and former civic administrators are available to provide advice and perspective to an incoming CAO. The executive directors of national, provincial, and state CAO/city manager associations can often connect a mentor and a mentee. Confidentiality is a necessity, and the relationship must be based on trust.

Be Visible

There is much mystery, uncertainty, and drama during the first 100 days, so be visible. If you remain bunkered down in your office or get pulled into the vortex of meetings and processes, the potential for angst and uncertainty increases proportionally to the time spent in your well-appointed office. If you are invisible, your persona and personal brand might be developed and defined by others. Therefore, spend the first 100 days getting to know the people in the organization and giving them the opportunity to get to know their new CAO.

Your entry into the workplace can take a number of forms. For example, departmental or divisional breakfast meetings or brown bag lunches can be arranged to give you an opportunity to tell your story – who you are, why you joined the organization – dispel any rumours, communicate some of your initial ideas, ask for theirs, and let them know how important they are as community builders and service providers. Some new leaders use YouTube videos to introduce themselves, but videos obviously do not provide the opportunity to be spontaneous and genuine; as well, they are a one-way form of communication, and the intended audience cannot respond or engage in a conversation.

Chris Murray, City Manager in Toronto, regularly attends the new-employee workshops organized by the human resources department. A typical meeting consists of a few dozen recent recruits receiving a basic orientation from HR. The city manager then describes some of the current issues and how as employees they relate to those issues. His style is very non-bureaucratic: laid back and conversational. New employees are put at ease and given ample opportunity to ask questions; the city manager provides honest and straightforward responses. He is also not shy about devoting precious but necessary time to listen to new recruits. In speaking to a recent attendee, I was told that the staff were pleasantly surprised that the city manager would take the time to outline the issues and, more important, to ask for their ideas. His brand and style of leadership were on full display, and the interactive exchange was far better than blogs, emails, or videos. Employees who attend these meetings are likely to convey positive impressions informally to a much wider audience.

The second way to remain visible is to employ "management by walking around," an approach first noted by management experts Tom Peters and Robert H. Waterman (1982). As part of their study of successful businesses, they noted that informal communications and interactions in hallways rather than boardrooms seemed to contribute to the success of the business. Sam Walton, founder of Walmart, visited stores and sought input from front-line staff. The payoff is often immediate when the new leader listens to the input and takes effective action.

Doug Oberhelman, CEO of Caterpillar, had a sign at the entrance of their headquarters that read "a desk is a dangerous place from which to view the world" (Jordan, 2020). The quote is from well-known espionage writer John le Carré, but it certainly applies to the sometimes mysterious world of municipal administration. During the first 100 days, it is natural to see the organization through the lens of budgets, operational plans, meetings, and reports. Although these are the traditional forms of communication and information, nothing is better than observing something on the ground and in real time.

Visit all the outside facilities, especially those that have been identified in the capital budget forecast. A tour of a water treatment plant, a public works yard, or a satellite office accomplishes two things: it helps you learn quickly about the operation during your entry period, and it demonstrates to staff that you care about them and their business. It is surprising to see that some CAOs remain confined to their offices, heads buried in spreadsheets and reports, claiming they are too busy to go out in the field.

"Management by walking around" also helps council make better budget decisions. For example, in a community I worked in there had been endless discussions about the need to replace some fire trucks and equipment as part of the capital forecast. According to the forecast, two very expensive trucks were due for replacement as part of the annual budget, and council was looking at the financial impact. All the discussion at committee focused on spreadsheets and budget options from staff. The chief was left trying to explain how the equipment necessary to deal with vehicle collisions on Canada's busiest freeway had changed since the last piece of equipment was purchased two decades ago. Council was viewing the issue from a dangerous place: the council chambers desk. After a short break, it was suggested that everyone meet at the fire hall, situated next to the municipal building. The firefighters at the hall were surprised when the entire council and the department heads arrived, and the chief explained the budget request. Councillors asked the staff better questions and received better answers during that visit than in the previous several hours spent reviewing budget actuals versus forecast reports in council chambers. The result after the site inspection was that the elected officials truly understood all the dimensions of the decision-making process, and this led to a well-informed outcome.

Secure Early Wins

There will be an expectation that the new leader will bring positive change and strive to improve the organization. Early wins, therefore, will help solidify your reputation, confirm that council made the right choice, and demonstrate to staff how you go about making decisions. The wins generally should be those where there is mutual benefit to the parties involved, and certainly not those that involve a clear winner and an obvious loser. Daly and Watkins (2006, p. 11) suggest that "you need to figure out where and how you will get early wins to build your credibility, create momentum and lay the foundation for achieving your longer term goals."

If you were recruited from another municipality and have experience as a CAO, it should not be difficult to apply successful strategies and policies to serve what appear to be longstanding grievances or irritants.

During the initial few months as a new CAO, I observed that the annual budget process was completely broken. It was mid-year and the budget committee of council was mired in unnecessary and often acrimonious debate. It was clear that the debate had become personal, and unfortunately staff had become casualties.

One department head believed he simply had to identify the risks involved in not obtaining the necessary funds for his department, and should the funding not be approved, the consequences would fall to council. As a result, he was asking/demanding a massive increase to solve the infrastructure deficit immediately. That request, coupled with the usual demands of the other departments, meant a double-digit tax increase in the year before the next election. It is no wonder the previous CAO left "to pursue other interests." The solution was to take the department head aside and ask him for a detailed briefing on how the budget process worked and what his ideas were to resolve things. It became apparent that he viewed his job as the protector of his silo first and a member of the senior leadership team a distant second. His communication style involved overwhelming council with technical-jargon-filled explanations that were not easily comprehended. As a result, some of the less patient councillors could not question his answers, so they resorted to attacking him personally, with a predicable outcome. It is no wonder that they were six months into the budget year with little prospect of having a budget decision. The only positive thing was that the snow-removal estimates were extremely accurate because the winter had passed!

In the end a budget was approved, and within a year the combative department head went on to pursue other interests. A post-mortem on the budget process involved interviewing each councillor and department head. It was clear that senior staff viewed the budget process as a competition for resources, and it was impossible to tie the budget to the strategic plan because that plan was fluff, with no measurable actions. Perhaps most strikingly, there was no opportunity for council to express what it would like to see in the annual budget.

The solution was obvious: a new policy was instituted that saw the preparation of a budget directions report, to be tabled in the six months prior to the budget deliberations. The report would outline the fixed costs in the operating budget, collective agreement obligations, benefits, pensions, utilities, and debenture payments. The capital budget would consist of those projects slated for commencement as part of a ten-year capital plan. Assuming service levels remained relatively constant, a tax increase range was estimated. It was made clear that, by approving the report, council was not pre-approving the budget; rather, it was giving direction for staff to build a budget based on a general strategy. The result was a much smoother and more rational decision-making process.

When I moved to another organization several years later, I was surprised to see that this community had precisely the same problem, although it was slightly earlier in the calendar year in its budget deliberations. Within a few weeks of my arrival, I suggested a new approach that was designed to solve the process problem and thus create an early win. The answer was to pause the process, ask council where the budget goal posts were, and, upon receiving some direction, to strike a budget a month before year-end using the lessons learned from the previous municipality. This "early win" helped, as Daly and Watkins would say, "build momentum in the short run and simultaneously lay the foundation for achieving your longer-term goals" (Daly & Watkins, 2006, p. 89).

An early win also provides a sense of how you deal with challenges, demonstrates your style, and answers the questions that staff and council might have had when you joined the organization.

Assess Your Team

The first 100 days will give you an opportunity to assess the senior leaders. Before you arrive to start the new job, it is useful to review the personnel files of members of the leadership group. The reviews, if done properly, will provide some indication of how they perform and behave. There might be executive assessments undertaken by third-party experts, 360-degree performance evaluations, and other items of interest in the file.

Given that your success might depend in part on your direct reports, it is crucial that you get to know the staff you have inherited during the on-boarding period. The most obvious way to do this is through formal and informal meetings and chats. Most senior staff work well beyond normal office hours, and after a long day I found it useful to drop in to their offices and have an informal discussion. The conversations could be work related, but more often tended to migrate to non-work topics – children, holiday plans, the state of hockey in Canada, and other important topics. Although I have made it a practice not to socialize with staff, there is no reason you cannot be sociable, demonstrate empathy, and be genuinely interested in your staff.

Invariably, you will discover that some of those who report to you directly might have competed for your job, so it is important to address that awkward dynamic very early in the relationship. I have had some senior staff tell me that they were very disappointed and that they wanted to find work elsewhere. Others have said that they applied only because they thought it would be an indication of a lack of ambition if they had not. Others said that they applied to block another member of the leadership group from getting the position – an early indication of dysfunction within the senior ranks. In each of these and a few other situations, I maintained a clear and consistent message to everyone: council made the decision, and although staff might have been disappointed with the outcome, the way they now choose to react to the decision will speak volumes about their ability to lead an organization in the future.

In some cases, council might appoint an interim CAO from among the current senior leadership team and leave the individual in place for an extended period. On one occasion, unbeknownst to me, a very competent senior leader was not selected for the position after having been the interim leader for a year. After discovering this, I arranged to meet with the individual weeks before arriving for the first day on the job. I explained that it was natural to be disappointed and angry but hoped that those feelings were not directed towards me. Councils make decisions and, for whatever reason, they might think that the internal candidate was not quite ready or did not have the skills to match the issues facing the organization at that point. Eventually, that person became my most trusted confidante and a worthy candidate for the CAO position one day, having blossomed and handled the "defeat" with class and dignity. In the months and years to come, I gave the individual responsibility for and direct oversight over a very large and complicated series of portfolios, which revealed the person's adeptness at leading a large municipality. Upon my retirement as CAO, council selected that individual as my successor.

Once settled into the new surroundings, you will be expected to assess the structure of the organization and the team within that structure. In the municipal world, there are essentially three models of senior leadership teams: a broad team consisting of the leaders of each business unit (seven to ten direct reports), one that has fewer direct reports and consists of a grouping of services or business units under three to five individuals, or one that has a very limited number of deputies (one to three), each with a large portfolio, who report to the CAO. There is no right or wrong model. You should not spend your first 100 days trying to determine which is best, since that would be to fall into the "sudden-move" trap. Rather, take time to assess the structure and just as important, the people within the structure carefully. During my career I have witnessed what at first glance appeared to be an unusual structure, but

I subsequently learned that it worked because of the quality and ability of the people occupying the positions. Although you should not base the organizational structure solely on individuals, it should be a consideration when designing the best way of delivering services and getting on with the business of civic administration.

The first 100 days should be a time to reflect on how well the leadership team works and how it is structured. This assessment should be structured and consistently applied. Daly and Watkins (2006, p. 107) provide a useful checklist of criteria for evaluating the team:

1. *Trust*. This is perhaps the most important quality – once lost, never found. Can you rely on this person to be honest and truthful? Will the person deliver on his or her commitments?
2. *Competence*. This is somewhat obvious, and should become apparent in the first few weeks.
3. *Judgment*. This is especially important in the municipal context: does the person exercise good judgment when making decisions? Does the person make evidence-based decisions or rely on intuition?
4. *Energy*. "Fire in the belly" and passion are excellent qualities but should be balanced with rational thinking and decision making
5. *Focus*. A scatterbrain simply will not survive in the complicated and stress-filled world of civic administration. There are many potential distractions, and a good leader knows how to manage time effectively.
6. *Relationships*. How well does the person get along with teammates? Is the person committed to supporting collective decision making or difficult to work with?

Daly and Watkins's list could be expanded to include two more criteria:

7. *Humility*. The business of municipal government is to "be of service." We are referred to as public servants for a reason, and successful CAOs are truly "leaders in the shadows," as Siegel (2015) notes.
8. *A sense of humour*. Some of the absurdities of local government require an antidote that can be supplied through a well-developed sense of humour. Nothing defuses the stress and pressure of a senior leadership meeting better than a well-placed bit of humour. Your team should take their jobs very seriously but not themselves nearly as much. A sense of perspective and humour are valuable qualities for a senior manager.

Towards the end of the first 100 days, you should be able to form a picture of the strengths and weaknesses of your team.

Managing Relationships with the Mayor and Council

Let's go back to the hourglass analogy and build it out to see what it means for you as a leader who must act, innovate, collaborate, change things (attitudes, culture, strategy, people, tools), and deliver results. Understanding the vision of council and investing in relationships during your first 100 days can help turn the hourglass from "us" versus "them" to "we." Three areas come to mind:

1. Untangle the complex structures, hierarchies, authorities, myriad job titles, and relationships and interdependencies among staff, council, vendors, contractors, and the community, and understand the boundaries. You should then be able to develop a strategy to collaborate across these boundaries before they become barriers.
2. Gain increasing confidence in your understanding of the vision of council. If that vision is unfocused or not clearly articulated, invest time in achieving that clarity, either for yourself or jointly along with the mayor and council.
3. Forge a relationship with the mayor and council, so you can agree on a common mission while acknowledging your differences. This is important, because while you work for the same corporate body and, one hopes, share the same vision for the municipality, your paths are very different, as are your motivations and your roles. You and the mayor must set an example for your respective teams (administration and governance) on how to work together. It is also helpful to understand and acknowledge differences beyond those defined by your roles and responsibilities. Tolerance of differences in personality, traits, leadership approach, and so forth between you and the head of council is critical to building a resilient relationship. Being aware of and respecting differences between two leaders who must work together to deliver value will help you create the space to work together effectively, and also give you room to disagree and ideate in different ways.

Work-Life Balance

During the first 100 days as the new CAO, you can expect to experience every human emotion imaginable. There will be the initial joy of landing the "big job," tempered with a bit of apprehension and sometimes even panic. There will be much to learn, many people to meet, and processes to understand. The days will fly by, and when you arrive home in the early evening the night will be spent doing more reading, researching, and thinking. The first 100 days will end far too quickly and the honeymoon period will rapidly come to an end.

Having a reasonable work-life balance is key to a successful onboarding experience. Although the pressures and stress of a new job are understandable, you must manage them. Take regular exercise at a local gym or an early morning walk – these are not only healthy for the body, they also help to clear the mind. You are probably entitled to a generous vacation package, so make sure you take advantage of it and learn how to disconnect from the office when you are away. The purpose of a vacation is to rest and rebalance. There is nothing more stressful or frustrating than checking emails in a place far removed from your place of work. One simply does not have access to all the information or resources, and the time spent recovering becomes filled with more frustration and stress.

Successful leaders understand the importance of a healthy work-life balance. Your municipality is important, but it places a distant second in life's priorities. A supportive family, staying in good physical and mental shape, and maintaining a positive outlook will help make the first 100 days and subsequent many years both productive and enjoyable. Keeping things in perspective is vitally important. As Keith Robicheau notes, "[t]he municipality is a body corporate. It's not a family member; it's not your wife, and you know what, you shouldn't care at the level I was caring" (quoted in Siegel, 2015, p. 171).

Conclusion

Managing a municipality can be one of the most rewarding, influential roles of your career. You will work with competent people dedicated to public service and elected officials who work hard to connect the municipality with its residents. You will affect the community you serve directly. You will see your successes and failures in near-real time – not on a corporate income statement, but in the spaces you manage and in your impact on the lives and experiences of people who live, work, and play in those spaces.

Use your first thirty days to establish relationships, broadcast your leadership style and core values, understand the issues, and map out the dynamics of the organization. Use the next thirty days to start formulating a vision, collecting data, and identifying internal innovators and change champions. Finally, focus on communicating clearly, openly, and often. In a word, if you can truly *engage* with the job, with your employees, and with council, you can set yourself up for success on strategy, structure, and sustainable, innovative change for the rest of your career and to ensure a healthy work-life balance.

The first several months will set the stage for the balance of time you work for the community. A successful first impression can lead to a lasting and positive effect if you have an entry plan, together with the energy and commitment to lead your staff and be of service to council and the community.

REFERENCES

Daly, P. H., & Watkins, M. (2006). *The first 90 days in government*. Harvard Business Review Press.

Jordan, R. (2020, 14 November). A desk is a dangerous place from which to view the world. *Forbes*. Retrieved from https://www.forbes.com/sites/robertjordan/2012/11/01/how-to-be-a-better-leader-ditch-your-desk/?sh=5025e291677c

Peters, T., & Waterman, R. H. (1982). *In search of excellence*. Harper & Row.

Siegel, D. (2015). *Leaders in the shadows: The leadership qualities of successful municipal chief administrative officers*. University of Toronto Press.

5 The Challenge of Leading Up: Strategic Alignment with Council

JEFF FIELDING AND KATE GRAHAM

Alignment is a critical aspect mentioned by most city managers for leadership success. Jeff Fielding, former city manager for the cities of Kitchener, London, and Burlington, all in Ontario, as well as Calgary, and Dr Kate Graham, a political scientist from Huron University College, describe Fielding's political relationship experiences. His sage advice covers aligning leadership expectations and strategic direction with council.

You take a sip from your coffee mug, only to find it cold – again. The council budget debate has waged on for more than four hours, with a number of the most contentious decisions still ahead on the agenda. The only people who seem pleased with this progress are the journalists, as the debate has been rich in quotable content from the most heated moments of the meeting. No one wanted to be in this position, most certainly not the elected officials: an already stretched budget as service demands increase and the costs of providing services continue to rise; a mounting infrastructure gap with no relief in sight; years of work invested in several high-profile projects requiring major new investment; and now, a major economic downturn leaving the community struggling and with dramatic impacts on municipal revenues.

These converging realities have created an inescapable fiscal pinch, with no "solutions" to be found – only a series of unpalatable trade-offs, none without community (or political) consequence. A motion had been tabled to delay a planned transit line extension, including laying off the team of engineers working on the project. On one hand, this would relieve some operating and capital pressure for the year ahead. On the other hand, years had already been invested in the project, aimed to provide transit service to a low-income and underserved neighbourhood. The project would never cost less than building it now, and the investment would support hundreds of jobs in the construction season ahead.

As councillor after councillor weighed into the debate, you could already tell the vote would be close. You could also feel the anxiety behind you in the gallery, including from your lead engineers, who had a particularly acute sense of what was at stake. The mayor caught your eye, with a mixed expression of anger and exhaustion. She had already been on the losing end of several important votes today and she had invested a lot of political capital in ensuring the transit project would proceed. With an election less than a year away, and a few potential mayoral contenders around the horseshoe, the debate was about more than a transit line.

When you accepted the position of city manager more than five years ago, you prided yourself on your ability to maintain strong relationships across the political spectrum. You had invested hours with members of council to understand their objectives, individually and collectively, and had done your best to align the work of the organization to their priorities. By and large, the mayor and councillors trusted you. Most considered you an ally and confidant. As with most important debates, you walked into today's meeting with a sense of which votes mattered most to each council member and, generally, where they stood on the major points of contention.

You and your senior team had contingency plans and alternative scenarios ready as options in case called upon. The budget presentation materials were clear, factual, and comprehensive – and yet you had sat through enough debates like this to know the moment was coming. You would soon be called upon to weigh in with "objective" advice, knowing full well that how you framed your response would be inherently and unavoidably political. Predictably, the question came from the mayor's leading presumed challenger. "Given our fiscal situation, frankly it would be utterly irresponsible to do anything other than delay this project. The city manager's report even lays out a plan for how this would be managed – but I'd like to hear from the city manager directly. Can you confirm for me that you can indeed manage this delay?" As you rise from your seat, you hear the media's cameras spin to focus on you, and you feel every pair of eyes around the horseshoe turn to you – full of expectation.

"Through you, Your Worship, to the councillor …"

The role of a city manager is unlike any other executive position in Canadian public administration. This chapter is about the *political dimensions* of this role: working with the mayor and council, in an effort to build strategic alignment for the organization and community. Unlike in other levels of government, navigating the dynamics of this political relationship is on display for public and media scrutiny. The city manager role is a tightrope walk of being intentionally apolitical while also appreciating that every public act is unavoidably political (Siegel 2020). The task is challenging, complex, fluid, and of paramount importance for effective local governance. Many people think the relationship between council and the city manager begins the first day on the job, or the first day after inauguration – but this relationship is in fact far more enduring, without a beginning or an end. The people in the roles will come and go, but the relationship between council and the city manager endures as an institutional foundation upon which local governance rests. For the individual city manager, this means being a steward of this relationship for a period of time. It means "leading up" (Siegel, 2015) with a group of elected officials who must find common ground and make difficult decisions in an environment defined by competing, and often unrealistic, expectations.

Purpose

In April 2004, I assumed the position of city manager in the City of London, Ontario, following a period of rapid turnover in the role. I was the fifth city manager in three years. The organization had been dogged by a series of high-profile scandals and faced constant public criticism. Early in my tenure, I was asked to deliver a speech on the future of the organization. I needed to be honest. We had a lot of work to do to improve, and we needed to acknowledge our shortcomings. But I also needed to do so without further deflating the fragile psychology of council and staff. I used a sports analogy to say that our team had missed the playoffs for a number of years, the players were afraid to step on the ice, the fans were staying away from the games and embarrassed by our play, and the media were critical of our performance. We needed to set our course to get back into the playoffs – to be ranked among the top municipalities in Canada. There was a high degree of scepticism, but four years later the City of London was ranked as the best-run municipality in Ontario (Coyne, 2009).

This was not my first city manager job. By this point, I had worked in several large cities in executive roles. In the City of Winnipeg, I had worked closely with council as we transitioned from a board-of-commissioners model to a CAO model. In the City of Calgary, I had worked on rebuilding the strained relationship between council and staff. As city manager of the City of Kitchener, I faced working with council in a challenged economy by taking risks and making public investment in the downtown. By the time I arrived in London, I had learned a few important lessons: chiefly, that a systematic approach is required to inherit and execute the city manager role effectively.

It is not enough to show up and do your best; as city manager, you have been hired by council to lead. They expect you to live up to your values and to instil in the organization the behaviours that you represent to them. I have found it useful to employ a model that sets out the roles, responsibilities, and results for council and administration (see figure 5.1), and to use a systematic approach to align the vision and direction of council with the management of the organization in order to deliver results (see figure 5.2). You then need to articulate clearly where the organization is headed (figure 5.3). In this chapter, I share the approach that I found delivered the best results for me – in the hope that other current and future city managers can use and adapt these tools to make them their own.

The Work

Three primary groups are engaged in local governance in Canada – council, administration, and the community – and we all wear "two hats." Clearly defining our roles and the relationships we hold with one another, as described in figure 5.1, is essential for success.

The first group is the community. Residents have hopes, dreams, and aspirations for the community in which they have chosen to lead their lives. They expect a high quality of life for themselves and for their families. Residents and businesses are also consumers of public services for which they pay a tax, rate, or fee. As customers, they expect value for their investment in those services.

The second group is council, which collectively holds the responsibility to interpret the aspirations of the community and establish a meaningful vision. Each city is different, therefore the vision for each city must differentiate the unique qualities of the community that are rooted in the aspirations of its residents. This is council's leadership role. Council also has a role in providing direction to administration to provide public services that add value to people's lives and contribute to their quality of life.

The third group is the administration, or staff. The public services provided by the local government must reflect the specific needs of the community. No two cities are the same, therefore the services provided to each community must be different to reflect their unique needs. Providing these services to the community, and managing the resources of the organization for council, are the main roles for administration.

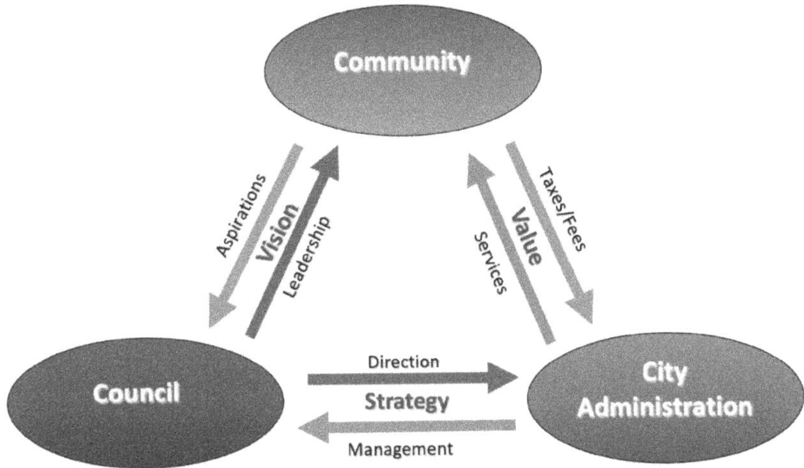

Figure 5.1 Fielding's View of Local Governance

The relationship between council and the administration depends on the strength of the direction provided by council and the ability of the administration to manage that direction. The outcome of this relationship is a *strategy for the local government* that enables the vision to be achieved through the quality of the public services in the municipality. The strategy drives public confidence and trust, and this outcome is dependent on the strength of the relationship between council and the administration, and the degree of cohesion in how they work together – or more simply, *strategic alignment*. Of course, in practice the relationship between council and the administration is more complicated than it appears in figure 5.1. It exists not as an abstract connection between two homogeneous bodies, but rather multiple relationships between individual actors within two heterogeneous groups. The city manager, however, occupies a special role as the sole member (or one of the few members) of the administration reporting directly to council. The city manager acts as the central conduit between council and the administration, and therefore must steward this important relationship.

What does this involve in practice? The task is akin to establishing (and then executing) a contract: a set of parameters defining the terms and boundaries of the relationship and a consensus on where the organization is headed. Figure 5.2 describes what this involves, where council and the administration collectively orient around a strategy by taking

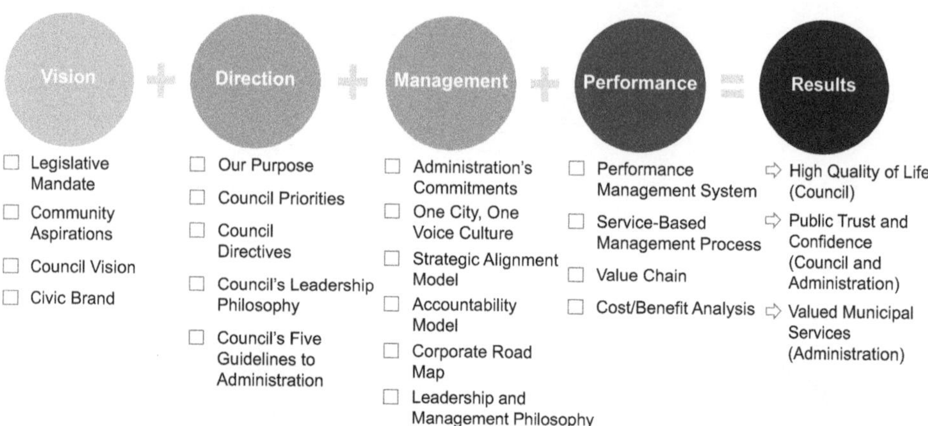

Figure 5.2 A Strategic Alignment Equation

on various functional roles in the process. Importantly, council is most involved in the elements to the left of the diagram, while the administration is most involved in the elements to the right. It is an equation designed to produce results. I have used it as a checklist to ascertain what is in place, what is missing, and what needs attention. An organization is like an assortment of puzzle pieces that can be assembled in a variety of different ways to create an assortment of different images. Each puzzle piece represents specific capabilities, and the city manager must assemble the puzzle pieces to fit the vision that the mayor and council have articulated – and fill in the gaps where they exist.

The equation starts with a clear vision, framed by the legislative mandate of the municipality and developed by council as a reflection of the collective aspirations of the community (Tindal & Tindal, 2019, p. 6). Council and the administration then translate this vision into direction, usually involving a strategic planning or another process where priorities, principles, directives, and other guiding directions are established. The administration is responsible for managing the resources of the municipality and putting performance management systems in place to increase and demonstrate the efficiency and effectiveness of local public services. When applied properly, the outcome of this effort should produce positive results: a high quality of life in the community, valued municipal services, and an increase in trust and confidence.

Establishing psychological safety within an organization is critical if transformation and innovation are expected. I have found it useful to articulate clearly a specific path ahead for the organization, as a way of leading change while also providing predictability and stability.

Stage One: Organizational Stability

Step 1: Articulate the leadership philosophy and approach
Step 2: Concentrate on priorities
Step 3: Establish goals
Step 4: Set specific objectives, measures, and targets

Stage Two: Organizational Effectiveness and Economy

Step 5: Align with strategic direction
Step 6: Clarify accountability
Step 7: Enhance organizational development
Step 8: Enable services integration
Step 9: Build organizational flexibility
Step 10: Focus on customer needs and public engagement
Step 11: Balance scope and scale of departments

Stage Three: Organizational Efficiency

Step 12: Address structural efficiency

Figure 5.3. An Organizational Road Map

If you have children, you are familiar with the question, "are we there yet?" Like parents in a family, organizations expect their leaders to know the journey ahead and how to get there. Building and sharing a road map establishes this path and timing (see figure 5.3). It informs the mayor and council about your pace of execution and ensures that the administration also understands the focus and timelines. As city manager, you must devote considerable effort to a logical and prioritized agenda that is challenging but doable. All too often, too much is promised, and an unrealistic timeline is proposed. Council will hold you to this timeline, so careful deliberation is your best ally. Your relationship with the mayor and council will depend on your success.

In Calgary, I committed to a services-based budget. I listened carefully to the team that would be executing the assignment. The team was concerned about the task and the timelines, so we rearranged the approach before we made our plans public. In the end the team developed the road map and regularly informed council and the administration when we finally would arrive at the destination.

Executing a road map – achieving strategic alignment with council, and then translating its vision into results – requires the effective city manager to have an impressive range of skills and abilities. As said at the outset, the city manager role is unlike any other executive role in Canadian public administration (Mouritzen & Svara, 2002, pp. 9–10). One reason for this is navigating the political dynamics occurs largely in a public setting: at council meetings. This means the city manager role also requires a particular kind of leader. A city manager is a 24/7 position. Ensuring you are present in the relationship with the mayor and council, being available when they need you (Manzie & Hartley, 2018, p. 24), willing to listen and provide advice, and maintaining a thick skin are necessary attributes in building and maintaining those relationships. I answer all my calls, emails, and text messages, and I committed to getting back to the mayor and council as soon as possible – always the same day without fail. When problems or concerns were raised, I would ask them to "leave it with me." My relationships depended on my follow-up and accountability to their concerns.

It also requires being comfortable with both leading and following, and knowing one's place. I have always considered the council floor to be the stage for a theatrical event. Sometimes it is scripted and sometimes it requires improvisation. The city manager's relationship with council depends on the city manager's ability to perform the role "on stage": providing solid advice, assisting in facilitating a difficult debate when council stalls, breaking the tension with an anecdote or a humorous comment, and assisting council in distilling the broad range of positions into a useful recommendation for its approval. The city manager's attention can never waver. You must listen and be engaged. You earn your place in these settings.

I learned this lesson the hard way a few times. When I was city manager in the City of Calgary, we faced a significant economic downturn that put enormous pressure on the city budget and operations – not unlike the dynamics described in the introduction of this chapter. During one committee meeting, councillors were discussing strategies to address the consequences of the downturn. The community had relied heavily on the oil and gas sector to generate economic prosperity, but the decline in oil and gas prices signalled the need for a different economic future. I challenged the councillors to be more assertive and invest more substantially in emerging technologies that would provide a more diversified economic base. Council was familiar with my encouragement to be more strategic, and generally had responded positively to my interventions. But on this occasion, I showed my frustration with the lack of progress. I went too far and jeopardized my relationship with the committee members. I had to swallow my pride and realize I had my place, and I needed to be both strategic and intentional in my remarks at council and committee in the future or the relationship would be jeopardized.

The city manager must be a master listener and relationship builder, and must earn the individual and collective trust of a large and often divided group of elected officials in the municipality (Ridge, 2020, p. 53). This trust is not a given; it must be earned. This often-challenging task requires you to have both range and scale: to be able to listen intently to both what is said and what is not said by those around you, to assess and reassess constantly the landscape of interests and motivations of the diversity of people around you, and to be able to align the interests of those people towards a strategy. It is not an easy job – and requires you to invest deliberately in relationship building at every stage of your role. Building these strong personal relationships will also help you influence elected officials, which is often needed.

In practice, mayors and councillors tend to focus less on their strategic roles and involve themselves more directly as an avenue for criticism and grievances about city services: council can become like a complaint department. In this circumstance, it is imperative that the city manager engage the mayor and council in undertaking their responsibilities to establish a strong vision for the community and clear direction for the administration that is meaningful and measurable. It requires skill and deliberate conversation by the city manager to persuade elected officials to do their highest value work.

Finally, effectively stewarding the political relationship requires a high level of self-awareness. This point cannot be overstated. When I was for Calgary during the late 1990s, I had the opportunity to have breakfast with the CEO of Canadian Airlines. The company had fallen on hard times, and his job was to wind down the airline. I wanted to know what was next for him. He told me that some headhunters were presenting offers, all of which were accompanied by a seven-figure salary. I wanted to know what offer he would accept. His answer? None of them. They were all with growth companies and his specific expertise was in downsizing.

I learned then and there that I needed to differentiate myself, to develop a skill set I could deliver and execute every time. I knew from my hockey days that very few coaches could move from one organization to another and be successful. The people and cultures, conditions, and ownerships all would be different. You need to be adaptable in executing your plans, but you need a core complement of strategies and tactics that are tried and proven. Your relationship with council will depend on your ability to deliver the outcomes you had promised. Differentiate yourself, but ensure you have the capability to back up your promises. Like any successful relationship, the political relationship for a city manager begins with a clear understanding of one's own character, motivations, and skills.

Many people aspire to leadership positions for the wrong reasons and are not truthful with themselves about what drives them to be there. Assessing your own personal fit to a city manager assignment – including the corporate culture, the task as council sees it, and the needs of the community at that moment in time – is absolutely essential. This includes when you take on a new role, and when you choose a time to depart. You will be more successful, and your work will have a higher impact, if you are in roles that are a fit for you as a leader. For city managers, you are, as they say about hockey coaches, ever only as good as your last game.

Changing communities frequently is a reality of the CAO role, and can be challenging from a personal and family perspective. Prospective and new city managers need to be aware that this is a part of the job – and make decisions accordingly, particularly if considering taking on a city manager role early in your career. Climbing to the top of the organizational ladder leaves no further steps to climb, and so at some point the city manager will need to find a new ladder. The vagabond city manager lifestyle is not for everyone, but for those who choose to accept it, the city manager role provides a unique and unparalleled opportunity to serve and shape a community.

Conclusion

Pericles once said, "fix your eyes upon the greatness of Athens, until you become filled with the love of her; and when you are impressed by the spectacle of her glory, reflect that this empire has been acquired by men who knew their duty and had the courage to do it." Pericles understood that the glories of Athens were the result of people who put the interests of their city ahead of the personal riches and power that accompanied position and hierarchy. In fact, Pericles chose his words carefully in defining the character of the people who made Athens great. He described the glories of Athens as having been "acquired" by those who had invested their hearts and souls in building a great legacy that would stand for hundreds of years. He also described these leaders as valiant, as brave and courageous in their beliefs, and as standing strong in their convictions regarding the value of public service. And finally, Pericles concluded by saying that these valiant people understood their responsibilities to the people of Athens, and they acted on the duties entrusted to them to make a difference in the lives of the citizens of that great city.

This remarkable insight holds true today. It is possible to place the name of any community that aspires to greatness in place of Athens. The responsibilities and duties assigned to those leaders by Pericles are the same today for the mayors, councillors, and administrators who lead and manage the democratic process on behalf of their constituents. Choosing a career in public service must be a conscious decision, because the work is not for everyone. Leaders must choose whether service in government aligns with their aspirations and personal character. The context for public sector leadership is changing. In the future, we hope to see a more diverse and representative group providing leadership in our communities.

Leading up is a challenge, even for the most experienced and skilled of city managers. The nature of the relationship with council – as being primarily about strategy, and requiring the CAO to aid council in focusing on a vision, providing direction, and then managing the performance of the organization to achieve results – must be well understood. This chapter has described this relationship (figure 5.1) and articulated an equation (figure 5.2) of how it can be put into practice. Of course, each municipality's circumstance is unique. City managers must adapt their approach to address the needs of the environment they are in and articulate this clearly to council and the organization (figure 5.3). In the end, success will rest on city managers' choosing assignments that fit their own values, character, and skills. The hopeful city manager should begin with a thorough personal assessment and consideration of the organizational "fit" between the responsibilities of the position and one's leadership style and philosophy.

This chapter began by describing an experience every city manager knows well: sitting in a long council meeting where tensions around the horseshoe are high, searching for "solutions" where only politically challenging trade-offs exist. This is the reality of life as a city manager. The city manager is the critical conduit in the council-administration relationship. An ineffective city manager will translate into a weakened relationship, with consequences that will live in the culture of the organization far beyond the tenures of the individuals in the role.

Effective city managers will forge a strengthened political relationship that will pay dividends for the municipality and broader community. They will create alignment between council and administration. They will establish an environment where council can trust staff to implement direction without meddling or interference. They will enable an environment where staff can do their work, including both successes and failures, without the paralysing fear of political or career ramifications. They will lead difficult but necessary conversations about strategic direction, policy choices, role clarity, and organizational challenges that occur in a productive and healthy manner. These are not easy tasks, and they require city managers to have incredible scale to do them well. Success rests on building strong relationships with council, both to deliver immediate term results and as an investment that extends long past the tenure of the incumbents in the role – a duty, a contribution, and an opportunity to "purchase the glories" of a great community.

REFERENCES

Coyne, A. (2009, July 22). Our best (and worst) run cities. *Maclean's*.

Manzie, S., & Hartley, J. (2018, October 11). Dancing on ice: Leadership with political astuteness by senior public servants in the UK. Open University Business School. Retrieved from https://oro.open.ac.uk/38472/

Mouritzen, P. E., & Svara., J. H. (2002). *Leadership at the apex: Politicians and administrators in Western local governments*. University of Pittsburgh Press.

Ridge, J. (2020). *Welcome to the hall*. Municipal World.

Siegel, D. (2015). *Leaders in the shadows: The leadership qualities of successful municipal chief administrative officers*. University of Toronto Press.

Siegel, D. (2020). Public servants and politics: Developing political acuity in local government. *Canadian Public Administration*, *63*(4), 620–39. https://doi.org/10.1111/capa.12381

Tindal, C. R., & Tindal, S. N. (2019). *Guide to good municipal governance*. Municipal World.

6 Council-Staff Relations: Forward Motion or Spinning Wheels?

TAMMY CROWDER

Most Canadian local governments are under 10,000 population and council-staff dynamics can be very different from those in larger municipalities. Tammy Crowder discusses her council relations experience as CAO in the Nova Scotia communities of Chester and Bridgewater. She reveals relationship challenges and strategies to foster and sustain a positive political-administrative interface.

Pedalling and just spinning your wheels, the feeling of going nowhere. I experienced this working as a CAO in municipal government where council and staff were unable to move forward together. Lack of trust, respect, and accountability fed the organizational culture, and nothing but dysfunction was achieved. It is possible to find a way out of this situation by building a relationship that enables council, the CAO, and staff to move forward.

Municipal government is the level of government closest to people, and can be the most effective and responsive to community needs. This, however, relies on an effective governance structure that enables effective service delivery. The relationship between council (politics) and staff (administration) is crucial to the success of this governance structure, as the functions rely on each other. In this chapter, I provide the context for an effective council-CAO relationship, key qualities of a successful political and administrative interface, and some CAO leadership strategies.

The Contemporary Context

The council-manager (CAO) governance structure was established in the United States in the early twentieth century as a reform effort to address corrupt practices and to separate service delivery from politics.

This system was adopted in some Canadian provinces around the same time, but rose to prominence only beginning in the early 1970s (Fenn & Siegel, 2017, pp. 11–12). Prior to this structural reform, the council committee system was predominant. In this model, council governed the municipality through a series of committees based on departmental functions such as public works, finance, parks, and planning. Legislatively, staff members were responsible to the full council, but in practice this system promoted a close relationship between the committee chairperson and the department head, so that there was an informal understanding that staff reported to committees and the committees directed their work. This often created a disorganized and fragmented approach to both policy development and service delivery. As needs and expectations of residents became more complex, it was clear that this uncoordinated approach was not sustainable. Service delivery crossed departmental boundaries and there was a need to break down silos, as well as to separate politics from the administration (Siegel, 2015, p. 408).

The council-manager structure was a way to remove political interference from coordinated service delivery. Under this system, the CAO is the sole person directly accountable to council. The CAO manages and coordinates the municipal departments to ensure council's policy direction is carried out. Furthermore, the council-manager structure could reduce council committee involvement and political influences in service delivery by staff (Fenn & Siegel, 2017, p. 8) . In theory, it is the notional division between politics and administration and separation of council and staff roles; in practice, this division is more nuanced.

The transition to the council-manager system was, and continues to be, fraught with challenges. In Nova Scotia, some municipalities made the transition on paper, but the practice was something very different. Kell Antoft and Jack Novack noted that, although municipalities opted for the council-manager structure, many continued to operate with council committees (Antoft & Novack, 1998, p. 72). In many cases, this practice has made quite difficult the transition from a structure in which council directs staff to one in which council works through the CAO, who directs staff.

My first introduction to the CAO system was in the mid-1990s in Nova Scotia. The one I joined had moved from a council-committee structure to a council-manager structure, but only on paper. Although there was a CAO's office and a CAO, it was clear that council wanted to direct staff and do so through a committee system. That council held onto the committee system for nearly a decade, undermining the role of the CAO, essentially using the CAO as a clerk position and directing staff through committees. Part of the issue was that the CAO actually was the former clerk, and had worked under the council-committee structure. Transition to a role in which the CAO, as opposed to a committee, directs staff was a challenge as both the now CAO and council were familiar with the council-committee structure.

When I arrived as the new CAO, I endeavoured to clarify the council-manager relationship. Eventually the council-manager system functioned better, but still not without challenges as the incumbent councillors had not changed and were not necessarily sold on the concept that the new system was a better governance structure. It required patience on my part to make incremental changes, develop policy guidance, and change traditional practices.

As Fenn and Siegel (2017, p. 16) note, the council-manager system has "shallow roots" in Canada given its relatively recent adoption, and thus is susceptible to failing. To transition successfully and maintain the division between policy and administration, a good working relationship between the CAO and staff is required. There is a tendency for some councillors to gravitate towards administrative matters, and sometimes staff can move into political matters. Having a good relationship enables the CAO and council to keep each other in check and do so in a respectful manner.

The aim of the council-manager system is to have the CAO as the sole employee of council and thus serving at the pleasure of council. The CAO is responsible for ensuring council is given the best advice to make informed decisions and ensure the effective implementation of political decisions. Undoubtedly, the CAO sometimes must provide advice council does not want to hear (Fenn & Siegel, 2017, p. 8), but to do this the CAO needs to feel secure in the relationship with council. Without this confidence, the CAO might not be candid in providing policy or strategic advice, negatively affecting key aspects of a good relationship such as respect, trust, and accountability.

I have found that sometimes I become the target of the frustration of council (or an elected official) if administrative advice does not align with its aims. I constantly remind myself and staff that our role is to provide objective advice and that it is council's role to make decisions. We should never tailor our advice to achieve political ends.

Dysfunctional Relationship

Council and staff rely on each other to fulfil their roles successfully. A poor council-CAO and, ultimately, council-staff relationship, has some clear signs, such as lack of strategic policy decisions, misalignment of council and staff priorities, dysfunctional meetings, the wrong type of media attention, lack of public trust, inability to provide the right services at the right level, and a revolving door to the CAO's office. Under such conditions, council is challenged to fulfil its role of policy development and community representation effectively. Staff are not in a safe environment that enables them to provide the best, unbiased advice to enable council to make policy decisions. This ultimately affects service delivery.

Local government functions properly when councillors and staff understand their respective roles. The framework developed by Gordon McIntosh depicts two realms: political and administrative (McIntosh, 2015, pp. 1–2; see Table 6.1). In the political realm, council sets strategic direction and makes policy choices such as setting service levels, approving budgets, and developing strategic plans. In the administrative realm, the CAO and staff deliver services and coordinate internal systems to implement council's policy and strategies, including daily decisions, staff allocations, and operational procedures to deliver services and programs.

While this model reflects the traditional dichotomous or "black-and-white" notion of role separation, it also portrays a "grey" zone to signify the contemporary reality of role overlap or duality between elected officials and staff. The effective navigation of the grey zone truly determines the success of the political-administrative interface, local government effectiveness, and consequently CAO leadership. Conversely, dysfunction occurs when there is confusion about roles, council-staff relationship principles, and poor processes.

When council does not understand or respect the role of the CAO, it starts to enter the administrative realm by directing staff, in essence rendering the role of the CAO ineffective. It brings back political interference into operations that prompted the local government reform movement to implement a council-manager structure in the first place. It can result in staff running in many different directions, none of which might be strategic or with clarity of purpose. It can further take council away from what it should be doing: connecting with the community and making policy and strategic decisions. Staff can become disengaged and discouraged with a significant effect on morale. In such "grey" circumstances, the CAO has little power and accountability and the dysfunctional symptoms inherent in the council-committee system return.

The transition of the municipality I first worked for from a council-committee structure to a council-CAO structure demonstrates what happens when politically provoked dysfunctions occur. In this circumstance,

Table 6.1 Local Government Functions Framework

The Political Realm	
Strategic Direction	***Policy Choices***
Vision for future Organizational mission Shared values Long-term goals Specific objectives	Legislative compliance Budget allocations Policy decisions Contract arrangements Short-term priorities
The Administrative Realm	
Systems Coordination	***Service Delivery***
Personnel practices Information systems Financial accountability Performance management Communications	Action plans Production systems Resource schedules Delivery strategies Service standards

a committee directed policy work, which was significant, using staff resources and with implications for the community. This was a politically sensitive piece of work and when it came forward to council the outcome was not great. The media took the story and ran with it and council was called to task by the public for something it did not even fully know about or direct. In such circumstances the CAO loses accountability to council when committee members direct staff, and staff lose accountability to the CAO. I have found that the CAO then must address the underlying cause immediately. This effort can be difficult and challenging but if left unchecked, it will result in dysfunction. It must be clear that council, not a committee, provides direction while the CAO directs staff to develop work programs

In a corresponding way, when staff enter the political realm, elected officials understandably wonder whether they are receiving thorough and unbiased technical advice or hearing staff's political opinion. If staff are perceived to have a "political agenda," confidence can be undermined; council might ask itself if its decisions will be carried out conscientiously should council take a course not recommended by staff. This loss of confidence can manifest itself in different ways: vigorous criticism of staff at council meetings, an unwillingness of staff to make authoritative recommendations for fear of council reprisal, or simply a pattern of individual council members or staff members bypassing the CAO and the chain of command.

All these symptoms are precursors to poor service delivery, insipid or low-quality policy advice, low organizational morale, and high turnover among staff, including the CAO position. This kind of conflict is good fodder for the media but bad for governance, ultimately tainting residents' view of local government – diminishing their trust in council and staff – and negatively affecting their quality of life. A municipality cannot successfully fulfil its long-term mandate under such conditions.

I observed an example of this dysfunction prompted by the administration when a municipality in which council and the CAO were not aligned was dealing with a decision about developing a major facility. The CAO did not respect the position's role of ensuring council had the relevant facts to make the decision. Rather, the CAO wanted to be the decision maker. This resulted in a delay in decision making, significant disagreement at council meetings, and negative media attention. During this time, staff morale and trust in council and the CAO were affected with staff being put in an uncomfortable position as council went around the CAO. The CAO spoke openly and critically about council's decision. Ultimately the CAO was terminated, but not before a legacy of damage was done.

Under the council-manager system, the theoretical roles are clearly defined on paper; in reality, the line that divides them will be crossed many times. As Gordon McIntosh notes in *What Is Black and Grey All Over?* (McIntosh, 2009, pp. 27–30), the notion that there are clear and distinct roles easily understood or followed in practice is false. Councillors, for bad or well-intentioned reasons, enter the administrative realm seeking information, advocating an interest, requesting work to be done, investigating concerns, or simply trying to help. The CAO and staff likewise enter the political realm seeking direction, championing a project, providing information, or making recommendations. While roles need to be respected, it is also important to recognize that there is a significant grey zone or blurring of lines for respective responsibilities. Understanding the push and pull of the relationship and knowing how and when to be flexible is important. So, how do a CAO and council walk the tightrope between the two roles?

I have found that using a model such as McIntosh's Local Government Functions Framework helps both staff and elected officials to visualize role clarity and deviations. Simple lists of responsibilities are harder to relate to and use as a training or diagnostic aid.

Functional Relationship Strategies

Integral to the success of the council-manager structure is the council-staff relationship. Respect, communication, accountability, and trust are the main elements that create the foundation of any relationship.

Respect

Councillors, the CAO, and staff need to respect one another's roles. Councillors are elected to represent the community in the development of policy, making decisions and setting strategic directions in the public interest. The political perspective, which involves being attuned to the political culture of the community, is the significant contribution councillors bring that helps shape policy and service delivery (Fenn & Siegel, 2017, p. 5). This is why they are elected and it is this very fact that keeps them accountable to the electorate. Councillors must compete for their positions in every election; if they get it wrong, the polls will tell them so. Ensuring that staff respect this role goes a long way to helping staff understand how and why council makes certain decisions.

The CAO and staff are not elected. They are hired to provide policy advice to council, implement strategic directions, and deliver services based on their knowledge. It is important that council respect that the CAO and staff are competent professionals whose role is to provide council with the best information and advice that it needs to make informed decisions, even if the advice makes elected officials uncomfortable. This does not mean council necessarily will approve the recommendation. The CAO and staff normally just want to do a good job and provide the best advice. As Fenn and Siegel note, "[t]he best public policy comes about not when one side defeats the other and gets its way, but when policy resides at the intersection of the two interests" (2017, p. 5).

Spending time on roles, responsibilities, and the rules of engagement at the beginning of a relationship between council and staff after an election is a good investment and will foster respect for the differing roles. Reinforcing these roles periodically is important as well in the following ways:

- *strategic direction* – how councillors achieve a strategic vision and goals for the organization and community, and staff execute strategies and report on progress;
- *policy choices* – how staff should prepare and present information, and how elected officials wish to conduct council meetings and debate;
- *service delivery* – how council sets service levels and responds to community needs while staff achieve efficient and effective operations;
- *systems coordination* – how council ensures fiscal and performance accountability while staff ensure reliable organizational processes and practices;

- *organizational member contact* – how councillors seek information about getting work done, while staff have protocols for contacting elected officials directly.

I have found that bringing in an outside expert advisor or facilitator is useful to help establish the ground rules with respect to roles and responsibilities. This party is neutral and has nothing to gain in helping the organization to establish some political-administrative interface guidelines. This might be particularly important if council has some strong players who are known not to respect the role of elected officials and/or staff. Likewise, these guidelines should be incorporated into staff orientation/onboarding practices. One should never assume that staff understand the roles of council and staff or the difference between politics and administration.

It is not uncommon to hear staff criticize council decisions. As noted, however, councillors are accountable to the electorate. Staff need to understand that councillors bring community (political) perspectives to the decision-making process that might not necessarily be reflective of staff's professional advice. Staff have fulfilled their role when they provide solid research, facts, and options. I reinforce with staff that it is council, not staff, that makes political decisions, and that it is the role of staff to execute all council decisions in a professional manner, whatever the personal opinions of staff members might be.

Staff need to understand the rules of engagement when councillors seek information. They need to feel comfortable referring a request from councillors to the CAO if it goes beyond seeking information. One method is to have all requests go through the CAO's office. This is a somewhat cumbersome process when a councillor is just looking for information, but it might be necessary if the information request is used intentionally or unintentionally to cause staff to undertake work. Another option is to reinforce staff's expectation that providing readily available information to councillors is acceptable, but requests that go beyond that and lead to the expenditure of time and resources must go to the CAO for authorization. The CAO, in turn, will decide when council direction is required. Constantly reinforcing these boundaries with staff is critical. Ensuring that council understands this process also will help. I do not think it is the role of elected officials to navigate the system; I expect staff to advise me when a political inquiry affects their workload, so that I can consider and address the situation.

Communication

Communication is also critical to a successful relationship between council and the CAO and staff. Lack of communication can negatively affect respect and trust, resulting in a dysfunctional relationship. The CAO needs to ensure that council is updated on matters in a timely manner. In doing so, it is important to treat all elected officials the same way. One councillor should not be privy to more information than others. This means that the CAO needs to ensure staff understand the importance of providing all councillors with the same information. This avoids the perception of one councillor having an advantage over others.

Conversely it is important for council to communicate concerns that need to be addressed through the CAO. The CAO cannot address concerns or issues if not aware of them: good communication will avoid "deer in the headlights" situations. There should be no surprises; everyone should be informed.

Establishing protocols for contact between council, the CAO, and staff can assist with communications, which can range from fairly routine matters such as pothole complaints or overflowing garbage bins to requests for information on policy matters such as affordable housing. It is important for the CAO to define clearly which information and requests should go through the CAO's office and which can be sent directly to staff. Conversely there need to be clear guidelines around when information can go directly to a councillor and bypass the CAO and council. As previously noted, it is important to ensure that all councillors are treated the same and are provided access to the same information. After every election, I review and modify the elected official contact protocols to best meet council's needs, while protecting any interference with staff workloads.

A useful tool for policy-related communications to council is a report template. A "request for decision" can provide prompts to ensure staff give the scope of information required for informed decision making. Staff in turn can use a "request for direction" if they are not sure of political expectations to guide their work in preparing recommendations. These two tools provide mutual confidence: council feels it is getting complete information, and staff are not left guessing what is on the collective mind of council. I make sure the request for decision is kept to one page with necessary attachments. It helps staff to highlight critical information while offering a mini-agenda and at-a-glance points to guide council's discussion.

Another useful communication tactic is to set time aside for council to provide feedback to the CAO on strategic matters. This will ensure that the CAO understands council's expectations and concerns and can adjust accordingly. One method to do this is through a CAO Update on each agenda, providing the current status of strategic priorities and emerging matters. It is also beneficial for the CAO and council to have regular sessions to discuss organizational performance concerns. My experience is that activity reporting can be informative, but it does not reveal underlying political concerns. I do quarterly council-CAO check-ins to focus on organizational performance and council-staff relations. These are done in camera since discussions might involve personnel matters

Accountability

Lack of accountability was one reason for the transition from the council-committee system to the council-CAO system. The CAO is the sole person directly accountable to council (Siegel, 2015, p. 418). Council thus needs to have confidence in the CAO's ability to make the organization efficient and effective.

Councillors sometimes feel that their requests disappear into a black hole. The CAO can demonstrate accountability by reporting to council on the progress of items. Quarterly reports on strategic priorities, including actions taken, metrics, and target deadlines are a good tool for ensuring accountability. In addition, each council meeting can result in requests that are not of a strategic nature. Periodic reports on the status of directions or actions requested through and endorsed by council will give councillors the confidence that neither their direction nor their idea was lost. I use both a strategic dashboard so that strategic priority targets and progress can be easily viewed, and a follow-up action list of other council directives. Both visuals serve as a reminder to council and councillors of the volume of requests that affect the staff workload and detract attention from council's strategic agenda.

As part of the accountability chain, the CAO should also hold staff accountable. This can be done by ensuring priorities are incorporated into performance reviews and clear goals are set that help the CAO meet council's goals. This is a way to keep everyone moving in the same direction and to maintain their accountability. It also gives staff a "line of sight" that the work they do contributes to organizational and community success.

The CAO cannot be held accountable to council if undermined by managerial decisions made by council. If this occurs, the CAO needs to reinforce the respective roles of council and staff. An example is an elected official who directs staff to modify a service. Staff should not entertain such a request without the CAO's support. If the CAO does not address this, it will happen again, and if the modification has negative consequences, the CAO will be blamed. Protocols should be in place to ensure such political influence over managerial decisions does not occur. Requesting a council member to secure a formal "council direction" can also reduce the risk that one member of council will give directions to staff or try to alter staff workplans or service delivery priorities and standards inappropriately.

Proper accountability of staff to the CAO requires that the CAO manage staff without political interference. When the CAO makes a decision that is unpopular with some staff, the staff should not have a receptive councillor's ear to try to have it reversed. By entertaining this, the councillor undermines the authority of the CAO and puts the CAO in a very compromising situation.

I worked in a municipality in which a senior-level staff member would meet often with an elected official to discuss strategic issues with the councillor and to get feedback on operational matters. The two formed a bond of trust and friendship. When I made decisions that did not sit well with this staff member, the topic often made its way to me by the councillor's visiting my office or raising it at the council table. This affected my ability to lead and to make operational decisions. It also challenged my ability to manage this staff member. As a result, I always ensure that roles and responsibility guidelines are regularly reviewed so that both staff and elected officials are accountable for behaviours or activities that detract from role clarity.

Trust

Mutual trust among council, the CAO, and staff is important. As noted, the best policy decisions are made when council receives the advice of staff and considers it with council's understanding of the community's needs. Staff members need to trust that council will receive the advice without reprisal or confrontation, even if it is not the advice that council wanted to hear. Councillors need to trust that staff are giving them the best professional advice and implementing council's policy directives, even if staff did not recommend a particular course. Sheryl Sculley notes that this is necessary to ensure that, together, council and staff can address complex and sometime controversial issues (Sculley, 2012, p. 536).

Trust takes time to gain, and a new CAO or a new council must build that trust. Trust comes from all the other elements: respect, communications, and accountability. Each new person adds a new dynamic; thus the relationship is in constant flux and must always be worked on. Complacency will not serve anyone well. Never get too comfortable.

One way to build trust is to ensure that the work of staff is aligned with council's priorities, which it should articulate clearly. Then a business plan should be developed to ensure that resource allocation and staff work programs match those priorities. Undertaking this exercise at the start of a council's term with quarterly updates or check-ins will ensure strategic alignment continues throughout the term.

Communicating progress in achieving council's priorities can build council's further trust in staff. Often, councils will say that things disappear in "a black hole, never to be heard of again." It is important to give council confidence that staff are aligned with its priorities and carrying out its direction. Quarterly reports highlighting progress and actions taken on strategic priorities are an effective method to do this.

Trust is evidenced through a relationship in which the parties are open, transparent, and accountable. A CAO can help build trust by being open, honest, owning mistakes, and seeking, receiving, and providing feedback in a positive, non-confrontational manner. Creating this type of environment and displaying these characteristics within the organization will foster the same characteristics among staff.

Conclusion

The council-manager system was created out of the need to separate the political role of council from administrative roles. As local government grew, it became evident that a professionally trained and skilled resource was needed for administrative functions. The council-manager system was established as a solution, but it does have its challenges. In theory, roles are clearly defined: elected officials perform the political role and the CAO and staff perform the administrative role. In practice, there is a constant push and pull as each crosses the line between the two roles. If this grey area is not navigated properly, dysfunction can occur that will ultimately affect both functions – and thus decision making and services. The council-CAO relationship is constantly in flux, influenced by external factors, new staff, and new council members. A relationship built on respect, trust, accountability, and communication will ensure that the CAO, staff, and council are able to navigate the uncertainty and challenges that arise. In the absence of such a relationship, it will be a challenge to ensure that the CAO and council work through the push and pull of politics and administration. The system works best when both groups rely on each other.

REFERENCES

Antoft, K., & Novack, J. (1998). *Grass roots democracy: Local government in the Maritimes*. Dalhousie University, Henson College.

Fenn, M., & Siegel, D. (2017). *The evolving role of city managers and chief administrative officers*. Institute of Municipal Finance and Governance Papers on Municipal Finance and Governance.

McIntosh, G. (2009). *Defining situational leadership for the local government CAO*. University of Victoria.

McIntosh, G. (2015). *What is black and white, and grey all over?* G.A. McIntosh.

Sculley, S. (2012). A view from San Antonio: A city manager's perspective. *Public Administration Review*, *72*(4), 536–7. https://doi.org/10.1111/j.1540-6210.2012.02606.x

Siegel, D. (2015). The public service bargain in local government: A new way of looking at relations between municipal councils and CAOs. *Canadian Public Administration*, *58*(3), 406–25. https://doi.org/10.1111/capa.12120

7 The Most Important Relationship in Local Government: Mayor and City Manager

BILL GIVEN

Bill Given has a unique vantage point on the relationship between mayors and city managers: he's been both. As former mayor of the Alberta city of Grande Prairie, and then Town Manager of Jasper, Alberta, Given uses a survey of his Alberta municipal colleagues to highlight how this crucial relationship should be structured and nurtured. Adding a new dimension to the foundational concept of the CAO-council relationship, Given describes how the mayor and the CAO can share leadership without coming into conflict, between themselves and with council.

At its core, government is a system of individual people, selected by other people, to address human needs in a coordinated fashion. So, while finances, processes, and technical knowledge are undoubtedly core elements of government, it is no stretch to say that human relationships are the foundation of any order of government. I believe this foundation in personal relationships is most important in municipalities because, at the local level, political and administrative officials undertake the day-to-day work of government in the community where they reside. This closeness of government officials to the residents they serve increases the importance of relationships over bureaucratic process. There are many human relationships at play in local government: elected official to constituent; elected officials to one another; constituents to frontline municipal staff; frontline staff to managers; and managers to elected officials. The last of these relationships, managers to elected officials, is the point in any government "within which politics has to be distinguished from administration" (Thornhill, 2005), and is generally referred to as the political-administrative interface.

Much of the current research discussing the political-administrative interface in municipal government focuses on the relationship between city managers (or chief administrative officers) and council. This historically has been seen as a dichotomous relationship between the policy role of elected officials and the administrative orientation of the CAO. Recently a more nuanced view has emerged that suggests a complementary relationship where responsibility and reciprocal influence are shared between political and administrative leadership within council-manager governments (Demir et al., 2012; Svara, 2001). Siegel (2015) suggests that this complementary relationship forms a "public service bargain" where each party gives up something in return for something from the other side. He further asserts that the bargain between the CAO and council is the most important in local government because it is the point where elected officials can ensure municipal administration accountability.

While I agree that the political-administrative interface is where the most important municipal government relationship can be found, with my previous experience of being a mayor, I do not believe that the most important relationship is CAO-to-council. In my view, this conceptualization of a complementary relationship between a CAO and council is not refined enough. It is based on an asymmetry of one individual relating to a group and does not account for the significant role that mayors play. Siegel (2015) acknowledges this shortcoming of the CAO-council relationship when he notes that, in an ideal form, the bargain would be between "the CAO and a homogeneous, or at least reasonably well-aligned, group of councillors" (Siegel, 2015, p. 413). He even shares an anecdote that illustrates the consequences when a manager's and a mayor's views come into conflict (p. 410).

My experience and research have confirmed my view that the mayor-CAO relationship is, in fact, the most important in local government. It is in this relationship where the political and administrative functions of local government converge most acutely, and it is where two individual actors relate to each other, as opposed to one individual with a group (municipal council).

Although this critical civic leadership relationship creates an environment with significant risk, I also contend that it presents an opportunity for a special kind of leadership, shared between two individuals, which I will call "co-leadership." In this chapter, I discuss the CAO and mayor roles, define and describe co-leadership, share my research that forms the basis of my assertion that this relationship is the most important in local government, and lay out some practical strategies that can be employed to nurture and strengthen the CAO-mayor relationship.

Contrasting Leadership Potential

Chief Administrative Officers

For simplicity, I refer to chief administrative officer, although across the country the position might be described as city administrator, city manager, chief commissioner, or director-general. No matter the title, a common feature of council-manager cities is that this single individual is appointed as the head of municipal administration and is delegated responsibility for administering the programs of the municipality and supervision of all municipal staff (Tindal & Tindal, 2004, p. 278). The CAO typically is entrusted with significant responsibility and formal authority as the leader of the entire municipal, corporate organization. Despite this well-defined authority, the significance of the position is not widely acknowledged by the public in Canada.

The CAO's position is similar to the position of mayor, in that both tend to be represented and conceptualized in overly simplistic terms that fail to convey the complexity and nuance inherent in the position (Boymton & Wright, 1971). CAOs in the council-manager system derive their influence from a combination of elements. These factors include: the CAO's dominant position of formal authority atop the administrative structure of the city; control over the preparation of the budget; the ability to influence the flow of information to council; the capacity to influence policy decisions by making recommendations to council (e.g., identifying policy options and their respective advantages and disadvantages); and by sometimes openly advocating with council for specific policies (Morgan & Watson, 1992; Selden et al., 1999; Tindal & Tindal, 2004). Despite their formal authority and the factors listed above, all CAOs realize that, when they enter into the political realm, they put themselves in a vulnerable position. They risk becoming too closely associated with a specific policy position that might fall out of favour with the majority of council (Morgan & Watson, 1992; Watson & Hassett, 2003).

CAOs also risk becoming too closely associated with the mayor or a specific group on municipal council. For example, CAOs might be at risk of losing employment should they be seen as too close an ally with an out-going mayor or council. Despite this risk, CAOs report that high levels of support from council are strongly correlated with high job satisfaction (Watson & Hassett, 2003). Interestingly, it has been noted that, compared to the mayor's, the CAO's power tends to have an inverse correlation with the population of the community. That is,

CAOs in larger communities tend to have less power than those working in smaller ones (Morgan & Watson, 1992).

Mayors

In the public imagination, mayors are often perceived to hold significant power. However, municipal legislation across Canada is generally clear that the mayor is simply "first among equals" on a council, and with a few modest exceptions the position's only formal legal authority comes in the context of chairing council meetings or potentially under emergency management protocols. As a mayor, this was occasionally a source of frustration for me.

Despite this limited formal authority, my experience in the role was that the perception of mayors as community leaders can imbue the position with significant influence and informal power with the public, council, and municipal administration. The literature supports this view and points to a model of mayoral leadership that is coordinative and based on consensus, while maintaining an active level of involvement and personal influence despite the position's limited formal powers (Goldsmith & Larsen, 2004; Svara, 1987; Tindal & Tindal, 2004; Wikstrom, 1979).

Seminal American works (Svara, 1987; Wikstrom, 1979) recognized the conflicting views of mayors in council-manager systems with assertions that these mayors are "commonly perceived to be doing less than they are, or capable of doing more than they can" (Svara, 1987, p. 207), and those descriptions of council-manager mayors based exclusively on formal powers are "undiscerning, simplistic and represent undue generality" (Wikstrom, 1979, p. 271). Svara (1987) asserted that mayors in council-manager cities have a significant ability to provide leadership beyond that which arises from formalized power granted to the position or through the office's traditional ceremonial functions. On occasion, this can be enhanced when the CAO willingly or strategically defers to the mayor's leadership, in order to give a matter greater impetus than the CAO can achieve.

Svara (1987) suggested that mayoral leadership can be conceptualized into ten different types of roles and that the kind of leadership a mayor provides depends on which of these roles the mayor "chooses (or happens) to perform" and how well she or he performs them; the most complete forms of leadership incorporate working with others to build consensus. This view of mayoral leadership in the council-manager structure is supported by the findings of Goldsmith and Larsen (2004) in their study of Nordic local political leadership, where they describe mayors as "key local leaders" whose influence is more significant than might be expected due to their ability to maintain a "consensual style of decision-making" (p. 131).

In my view, it is clear that both CAOs and mayors can exhibit leadership in the context of local government, although each derives that ability from different sources. The literature points to a model of influential mayoral leadership, rooted in public perceptions of the position, that is coordinative and based in consensus while maintaining an active level of involvement and personal influence, despite limited formal powers. In contrast, the CAO is granted significant responsibility and formal authority as the leader of the entire municipal, corporate organization. Despite this well-defined authority, however, the CAO position's significance is not widely acknowledged by the Canadian public. My personal experience with this intertwined leadership dynamic drove me to explore the CAO-mayor relationship more systematically.

Case Study Findings

To test my views on the relationship between mayors and CAOs, I chose to examine the mayor-CAO relationship in Alberta's mid-sized cities. I wanted to consider if there might be a form of shared leadership at play and, if there was, what steps might be taken to nurture growth in the relationship. I studied twenty-two urban and mixed urban/rural local governments ranging in population from approximately 10,000 to just over 100,000. Limiting my inquiry to mid-sized cities ensured that all organizations operated on a similar scale and with similar resources. This research focus also allowed me to compare my research findings with my own experience as the mayor of a mid-sized Alberta city and the working relationships that I developed with three quite different city managers during my term as mayor.

This similarity in scale was necessary because the literature indicates that, as a city's population approaches 250,000, power begins to shift from the manager towards the mayor (Morgan & Watson, 1992). All mayors, CAOs, and council members from these twenty-two communities were invited to participate in an initial survey to assess their views of the leadership potential of the CAO's and mayor's positions and attend a follow-up, in-person event held at a convention of the Alberta Urban Municipalities Association. These two engagements produced the following findings.

Survey Findings

A majority of all participants (mayors, CAOs, and councillors) affirmed the mayor-CAO relationship as both important on its own and more important than the CAO's relationship to council as a body. The mayor-CAO relationship was rated as either "important" or "very important" by 100 per cent of respondents. There was also strong agreement that the relationship was at least "to some extent" more important than the relationship of the CAO to council as a whole: 93 per cent of mayors and CAOs felt this was the case, while even 64 per cent of councillors held the same view.

Although the findings make clear that a majority of participants perceived the mayor-CAO relationship to be of greater importance than the relationship between the CAO and council as a body, the findings also show that councillors had a desire to be informed and engaged. The findings suggest that, while there is broad agreement on the importance of the mayor-CAO relationship, efforts to nurture the relationship still need to be sensitive to councillors' concerns and perceptions.

These findings further indicate that mayors and CAOs hold different views concerning each other's leadership potential, that elected officials attribute to CAOs more leadership potential in the political realm than administrators give themselves credit for, and that, despite these broad trends, individual mayors or CAOs might hold more rigid views of which party should lead in specific contexts. The findings also suggest a high degree of overlap in the mayor-CAO leadership dynamic and that this role duality could leave the relationship vulnerable to misunderstanding and unchecked assumptions. These findings confirm my own experience as mayor of my city.

Risk of Misunderstanding and Confusion of Roles

A significant contributor to the risk of misunderstandings arises from the finding that each role can provide leadership in any domain, including with council, the public, community groups, senior staff, and frontline staff. In each of these five domains, over 65 per cent of each respondent class agreed that both the mayor and CAO could, at least sometimes, be perceived to be a leader. In fact, for most domains, the level of agreement that both the mayor and CAO could be perceived to be a leader exceeded 80 per cent. Thus, regardless of the narrowly defined authorities generally described for either position in typical municipal legislation, all parties agreed that both mayors and CAOs have some ability to lead in any domain in real-world practice.

This overlapping view is further supported by the literature, which suggests that, in Canadian municipalities, administration and policy matters can often be interwoven and difficult to distinguish (Tindal & Tindal, 2004).

In addition to the potential confusion that arises from this overlapping dynamic, additional risk comes from the finding that CAOs and mayors expressed slightly differing views of each other's ability to lead within specific contexts: CAOs held a lower view of the mayor's leadership with frontline staff, while mayors held a lower view of the CAO's leadership with community groups. Interestingly, both groups of elected officials (mayors and councillors) expressed a greater openness to the CAO as a leader with council than the administrators gave themselves credit for. Finally, despite these broad trends confirming the overlapping nature of mayoral and CAO leadership, some individuals held significantly differing views, including those who expressed particularly rigid views of the separation of political and administrative leadership, and those who, relative to their peers, appeared to downplay the leadership potential of their position.

Taken together with the finding that participants viewed the relationship as highly important (on its own and relative to the CAO-council relationship), the mayor-CAO dyad must be considered the most important relationship in municipal government. Nurturing this relationship and ensuring its success should be a priority for all parties, but that effort requires an openness to a non-traditional leadership model called "co-leadership."

Shared Leadership

Defining "Co-leadership"

Examples of co-leadership stretch back to Roman times (Sally, 2002), but it is only since the turn of the century, when Heenan and Bennis (1999) described it as "two leaders in vertically contiguous positions share the responsibilities of leadership," that the concept has become a more significant focus of leadership research.

Denis et al. (2012) note that "leadership in the plural" is described by scholars using a variety of terms, including "shared," "distributed," "collective," "collaborative," "integrative," "relational," and "post-heroic" (p. 213). Developing a common or shared understanding between individuals of what co-leadership means requires a definition with a greater level of specificity.

Sally describes Roman expressions of co-leadership (e.g., two "consuls" elected annually by Roman citizens) as dyads of equals where "power asymmetries" (Sally, 2002, p. 87) were studiously avoided and, by design, co-leaders would have no chance of "ascending to solo leadership" (p. 88). This view is similar to MacNeill et al. (2012), who describe a form of co-leadership found in arts organizations where artistic directors and general managers have very different responsibilities within the organization and cannot easily be said to be above or below each other in the hierarchy. These two characterizations of co-leadership seem to be most closely aligned with the mayor-CAO pair's structural realities.

Similar to the concept advanced by Sally (2002), it is not possible for either the mayor or the CAO to "ascend" within the organization to take on the other's position. Furthermore, closely resembling the condition described by MacNeill et al. (2012), the mayor and the CAO have very different responsibilities from each other within the municipal organization.

Although there is currently no definite agreement on a unifying definition of co-leadership, I suggest this: *co-leadership is two individuals who, by design, hold different responsibilities at the top of one organization, sharing power and jointly leading.*

Benefits of "Co-leadership"

Although literature explicitly considering co-leadership in the mayor-manager context is limited, inquiry into the topic from a diverse variety of other settings offers some indication of co-leadership's potential benefits. There is broad agreement in the literature that co-leadership has several benefits. It can make leadership less lonely by sharing the burden. It can allow for the division of responsibilities according to the skills, knowledge, or interests of the individual leaders. It can act as a sounding board, serving as a reality check for the two roles. It can provide the opportunity for the pair to benefit from figuratively being in two places at once. It can act as an insurance policy that supports continuity and stability within an organization. Outwardly to council, the municipal staff, and the broader community, it can convey the perception of civic leadership at the apex as balanced and complementary (Hartshorn-Sanders, 2006; Heenan & Bennis, 1999; Kocolowski, 2010; Miles & Watkins, 2007). Additionally, it was my experience that some specific benefits appear in (or have more relevance in) specific contexts. Hartshorn-Sanders (2006) examines formalized co-leadership at the political level in the New Zealand Green Party, and notes that co-leadership acts to reinforce a team approach across the rest of the organization.

Specifically speaking from the corporate business context, Vieito (2013) found that firms with co-CEO arrangements demonstrated better performance and higher returns to shareholders. Heenan and Bennis (1999) asserted that co-leadership arrangements can act as a form of mentorship by allowing one member of the dyad to see first-hand how the other handles the "duties and pressures" of leadership (p. 15), and that close personal bonds based in shared accomplishment are likely to arise. Kocolowski (2010) notes that two leaders acting together can be helpful in times of change and for organizations facing complex challenges. Finally, two somewhat interrelated views come from outside the business world. Hartshorn-Sanders (2006, p. 53) asserts that co-leadership "allows leaders to play to their strengths and remain genuine," which seems to support the conclusion arising in the consideration by MacNeill et al. (2012, p. 14) of co-leadership in arts organizations, where they find that successful co-leadership arrangements might demand or in fact "build authentic leaders." These academic perspectives confirm the real-life lessons that I learned as mayor.

Since the municipal participants in my research indicated that CAOs and mayors both seem to be providing leadership in local government, and that co-leadership offers the potential benefits described above, I dug deeper to uncover what risks might be associated with explicit efforts to forge a shared leadership dynamic among mayor/CAO pairs.

Risks

Following my online survey, which was meant to establish a baseline understanding of participants' views concerning the mayor-CAO leadership dynamic, my in-person sessions with participants sought to solicit their views on barriers, strategies, and opportunities. In particular, respondents suggested that role clarity, ego, political change, personalities, values, and age could present barriers to implementing mayor-CAO co-leadership. The discussion below contains "in their own words" direct quotations collected anonymously from participants during the in-person events.

Role clarity issues emerged as the most often cited barrier to implementing mayor-CAO co-leadership effectively. Comments from mayors such as "lack of understanding of roles," "who is the boss?" and "not knowing whose job is whose" aligned with the role clarity theme, as did councillors' comments such as "different views of their roles," "blurring of roles and responsibilities," and "crossover of governance and operational matters." While fewer comments related to role clarity arose from the CAOs, those that did were direct and explicit, including "critical to reach a clear understanding of roles and expectations" and "to avoid problems."

As a mayor at the time and knowing the personalities that can be drawn to the role, I was not surprised when themes related to ego did not show up often as a potential barrier from mayors' perspective, but it did frequently arise from both CAOs and councillors. These two latter classes of respondents provided comments indicating ego-related concerns, such as "ego clash," "one has too much ego," "ego," and "recognition." In contrast, mayors shared concerns related to political change far more often than did CAOs or councillors. Comments from mayors on this theme included "election cycles," "new mayor may have agenda," "change in leadership + election," and "change in mayors readjust CAO."

A smaller number of each of the three participant classes (mayors, councillors, CAOs) also identified somewhat unusual themes as potential barriers. For mayors, this theme was related to "age" or "generational differences"; for CAOs, it was "values" or "conflicting values." Among councillors, two themes arose, the first related to the personalities of the individuals in the relationship, which surfaced with comments such as "personality conflict," "strong personalities," or "personality styles (different)." The second theme was a more general sense that implementing mayor-CAO co-leadership came with risks. This concern was highlighted in straightforward comments such as "there is risk to mandate this" and "do not necessarily agree that this should be institutionalized."

Addressing Barriers to Co-leadership

When the discussion turned to asking participants to identify what strategies might be employed to address co-leadership barriers, mayors, CAOs, and councillors highlighted dialogue, education, and defined agreements as preferred approaches. The preference for dialogue was evidenced in comments such as "clearing the air," "clear open/honest discussion," and "initial sit down to identify/clarify roles." The theme of education arose in comments suggesting things such as "common training," "professional development," and "mayor and CAO complete, consistent training on leadership." Additionally, with suggestions such as "Memorandum of Understanding (MOU)/ Policy/Procedure/Code of Conduct," "defined agreements on objectives," and "written protocol/statement of leadership principles/role definition," councillors and CAOs specifically expressed a clear desire for defined agreements. Comments that can be interpreted to be related to this desire, such as "setting strategic goals together," also came from mayors, albeit with somewhat less clarity or frequency.

Participants highlighted municipal policies, provincial legislation, and council orientation as potential opportunities to institutionalize co-leadership in Alberta's municipalities. Municipal policies emerged as the top theme for each class, with examples such as "CAO by-law," "council procedure by-law," and "code of conduct" being offered. Provincial legislation was identified by repeated comments pointing to the Alberta Municipal Government Act (MGA): "put it into the MGA (process procedures)," "urge MGA legislation," and "roles defined in the MGA and is part of the required annual CAO performance feedback." Finally, CAOs in particular and mayors to a lesser extent identified "council orientation" as a critical opportunity to institutionalize mayor-CAO co-leadership. Interestingly, council orientation also arose from councillors, but it was suggested more frequently as an opportunity to increase understanding and to transfer best practices.

Participants indicated some opportunities to address perceived barriers to effective mayor-CAO co-leadership models, including increasing dialogue, providing education, and developing defined agreements. Below, I discuss two practical, transferrable approaches I have used to increase dialogue as a means of building the CAO-mayor relationship.

Tactics in Practice

In my experience, when it comes to operational tactics to nurture the mayor-CAO relationship, the reality is more an art than a science. Although the survey data and literature discussed above provide helpful insights into the nature of the relationship and its challenges, actualizing the opportunities to address the challenges in practice depends on many variables. In my view, these variables include whether the relationship is pre-existing or just newly forming, the length of tenure of each party, and, of course, willingness to participate.

That said, I believe two highly transferable approaches can reduce conflict and improve the ability of mayors and CAOs to work together successfully. In my experience as mayor, these strategies form a kind of continuum from the informal to formal and include creating space for dialogue between the parties through the use of what I call "first-night questions" and making intentional efforts to build trust and bridge differences in age, personality, and background by explicitly setting aside time to discuss values.

"First-Night" Questions

Many years ago, I had the privilege to spend a year abroad as a Rotary youth exchange student. Rotary International is a sophisticated organization with over 35,000 local service clubs spread worldwide (Rotary International, 2020). In the youth exchange program, a sponsor club in one country selects a young person (typically of high school age) to spend a year in the care of a receiving host club in another county with "the aim of promoting international understanding and friendship" (Glavinskas, 2020).

I found the experience to be transformative but intimidating in the beginning. Incredibly tricky was the process of getting to know new "host families" as I moved from the home of one Rotarian to another every couple of months. These moves required navigating new sets of expectations and household rules. Thankfully the Rotary exchange program was well developed and equipped me with a helpful tool in the form of a photocopied page with a list of "first-night questions." Today you can find these questions on the web in many places, but in my day a single paper sheet listed approximately thirty questions to ask of my new host family as I moved in. The questions covered a range of topics from "what should I call you?" to "should I wash my own underclothes?" and "what areas of the house are strictly private?" – all with the same ultimate goal: to reduce the risk of unintended conflict by ensuring that expectations and preferences were openly stated and clearly understood by both parties.

Over my time as mayor, I have had the pleasure of working with three different CAOs, and this very same tactic was helpful in the early stages of my relationship with each. When I first became mayor, the CAO had been in his role for about two years. He had previously served in another senior leadership role, so we knew each other quite well from my time as a councillor. Likely because of this familiarity, our initial conversation as CAO-mayor pair was brief and informal. However, we covered a few basics, such as whether it was appropriate to refer to me as "your worship" in the office (only during a council meeting, please, and maybe "Mr Mayor" around staff, but when it is only the two of us, "Bill" will do just fine).

Since that CAO retired near the end of my second term, I have worked with two others. I have been much more intentional about using my "first-night-questions" approach to clarify a broader range of issues beyond formalities such as titles. On a CAO's first day, we sit down and discuss basics: how often we might set aside time for one-on-one meetings, how we each like to send and receive information, whether it is a problem to walk into the other's office unannounced, and a variety of other topics.

Either party can initiate this approach, and the answers to any particular question can vary from person to person. As working professionals, we should be capable of adapting to each other if we take intentional steps to ensure everyone knows the ground rules. In mayor-CAO pairs, the "first-night-questions" process can serve the same purpose it did for me as a youth exchange student: to reduce the risk of unintended conflict by ensuring that expectations and preferences are openly stated and clearly understood at the beginning of a relationship.

Values Discussion

I started my career as an elected official at an early age, and for much of the time, I was regularly the youngest person in the room, even as mayor. Consequently, every CAO I have worked with has been older than I, sometimes by a number of decades. My most recent CAO was also from a different cultural background, having been born and educated in South America. These differences in age and life experience could have signalled that our relationship was headed for troubled water. Thankfully, each CAO I have worked with has demonstrated respect for me as a person, while willingly sharing their experiences and remaining open to learning from mine.

Personal respect is a solid foundation for any relationship, but I have found that bridging differences in age, personality, culture, and background to build trust can take more than just personal respect. In an era when diversity, inclusion, and reconciliation are at the forefront of progressive civic leadership and municipal management, I can attest to the fact that working closely with those from other backgrounds, both in city hall and in the community, has made for better decisions, a more respectful organizational environment, and more responsive local government.

Schwartz asserted that "values serve as standards of criteria. Values guide the selection or evaluation of actions, policies, people, and events" (Schwartz, 1992, p. 4). Put another way, our values are always with us and they influence how we see the world and how we behave. I believe having some understanding of people's values is key to getting a sense of their intrinsic motivations, and gives you a leg up on understanding why they might make the decisions they do. Although it might not be a typical thing to do in a newly forming dyad, I have found a simple way to create space to discuss values with each of my CAO partners explicitly.

Not everyone might be as immediately open to discussing values as I am, so the first step is always a casual verbal check-in to see if the CAO is open to the idea; no one has yet declined. After this gentle introduction, I follow up with an email defining the activity and sharing a list of about two hundred words describing various values. Such lists of values are widely available on the Internet. Each of us independently reviews the list to select just five that we feel are most important in approaching our work and the professional working relationship between us. Then we sit down to share our lists and discuss the values we chose.

Because two people might take different meanings from the same word, we do not just compare lists; we also share a bit of context on why we chose each word and how we imagine their coming to life in the day-to-day sense. The process from verbal inquiry to comparing lists can happen over a week or more as time permits, and allows us to identify any commonalities and avoid some of the pitfalls that can come from not understanding where we are coming from as we begin working together. Even though my CAO partners and I have been of different generations and backgrounds, the process of sharing our values has helped me gain a better sense of what drives them, and I hope it has helped them understand my motivations and preferences as well.

Conclusion

The two approaches discussed – "first-night" questions and a discussion of key values – have helped me set a solid foundation for the mayor-CAO relationships of which I have been a part. Although prevention can be challenging to measure, I believe taking these steps has helped reduce conflict and improve our ability to work together. First-night questions and values discussions create space for dialogue, help us learn about each other's motivations, and ensure our preferences and expectations are openly stated and clearly understood at the beginning of our relationship.

I believe these two practices are highly transferable. No onerous time commitments, technology, or training are required, making them simple to deploy in local governments of any size. The processes can be initiated by either the CAO or the mayor. For example, a wise CAO might wish to use these tactics with a newly elected mayor proactively or as the CAO begins work in a new municipality. The reverse is also true: an incumbent mayor might wish to start the discussion with a new CAO. In any case, the key is to reduce the potential for misunderstandings and conflict by creating space for dialogue at the beginning of any new CAO-mayor relationship.

The interview process of a new city manager provides the first opportunity to assess the compatibility of the personalities of the candidate and mayor and the degree of flexibility each might have while working together. During one interview for a new city manager in my second mayoral term, I began to feel comfortable that one candidate would be a good fit for our city. During his presentation and in answering questions, the candidate continually referred to accomplishments in previous municipal positions by using the word "we" rather than "I." Even when challenged on this point as to why he only used "we," he hesitated to say "I." This unconscious choice of words indicated that his demonstrated style was genuine and in character. In addition, he acknowledged the importance of *working for and with council*. He also stated that one of his tasks was to keep council out of trouble because "when you [council] look good, we [staff] look good." He got the job because he had the required professional credentials, provided strong references, appeared to be a team player, and was expected to bring a fresh and respectful approach to working with staff and council.

The Role and Responsibilities of the City Manager

This section highlights many of the key duties and responsibilities of the city manager and uses anecdotes from my experience as a municipal councillor for nine years and mayor for seventeen years.

First and foremost, a city manager is responsible for all administrative matters, and must have the capacity to lead and manage administrative staff ethically by genuinely respecting all staff and, as much as possible and appropriate, by delegating responsibility for completing tasks. Regardless of professional expertise, the city manager needs to have a clear understanding of the basic goals and functions of each department in the organization. Keeping the pulse on major files within each department is paramount to being a successful manager, but it does not mean having to know or get involved with each activity. The basic premise is that the city manager is a manager of people and strategy, rather than someone who performs tasks.

As a leader, the city manager must be a good and effective communicator, and able to listen, understand, and respond with confidence to a wide variety of internal and external settings. The ability to deal with issues in a calm manner and not to act impulsively will in itself demonstrate a sense of confidence to others that the subject matter will be dealt with appropriately. It takes courage and patience to stand up in front of a vocal and dissatisfied group of residents while assuring them that their opinions have been heard and the matter will be handled in a fair manner.

Interpersonal and relationship skills will be put to the test on a daily basis. Internal personnel matters are normally dealt with by department heads; however, there will be occasions when the city manager needs to intervene in disputes between a staff member and the department head or even between department heads. The ability to identify and understand the real underlying causes of a dispute will go a long way towards avoiding a toxic atmosphere that could fester within the staff ranks. I recall a circumstance when a second-tier supervisor was creating a disruptive environment in the department by taking a negative approach to supervision of staff and critical of the direction taken by senior management and council decisions. The department head was reluctant to take timely and decisive action to deal with the matter. This led to the city manager's having to step in and encourage the department head to remove the disruptive person so that the department could return to a productive staff unit.

The Public Profile of the City Manager

The city manager should also establish a public, but not political, profile, since, when directly interacting with community members, these same interpersonal and relationship skills will be required. These skills, it is hoped, will show that the city manager is approachable, trustworthy, and committed to listening to residents and businesses with an open mind as well as being prepared to resolve issues within the city manager's jurisdiction. While not a political position, a city manager should be able to inspire confidence in the public that the municipality is there to serve residents to the best of its ability.

The city manager might be called upon to negotiate a contract with an external person, organization, or other order of government, or even to repair a broken relationship between the municipality and an external body. The city manager should make it clear that discussions and actions will come from an administrative and professional perspective and within the bounds of the municipality's policies and by-laws. Notwithstanding this, and if instructed to do so, the city manager should be forthright if his or her comments are being given under the mayor's direction.

A city manager should be able to recognize and understand the difference, sometimes subtle, between recommending a policy or action that could put the municipality at risk and maintaining the status quo, and when to use either one. An example of a potential risk for the City of Kitchener occurred when the city manager and senior staff recommended a bold and transformational $110 million Economic Development Investment Fund to initiate an education and knowledge-creation cluster. The plan could have failed totally and put the city in a difficult financial position; instead, it has fundamentally transformed and broadened the economy of the city, particularly in the downtown. The results, over a number of years, have had a dramatic and positive impact on employment and new construction as well as attracting innovative companies. Knowing that this was a risky proposition, the city manager proposed a plan to ensure the public was involved in final decisions. By this time in the position, the city manager had earned the trust and confidence of the mayor and council, as well as inspiring and empowering staff to up their game. This is a good illustration of how a city manager can encourage an innovative culture throughout the municipal organization.

Setting the Organizational Culture

The working atmosphere or culture within a municipal bureaucracy undoubtedly has an impact on the outcome of services to the municipality's residents and business clients. The staff leader of the organization, the city manager, must set the tone of the workplace culture, with variations on either authoritative or collaborative. It is widely accepted that an organization's long-term success depends on respect and the involvement of all staff, regardless of status or rank, whether a frontline worker or a department head. The enlightened city manager will manage issues or develop potential policy recommendations in a collaborative manner, but when final determinations are to be made, they should be decisive. After all, the city manager should be and will be held accountable for such decisions.

I recall when a senior director was promoted to become the new city manager and immediately recognized the need for a structural change of administration to eliminate the traditional silo mentality among departments. The plan began with a revised administration strategic plan that morphed into a new corporate plan. The next phase involved multiple employee surveys that highlighted a lack of trust of senior management. This insight resulted in the decision to pivot the process to invite high influencers throughout the organization, below the rank of managers, to work together on projects in cross-departmental groups. The final result was a *People Plan* document that empowered staff members to make many operational decisions independently, which led to a more collegial and productive work environment.

Understanding the Roles of the Mayor and the City Manager

Clarity of the contrasting roles of the city manager and the mayor is absolutely critical. It is imperative that the distinction between governance and administration is understood and followed. By the very nature of the services provided by a municipality, from time to time politics will enter into the discussions between the mayor and city manager. This is also a danger zone, however, which the city manager must approach with great care and wariness because of unpredictable minefields. This is particularly troublesome if council has a partisan approach to dealing with issues. It is not the responsibility of a city manager to provide political advice to the mayor or any member of council. It is also not the role of the city manager or other administrative staff to educate council politically. It is prudent and advisable, however, to provide a program of orientation to a new council on legislated municipal rules and procedures, as well as the municipality's administrative operations.

The city manager is technically the only direct employee of council, and therefore the formal conduit between council and administration, and thus the staff advisor to the mayor and council. At the beginning of each council term, I met privately with each councillor to gain an understanding of their goals and objectives for the upcoming term. One new councillor suggested directing some individual staff members to study a particular issue. I strongly reminded the councillor that protocol had to be followed and that the matter had to be discussed with the city manager, who – and not the councillor – would direct staff to do the work if it was seen as worthy of study. Depending on the time required to do the work, it might also require council's direction to the city manager to proceed. It is absolutely imperative that the city manager remain impartial in dealings with all members of council.

A close and professional relationship requires open and candid discussions between the city manager and council in order to build mutual trust and respect. This forthright relationship becomes even more critical between the city manager and mayor. In order to have a productive working relationship, the mayor should feel intuitively that the city manager will always be totally honest in providing the best professional advice and has the courage to challenge respectfully the mayor's thinking – knowing that, in the end, a level of comfort will exist for both parties that they are in sync as they move forward. This is not to suggest that they become clones of each other, but rather that a high level of trust between them should never need to be questioned.

There are times, however, when that relationship could break down. A city manager was less than forthright with me once in a private discussion before a council meeting. Just a couple of hours later, during the meeting and to my surprise, the city manager announced a previously unrevealed study he and other colleagues had completed regarding our regional governance structure. This ought to have been shared with me, as mayor, prior to the council meeting. Beyond the fact that city managers should never cross the line into fundamental political matters, there should never be surprises. This is particularly important in the relationship between the city manager and mayor, unless one is willing to risk that council will begin the process of seeking a new city manager.

Performance Evaluation of the City Manager

In my experience, it is essential to have a regular and formal performance evaluation process to develop and maintain a healthy relationship between the city manager and council, as well as the organization as a whole. At the beginning of the performance evaluation process, it should be recognized and understood by the city manager and all members of council that all aspects of the review will be treated as a personnel matter and therefore as totally confidential.

Although the format and process can vary, the evaluation should start at the very beginning of an established twelve-month period, when the city manager presents a work plan and goals for the forthcoming year. This should include a plan for leading and managing staff in order to improve the effectiveness and efficiency of the entire administration during the coming year. The report normally would include how the council-approved corporate strategic plan and objectives will be implemented. And finally, the document should also include the city manager's personal assessment of whether or not the prior year's goals and objectives were met, as well as grading the results using the same methodology as members of council.

All members of council should then review the report and grade the city manager's performance. This would be accomplished by answering a number of pre-established questions by using either a numeric scale or word categories indicating the manager's perspective on how each area in the performance evaluation questionnaire was met or not met. The mayor then should summarize the evaluations of all members of council, as well as the city manager's self-assessment. The summary should include the average grade and range of grades for each question, as well as all unattributed comments.

Perhaps the most important part of this process is a confidential meeting of all council members and the city manager to discuss further the substantive aspects of the performance evaluation. In addition to the city manager's goals and objectives, the discussion should cover other matters relating to how the city manager fulfilled his or her role. Topics should include the city manager's relationship with the management team, all other staff, and the public, ability to encourage a service-oriented culture within the organization, communication skills, strengths and weaknesses, areas for improvement, financial accountability, and overall assessment of the city manager's performance.

All documents related to the performance evaluation should then be retained in the mayor's private files and remain confidential.

The Relationship between the City Manager and the Mayor

A healthy and respectful relationship between the city manager and the mayor is absolutely essential to set the tone for a respectful and effective organization. To dismiss this important human dynamic as irrelevant could put the municipality in danger of creating a dysfunctional organization and diminishing the level and quality of services provided to residents and businesses. One of the first things I did upon becoming mayor was to schedule regular weekly meetings with the city manager. The flexible agenda was to discuss openly current issues, keep each other informed of actions being taken in our respective areas of responsibility, and ensure collaboration of both the administrative and political arms of the municipality. There was always an unspoken understanding, however, that the city manager was the leader of the administrative staff. The overriding objective of these weekly meetings was how to make our city better.

There is a line in the relationship between the city manager and the mayor that both parties must watch very closely. It is dangerous for these two officials to socialize together on a regular basis because it ultimately might erode the professional relationship to the point where staff and councillors could no longer differentiate the positions they take on issues. Although I frequently talked with the city manager and sought out the manager's professional advice, councillors also deserve and require independent thought, perspective, and advice from the city manager on an ongoing basis. This delineation of responsibilities and authority upholds my view, as stated earlier, of a democratic governance ethos.

My mayoral experience with four different city managers over seventeen years has shown that there are varying levels of respect that require continuous attention by both parties. This certainly does not mean that both parties need to agree on how to deal with a particular issue. The city manager should be willing and strong enough to challenge the decision of council or the mayor if it contravenes other laws or could lead to unintended consequences. In fact, diversity of opinion is healthy and should be embraced as a normal part of the process of coming to the optimal position or decision.

The concept of the city manager and the mayor as *independent partners* in the municipal hierarchy is foundational to create or maintain a healthy municipality and its administration. *Independent* people could be called unconventional, mavericks, free-spirited, or unrestrained; *partners* could be referenced as colleagues, associates, collaborators, or teammates. In some situations, combining these two words could appear incompatible and irreconcilable. However, when thought of in the context of municipal government, where two distinct bodies of authority and responsibility exist, they could be viewed as the quintessential model of good governance. The city manager is an employee of the municipality, while the mayor has a term-by-term implied contract by virtue of being elected by the citizens. So, in legal terms, the city manager and mayor are independent officials, but in their functional roles they could be viewed as partners who are interdependent and work within an environment of interconnectedness.

When the attributes of leaders – respect, trust, collaboration, candor, flexibility – are brought together in the city manager–mayor relationship, there is the potential to create a vibrant and robust culture within the municipal organization. This healthy interdependent relationship, comprising independent officials, can lay the foundation and tone for building a healthy administration that exhibits the same attributes.

REFERENCE

Graham, K. A., Phillips, S. D., & Maslove, A. M. (1998). *Urban governance in Canada*. Harcourt, Brace & Company Canada.

9 What Does Diversity-Inclusion Look Like in Action?

SHIRLEY HOY

Although there are bigger cities in North America, Toronto is the largest with a city manager. With tens of thousands of employees, a budget in the billions, dozens of full-time councillors, and a population so diverse that half of its residents were not born in Canada, the job of Toronto's city manager is daunting. Dealing effectively and creatively with issues of diversity and gender came naturally to former Toronto city manager Shirley Hoy, growing out of the challenges and successes of her own career progression to the biggest city manager job of them all. Her chapter offers insights that apply to all contemporary municipalities, whether large or small.

In the late 1980s, I worked as the Director of Policy Development in the Community Services Department of the former Metro Toronto government (an upper-tier regional government). During that time, I was offered a secondment opportunity to serve as the General Manager of Administration at the Metro agency responsible for programming and managing the lands and buildings at Exhibition Place. The Canadian National Exhibition (CNE) is the main high-profile tenant.

The main purpose of the secondment was to re-establish Metro administrative and financial policies and procedures at this agency. It had gone too far on its own in developing systems and policies, with limited accountability to Metro Toronto Council. The chair of the Exhibition Place board scheduled a meeting with the senior management team for me to be introduced to them. As we walked into the room, one of the senior executives said: "Well, the chair and the secretary are here, where is this new GM we are supposed to get from downtown?"

The two-year secondment was an arduous journey in gaining the trust and respect of the senior management team. But at the end, the objectives were achieved, and I gained valuable insights into gender and cultural diversity issues at the senior ranks.

Throughout the 1990s, as I assumed new challenges at the Metro Toronto government, at the Ontario government, and then in the amalgamated City of Toronto, I found that navigating gender and cultural diversity issues was an integral part of striving to be an effective manager and leader. In this period of my career, I would experience a few more times that quizzical look that said: Could this small Asian woman be the new assistant deputy minister, or the CEO of the Ontario Housing Corporation, or the city manager of the City of Toronto?

On many occasions, this experience made me reflect on the importance of diversity-inclusion in our society, and specifically in the public sector. These are noble concepts, which are often enthusiastically embraced by decision makers and a majority of members of our society. In a turbulent world, as we have battled the unprecedented COVID-19 pandemic and witnessed the global protest against anti-Black racism and racial violence following the horrific killing of George Floyd in Minneapolis, we have seen residents demand that their governments deal with systemic injustice and demonstrate an institutional commitment to diversity-inclusion redress. Political leaders' immediate response has tended to be symbolic – for example, the removal of offensive statues or the appointment of a Black leader to a police service. Unfortunately, sometimes that is the inadequate extent of the response.

In this chapter, I want to dive deeper into the following questions: what do the concepts of diversity-inclusion really mean in action, and how does progress in diversity-inclusion improve civic decision making and the functioning of the public service? From the outset, I should state my bias that just understanding and applying specific special diversity-inclusion initiatives are not enough. They are sometimes a flash in the pan, often to placate the public following difficult protests. I believe that, in order to achieve sustained and meaningful outcomes, the more tedious work of transforming the very core structure of the public service must be done. This premise has influenced the selected readings I cite in this chapter and the practitioner's perspective I present.

I begin with a review of selected readings on research, findings of the effect of diversity-inclusive initiatives, and evidence of outcomes in public organizations – in particular, municipal governments. I then offer a discussion and analysis of the approach that, in my experience, has been effective in dealing with diversity-inclusion issues. This practitioner's perspective starts with a solid understanding of the key responsibilities of the CAO position and the functioning of the public service in municipal government. I propose a framework for this discussion, and offer examples from the early stages of development of the new City of Toronto public service following amalgamation.

A Literature Review

Lisa M. Leslie, in her article "Diversity Initiative Effectiveness: A Typological Theory of Unintended Consequences" (Leslie, 2019), provides a comprehensive analysis and compelling theory of unintended consequences of diversity initiatives. She notes that the main purpose of such initiatives is to help disadvantaged groups in society to achieve better outcomes in organizations, but they do not necessarily work as intended. Her typology includes four unintended consequences: backfire, negative spillover, positive spillover, and false progress. Reflecting on my own experience, I certainly can relate to each of these unintended consequences. In both public and private sector organizations, special diversity offices are often established to research and develop such special programs. This innovation has proven to be helpful in formulating specific diversity strategies, but it does not guarantee that unconscious, unintended bias in organizations will be addressed. As Leslie notes, depending on how implementation is done, such action will either yield good progress or fall into one of her four "unintended" categories.

Rhys Andrews and Rachel Ashworth find that gender representativeness and minority ethnic representativeness are related to perceptions of inclusiveness and the experience of discrimination and bullying within UK civil service organizations (Andrews & Ashworth, 2015). Public service organizations that more closely resemble the population they serve are perceived by their employees to be more inclusive environments in which to work and, as a result, had fewer incidents of discrimination and bullying in the workplace.

Niels Opstrup and Anders R. Villadsen confirm my own experience in the public service in their article, "The Right Mix? Gender Diversity in Top Management Teams and Financial Performance" (Opstrup & Villadsen, 2015). They examine gender diversity in top management teams of public organizations and its relationship to the organizations' financial performance. Their key finding is that management diversity is a positive asset, allowing for more diverse knowledge and skill sets. In their longitudinal study of top management teams in ninety Danish municipalities, they find that gender diversity led to higher financial performance, but only where management structure supported cross-functional teamwork.

Patrick Eamon O'Flynn and Tim A. Mau's article, "A Demographic and Career Profile of Municipal CAOs in Canada: Implications for Local Governance" (O'Flynn & Mau, 2014), find recruitment challenges regarding the representativeness of the bureaucratic elite in the municipal sector, and note that their "research reveals that municipalities have some way to go to ensure representativeness in the CAO community" (p. 157). In particular, the results of their 2010 survey point to the severe underrepresentation of women in the municipal CAO position. My informal canvass of the municipal scene across Canada over the past five years or so leads me to believe that there has been significant progress in gender and cultural diversity in the senior ranks of municipal public services, including in the role of CAO. More formal research should be undertaken in this area in the future.

A Practitioner's Perspective

The key question is: Do diversity-inclusion actions improve civic decision making? If so, how?

An insightful way to address this question would be to focus on understanding the key roles of the management ranks in the municipal public service, starting with the CAO position. David Siegel's article, "The Leadership Role of the Municipal Chief Administrative Officer" (Siegel, 2010), is comprehensive and detailed in describing the leadership responsibilities of the CAO's role. He outlines clearly the complexity of the position as he describes how "the incumbent must lead in three different directions simultaneously, down (dealing with subordinates); out (dealing with residents' groups, media, and other governments); and up (dealing with mayor and council)" (Siegel, 2010, p. 139).

This structure can be applied not only at the CAO level, but at all management levels of the bureaucracy. To effect good governance, there is a need to manage constantly in all three directions and at all levels of management, including the CAO position. It is absolutely critical to a sound implementation of gender and cultural diversity goals and strategies that they be applied at all levels of the public service (managing down) and in the community (managing out). As it relates to the mayor and council, the situation is much more complicated. As Siegel notes, "leading up" for the CAO is very different from the other two directions, as the CAO is accountable to the mayor and councillors and the power of the CAO comes from exercising influence (Siegel, 2010, p. 152).

To achieve a successful relationship with the mayor and council, the CAO must foster trust and respect, focus on both the short- and long-term priorities of the mayor and council, be creative and resourceful in policy development while adhering to solid principles, and always be transparent, clear, and open with decision-making processes. With such a relationship established, the CAO can then focus on "leading down" and "leading out."

Leading Down

Over the years, I have learned that the fundamentals of a robust public service must be in place in order to institute gender and cultural diversity strategies. The key characteristics of a solid public service foundation encompass the following: clear shared values; a culture of competence, professionalism, and talents; a deep understanding that the decision-making process in the public sector is hardly ever a straight line, but often a long and winding road; a recognition that many variables are not in the control of the mayor, council, and the public service; a certain comfort level in dealing with ambiguity; a passion for implementing well; and, above all, trust and respect in working relationships at all levels of the bureaucracy.

I would like to illustrate this contention by describing my experience in the initial phase of the amalgamated City of Toronto (1998–2008). (Six predecessor local "city" municipalities and the metropolitan government were merged into a single municipality by provincial government legislation in 1998.)

The first three years were chaotic, with seven cultures co-existing side-by-side and seven legacy systems to manage human resources, finance, and service delivery. The prime goal was to ensure no service disruption to the residents, but some staff and councillors, many of whom had opposed the merger, held the expectation that the amalgamation could still be reversed.

Despite this turmoil, the new council established a Task Force on Access and Equity, partly in response to the protests and demands of community organizations opposed to amalgamation. It also approved the City of Toronto's motto, "Diversity Our Strength." In addition, there was a Diversity Management and Community Engagement Unit in the CAO's office. Accordingly, some of the basic and necessary building blocks were in place to implement gender and cultural diversity strategies.

Unfortunately, the foundation of the new City of Toronto public service had not yet been built in the first three years following amalgamation – that is, seven very different public service cultures co-existed. Therefore, between 2001 to 2004, as the CAO, I worked with the senior management team to set up a multiyear process of developing and communicating a new shared set of values and culture for the public service. Work started with instilling trust and respect among the senior management ranks. Then managers undertook field visits to all work sites, and different types of staff development and engagement initiatives were employed, including mentoring/coaching programs, town hall meetings, public sector quality fairs, and focus groups.

The fact that we were building a new unified, single public service and an accompanying value system gave us an opportunity to embed diversity-inclusion policies and procedures in the foundation. The vision and mission were to implement the city's motto. The central questions for discussion and, indeed, debate with public servants at all levels of the organization were the following: What does this motto mean to you? How do you think it will affect your own job? And how will it affect the Toronto public service?

During those three years, there were some difficult conversations at all levels of the organization. In response to the specific statement that we would like to see the Toronto public service reflect the diversity in the community, questions from staff included: Is management looking at requiring affirmation action, a quota system? If I am not a person of colour or a woman, should I even try for a job competition? Is this not reverse discrimination? How do I know the process will be fair?

In discussions with staff, mainly male, in the more traditional departments of fire, paramedics, transportation, water, and waste disposal, I was asked a few times how I became the CAO for Toronto. There seemed to be some surprise that a woman with a background in social policy and public administration had become the CAO. It was interesting that I did not get the same line of questioning from the community services departments, such as childcare, long-term care, social services, public health, or recreation, that are dominated by female staff.

In reflecting on the selected readings I outlined earlier in the chapter and on my own experience in the Toronto public service, I want to highlight certain lessons learned.

The symbolic value of council's Task Force on Access and Equity and the new Toronto motto of "Diversity Our Strength" was immense in providing the vision and, even more important, the permission for the public service to take action. The Diversity Management & Community Engagement Unit in the CAO's office was vital in seeking out new ideas and developing strategies for implementation. To be truly effective, however, the strategies should be embedded in robust human resource policies and procedures, and the human resources department needs to report directly to the CAO. Moreover, diversity-inclusion strategies must be implemented at all levels of the organization, with constant review, assessment, and adjustments. Evidence-based approaches should be adopted from the beginning and a commitment and appropriation of the financing requirements allocated in order to secure solid data. In implementing the strategies, it is necessary to deal expeditiously with issues, concerns, and complaints that arise.

During those years of building the new public service in the amalgamated city, I lost many nights of sleep, worrying whether I was an effective leader. Now, with 20/20 hindsight, I would offer that a CAO needs the following strategies in undertaking major transformation in an organization:

- be comfortable, indeed enthusiastic, with focusing on the collective, the team, and consensus building;
- welcome diverse views and strong opinions in discussions and debates, as such honest and open interactions will lead to stronger consensual directions;
- foster strong working relationship with the union leadership, and ensure that they are fully consulted on the purpose, directions, and timeline of the diversity-inclusion strategies to be implemented; most important is the need to demonstrate that such strategies are in keeping with the requirements of the collective agreements;
- govern by listening, reflecting, connecting, and collaborating, an approach that should be employed by the senior management team at all levels of the organization, in all different work settings; and
- do not rely on a command-and-control approach, as feedback would be inadequate; instead, recognize the tendency for some staff to "manage up" as a way to avoid uncomfortable conversations or conflicts.

Finally, an effective feedback system must be built in to ensure regular and timely communication of clear, simple messages repeated often in all parts of the public service. If a misunderstanding occurs, immediate corrective action needs to be taken before it takes hold in the organization. I would suggest that, in our current environment of ubiquitous and powerful social media, it is even more difficult to establish an effective feedback system.

Leading Out

Siegel defines "leading out" as "the CAO's relationship with individuals or groups, such as the media, residents' groups, business organizations, and the other governments, that are outside the municipal structure" (Siegel, 2010, p. 147). In the twenty-first century, the CAO and municipal public servants at all levels of management must understand the importance of the set of responsibilities that are involved in "leading out." The breadth and depth of the mandate of municipal governments have become so much more complicated that the knowledge, competence, and skills of municipal workers must be diverse in order to address issues ranging from global pandemics to economic recessions, social justice, and climate change.

To achieve success in dealing with these thorny, complicated public policy issues, municipal governments must always be in partnership and collaboration with others – other orders of government or other community and civic organizations.

What I gleaned from my experience in the amalgamated City of Toronto was that, if the public service at all levels reflects the diversity in the community, then forging partnerships and collaboration and gaining trust and respect with key partners are much easier to attain. Greater gender and cultural diversity at different levels of the administrative structure provided the knowledge and skills necessary to secure the trust of the community in dealing with impending issues, developing more creative solutions, and facilitating implementation. The success of two important council initiatives – "Clean and Beautiful City" and "Community Safety" – relied on outcomes at the neighbourhood level. They were only possible with strong collaboration across departments and a deep understanding of community dynamics at the local level.

Finally, one other dimension that enhanced the public service's ability to "lead out" was the strategy to move from a permanent hierarchical structure to nimble networks for implementation. In their study, Opstrup and Villadsen (2015) note that increased gender diversity improved decision making, but only if it was accompanied by a move to a lateral, cross-departmental structure. Their research also indicates that gender diversity in top management positions had no effect in traditional hierarchical organizations, mainly because cross-functional management structures promote what they term "behavioral integration" in decision making, leading to better results.

This certainly was my experience in the amalgamated City of Toronto. In the first five years following amalgamation, the consolidation of all the departments from the former seven municipalities followed the traditional program/service delineations, with commissioners and general managers forming the senior management ranks. Although this organizational structure clearly emphasized the service delivery role of the public service, it was too rigid to deal with the need to eliminate some legacy public service cultures in parts of the organization or purposefully embrace innovation, diversity, and a new unified public service culture.

In 2005, the mayor and council approved a new administrative structure for the Toronto public service to replace the traditional system of commissioners as heading major service departments. The new one renamed the CAO as city manager and installed a new executive level of deputy city managers to whom a number of former departmental commissioners would report. Major policy and program issues that cut across service areas would be led by the deputy city managers. In my view, this new structure improved decision making in "leading down" and "leading out" by capitalizing on the diverse skills and knowledge at different levels of the bureaucracy.

To "lead out" well is vital, as the public's expectation of government – in particular, at the municipal level, the one closest to residents and the one having the greatest impact on their day-to-day activities – has increased year after year. And in a world of intense social media scrutiny and instant responses to questions raised, effective collaboration is a must. A key ingredient for success is having diverse public servants in all areas of the bureaucracy in order to anticipate, plan, respond, and implement well.

Conclusion

To be effective, diversity-inclusion initiatives must go beyond the rhetoric, the symbolic gestures, and the one-off special projects. They must be embedded in the foundational elements of the public service. Key to this is the tone from the top – that is, the CAO position – and robust human resource policies and procedures that can withstand the challenges of transparency, fairness, and commitment to community representativeness. Above all, it requires an active management at all levels of the bureaucracy committed to diverse talent development and retention.

There are no quick fixes. The definition of the problem is clear: in both the public and private sectors, gender and cultural diversity in C-suites and boardrooms still fall short of representing the demographics in society. A 2020 *Toronto Star* article headlined "Canada has a problem in its boardrooms. A new study shows racialized voices are missing." The study was the first of its kind by the Diversity Institute at Ryerson University (now Toronto Metropolitan University), which took a snapshot of gender and racial diversity in Canadian board positions. It found that "women occupied 40.8% of board positions across the country, but few women of colour share the standing," and "racialized people accounted for 10.4% of the [board positions]." Professor Wendy Cukier, the founder of the Diversity Institute, commented: "progress is slow but moving forward" (Keung, 2020).

Since 1998, the City of Toronto Public Service has made many achievements, and gender and cultural diversity in its senior management ranks is certainly one of them. It is not, however, an achievement that one can just check off; it is always a work in progress.

My deep belief is that permanent structural reform to realize the gender and cultural representativeness of Canadian society requires constant vigilance and action at all levels of management in an organization and a commitment to leading and managing well – down, out, and up!

REFERENCES

Andrews, R., & Ashworth, R. (2015). Representation and inclusion in public organizations: Evidence from the U.K. civil service. *Public Administration Review, 75*(2), 279–88. http://doi.org/10.1111/puar.12308

Keung, N. (2020, 6 August). Canada has a problem in its boardrooms. A new study shows racialized voices are sorely missing. *Toronto Star*. https://www.thestar.com/news/gta/2020/08/06/canada-has-a-problem-in-its-boardrooms-a-new-study-shows-racialized-voices-are-sorely-missing.html

Leslie, L. M. (2019). Diversity initiative effectiveness: A typological theory of unintended consequences. *Administrative Science Quarterly, 44*(3), 538–63. https://doi.org/10.5465/amr.2017.0087

O'Flynn, P. E., & Mau, T. A. (2014). A demographic and career profile of municipal CAOs in Canada: Implications for local governance. *Canadian Public Administration, 57*(1), 154–70. http://doi.org/10.1111/capa.12055

Opstrup, N., & Villadsen, A. R. (2015). The right mix? Gender diversity in top management teams and financial performance. *Public Administration Review, 75*(2), 291–301. https://doi.org/10.1111/puar.12310

Siegel, D. (2010). The leadership role of the municipal chief administrative officer. *Canadian Public Administration, 53*(2), 139–61. https://doi.org/10.1111/j.1754-7121.2010.00122.x

10 Diversity from Bottom to Top: The City Manager and Workplace Diversity

SHEILA BASSI-KELLETT

Working for the federal government and the territorial government in the Northwest Territories and as Yellowknife's city manager, Sheila Bassi-Kellett has a particular perspective on thriving in an environment where women in leadership roles remain uncommon and where responding positively and respectfully to Indigenous issues is always top-of-mind. Like other public sector executives, Bassi-Kellett has been an innovator but has also paid the price for principled stands. It has earned her the respect of those she leads for her integrity and for her collaborative approach to "making a difference" through professional city management.

Municipal governments in Canada are mandated to ensure safe and efficient community services, including water and sewage, waste management, fire and ambulance – and have evolved to be "ground zero" for addressing many of the significant issues of our times. Strategic, thoughtful leadership is needed to navigate the issues facing municipalities, including climate change, homelessness, sustainability, economic development, reconciliation, anti-racism, and, after the experience of the COVID-19 pandemic, pivoting to provide safe options for urban necessities such as public transit and recreation, accessibility, and public engagement. Diversity in the administrative leadership of municipal governments is critical, and influences how municipalities position themselves to navigate issues positively and productively.

After spending more than thirty years working in the Northwest Territories (NWT) across three orders of government as well as in the private sector, I remain convinced that the most exciting, nimble, and responsive order of government is the municipal. Nobody who has worked in the realm of municipal government has ever said it was boring – the scope of issues is broad and the context for addressing these issues is constantly evolving. Having worked in two NWT communities – as chief administrative officer in the 1990s in Tulit'a, a small predominantly Indigenous community located on the traditional lands of the Sahtu Dene and Métis, and now as city manager for the City of Yellowknife, located on Chief Drygeese Territory of the Yellowknives Dene – I can attest to how the role is dynamic and far more expansive in scope than is often assumed. (While municipal chief administrative officers use a variety of titles across Canada, for purposes of simplicity, in this chapter I generally use the term "city manager.")

City managers play a key leadership role in navigating the complex and nuanced context of local government – aligning council's political perspective with long-term stability and continuity, balancing residents' interests with delivering cost-effective programs and services, all the while leading a functionally diverse workforce. Given the scope of the impact city managers can have, it is puzzling that the role is still such an afterthought. O'Flynn and Mau have noted that, "[d]espite the growing importance of municipalities in our federal system of government and the critical role that chief administrative officers ... play therein, it is perhaps the least studied and understood senior government position in Canada" (O'Flynn & Mau, 2014, p. 154).

The Role of City Managers Is Evolving and the Scope Is Broadening

Local governments in the NWT have undergone significant evolution and transformation in their relatively short history. Although Indigenous peoples have lived nomadically in the area since time immemorial, settled communities are a recent development. Public, or municipal-style, government was first formally instituted with the passage of the Municipal Ordinance in 1963 with administrators – male and from "south of 60" – hired to run local settlements.

Over time, residents' escalating interest in ensuring community control over the programs and services directly affecting them, coupled with a need to address an ever-expanding variety of significant issues such as Indigenous rights, devolution, and resource development, mean that the mandate of local governments in the NWT has evolved to include a much more diverse range of responsibilities. Further, it can be argued that offloading from other orders of government to the local level has contributed to the mandate creep. Consequently, city managers are called upon to advise elected leaders on a broad range of increasingly strategic, complex, and technical issues, and to follow through on implementing the broad direction of council in tactical ways. While the provision of core municipal services is the foundation of local governments, mandates have expanded to include broad matters of relevance and importance to residents and communities. At the City of Yellowknife, the majority of my time as city manager is spent on strategic issues, including sustainable development, intergovernmental relations, economic stimulus, and social issues; no day is ever the same and the challenges are diverse and exciting.

Diversity of Backgrounds: City Managers Need Distinct Characteristics and Competencies to Be Effective

Reflecting on my personal career path prior to joining the City of Yellowknife, from officer level positions in the Government of Canada and the Government of the Northwest Territories to CAO in Tulit'a, to deputy minister and then private consultant, I can wholeheartedly support O'Flynn and Mau's statement that "there is no clear pathway to becoming a municipal CAO" (O'Flynn & Mau, 2014, p. 167). Many of my CAO peers in the larger NWT communities tend to come from either an accounting or engineering background; they fell into municipal management as a result of a circuitous professional path. Regardless of professional background, certain common competencies and personality traits contribute to an individual's success as a city manager. Research for my 2009 Master's thesis on developing local government administrators in the NWT affirmed for me the importance of managerial leadership competencies – to manage people, resources, and organizational performance – along with political acuity and the ability to sustain a productive relationship with council.

One of my mentors blazed a professional path that I have inadvertently followed, moving from a deputy minister role in four portfolios within the Government of NWT to become city manager in a capital city elsewhere in Canada. She expressed to me how she enjoyed the immediacy and diversity of this new role, and recognized the need for political acuity equally within both municipal and territorial governments. Some might see moving from a city manager position to become a deputy minister as a career advancement. In terms of job satisfaction, however, there is much to be said for the experience a senior public servant brings to a city manager position.

The similarities between the roles of city manager and deputy minister are numerous. It could be argued that, given the reporting relationship to mayor and council, a city manager's function could be seen as more similar to the role of secretary to cabinet, which reports to the premier and cabinet. Both

- are the conduit between the political and administrative, balancing the interests of each;
- require strong political acuity, strategic leadership, policy facilitation, ethics, and a commitment to democratic advocacy and constituent engagement;
- need a balance of people skills to manage their relationship with the public, along with project management skills to move the machinery of government forward coherently towards corporate goals; and
- are subject to the political vagaries of their respective contexts and as a result can be publicly and hastily shown the door and thanked for their service.

Ensuring diversity of perspective, as well as experience, in the top roles within municipal and other orders of public government contributes to better leadership in the complex and nuanced interface between the political and administrative realms.

Gender Affects Leadership Style

Gender differences in leadership have been studied extensively, including the position put forth by Chamorro-Premuzic & Gallop (2020) that women have more leadership effectiveness (what it takes to perform well), while men typically dominate leadership emergence. They propose that "the real problem is not a lack of competent females; it is too few obstacles for incompetent males, which explains the surplus of overconfident, narcissistic and unethical people in charge."

As the first female city manager for the City of Yellowknife, the simple act of my appointment in 2016 after a competitive process can be seen as a statement on management culture by council. Although the recruitment process is confidential, various comments councillors raised during their deliberations on the candidates made their way to me. Based on this anecdotal information, even in the twenty-first century gender perceptions remain an issue – with council members ranging across the spectrum from pro to con for a female city manager. Perceptions of leadership abilities based on gender are not new, particularly in the municipal context, where many of the hard services that municipalities offer are seen as the traditional professional bastion of men.

When I came on the scene, councillors might have been seeking a more collegial environment in the wake of a particularly combative working context previously, as noted in local media (Rendell, 2015). A competency I bring to the city manager role is collaboration, which Opstrup & Villadsen (2015) cite as a typical female leadership behaviour. Prior to officially starting as city manager, I met with each councillor individually in order to seek to understand respective priorities and concerns, and to align these, to the greatest extent possible, with my plan for the first ninety days on the job. These meetings were intended to enable connection with all council members, particularly those who did not endorse my appointment, and to lay the foundation for relationships going forward based on trust and respect.

More Gender Diversity Is Needed at the Top

The top position in municipal administrations across Canada remains dominated by men. As O'Flynn and Mau affirm, "[t]he results of our survey point to a severe underrepresentation of women in the municipal CAO position ... only about one quarter of our respondents (55 out of 219) were female" (O'Flynn & Mau, 2014, p. 157). It is disheartening to think that, in the twenty-first century, "the numbers support the notion that was repeated by our interviewees that senior municipal management positions were a sort of 'old boys club'" (p. 159). This is not surprising, as I vividly remember the sea of grey balding heads in the crowd at my first Canadian Association of Municipal Administrators' annual meeting in 2017.

The nature of the city manager role is such that the competencies and skills required are more diverse and less focused on professional skill sets historically dominated by men, such as accounting or engineering. Municipal governments can expect to benefit from the recruitment of female CAOs given that "women in top management are likely to be highly skilled, as they typically have to overcome significant challenges to break the glass ceiling and get promoted to higher ranks" (Opstrup & Villadsen, 2015, p. 293).

At the City of Yellowknife, the dynamic of managing a majority male workforce is not lost on me, and I customize my approach for the various work contexts across the organization. My more collaborative leadership style was new to many of the directors. Many attribute the drive for increased interdepartmental collaboration to a female city manager and gender balance at the top. The senior leadership meetings have evolved from a weekly hour-long session – simply to review agendas for upcoming council and committee meetings – into one morning per week for interdepartmental initiatives to be collectively reviewed and enhanced by the collective "brain trust." Full participation is expected, and constructive comments on initiatives from other departments are required. At first, some directors were non-plussed at the lengthened weekly meetings, but my emphasis that these provide the opportunity for us as the senior leadership team of the organization to bring the collective expertise to the overall corporate interest has ultimately been appreciated.

Gender Balance in Senior Leadership Makes a Difference

Having worked at both ends of the spectrum – within an all-female organization and managing an all-male work force – I strongly believe that blended workplaces which aspire to gender balance are ideal. Either extreme struggles with a lack of diversity of perspective. Opstrup and Villadsen support this with their observation that, "compared with men, women's cognitive style tends to emphasize harmony … this gender difference may lead to superior team dynamics when men and women are brought together in continuous interaction, where the distinct strengths of each gender can be leveraged" (Opstrup & Villadsen, 2015, p. 293).

Creating a gender-balanced senior leadership team at the city changed the way in which departments engaged and how issues are analysed and presented to elected leaders. Engaged debate around the issues takes place, with the key interest being to produce the best possible product for council and the community. It might be argued that this contributed to a healthier dynamic between administration and council, with a far less combative tone.

The Organizational Culture of the Municipality Is Driven by the CAO

All organizations have an organizational culture, but exactly what constitutes culture and what is its effect on the organization garner very diverse opinions. If culture is the way in which an organization does things – the "how" more than the "what" – then the CAO leads in shaping the agenda of the municipal government. As Fenn and Siegel note, "[t]he CAO helps establish the organizational culture of the municipality, which defines the behaviour expected of public servants … One person at the top can have a profound influence on the behaviour that is encouraged or discouraged in an organization. The tone is set from the top" (Fenn & Siegel, 2017, p. 10).

When I started as Yellowknife's city manager, my leadership style – upward with council, downward with staff, and outward with constituents – was different from that of my predecessors; of course, this is as expected with any new corporate leader. Bringing transparent, open, and accessible administrative leadership, along with systems thinking, regular communications, and aspirations for a learning organization, garnered reaction from all sides. Moving from a stove-piped operational approach where each department did its own thing was perhaps the most immediate cultural shift. It was achieved by reaffirming expectations around systems thinking, analysis of functional interrelationships, and corporate consistency. As Opstrup and Villadsen note: "Research has provided numerous studies of how leadership styles differ between men and women. Generally, studies find that women engage in leadership behavior that is more participatory, collaborative and democratic than men's" (Opstrup & Villadsen, 2015, p. 293).

Being open and accessible to staff and establishing regular direct communication was noted as a big change within the city administration. Implementing monthly all-staff meetings that are videotaped and available on the city staff intranet ensured consistent information and engagement with staff. At these meetings, I update staff on key decisions before council and current issues for city administration, and openly welcome questions from staff, which can be raised at the meeting or in advance, in person or electronically, and with the option to do so anonymously. Many staff have expressed their appreciation for consistent communication across the organization, as well as having avenues to raise their issues in an environment where there is a commitment to respond. The intent is to engage with all staff through a lens of openness, respect, and collaboration, and in turn to reaffirm the value they bring to the organization and the community. Culture can be influenced by signals such as this. Andrews and Ashworth note that inclusion happens when "an employee considers himself or herself an 'esteemed' member of an organization if he or she experiences 'treatment that satisfies his or her needs for belonging and uniqueness'" (Andrews & Ashworth, 2015, p. 280).

Throughout the organization, most staff appreciate an accessible and responsive city manager, more so than consciously responding to the fact that I am female. The link between these two, however, is likely implicit, given the observation by Opstrup and Villadsen that "women are more likely than men to be perceived as leaders in environments that involve a significant degree of social interaction. Public sector organizations exist in highly diverse and complex environments, which may make female leaders an asset" (Opstrup & Villadsen, 2015, p. 293).

Working with a council that consciously values a diversity of voices – in both public engagement and staff perspectives – is a gift, and can strategically position a city manager to shift the culture of the organization. Alignment with elected leaders on the culture of the municipality expedites change and can help define the municipality's "brand." A council that does not trust the city manager to build the culture and feels it is wholly on the elected leaders to do so will not be productive in establishing the sort of organization where people want to work. However, a council that sets broad goals of diversity, staff retention, continuous improvement, and reconciliation, and that expects the city manager to realize these in meaningful ways, sets a constructive dynamic that is apparent both outside and within the organization.

A Representative Workforce Makes for Better Government

Across the municipal corporation, diversity beyond gender is important. The concept of representative bureaucracy explores the connection between effective governance and having a workforce that personifies the population it serves. In the research for my 2009 Master's thesis, I found that "[s]cholars of representative bureaucracy recognize that bureaucrats exercise discretion in policy implementation. Where discretion exists, the values of the decision-maker become important" (Bassi-Kellett, 2009, p. 30). As such, representative diversity of city staff is essential to ensure that the vision and goals of council are implemented and translated into action in ways that align with the community overall. There is more work to be done in this area; as O'Flynn and Mau note, "[u]nlike the federal public sector … where tremendous progress has been made in the past decade in particular to ensure that the senior ranks of the bureaucracy reflect the diversity of Canadian society, we discovered that local governments have collectively yet to embrace representativeness in the same way" (O'Flynn & Mau, 2014, p. 168).

Andrews and Ashworth (2015) note that "representative bureaucracies do not lead to improved benefits for one societal group at the expense of another but rather improve benefits for society as a whole, as a representative bureaucracy tends to be a more qualified organization that makes better decisions" (p. 286). Not surprisingly, "researchers have highlighted the potential significance of organizational culture and the work environment as critical concepts within the study of representative bureaucracy" (p. 286). The benefits for Yellowknife include a manifestation of reconciliation, where Indigenous people are fully included and Indigenous ways of being infuse approaches to key policy issues and directions.

Exploring ways to enhance the representativeness of the city workforce so that it is a reflection of the diversity of Yellowknife became a key action for the city with the renewal of the human resources framework in 2020. Yellowknife is a surprisingly diverse community given its size, with 25 per cent of the population being Indigenous, living alongside people from across the world. Strategies to attract and retain a diverse representation of the community in the city workforce have been built into a comprehensive overhaul of the city's human resource directives, including recruitment and employment outreach protocols that specifically seek to attract Indigenous persons, persons with disabilities, and visible minorities.

As city manager, having the opportunity to align my personal values around reconciliation and diversity with the overall goals and corporate culture of the city is deeply rewarding. In particular, recognizing and enhancing the unique relationship between the city and the adjacent Yellowknives Dene First Nation (YKDFN) through practical actions that advance reconciliation and shared interests has been productive for both governments. Together we have introduced significant changes to the boundary between our two communities, which advance YKDFN interests for self-government, while also anticipating future city growth, driven by the Indigenous rights process that YKDFN and the Government of Canada are currently negotiating. In Spring 2021, YKDFN and the city finalized a joint economic development strategy, and are mutually supporting infrastructure projects in each other's communities. At the end of the day, diversity in the workforce makes for better policy decisions and better operational implementation. Community members who see themselves represented in their government will be more engaged and trust that a broad spectrum of perspectives across all types of diversity will inform policy and program decisions.

Looking Ahead: Mentorship and Sponsorship

The mentors and coaches I have had the good fortune to connect with have been invaluable on my professional journey and have opened doors that I might otherwise have walked past. They inspired me to think about the honour of public service, the excitement of administrative leadership in a political context, and the ability to influence change. They also sponsored me in providing opportunities to develop skills and to pursue advancement. This type of professional support can amplify the outcomes of policies, strategies, and organizational culture that seek to increase representation.

From where I sit now, the opportunity to mentor up-and-coming professionals from diverse backgrounds is a pleasure and a privilege. When this includes the opportunity to showcase the scope, breadth, and impact of the city manager role, that is even better. More women will continue to assume the city manager role across the country as the value of women's leadership behaviours to address the complex policy and operational issues facing municipalities is recognized. The societal pivot caused by the COVID-19 pandemic has made us think about effective leadership, where empathy, transformation, and team engagement – all traits associated with female leadership – are recognized as valuable and have reinforced diverse leadership role models around the world. The world of municipal management benefits from diversity in the same way that other governing institutions have done. All of us currently in the field have the ability to lead the way.

REFERENCES

Andrews, R., & Ashworth, R. (2015). Representation and inclusion in public organizations: Evidence from the UK civil service. *Public Administration Review*, *75*(2), 279–88. http://doi.org/10.1111/puar.12308

Bassi-Kellett, S. (2009). *Building and sustaining the capacity of local government administrators in the NWT*. Royal Roads University.

Chamorro-Premuzic, T., & Gallop, C. (2020, 1 April). 7 leadership lessons men can learn from women. *Harvard Business Review*. https://hbr.org/2020/04/7-leadership-lessons-men-can-learn-from-women

Fenn, M., & Siegel, D. (2017). The evolving role of city managers and chief administrative officers. *IMFG Papers*. University of Toronto, Institute on Municipal Finance and Governance.

O'Flynn, P. E., & Mau, T. A. (2014). A demographic and career profile of municipal CAOs in Canada: Implications for local governance. *Canadian Public Administration*, *57*(1), 154–70. https://doi.org/10.1111/capa.12055

Opstrup, N., & Villadsen, A. R. (2015). The right mix? Gender diversity in top management teams and financial performance. *Public Administration Review*, *75*(2), 291–301. https://doi.org/10.1111/puar.12310

Rendell, M. (2015, 18 November). Whistleblower tension: Things get a tad contentious at council over employee protection protocol and advertising policy. *Edge North*. https://edgenorth.ca/article/city-briefs-whistleblower-tension

11 Indigenous and Municipal Relationships: The Art of Collaboration

ANN MITCHELL

The notion of "community of communities" now more than ever involves Indigenous people and governments. Ann Mitchell, Lethbridge County, Alberta, CAO shares her experiences while at Sioux Lookout, Ontario, to foster collaboration with Indigenous communities and leaders. Her primary premise is the requisite relationship building for shared services and joint strategic efforts to enhance the sustainability of all communities within a region.

Canada is experiencing a sea change in the relationship between Indigenous people and other Canadians. Canada is a signatory to the United Nations Declaration on the Rights of Indigenous People and the federal government has generally accepted the calls to action set out in the Report of the Truth and Reconciliation Commission of Canada (2015). Local governments have a significant role to play in this changing relationship. The municipal chief administrative officer needs to take a leadership role in this initiative. This new way of thinking about the Indigenous–non-Indigenous relationship makes some people uncomfortable. As a community leader, the CAO is uniquely positioned to lend support to – or sometimes to lead – local government reconciliation efforts in the face of discomfort or outright hostility.

As a CAO, I have worked in mostly small, rural, or remote communities that challenge you to find innovative solutions. To increase economic opportunities for all, municipalities must create partnerships when traditional revenue streams are not accessible. A proactive CAO continually endeavours to find ways to ensure that her or his community remains viable. It was during my time as CAO in the community of Sioux Lookout (from 2012 to 2018), in northwestern Ontario, that I grew to appreciate the nuances and benefits of First Nations–municipal partnerships and enhanced Indigenous–non-Indigenous community relations. We used these partnerships to break down barriers between Indigenous and non-Indigenous people in our region, to establish joint service provision, and to leverage external funding,

The purpose of this chapter is to tell the story of how one CAO in one municipality navigated these shoals, in the hope that it will provide advice and inspiration to other CAOs facing similar issues. The first section provides context by describing the community of Sioux Lookout and the development of a foundation – the Friendship Accord – for Indigenous–non-Indigenous relations and partnerships. The next two sections discuss the Truth and Reconciliation Commission and the Calls to Action and Call for Justice of the National Inquiry on Missing and Murdered Indigenous Women and Girls (NIMMIWG) as they relate to local government. The next two sections describe the organizational readiness of Sioux Lookout to engage with the local First Nations, followed by a discussion of the rationale for local partnerships. The final section describes various strategic initiatives and shared services with First Nations. Through several case studies, I highlight the importance of relationship building as the cornerstone of joint ventures with First Nations.

There is an art to creating and sustaining these alliances. It was through these First Nations–municipal partnerships that I truly began to understand the importance of regional collaboration as well as the CAO's leadership role in developing and sustaining such partnerships. CAOs must be able to balance the directions of elected officials and the needs and wants of staff, stakeholders of First Nations, and local governments for the benefit of their respective communities.

Context

Sioux Lookout, Ontario, has approximately 5,300 residents, over 60 per cent of whom are Indigenous (Statistics Canada, 2016). Additionally, Sioux Lookout is surrounded by twenty-nine First Nations communities with about 30,000 residents.

As in many municipalities across Canada, at one time the seven-member Sioux Lookout municipal council did not reflect the demographic (or gender) profile of the community that elected it. Although the majority of the population was Indigenous, there was no corresponding representation on council; as Heritz (2018, p. 596) has noted, "[d]espite their growing numbers, Indigenous people remain underrepresented in municipal government." This led to a further disconnect between the municipality of Sioux Lookout and the surrounding Indigenous communities, mirrored by a divide within the Sioux Lookout urban area between the Indigenous and non-Indigenous populations. Although attempts had been made over Sioux Lookout's one-hundred-year history to strengthen relationships, there was still much more to do. And relationships are especially crucial for positive dealings with Indigenous communities.

Wilson (2008) provides the Indigenous perspective when he emphasizes the value of relationships in Indigenous culture: "The importance of relationships, or the relationality of an Indigenous ontology and epistemology, was stressed by many people who talked to me about this topic. Several stated that this relational way of being was at the heart of what it means to be Indigenous" (p. 80). Wilson further specifies that, often, when meeting new people, Indigenous people will try to find connections through common acquaintances or relatives. This gives comfort to those you are dealing with and paves the way to commonalities.

Many meetings between the municipality and First Nations, whether casual or formal, would begin with conversation and usually laughter. It brought a relaxed feeling and underscored the importance of rapport. It was extremely beneficial for us, collectively and individually, to intermingle and adopt the Indigenous way of interaction and ceremony. Often meetings would be accompanied by a meal, ceremonial drumming, or storytelling. This allowed us to gain a richer insight into Indigenous culture and deepened our relationships, which made the partnerships stronger.

In 2015, a new mayor was elected who understood the benefits of the collaborative relationship. He often acknowledged that "what is good for the North is good for Sioux Lookout" (D. Lawrance, personal communication with author, 2016). Since the economy of Sioux Lookout and region relies mainly on Indigenous communities, he was correct in his assessment. A very important point is that our approach was to work with the communities, not simply to use them. The key to partnerships is how we adjust or adapt to change. The key to understanding and developing Indigenous–non-Indigenous relationships is not to repeat what was done in the past. We need to forge new paths, and there is an art to this. We must also remember that each Indigenous community is at a different place in its history.

The Friendship Accord

In 2012, Sioux Lookout entered into a Friendship Accord with Lac Seul and Slate Falls First Nations. This historic framework was an overarching document that outlined how we would work together. The Friendship Accord had four pillars or areas of focus: resources and economic development; long-term care beds; public and community awareness and education; and a review of the judicial process. The agreement has since been expanded by the addition of the Cat Lake and Kitchenuhmaykoosib Inninuwug First Nations. The Friendship Accord was a direct result of a workshop held in Lac Seul on 4 November 2011 by the Federation of Canadian Municipalities to highlight the First Nations-Municipal Community Infrastructure Partnership Program. Chief Bull of Lac Seul and Mayor Dennis Leney of Sioux Lookout made a presentation on the Friendship Accord to the Federation of Canadian Municipalities annual conference in Niagara Falls, Ontario, in June 2014.

During the discussion period that followed the presentation, many municipalities expressed their concerns about working with their First Nations neighbours. This made it clear to us how far ahead of other local governments we were, while at the same time realizing that we were only beginning. One common obstacle mentioned by session participants was that they had never sat down with First Nation members to discuss common obstacles and opportunities. Continuing relationship building seemed to be the crux of the successful partnerships. For example, the Friendship Accord recently became an incorporated entity that is now working on land purchases for large projects such as a conference centre and hotel.

For many years the location of Sioux Lookout made it a hub for Indigenous communities. Health Canada used the area as a base to provide both health and dental care to the twenty-nine communities north of Sioux Lookout. Since Sioux Lookout was incorporated as a town in 1912, there have been many overlapping efforts to solve some of the outstanding social and economic issues. However, I believe that from 2010 onward there has been a strategic and conscious effort by the municipality to be involved more deeply. This is reflected in Sioux Lookout's vision statement from the 2014–2018 Strategic Plan: "Through innovation leadership we engage our diverse population to create a caring, prosperous place to live, invest and be a desirable destination for regional services and tourism."

The Friendship Accord was a critical starting point in our partnerships. This mechanism gave us the opportunity to have difficult conversations about the social issues besetting the community. It also gave us familiarity with our Indigenous community neighbours and started the process of building trust. Although this historic agreement is important, we must also understand that what triggered subsequent partnership efforts was political and community momentum.

One of the difficulties encountered in the accord process was arriving at communication protocols. This is where "adaptive leadership" plays a role – the municipality and the First Nations had very differing views on how to communicate our successes. After several attempts to collaborate on a standard communication protocol, our Indigenous partners did not want to sign the document as they did not agree with the format. This further underscored the differences in our governance models. In the municipal forum, communication protocols are standard and the mayor speaks for the municipality. Indigenous cultures feel this is too formal of a process. For the good of our partnership, we had to let this piece go.

Truth and Reconciliation

During my time as CAO in Sioux Lookout, the Truth and Reconciliation Commission of Canada, which operated from 2008 until 2015, was drawing to a close. We knew this was an opportunity to rebuild relationships both in our town and in the surrounding Indigenous communities. In the words of Commissioner Mr Justice Murray Sinclair, "Reconciliation is about forging and maintaining respectful relationships. There are no shortcuts" (Truth and Reconciliation Commission of Canada 2015, p. 1). In June 2015, the commission released its ninety-four calls to action, which were divided into two themes – legacy and reconciliation. In 2016, Sioux Lookout set up the first Municipal Truth and Reconciliation Committee in Canada.

The primary goal of the committee was to educate the public and be a force for change in relations between the Indigenous and non-Indigenous communities. Few of the Truth and Reconciliation Committee's ninety-four calls to action fall under municipal jurisdiction, so the intention was to lobby the provincial and federal governments for changes in areas such as education and the legal system, which fall under their jurisdiction. This included attending municipal and Indigenous conferences to spread the work of the committee, and ongoing advocacy with the Ontario Attorney General for alternative justice and for a community justice centre to be located in Sioux Lookout. The committee also advocated with the Far North Electoral Boundary Commission for a new northern riding in the Ontario Legislative Assembly.

We concentrated our work within the community on educating stakeholders. For example, the committee hosted a viewing of the *Secret Path*, the graphic novel by Jeff Lemire with music by Gord Downie, which was made into a film. Pearl Wenjack, sister of the main character in the novel was in attendance. This is the story of an Indigenous youth who tried to run away from a residential school and perished. His death was the impetus for investigations into residential schools. The committee also attempted to educate the community and region to gain greater understanding of the impact of the residential schools on the Indigenous population. Although our efforts were well received, a contingent of the community continued to be resistant to accepting and adopting the work of the committee.

The committee was only possible due to the relationships we had built through the earlier Friendship Accord process. The committee started slowly and attempted to begin by breaking down the ninety-four calls to action into four themes: business, historical, social, and political. The committee then split into subgroups to discuss actions within each theme. It was a privilege and honour to be part of this historic group. An endeavour such as this seems far outside the scope of the duties of a CAO, but it is this type of situational leadership or shape shifting that helps us to make a difference.

Setting up the Municipal Truth and Reconciliation Committee was extremely beneficial to relationship building with the First Nations in our community and the surrounding area. The committee helped many stakeholders gain a greater understanding of the Indigenous perspective. One of the drawbacks of the committee was that, like any organization or group, it needed champions to commit to and sustain forward momentum. Events can slow progress, such as changes to elected officials from the First Nations band councils or on the municipal council, illness among leading Elders, or even a change of municipal CAO. Having experienced these events in Sioux Lookout, there has been little traction with this committee since 2018.

Missing and Murdered Indigenous Women and Girls

The National Inquiry into Missing and Murdered Indigenous Women and Girls was set up by Prime Minister Trudeau in 2016 to investigate the high rate of violence that was being inflicted on Indigenous women and girls. "Indigenous women are between 3 and 3.5 times more likely to be victims of violent crime than other women, and the violence they face is often more severe" (Native Women's Association of Canada, n.d.). Because of the high number of missing and murdered Indigenous women and girls in northwestern Ontario, both the Sioux Lookout Municipal Truth and Reconciliation Committee and the municipality had urged the federal government to open such an inquiry. In 2019 the inquiry issued calls for justice.

However, progress in Indigenous–non-Indigenous relations can also be easily undone. The municipality's relationship with our Indigenous partners suffered when a member of municipal council voted against the resolution in support of the inquiry, saying, "Spending millions of dollars on lawyers and judges and university professors won't get us any closer to the solution. I think we know what the solution is. The system has to change" (*CBC News*, 2014). This occurred at the first meeting of municipal council after the 2014 election, which returned all but one of the previous councillors and produced a new mayor. The new mayor brought a different perspective to the office because he wanted the municipality to embrace First Nations relationships. Although CAOs report to council as a whole, we must also have relationships with individual council members. This issue could have created a split on council, but adept CAOs understand that, while we do not set the vision, we do try to smooth the waters. As council's principal advisor, we must understand the current climate. We cannot control or contain all situations; however, we must endure the consequences.

The resolution came back to council and was passed in January 2015. The fact that the council and new mayor were supportive of building relationships with the Indigenous communities was highly beneficial to renewed First Nation connections.

CAOs need to maintain an arm's-length relationship with councillors, but the relationship should become one of trust that allows them to have frank discussions with councillors. The CAO with that kind of relationship sometimes can play an intermediary role in awkward situations precisely for being removed from the fray that can occur among councillors. In this case, I was able to have a conversation with this councillor that left him comfortable to voice his opinion, but in a more respectful manner that was not detrimental to the organization's strategic vision.

Organizational Readiness

My time in Sioux Lookout was characterized by innovative initiatives concentrated on our First Nations neighbours. This was highlighted by the signing of the Friendship Accord, the culmination of years of work and conversations. In addition to ours, there are now many examples of Indigenous-municipal partnerships not only in Canada but across the world that are attempting to qualify and quantify these partnerships to better understand and replicate successes.

From my experience in Sioux Lookout, it was evident that, although you might have a framework such as the Friendship Accord, there is no established road map that guarantees successful partnerships. Further, some of the communities that we dealt with were further advanced along the process of modernizing their communities, and certainly there was a variety of differing philosophies and leadership styles. Some communities had year-round road access, while others had only winter ice roads.

As an example of differing philosophies, the community of Mishkeegogamang felt that signing the Friendship Accord would somewhat diminish their independence. Therefore, although not a signatory to the accord, they were consulted on joint ventures and kept up to date on progress. These types of situations would often occur, and certainly could not be contained under a conventional scope. One must understand the time and place to have a sense of how these partnerships are formed and maintained.

The 2006–10 council was extremely progressive and implemented several mechanisms to enhance and encourage partnerships with our Indigenous neighbours. There was, however, growing concern by some of the residents and stakeholders that the municipality was expending too much time and energy on First Nations relationships, and this concern showed up in the 2010 election results.

The 2010–14 municipal council had a very different philosophy towards vision setting, and more specifically the relationship with the Indigenous communities surrounding Sioux Lookout. As CAOs we must be consensus builders between council and staff and between the entire organization and the whole community. "As the highest-ranking appointed person in the municipal hierarchy, the CAO plays a significant role with regard to the linkage to the political arm of government (the mayor and councillors) and the administrative arm of government (the appointed public service)" (Siegel, 2015, p. 17). This clearly underlines the importance of the CAO's embracing the development of relationships with the Indigenous communities.

My objective was that this belief would permeate the organization and flow out to the public. I never wavered, and was strong in my belief that we were better together. It was not simply about leveraging funding, although this was certainly a benefit for the region. It was really about the weaving together of our communities. My personal belief is that as CAOs we should endeavour to leave every organization, community, and region in a better position than we found it.

My employment as CAO started in Sioux Lookout in 2012, and I walked into a highly dysfunctional situation. There was strong mistrust between council and staff, low staff morale, and the stakeholders wanted lower taxes and a tightening of the reins in municipal operations. While a few stakeholders understood the importance of collaboration with the Indigenous communities, there was a contingent that felt that the municipality should be concentrating on other goals, such as lowering taxes and lobbying other levels of government for infrastructure funding. Although these objectives were critical, the Indigenous communities were so vital to our existence that this needed to be high on the priorities list. My first order of business was to shift the corporate culture. We needed to highlight that, in our community, Indigenous relationships and First Nations-municipal partnerships were to be welcomed, enhanced, and honoured.

Although the CAO is the head of the administration and sets the organizational values, it is another matter to align staff with the organization's vision. According to Kouzes and Posner, "[t]he truth of leading by example is accepted worldwide. It's ancient wisdom" (Kouzes & Posner, 2010, p. 108). Since CAOs are often tasked to "set the tone at the top," this was essential when dealing with our municipal-Indigenous relationships. Working with a new council, some of whom could not see the benefit of this initiative, was a challenge. Highlighting the overall concern from the stakeholders regarding the social issues as well as the benefits of working together, I, along with several champions on council who had remained from the 2006–10 term, worked on a strategy that eventually became embedded in our strategic plan. With the senior management team generally and the economic development officer specifically, we worked together to convince the newer members of council and the community of the importance and benefit of these alliances. Leading off with the social issues allowed council and the community to have confidence that their concerns were being taken seriously.

The Rationale for Municipal-Indigenous Partnerships

When I was in Sioux Lookout, the municipality derived minimal tax revenue from its limited industrial and commercial bases. Its economy relied heavily on service provision – mainly health care for the First Nations communities. This was the backbone of our economy. Our largest employer was the Meno Ya Win Health Centre, a hospital that was built under a four-party agreement (municipal, provincial, federal, and First Nations). The hospital employed approximately 450 people and the surrounding campus had a large footprint. As our largest employer and certainly a very important piece of the fabric of our community, it was disconcerting from a financial perspective that the hospital paid the municipality only approximately $6,000 in yearly property taxes. This was due to Ontario's heads-and-beds payments-in-lieu of tax legislation, which applies to hospitals, universities, and prisons, the amount of which has not changed since 1987.

The neighbouring municipalities of Red Lake and Dryden brought in millions in property taxes from their gold mine and pulp and paper mill, respectively. We had to be inventive to leverage funding for our community, keeping in mind the importance of the relationship building that was needed with the Indigenous communities. The concept of "systems thinking" is appropriate when collaborating with Indigenous communities because you need to look at the entire Indigenous system, including the governance model as well as their culture. For example, ceremony is deeply embedded in Indigenous culture.

While it is tempting to apply the regular playbook for municipal partnership agreements, it is not effective when dealing with Indigenous systems. Stroh's theory on systems thinking is relevant when viewing municipal-Indigenous partnerships in a holistic manner: "Most people are more accustomed to advocating than inquiring, so then it helps to begin with inquiry – the art of asking others how they see the world and then listening deeply" (Stroh, 2015, p. 87). To join forces, we first needed to understand both Indigenous culture and Indigenous governance systems.

The municipal council and staff embraced the notion of alliance and cooperation, but we realized that we had to adjust our thinking, because our governance structure and mindset were very different from those of the First Nations. One of the most profound comments I remember was by Chief Clifford Bull of neighbouring Lac Seul community, who asserted, "You are trying to rush us down the aisle when we are only on our first date" (C. Bull, personal communication with author, 2013). This comment echoed the concept of systems thinking; we were looking at the individual parts, but we missed the entire system that was based on the importance of rapport and ceremony to Indigenous people.

There was a definite need for greater understanding by both parties. Setting up the Friendship Accord working group and holding quarterly meetings allowed us the opportunity to discover each other's mandates, needs, and priorities, and to figure out how we could collaborate for mutual benefit. The working group was a safe space in which we could discuss difficult subjects, such as homelessness and other social issues that were concerning to the residents and stakeholders of Sioux Lookout, as well as to the Indigenous communities.

I was able to transfer this insight to influence both staff and council of the importance of relationship building as the foremost step towards establishing partnerships. CAOs must be aware of the trends in their communities, regions, and even globally. In Sioux Lookout, the relationships with our neighbouring First Nations were critical to a strong community and region.

Collaborative Benefits

Having these connections with the Indigenous communities that surround Sioux Lookout was extremely advantageous. If a funding application had the support of a First Nation, it was generally well received no matter the level of government or type of funding agency. Further, the collaborative aspect of these partnerships made an impact on these funders. These joint ventures were generally good news stories that the politicians loved to share. Joint-venture funding helped the municipality to leverage its limited resources for projects and services.

The First Nations often did not have sufficient depth of personnel and experience on their staff, so we were able to support them through our municipal workforce. As a result, their staff gained new skills and knowledge to enhance organizational effectiveness. The First Nations had much more experience dealing with the federal government than with the provincial government. As a municipality, we had a solid understanding of the various levels of government and how to lobby and approach both provincial and federal ministers and Members of Parliament as well as funding agencies. The expectation from the Indigenous communities was that we would have more traction with the province. Although sometimes this was accurate, often the First Nations had more success.

Some of the wounds in the relationship between Indigenous and non-Indigenous people in our community were deep, and the benefits of partnerships started us down the path towards reconciliation and mutually respectful relations.

Strategic Initiatives

Building on the Friendship Accord, the municipalities of Sioux Lookout and Pickle Lake joined with the Friendship Accord partners of Slate Falls, Lac Seul, Kitchenuhmaykoosib Inninuwug, and Cat Lake to expand our economic partnership. "Working together," said Chief Clifford Bull of Lac Seul First Nation, "is the best way for all partners to meet their goals and aspirations. Lac Seul First Nation is happy to be part of the process" (Newsnetledger.com, 2017). It was these ongoing collaborations that continued our forward trajectory.

The following are some of our early collaborative efforts, which I outline and explain both the benefits and the drawbacks. CAOs by their very nature must be strategic thinkers – we need to assist council, staff, and stakeholders to think broadly. This is the only way we will be able to keep our communities sustainable.

The Ring of Fire

The resource industry is critical to northern Ontario's economy. The "Ring of Fire" is the name given to a massive planned chromite mining and smelting development project in the mineral-rich James Bay lowlands. The development would affect nine First Nations, and potential developers are required to negotiate an impact and benefit agreement (IBA) with these communities prior to development (Ontario Chamber of Commerce, 2014). A regional framework was in place with the First Nations, the mining company, and the provincial government in 2014, but it was dissolved in 2019.

Sioux Lookout was not involved in this agreement, but since it had branded itself as "Hub of the North" and in order to respect our partnerships, we worked together to procure funding and broker meetings between the communities and various provincial and federal ministers. Sioux Lookout also participated in joint trips to Toronto with our Indigenous partners to attend the Prospectors & Developers Association (PDAC) of Canada conference. This international event, held for the minerals and mining industry, gathers 25,000 people from over 135 countries each year. As a municipal entity, we secured funding to attend this event annually with our Friendship Accord partners.

We also lobbied to change the access route to the Ring of Fire in a way that would be more viable for the area north of Sioux Lookout. The previously proposed route would not have been as beneficial to our Indigenous partners as it would have bypassed many of the communities with which we were working.

When the Ring of Fire does start producing, the area north of Sioux Lookout will become much more economically viable. This was an extremely time-consuming endeavour for the municipality, and it has yet to produce any economic development for the region. The municipality spent considerable time in writing grants for the PDAC conference and setting up meetings with various types of mining companies and federal and provincial ministers. This reality of First Nations–municipal partnerships highlights the risks associated with municipal support for ventures that might not materialize or might take many years to bear fruit. Again, the delicate balancing act of the CAO is how to determine where to expend precious workforce resources.

Healthy Communities Task Force

The geographical position of Sioux Lookout lends itself to various social issues – for example, we had extremely high policing costs prior to the change in the Ontario policing model (Tbnewswatch.com, 2015). To bring together the parties most affected by the social issues facing our community, we used the Friendship Accord to start a Healthy Communities Task Force. The municipality's participation in the messaging made it clear that we intended to be part of the solution. Municipal governments traditionally provide a standard set of services, but given the situation in Sioux Lookout, council decided to expand its role. It was a risk worth taking. The mandate of the Healthy Communities Task Force was to develop and implement a holistic, community-based strategy to address drug and alcohol misuse, housing and homelessness, and mental health challenges. One of the earliest initiatives was a conference that included a presentation by world-renowned addiction specialist, Dr Gabor Maté. It was a catalyst for greater understanding between the parties.

One of the outcomes of the task force was the combining of several organizations that were performing similar services. The major challenge of the task force was that no one group wanted to be the lead agency, and although good work was accomplished, much more could have been achieved if there had been a head organization, such as the Meno Ya Win Hospital, but its management felt that this activity fell outside its mandate. Looking back at this, it is clear that, although the CAO might envision relationships and partnerships evolving in a particular manner, they often head in an unexpected direction. There can still be great benefits, however, even if the project does not meet intended expectations. Instead of collateral damage, there can be collateral benefits. As an example, many groups discovered efficiencies through eliminating the duplication of services.

Economic Development

One of the first initiatives of the Friendship Accord was a joint economic development initiative through the Council for the Advancement of Native Development Officers (CANDO) under its Canadian Economic Development Initiative (CEDI). Through this funding, the parties of the Friendship Accord were able to meet and build relationships that could lead to joint projects.

One such project is a distribution centre for northern communities operating out of the Sioux Lookout airport. This began with an idea of a local youth who was concerned about the cost of goods being sent to the communities. It turned into a $2.2 million venture with four partners – Kitchenuhmaykoosib Inninuwug First Nation, Sioux Lookout First Nations Health Authority (SLFNA), Health Canada, and

Morgan Fuels, a long-time Sioux Lookout family company. Health Canada and SLFNA both regularly ship supplies to the far northern communities. When completed, the distribution hub will transport goods to and from Indigenous communities in the north in a more cost-effective manner. As SLFNA and Health Canada also send goods, economies of scale will be realized. The municipality also will gain some tax revenue from the distribution centre.

Many hours were spent on this project. The municipality's economic development officer worked on funding applications and travelled to various sites to examine similar models. Although the municipality will benefit from tax revenue, it is doubtful that the payback will cover the time and effort that was put into it. The true benefit of a partnership, however, is that it benefits the entire community, even if the municipality must bear some short-term costs. Collaboration requires both flexibility and patience, and some initiatives take time to come to fruition. As stated by Cat Lake Chief Ernie Wesley in 2017, "One of the elders who's not around anymore told me about the ripples. It's how things get started. You know how the ripples go. If we can do that in such a way, everyone will benefit" (TBnewswatch.com, 2017).

Shared Services

Unexpected partnerships will arise if you are receptive. As the administrative leader of the municipality, you must set the tone for innovation. You create the environment to foster inventiveness. If you are an innovator as CAO, others will echo this behaviour. The following are some examples that occurred in Sioux Lookout. Although these might have occurred independent of our relationship with the Indigenous communities, the groundwork of collaborative efforts certainly paved the way for dialogue that led to various unique solutions.

YOUTH SERVICES

At one point the municipality had two youth centres, one located in the lower level of a municipally renovated old hotel, renamed the Centennial Centre, the other at the Nishnawbe-Gamik Friendship centre. The intent was to encourage youth to call a space their own, but a social division had occurred, which was concerning because the community is too small to be divided and the mandate of the Centennial Centre was to bring youth together.

As a solution, the town arranged with the executive director of the Friendship Centre to run that centre's programs in the municipality's location. The joint venture was beneficial on several levels. The municipality was able to eliminate a staff position, and the Friendship Centre now had sufficient space to administer its youth program. The fact that this brought youth who previously had been divided into one location was the kind of unexpected benefit that often arises in partnership situations. When an opportunity presents itself, you need to act on it if the time is right. Having solid relationships in place and having a 360-degree view of your community is critical. A CAO's connections in the community are an essential component of success. The alliance of the two centres would not have been realized if the executive director and I had not met regularly and discussed shared aims and challenges.

There were challenges in this arrangement because our facility was governed by certain policies and procedures, and there were times when the building was not staffed, unlocked, and generally not being looked after to our standards and expectations. As mentioned earlier, CAOs need to use their influence while leading down, and this was an ideal example. Municipal staff did not want to deal with these issues, so it took convincing from me to help them understand the greater vision and the importance of our relationship with our Indigenous partners.

Collaboration is an art form: there are no rulebooks to follow and past practices might not apply. As CAOs we must find the time to interact continually with various stakeholders in the community. Although CAOs are not the voice of the town, we are a representative, and how we conduct ourselves plays an important role in the success and vitality of our municipalities.

BUSINESS HUB

The renovated Centennial Centre also housed our economic development officer. Much of her work with the First Nations partners was coordinated with their economic development officers. She discovered quickly that most of the chiefs and economic development officers coming from the northern communities had no office space in which to meet when they were in Sioux Lookout. As the "Hub of the North," we quickly made office space available. We also lobbied for the Member of Parliament to house his office in the same building. This created many synergies between the First Nations and the municipality as well as the federal government. This was extremely successful and led to various opportunities that would not have come about otherwise. It also allowed for significant community engagement because of the large number of Indigenous people who live in and frequent our community.

One challenge was that our economic development department consisted of one full-time and one part-time staff member. Generally, most of the First Nations had minimal staff, and it was mainly the progressive First Nations that retained an economic development officer. Given the extensive number of joint projects, municipal staff had to absorb the strain and expectations.

LOCAL TRANSIT

Sioux Lookout had local transit operated by a group of volunteers. The municipality provided a subsidy, but it was proving unsustainable. Many residents relied on this service to attend to medical appointments and to run errands. If this service had ended, it would have forced the seniors who depended on it to take much more costly taxis.

Lac Seul Band was facing transportation challenges because it was the sole owner of the Tim Hortons franchise located in Sioux Lookout and was struggling to find staff to work there, as securing transportation to and from work – approximately 47 kilometres – was challenging. This resulted in a shared service born of necessity and convenience. The transit service was renamed Hub Transit, and approximately $1 million in provincial funding was obtained. Partnering with Lac Seul provided the volume of ridership needed to keep the transit afloat.

AIRPORT EXPANSION

The municipal airport at Sioux Lookout, meant to be the "Hub of the North," was overburdened almost immediately after it was built in 1985. We recognized the need for an expansion, but we did not have the capital needed to complete the project. We worked with the First Nations to lobby both the federal and provincial governments to complete a $17 million retrofit.

Collaboration with the First Nations and other stakeholders was extensive and very consultative. For the majority of the Indigenous communities, air service was their only means of transportation, and it was critical that we involve them in the project. We developed a greater understanding of what was needed from stakeholders, including air ambulances, airlines, leaseholders, and, most important, the Indigenous communities and residents of northwestern Ontario who frequented this service. We understood that this was a regional airport, a place where often a loved one who had passed away would be taken back to the community; these types of services were incorporated into the design.

Although the airport was owned by the municipality, it was always our contention that it was a regional transportation hub. Meaningful and broad consultation with the Indigenous communities meant that they were able to make a connection to the airport as their asset, not just Sioux Lookout's.

Most municipalities benefit from valuable community services operated by non-profit civil society groups. When the services become unsustainable, the operator frequently will look to the municipality for assistance, but adding another service to an already-overburdened workforce needs serious consideration. When faced with these contradictory pressures, councils frequently look to the CAO for a creative solution. The case studies above provide examples of situations where we were able to find such solutions by working with the Indigenous community, amounting to win-win situations for all stakeholders.

Conclusion

Building partnerships between municipalities and First Nations takes time, patience, and understanding. Finding common ground is vital. Listening to Indigenous voices is essential to the development of these partnerships. A supportive council and administration are also necessary to implement this vision, along with community backing.

The CAO needs to look beyond the conventional municipal services lens. CAOs are encouraged to attend various professional development sessions to enhance their competencies and grow their skill set, but Indigenous–non-Indigenous relationships and First Nations partnership development require on-the-job experience. As Daniel Coyle states in his book, *The Culture Code*, when referring to innovation: "It's about building ownership, providing support, and aligning group energy towards the arduous, error-filled, ultimate fulfilling journey of making something new" (Coyle, 2018, p. 226). Being open and receptive to possibilities allowed us to thrive. The benefits of enhanced Indigenous–non-Indigenous relationships and First Nations partnerships are unquestionable, which leave you open to a world of prospects. You begin to think differently, and you become more inventive through the process. It truly is an art form.

Municipal and Indigenous partnerships are unique and should be treated as such. CAOs need to step out of their traditional scope and look at their mandate along a broader spectrum. We need to be inventive, adventurous, and occasionally throw caution to the wind. As I have laid out throughout this chapter, these relationships need to be viewed holistically. Additionally, not all benefits are tangible, but they certainly cannot be discounted. As the Report of the Truth and Reconciliation Commission of Canada (2015, p. vi) states: "Reconciliation is not an Aboriginal problem, it is a Canadian one." These partnerships were undertaken in northwestern Ontario, and I believe they are a path that communities across Canada can follow. By undertaking these partnerships, both our community of Sioux Lookout and the Indigenous communities in its surrounding region are now better off. More important, as individuals, we have gained a greater understanding of each other, and that, I believe, is true reconciliation.

REFERENCES

CBC News. (2014, 28 November). Sioux Lookout council encouraged to be more "culturally aware." https://www.cbc.ca/news/canada/thunder-bay/sioux-lookout-council-encouraged-to-be-more-culturally-aware-1.2853558

Coyle, D. (2018). *The culture code: The secrets of highly successful group*. Bantam.

Heritz, J. (2018). From self-determination to service delivery: Assessing Indigenous inclusion in municipal governance in Canada. *Canadian Public Administration*, *61*(4), 596–615. https://doi.org/10.1111/capa.12277

Kouzes, J., & Posner, B. Z. (2010). *The truth about leadership*. Jossey-Bass.

Native Women's Association of Canada. (n.d.). Fact sheet: Violence against Aboriginal women. Native Women's Association of Canada. https://www.nwac.ca/wp-content/uploads/2015/05/Fact_Sheet_Violence_Against_Aboriginal_Women.pdf

Newsnetledger.com. (2017). Sioux Lookout Partners for Economic Development Opportunity. http://www.netnewsledger.com/2017/04/04/sioux-lookout-partners-economic-development-opportunities/

Ontario Chamber of Commerce. (2014). Beneath the surface: Uncovering the economic potential of Ontario's Ring of Fire. https://occ.ca/wp-content/uploads/Beneath_the_Surface_web-1.pdf

Siegel, D. (2015). *Leaders in the shadows: The leadership qualities of municipal chief administrative officers*. University of Toronto Press.

Statistics Canada. (2016). *Census profile, 2016 census*. https://www12.statcan.gc.ca/census-recensement/2016/dp-pd/prof/details/page.cfm?Lang=E&Geo1=CSD&Code1=3560034&Geo2=CD&Code2=3560&SearchText=Sioux%20Lookout&SearchType=Begins&SearchPR=01&B1=All&TABID=1&type=0

Stroh, D. (2015). *Systems thinking for social change*. Chelsea Green Publishing.

TBnewswatch.com. (2015, 5 October). "Small town trying to make police costs a federal issue." https://www.tbnewswatch.com/local-news/small-town-trying-to-make-police-costs-a-federal-issue-403015

TBnewswatch.com. (2017, 3 March). "Sioux Lookout reconciliation partnership growing." https://www.tbnewswatch.com/local-news/sioux-lookout-reconciliation-partnership-growing-551935

Truth and Reconciliation Commission of Canada. (2015). *Honouring the truth, reconciling for the future. Summary of the Final Report of the Truth and Reconciliation Commission of Canada*. https://ehprnh2mwo3.exactdn.com/wp-content/uploads/2021/01/Executive_Summary_English_Web.pdf

Wilson, S. (2008). *Research is ceremony: Indigenous research methods*. Fernwood Publishing.

12 The Gift of Clarity and the Freedom to Innovate

ROBERT EARL

Hiring the right employees is important, but the job isn't complete until you have moulded them into a team and created the right organizational culture. Robert Earl has always emphasized team building during his time at several municipalities in Alberta and British Columbia. In this chapter, he describes how he creates an environment for developing a team by combining the principles of clarity of purpose and freedom to innovate. This ensures that team members are free to take risks at the same time that they are oriented to act in the interest of the organization.

In this chapter, I address the question, What are important elements for creating successful teams in the municipal context? I explore different types of municipal teams and argue that there are two fundamental conditions for creating an environment for great teams to emerge: clarity of purpose and the freedom to innovate. The first – clarity of purpose – might seem self-evident, but it is often elusive in the municipal realm. The second – freedom to innovate – is a practice that seemingly fights against our natural instincts to survive inside an organization.

Municipalities in Canada are charged with delivering a wide range of programs and services. It is the order of government that is closest to its constituents and is well positioned to help set the stage for residents to lead fulfilling lives. From safety-oriented services such as policing and fire protection to recreational and cultural programming, municipalities help to create the conditions for society to thrive. Outwardly, communities are gatherings of buildings, roads, and the public spaces that fill the in-between. The reality, however, is that we are collections of people, and when done well, municipalities create the foundation for people to flourish. This is a compelling reason for municipal governments, and the teams that form them, to strive to build the best possible communities.

Community building is a complex process that is both constantly evolving and difficult to define. Ask ten people the question "what makes a community great?" and you are likely to get ten different responses. The metrics of success for a community are neither obvious, nor are they stable. Furthermore, in the Canadian municipal context, the elected leadership of a community changes regularly, often resulting in a change of dynamics, culture, and direction.

The Essential Role of Teams

One constant is that municipal policies, programs, and services are developed and delivered by teams of individuals. There are specific service delivery teams, such as the parks or the engineering teams; there is the senior leadership team and the team of elected officials; and there are times when ad hoc teams are formed from various departments or organizations to tackle a specific project or initiative. Each of these different teams must be set up for success if the organization and community are to thrive. Given a constantly changing municipal environment, the ideal team is optimized both to fulfil the purpose of the team and to be changing and dynamic; these can be conflicting directions. Establishing clarity of purpose and supporting the freedom to innovate are two fundamental organizing principles that optimize the conditions needed for great teams to emerge in any organization. In the municipal context, these conditions can help to bridge the gap between daily service delivery and long-term objectives.

Clarity of purpose helps individuals and the teams they are part of connect their efforts to the broader vision of the municipality. I will explore a series of long- and short-term tools that can help a CAO deliver such clarity. Supporting the freedom to innovate is taking care of the conditions needed for team members to feel confident in their use of their own wisdom and judgment. Teams perform best when all voices contribute to the effort. It takes careful attention by the CAO to select the right conditions, from among many possibilities, for team members to feel confident to exercise their judgment.

Clarity of Purpose

Defining clarity of purpose in the municipal realm seems straightforward, as there is much common ground in the service offerings of municipalities. Policing and fire services, water and wastewater, roads, public transit, recreation, solid waste, parks – the list goes on and on. Being clear about which programs and services a specific municipality delivers, and at what level, is of paramount importance to the team or teams charged with the delivery of those services. Despite this, many municipalities do not take the time needed to be clear about their service offerings. When teams are given a clear purpose, it becomes much easier for them to thrive. "We all seek purpose and meaning in what we do and how we live. When someone articulates a set of aspirations that elevates our purposes or deepens the meaning we find in our lives, the motivational juices flow" (Hackman, 2002, p. 63). Most Canadians have chosen to situate their lives in organized municipalities. Delivering services to these community members in a way that meets their expectations is work that matters.

Given this imperative, I believe that clear direction is a condition that must be well established for a municipality to have truly effective teams. "Authoritatively setting direction about performance aspirations has multiple benefits: It energizes team members, it orients their attention to action, and it engages their talents" (Hackman, 2002, p. 63).

There exists a hierarchy upon which clear direction can be established in the municipal realm. In the Canadian context it starts with enabling legislation at the provincial level that governs what a municipality can do. This is then followed by an official community plan (created with substantial community consultation) and adoption through a by-law. It often has a twenty- or thirty-year planning horizon and sets out high-level direction for how the community should evolve over that period. The community plan addresses more than the physical and geographical; it also addresses what role the municipality will play in optimizing the capacity of residents to be at their natural best. From there, a tool that I have found to be effective is a strategic plan that then spans a three-to-five-year planning horizon. A strategic plan is not meant to be a comprehensive list of everything that the municipality does. It is rather a list of areas where change is needed and where the organization would like to focus resources in an effort to be more effective at achieving the vision articulated in the official community plan.

The Role of Strategic Planning

Early in my career I made it a practice to create strategic plans every year. This was likely born out of the annual budget cycle, as budgets are ultimately the true measure of municipal focus. Annual strategic plans create two risks. The first risk is that progress is not achieved within the year, as many municipal initiatives can take time to get off the ground. The second risk is that focus changes each year, with new priorities added without old priorities being removed. This creates too many priorities for the organization and results in a lack of focus and progress. This taught me to try to create multiyear strategic plans as a hedge against these risks.

A strategic plan longer than the current term of office, however, runs the risk that the next leaders might not agree with the direction and resources might be wasted.

A strategic plan (led by council) that contains objectives, strategies, and tactics can then be tied to departmental performance planning. It can be further tied to team and individual performance plans. A top-down council-led strategic plan complements, contrasts, and brings focus to a community-driven community plan. Connected in this way to the official community plan, with tasks articulated within the five-year horizon, allows a team or an individual to understand more clearly how their role fits within the organization's vision, and why it is important for them to be successful.

Early in the mandate of a newly elected council, the CAO has an opportunity to facilitate a process with council to identify gaps between where the municipality is and where it wants to be, and then create a strategic plan to fill the gaps. This process requires council to come together as a team to create a shared vision for the future. This is not always easy, as there can be disparate views of where the municipality should be going or how it should get there.

Appropriate care needs to be taken to come together to create this shared vision. This also might require spending time to create a safe environment for councillors to debate their various policy perspectives and approaches. It can be challenging to balance the need for transparency in governance and the provision of a safe place where individual elected leaders can admit that they might not know the answer or that they might need help. Creating such an environment at the elected table, where the focus is on being helpful rather than being right, is tricky business. I would argue that this culture is best created *in camera* and that the role of the CAO is to fashion it.

A further risk associated with a municipal strategic plan is that, once the plan is created, administration might be accused of "running the show," or of being the "tail wagging the dog" – more than once in my career, I have heard such an accusation from community members. The CAO needs to take care to ensure that the elected leadership remains front and centre in driving the strategic plan forward. The clarity created by using a multiyear strategic plan, however, is worth the risks that come with such a plan.

Municipal Service Review

Although a strategic plan can do a great job of articulating clear direction in areas where the municipality wants to create change, most of the municipality's work is ongoing in its current form. A tool to help establish clarity of direction for ongoing municipal services is a municipal service review. In this process, a municipality reviews which programs and services the municipality delivers and at what level. In the municipal context, defining the problem to be solved is a key step often overlooked. Without a clear understanding of council's service-level expectations, measuring success is nearly impossible.

I have found the five important components of such a service review process to be:

- description of the program or service;
- revenue and expense information for the program or service (including capital);
- a list of council's service-level expectations for that program or service;
- benchmarking of service efficiency and effectiveness against previous years or other organizations; and
- a "what's working well" and "areas for attention" conversation between council and the frontline service delivery team.

Incorporating a service review process into the annual planning cycle helps the service delivery teams stay connected through council to the community's service-level expectations. The process of the service review is beneficial as it opens all team members' minds to the various political perspectives on the service, and the product of the service review is beneficial as it creates a compendium of municipal programs and services for newcomers to the conversation, both elected and administrative.

Setting Agendas and Leveraging Data

Further tools to support clarity of purpose are processes that I have been calling the "near-term" and "long-term" agendas. The near-term agenda is a schedule that maps out the next four months of council meetings with specific items scheduled for each meeting in that period. Through this, council can see how its strategic priorities are stacked up against the ongoing work of the municipality. This helps council stay "in control" of municipal strategic direction.

The long-term agenda is a document that maps out items from the strategic plan and where they will appear by quarter for the upcoming year. Both the near-term and long-term agendas can be published as part of regular meetings of council. This allows for council to be transparent about its strategic direction and creates clarity for teams that are charged with delivering on council's vision. Further, this process creates the opportunity for ongoing feedback with respect to the organizational capacity to be resilient to new or emerging issues.

Another tool to help create clarity of direction is a common "request for decision" format. Such a reporting format includes sections such as Recommendation, Summary, Background, Options, Communication, Financial, and Policy – all laid out in a consistent pattern. Having an established format for reports helps to provide council with a consistent body of information when it is considering a decision. It also helps the team that is supporting council to understand better how the elected body will make its decision. This practice leads to fewer surprises in council chambers and builds the confidence of both the elected and appointed teams through clarity.

A final tactic that can help to illuminate clear direction for municipalities is the use of data. Technology advancements in recent years have provided opportunities to use new sources of data to help in decision making. The long-time motto of Mike Bloomberg, former mayor of New York City, was "In God we trust. Everyone else: bring data" (Bloomberg, 2015). Municipalities should add real-time data where possible to other sources of information to aid in decision making. This will put into context anecdotal information and vested opinions. Real-time, Bluetooth-enabled traffic counters are a current example of how municipalities can bring data into decision making, as is postal-code-level demographic, financial, and psychographic analysis of neighbourhoods and their households.

To sum up, the first component of creating the conditions for teams to thrive is to provide clarity of purpose. Tools that can be used to help achieve this include:

- a community plan (ten-year plan, thirty-year planning horizon);
- strategic planning (five-year plan, ten-year planning horizon);
- a service review (annual);
- near- and long-term agendas (quarterly);
- a common format for a request for decision (as required); and
- data (whenever possible).

These tools help take the thirty-year vison in the community plan and break it down into near-term objectives, strategies, and tactics that can provide the clarity of direction needed to create a compelling call to action for the various municipal teams. These tactics and plans are interdependent, and although one is possible without the other, the combination of them keeps everyone focused, from the 35,000-foot level to the 5-foot level. The CAO plays a pivotal role in helping to orchestrate the layering of these tactics and in being a champion for interconnected planning at all time scales. The CAO needs to be able simultaneously to stay focused on both the near and far terms and to build organizational continuity between the two and across the political-administrative divide.

Freedom to Innovate

The second component needed for municipal teams to thrive is the freedom to innovate. Governments at all levels are more often risk averse in their approach than they are innovative, yet innovation is needed to advance big ideas. Municipal team members who practise this precautionary approach to management will indeed be safer, as they will not "stand out" – but I would argue that such will also be the fate of their municipalities "not to stand out."

Amy C. Edmondson describes organizations that have created "stand out" cultures as "fearless organizations," with psychological safety the key ingredient (Edmondson, 2019). Without a psychologically safe workplace, organizations run the risk of losing out on the critical thinking capacities of team members. "The brain processes a provocation by a boss, a competitive co-worker, or a dismissive subordinate as a life-or-death threat. The amygdala, the alarm bell in the brain, ignites the fight-or flight response, high jacking higher brain centres. This 'act first, think later' brain structure shuts down perspective and analytical thinking" (Delizonna, 2017, p. 2). Team members will fail to participate when they feel threatened, and innovation and creativity will suffer. Whether in a meeting room among peers or in council chambers, a precautionary culture will stifle the capacities of individuals and the teams of which they are a part.

In 2012 Google embarked upon "Project Aristotle," which asked researchers to discover the secrets of effective teams at Google. The research name was a tribute to Aristotle's quote, "the whole is greater than the sum of its parts." Prior to this research, like many other organizations, Google believed that "building the best teams meant combining the best people" (Duhigg, 2016, p. 2). Google reviewed academic studies, the demographics of their team members, their educations, hobbies, personality traits, and patterns of behaviour. One of the surprising findings was that "the most productive employees tended to build larger networks by rotating lunch companions" (p. 2). Another finding was that high-functioning team members were "skilled at intuiting how others felt based on the tone of their voice" (p. 4). These traits seemed to have little to do with team members' education or experience, and more to do with how team members participated as part of an organization. The municipal CAO plays a pivotal role in helping to define how team members participate with one another.

Breaking Down Barriers to Innovation

In my role as a CAO, I have worked to break down traditional barriers, seeking to connect and build relationships at all levels of the organization and community. This is not done to micro-manage, but to understand how I or the organization can help. It creates an analytic, non-judgmental approach to better understand situations, encouraging folks to ask questions, take risks, and explore new approaches to municipal governance and service delivery. Many municipal organizations are steeped in institutional momentum. Previous council direction combined with a "we've always done it this way" culture can keep organizations stuck. Finding a way to get "unstuck" is often a prerequisite to success.

Google discovered that team composition was not a good predictor of success. Its research determined that five characteristics of team culture, other than team composition, mattered the most. By far the most important was psychological safety.

Psychological safety is a "group culture"; it "describes a belief that neither the formal nor informal consequences of interpersonal risks, like asking for help or admitting a failure, will be punitive" (Edmondson, 2019, p. 15). In a psychologically safe workplace, team members will know that their voices matter, and will be quick to speak up and add their perspectives to solving the problem at hand. When team members feel comfortable speaking up, better solutions will result as more knowledge and experience will be applied to the problem at hand. Without a culture that enables team members to engage in the conversation, other behaviours such as collaboration, experimentation, and reflection cannot happen. The CAO can advance this approach by establishing a culture where the status quo is regularly challenged in the pursuit of finding a better way. Change can be hard, however, for organizations steeped in a precautionary approach to management. Pilot projects with short timelines and small budgets are great ways to experiment in a fashion that creates less discomfort at both the elected and administrative tables.

In *The Structure of Scientific Revolutions*, Thomas S. Kuhn makes the case that revolutionary leaps in our knowledge of the world can occur only when bold thinkers challenge the status quo and replace the old paradigm with a new one: "Truth emerges more readily from error than from confusion" (Kuhn, 2012, p. 18). On a team where you can feel safe challenging the majority or prevailing perspective, true insights and radical approaches can emerge. Although it might be unusual to view municipal service delivery teams as revolutionary, real progress is best achieved when the status quo is challenged. The maxims "curiosity is king" and "all voices matter" should be celebrated on all teams within the municipal organization.

Climate change is an example of a new paradigm that is increasingly influencing municipal decision making, and teams that incorporate it will be more successful in delivering a changed municipal mandate. The CAO needs to set high expectations with respect to how teams scan the environment for intended and unintended consequences, including how progress will be measured and what "bottom-line" success looks like. Greenhouse gas reductions, for example, have become an additional bottom line, rather than cost efficiency or program effectiveness alone.

"In an increasingly competitive, complex, and fast paced world in which information and expertise are distributed across multiple individuals and firms, distributed leadership, throughout the organization is crucial" (Ancona et al., 2007, p. 58). Municipalities are best served when all team members contribute to their fullest capacity, collectively providing leadership to their team, and by extension to their community. The CAO needs to help set the stage for all members of the organization to know that their voices matter. This can be achieved by building systems that seek the input of all involved in service delivery, policy development, and governance.

To take this notion even one step further, municipal teams must also seek perspectives beyond their membership. The CAO needs to create an expectation within teams such that they seek out perspectives and approaches from beyond the usual sources: who is doing it best, how, and why? This culture of constant challenge needs to be at the foundation of the mandate of the team.

Failure Is Not the Opposite of Success, but a Complement to Success

In *X-Teams*, Debora Ancona and Henrik Bresman make the case that teams that are too internally focused run the risk of failure, and that high-performing teams are externally as well as internally focused. In the municipal context, this external focus can be with another department within the organization, another community, residents of a neighbourhood, or users of a municipal program or service. Ancona and Bresman introduce the notion of scouting as a tool for external focus: "Getting a sense of what a team's task actually is, who the key players are, and what everyone's expectations for the final product are is scouting's key task" (Ancona and Bresman, 2007, p. 69).

In-House Psychological Safety Survey Questions

1. People at this organization can bring up problems and tough issues.
2. I feel safe to take a risk in this organization.
3. It is difficult to ask other members of this organization for help.
4. No one at this organization would deliberately act in a way that undermines my efforts.
5. Working with members of this organization, my unique skills and talents are valued and utilized.
6. If I make a mistake at this organization, it is often held against me.
7. People at this organization sometimes reject others for being different.

Edmondson's third behaviour of effective "teaming" is experimentation. In the municipal context, this can come in the form of pilots or trials. Without a psychologically safe work environment, individuals and teams will be reluctant to embark upon a trial, as "failure" is indeed a possibility within all trials. Indeed, "[f]ailure and fault are virtually inseparable in most households, organizations and cultures" (Edmondson, 2011, p. 2). Individuals naturally will avoid situations where fault can be assigned to them. For innovation to thrive, a culture needs to be created where fallibility is presumed and individuals and teams have the freedom to fail.

When a trial or pilot fails, there should be no thought of assigning fault, as everyone owns the outcome and the learning it provided the organization. I have been involved in many pilot projects involving traffic and parking. Many have led to permanent installations and many other ideas were abandoned, but all led to a better understanding of the issues at hand. Trials and pilots make it easier for decision makers to move forward when accompanied with a start-stop timeline, an evaluation process, and a trial-sized budget before the big budget is considered.

Measuring the current level of psychological safety in your workplace is a good way to start to see if your organization, or parts within it, are "fearless." Shannon Howard (2019, p. 1) recommends a simple in-house survey, with a one-to-five scale from strongly agree to strongly disagree, to determine your current state.

Edmondson suggests that there are three parts to creating a psychologically safe workplace: setting the stage, inviting participation, and responding productively (Edmondson, 2019, p. 154). Setting the stage in the municipal context could be an acknowledgment of how complex community building really is, and that no one correct solution exists. Shifting the focus to the notion that failure is expected, but that "those that catch, correct, and learn from failure before others do will succeed. Those that wallow in the blame game will not" (Edmondson, 2011, p. 9). Inviting participation is about honouring the maxim that "curiosity is king." Asking questions at team meetings that create debate and confront difficult topics is an important part of this. Evidence that this might be working is robust debate and conversational "turn taking," a feature of good teams, as Google's research discovered (Duhigg, 2016, p. 4).

The second component for setting the stage for great teams to emerge – the freedom to innovate – is fundamentally about supporting a psychologically safe workplace. The CAO is uniquely positioned to model this by demonstrating that all voices matter and that true success requires some failure along the way. IBM's Thomas Watson Sr is quoted as saying "the fastest way to succeed is to double your failure rate" (Parks n.d.). The tradition in government, however, has been one of failure avoidance. When taken to its extreme, an organization steeped in failure avoidance eventually can become lost in decision resistance.

One of the roles of the CAO is to help municipal teams (both elected and appointed) embrace the benefits that failure will bring to avoid getting stuck in failure or decision avoidance. The CAO needs to help position failure not as the opposite of success, but as a complement to success. Build pilot projects and trials with goals associated with the experience that the trials will provide, rather than solely with the benefits the service or program is intended to deliver. When done well, the organization will thrive and the individuals who form the teams will feel more connected to one another, and their careers and the community will benefit.

Conclusion

At the beginning of this chapter, I suggested that I would address important elements for creating successful teams in the municipal context, which I argue are clarity of purpose and the freedom to innovate.

Municipal teams are charged with delivering a dizzying array of programs and services with bottom lines of success that are often unclear and constantly evolving. Creating clarity of purpose for those teams (both appointed and elected) is key to their ability to understand what it is they are trying to achieve, and how they will know if they have succeeded.

We all seek to avoid failure, yet real progress is rarely achieved without trial and error. Creating a culture where error is seen as a necessary step on the road to success is fundamental for great municipal teams to emerge.

REFERENCES

Ancona, D., & Bresman, H. (2007). *X-Teams*. Harvard Business School Publishing.

Ancona, D., Malone, T., Orlikowski, W., & Senge, P. (2007, February). In praise of the incomplete leader. *Harvard Business Review*. http://doi.org/10.1109/EMR.2009.5235483

Bloomberg. (2015, 13 November). Bloomberg's global data team takes a deep dive into ocean data. Retrieved 16 November 2020, from https://www.bloomberg.com/company/press/bloombergs-global-data-team-takes-a-deep-dive-into-ocean-data/

Delizonna, L. (2017, 24 August). High-performing teams need psychological safety. Here's how to create it. *Talent Management*.

Duhigg, C. (2016, 25 February). What Google learned from its quest to build the perfect team. *New York Times Magazine*, p. 8.

Edmondson, A. C. (2011, April). Strategies for learning from failure. *Harvard Business Review*. https://hbr.org/2011/04/strategies-for-learning-from-failure

Edmondson, A. C. (2019). *The fearless organization*. John Wiley & Sons.

Hackman, J. R. (2002). *Leading teams: Setting the stage for great performances*. Harvard Business School Publishing.

Howard, S. (2019, October). How to measure psychological safety at your company. *Predictive Index*. https://www.predictiveindex.com/blog/how-to-measure-psychological-safety/

Kuhn, T. S. (2012). *The structure of scientific revolutions*. University of Chicago Press.

Parks, N. (n.d.). The fastest way to succeed is to double your failure rate. Retrieved 16 November 2020 from https://legacycultures.com/the-fastest-way-to-succeed-is-to-double-your-failure-rate/#:~:text=The%20above%20quote%20by%20Thomas,%E2%80%9D%2C%20laugh%20and%20try%20again

13 Rowers, Coasters, and Drillers: How Team Building Can Improve Your Crew

JOHN LEEBURN

What do you do when you come into a new organization and the culture you inherit is not working well? How do you change that culture and create a team of people who work together well? This was the challenge facing John Leeburn when he took on a new position in Port Coquitlam, British Columbia. In this chapter, he provides a case study of how he went about changing the problematic organizational culture he inherited and creating a strong team.

The Context

I begin this chapter with the first of many references to proverbial boats and buses. In September 2012, I was hired as the CAO in Port Coquitlam, British Columbia, and given a mandate by council to turn around the history-laden, glacial moving, don't-rock-the-boat good ship "PoCo." My mandate was twofold: improve the city's systems, processes, and work methods; and tap into the unused potential of the city's employees. Within weeks I knew that to turn the ship around I would need a high-performing executive team whose experience, intelligence, and creativity I could harness.

This chapter shares the story of how I built a new executive team of department heads in PoCo. My story includes my assessment of the team I inherited, my changes, the team building model we followed, and the efforts we made to sustain the team. At the end of each section, I offer some reflections on each phase of our journey.

Assessment

I spent the autumn of 2012 getting to know my direct reports and observing the organization. I held one-on-one meetings with each executive team member, attended every advisory committee meeting, and invited myself to many departmental staff meetings and working group meetings. I took every opportunity to watch my executive team in action.

Early in 2013, I shared my diagnosis of the organization with the executive team and started conversations with them about what we needed to change. This approach enabled me to get a good idea of who was buying into a different future, who was sitting on the fence watching and hedging their bets, and who was not getting onside. A few months later, shamelessly adapting Gallup's employee engagement categories,[1] I created the PoCo version of the three levels of engagement:

1. Rowers: Those working hard, in unison, to speed in the desired direction.
2. Coasters: Those in the boat whose oars are occasionally in the water (usually when someone is paying attention) but most of the time they are happy to enjoy the ride propelled by the rowers.
3. Drillers: Those who are actively trying to sink the boat and work at cross-purposes from the desired direction.

As the executive team started to introduce our ideas and programs to council and the organization, and as we started to work together, it became increasingly clear to me who was rowing, who was coasting, and who was drilling.

Reflections: By actively observing the organization and your team during the first two to three months on the job, you will have a good feel for the culture of the organization and the people on your team. You will have a clear sense of the practices and norms that contribute to high performance and those that impair high performance. You will also have a good handle on who will row for you and who is drilling. There will also be a few coasters for whom you will need more time to determine if they are capable of rowing. My advice is to trust your assessment and act sooner than later: you do not need to wait six months.

---

1 Gallup's Q12 employee engagement survey categorizes employees as "engaged," "not engaged," and "actively disengaged." "Rowers," "Coasters," and "Drillers" created needed imagery for PoCo employees and was consistent with the *Port* in Port Coquitlam. More information on Gallup's work is available at https://q12.gallup.com/

First Who

Throughout my career, no piece of advice has served me better than Jim Collins's often-quoted bus analogy from his 2001 book *Good to Great*: "First Who … Then What. We expected that good-to-great leaders would begin by setting a new vision and strategy. We found instead that they first got the right people on the bus, the wrong people off the bus, and the right people in the right seats – and then they figured out where to drive it. The old adage 'People are your most important asset' turns out to be wrong. People are not your most important asset. The right people are. Confront the Brutal Facts (Yet Never Lose Faith)" (Collins, 2011, p. 13). From early 2013 to mid-2014, three members of the executive team got off the bus because, unfortunately, they were the wrong people for the journey ahead. I have three observations regarding ending an employee's employment. One, reaching the conclusion the employment needs to end is usually quite straightforward. There is objective evidence the performance is not acceptable, your gut is telling you it is the right thing to do, and likely your colleagues are telling you change is needed. Two, the days and particularly the hours before the termination meeting are stomach churning, angst ridden, and you might second-guess yourself. The meeting itself is solemn and awkward. Three, it will not take very long after the departure before you realize you have made the right decision, and you will be asking yourself why you did not act sooner.

Before inviting new executives on-board the bus, I asked the remaining team members to define what we needed. We wanted to create an organizational culture that:

- enabled employees at all levels of the organization to have input into decisions and directions;
- was passionate about continually getting better;
- had high standards and held each other accountable to the standards;
- took our work but not ourselves seriously; and
- took a "one-city" view that put the interests of the whole ahead of the interests of any one department.

This meant recruiting new executives who were collaborative, courageous, and confident when upholding their values and beliefs, innovative, self-aware, self-deprecating, and team players. In addition, as a team, we enjoyed applying amateur psychology to ourselves, and we were familiar with the Myers-Briggs Type Inventory personality inventory and the Insights Discovery psychometric tool (both assessment approaches are based on the same Jungian psychology). We knew the composition of our team in terms of our individual personality preferences and we knew what personality types were underrepresented at our table. This knowledge enabled us to create specific profiles of our desired candidates in terms of technical skills, behavioural competencies, and personality type. We conducted robust recruitments that promoted our culture change journey, heavily involved the executive team, used personality (psychological) assessments, and checked references rigorously.

Reflections: Getting the right people on the bus is critical. Local governments are underresourced at the executive level. Executive team members produce a disproportionate amount of the net new work to accomplish the ambitious and ever-changing agendas of councils. The executive team and the next level down (i.e., the senior managers who report to executives) must all be rowers to deliver the goods, share the workload, and emotionally support one another.

Make your changes to the executive team before you begin to make significant changes in the systems and processes. Change is hard. It is near impossible in stagnant, entrenched organizations.

Team-Building Model

Even after getting the right people on the bus, strong and effective teams do not happen just because you slap a "corporate management team" or "executive management team" label on a group of employees. Team building does not happen by chance or with the passage of time: it requires deliberate actions and dedicated time and resources.

In late 2013, with almost all of the executive team changes in place, we began our team-building journey. Over the next eight months, with the aid of a fabulous facilitator, we held four half-day sessions and two one-hour follow-ups with the facilitator to monitor progress. Our half-days had two components: to develop strategies and implementation plans to achieve council's mandate and agenda, and to accelerate our effectiveness as a team. Our facilitator used Patrick Lencioni's *The Five Dysfunctions of a Team* (2002) as our model for team building. The model, figure 13.1, identifies five sequential steps a team must take to become highly functional.

The five steps are explained in the following sections.

Reflections: Hiring the facilitator to help build the 2013–14 executive team was one of the best decisions I made in my six years at PoCo. The director of human resources and I had worked with the facilitator

Figure 13.1 The Five Dysfunctions of a Team

many times: we knew her style, her philosophies, and we shared her beliefs about what was critical for team success and cultural change. Investing the time and resources into targeted team-building activities significantly increases the likelihood of creating a highly functional team.

Step 1: Develop Vulnerability-Based Trust

The reason this model worked so well for us was our ability to develop vulnerability-based trust, which "is predicated on the simple – and practical – idea that people who aren't afraid to admit the truth about themselves are not going to engage in the kind of political behaviour that wastes everyone's time and energy, and more important, makes the accomplishment of results an unlikely scenario" (Lencioni, 2005, p. 14). In a 2018 presentation to the Nordic business forum, Lencioni described it this way: "Vulnerability based trust is the kind of trust that comes about when human beings on a team can and will genuinely say things to one another like 'I don't know the answer,' 'I need help,' 'I think I screwed this up,' 'You're much smarter than I am, teach me to be how to be like you' or even 'I'm sorry, what I said yesterday was totally unfair.' When people can be that buck naked, if you will, with each other – that emotionally transparent, it changes everything on a team" (Lencioni, 2018).

Our passage to "buck nakedness" began cautiously but ramped up quickly. Over the course of eight months, the executive team engaged in four trust-building exercises, and each exercise was more emotionally revealing than the previous one. In the first exercise, we shared three things the team likely did not know about each of us. In the second exercise, we shared the results of our Myers-Briggs Type Inventory and how our types present in the workplace. In the third exercise (and now we are starting to show some skin), we shared our personal history: where we were born, where we are in the birth order of our siblings (first born, baby of the family, middle-child …), and one thing that happened to us as a child that influenced or impacted us as adults. The fourth exercise was the "item of importance exercise," where we brought something tangible and explained to the team why it is important or meaningful to us. One of the critical elements of the exercises was that the leader (i.e., me as the CAO) must go first. If the leader is serious about building vulnerability-based trust, then there is no greater opportunity to do so than by opening the proverbial kimono first and fully.

Before you run off thinking vulnerability-based trust is some sort of competition to see who can evoke the greatest volume of tears, let me be clear that it is not. The purpose is to get to know each other at a deeper human level, to open the book on who each of you is. When you know more about your teammates, their struggles and their motivations, you are more likely to be forthright and transparent with them, offer help, ask for help, and apologize. If your relationship with your teammates more closely resembles what I call the bus driver relationship (characterized by frequent mindless exchanges such as "good morning," "lovely sunny day isn't it?" "have a great weekend"), then you will focus on your needs and agenda at the expense of achieving the team's goals, because you will have less buy-in and commitment to the team and the team's goals.

Reflections: When the organization is running smoothly and relationships (e.g., with council, interest groups, the community at large, city unions, and city employees) are solid, then there is less need for the executive team to be a high-trusting unit. There might be room for a bit of individualistic thinking and acting and small "p" political shenanigans, and the consequences of these behaviours might not be terribly detrimental to the city's goals. When the executive team is under pressure, however, the need for trust, cohesion, and collaboration is high. When the members of the executive team feel they are constantly being tested, as we did for most of my time in PoCo, there is no time for internal fighting or second-guessing. Every ounce of energy, brainpower, and creativity must be spent on the work in front of you. It cannot be wasted on backroom internal mischief. If you walk away from this chapter with just one thing, let it be this: build vulnerability-based trust on your team; it is the difference maker.

Step 2: Conflict Is Inevitable (Combat Is Optional)

A strong foundation of trust enables passionate, unfiltered debate about the ideas important to the team. Because there is a high level of trust in the room, disagreements and counterarguments are not taken personally or viewed as trying to advance a personal agenda; rather, they are seen as part of the process "to produce the best possible solution in the shortest period of time" (Lencioni, 2002, pp. 202–3). To help the PoCo executive team engage in passionate debate during our work with the facilitator, we created a one-page list called our Interaction Guidelines that defined our agreed-to commitments regarding how we would behave in our meetings. The topics covered were language, tone of voice, body language, emotional content, involvement and participation, distractions, and timeliness. The guidelines allowed anyone at the table to call out a team member who violated our agreement

While, in theory, our high level of trust and agreed-to guidelines should have resulted in entirely free-flowing conversations and contributions from all, I still needed to temper the contributions of some team members and invite contributions from the less vocal. At one end of the spectrum, I prohibited one team member from speaking first on any issue; at the other end, I had to keep inviting one team member to speak.

Reflections: The level of trust and the diversity of experience and personalities on the team helped us look at our challenges and opportunities from multiple angles. We had diversity on risk tolerance, speed of change, need for consultation, employee centrism, and capacity to take on new work. We certainly did not get everything right, but our missteps were not as a result of group think or one person's railroading an opinion over someone else's – sometimes we just missed an option or a source of information.

Step 3: Commitment

The desired outcome of the passionate debate is a decision or direction everyone can commit to and quickly act upon. The basic concept is: with full weigh-in, you get full buy-in. Even team members not in favour of the decision are able to "disagree and commit," a phrase attributed to a number of CEOs in the high-tech field, including Scott McNealy (Sun Microsystems), Andrew Grove (Intel), and Jeff Bezos (Amazon). The idea is you do not have to waste time reaching consensus; you simply have a robust discussion, ensure everyone has been heard, then decide.

Reflections: Most of my executive team members were anxious and ready for decisions sooner than I was. My desire to get everyone on board with a decision often delayed action. Generally, executives can "disagree and commit" except in circumstances when a decision is contrary to their core values or principles. Don't be afraid to force clarity and closure once everyone has been heard.

Step 4: Accountability

The executive team met two or three times a week, and I met individually with team members weekly or bi-weekly. This level of communication ensured expectations were clear and progress and behaviours were monitored and discussed. This near-constant feedback approach significantly reduced the need for difficult conversations and formal performance management because issues rarely escalated to the point where that was necessary. We were not perfect, and when our performance did not meet expectations, I never thought it was a result of incompetence, carelessness, laziness, or apathy by one of the team members. I believed all team members gave their best effort. Our missteps were dealt with from the perspective of what we can learn from them and what we need to do differently.

I remember three occasions in six years when I had to take action to correct inappropriate behaviour by an executive team member. These were occasions when team members made decisions or engaged in behaviour that was inconsistent with city policy and/or leadership expectations. My actions involved giving clear direction regarding expectations and outlining possible consequences if the expectations were not met. The conversations did not result in hard feelings or subsequent awkwardness between the department head and me because of the high level of trust between us. An isolated mistake was made, it was dealt with, and we went back to leading the city.

Those who report directly to you might try to hide interpersonal conflicts or struggles: they might be concerned that you would interpret such difficulties as a negative reflection on them. Yet it is important you become aware of such issues. I had two communication channels to learn such information. First, my regular one-on-one meetings with each team member provided the opportunity for a confidential, "heads-up" if something was going on within the team that I might want to pursue. Second, I established relationships with a few managers who reported to the team members, and shared with me what was going on in their department. I did not seek out managers to be my "moles" – these relationships grew organically and, I honestly believe, the managers shared with me with the best interests of the city at heart. On those rare occasions when I did get the feeling the information being shared with me by the manager was self-serving (i.e., to boost my opinion of a manager at the expense of a department head), I would "act" on that information much more cautiously and my trust in that manager would be diminished.

Reflections: The executive team had a difficult relationship with council for most of my time in PoCo. This forced us to meet frequently as a team. The silver lining to the frequent meetings was that our expectations of each other were clear and our progress monitored. The combination of having the right people on the bus and, frankly, the fear of the consequences of "failing" council and each other kept us all on the proverbial straight and narrow.

Step 5: Focus

The fable part of Lencioni's *The Five Dysfunctions of a Team: A Leadership Fable* is about a CEO who joins a dysfunctional high-tech company and is mandated with improving company performance. The new CEO and the executive team set the goal of acquiring eighteen new customers in one year, and devise strategies and tactics around how each department will contribute to the achievement of the team goal. If only the local government world were so simple that each department could support such a unifying, compelling, SMART[2] goal.

From a team-building perspective, difficulty setting measurable goals at the corporate level and a lack of focus increase the executive team's challenge to think and act in the city's best interest, rather than that of their department. Local governments are in multiple and diverse lines of business. Our strategic planning and business planning processes drive us to set departmental goals and measures because the corporate goals are so overarching and imprecise. Executive team members are rewarded or held accountable by council for the achievement of department results, and this leads executives to pursue their departmental agenda rather than the corporate agenda.

Local government corporate goals will never be as simple as "land eighteen new customers in one year," but increased corporate focus is possible if councils agree to a small, manageable list of priorities within the corporate strategic plan for a three-to-four-year time frame. Finding ways for each department to contribute to the priorities will increase corporate focus. Obviously, not every department will contribute equally, but having the organization rally around three broad goals is much more effective than dispersing energy on ten or twelve.

I also think there is an opportunity to rethink how we approach our business plans to align them along priority lines rather than departmental lines. For example, how do we present the common challenge

2 Specific, Measurable, Achievable, Relevant, Time-bound.

of downtown revitalization? Typically, the planning department would report on its initiatives, and then the engineering department would take the stage and talk about the projects it will do, and then by-laws would highlight its enforcement activities, and on we would go. Instead, we need to talk about what are we doing collectively and with one voice: the voice of the executive team.

Reflections: I said earlier in this chapter that change is difficult, and this is true, but maintaining corporate focus is just as difficult. In my opinion, lack of focus is the second-biggest risk to team cohesiveness, after lack of trust. We set our goals, objectives, and measures along departmental lines, and the pursuit of these outcomes encourages competitive rather than collaborative behaviour, departmental rather than corporate thinking (and acting). To the extent possible, the CAO needs to work with council to agree to a limited number of strategic priorities, and then help to connect each department to its role in the delivery of these priorities.

Sustaining the Team

Once great teams are created, they need nourishment to stay great. We took three approaches: team retreats, one-on-one meetings with the CAO, and social get-togethers.

Twice each year we held off-site retreats where we navel-gazed. We used the Team Effectiveness Exercise (Lencioni, 2005, p. 139), which provides an avenue for each member of the team to receive feedback from the rest on how that person is contributing to the team's success and what the person is doing that detracts from the team's success. At the subsequent off-site session, there was a review of the previous feedback and an opportunity to discuss progress made towards addressing detracting performance or behaviours.

I also held regular (i.e., weekly or bi-weekly) one-on-one meetings with nearly every team member. In my case, most of the meetings were held in my office, but there is great value in going to your department head's office. It is likely a more comfortable or less formal setting, and it also makes you more visible to the organization when you are out visiting the departments. The one-on-one meetings allowed me to keep up to date both on what was going on in the team members' areas of responsibility and on the executive team generally. When I noticed slight changes in behaviour or attitude, I asked about the cause of the change. As noted previously, I am convinced these one-on-one meetings were a large part of why there was minimal interpersonal conflict on the executive team: we identified conflict early and dealt with it swiftly.

Across the street from city hall in PoCo is a neighbourhood pub, known in city hall as the staff cafeteria and healing centre. The executive team frequented the pub for post-council meetings therapy and to celebrate work and personal milestones. Two or three times a year, we also got the executive team together with spouses for summer BBQs and Christmas parties. The social time allowed us to continue to open our book to each other, thus enhancing the trust building we began in 2013–14. Let me be clear: I am not suggesting that you as CAO need to become best friends or drinking buddies with those who report to you; I am saying that it is important to get to know them at a personal level and for them to get to know you – to show an interest in their family and their avocations and to share yours. For us, the pub was a convenient and comfortable place. I appreciate a pub might not be appropriate for many teams for many reasons. The key here is not the venue but the outcome of getting to know each other at a deeper level.

I do want to share one important lesson I learned about socializing with your direct reports, and that is to share social time as equally as possible and not to spend noticeably more time with one subgroup. The risk of spending more time with some than others is that it can create the perception of an "A-team" and a "B-team" within the team. It is natural to gravitate to people with whom you share an interest, a hobby, or other connection. Instead, I encourage you to engage with such people in your community, rather than on your team.

Reflections: Two things were critical to sustaining our team: taking time to talk about how we were working together (this navel-gazing can be done in group and one-on-one sessions), and deliberately cultivating and nurturing your personal relationships with team members (be interested in the person, not just the peer).

Conclusion

Having docked the boat and parked the bus, I want to share my reflections on the PoCo journey:

- You don't need much more than three months to get a good read on your existing team and their suitability for the journey ahead.
- Get the wrong people off the bus quickly and dedicate the time and energy needed to recruit the right replacements.
- Invest in a deliberate team-building process and go first in every awkward, soul-revealing exercise.

- Use your team at every chance. You do not have to have all the answers and be seen as the smartest person in the room. Harness and highlight the brains and creativity of your team.

And, most important, open yourself up to your team. Employees want to relate and connect to their boss; they want to know you are a real person with a heart, a sense of humour, and a big dose of humility. Invest in the relationships, and the results will follow.

REFERENCES

Collins, J. (2011). *Good to great: Why some companies make the leap and others don't*. Harper Collins.

Lencioni, P. (2002). *The five dysfunctions of a team: A leadership fable*. Jossey-Bass.

Lencioni, P. (2005). *Overcoming the five dysfunctions of a team*. Jossey-Bass.

Lencioni, P. (2014, 20 November). "Why Great Leadership Fuels." https://www.inc.com/magazine/201412/patrick-lencioni/innovation-wont-get-you-very-far.html

Lencioni, P. (2018, February). *Build vulnerability-based trust on your teams (Part 2)* [Video]. YouTube. https://www.youtube.com/watch?v=ACCn1sNYpVc

14 Five Strategies for Successful Municipal Intergovernmental Relations

JOHN E. FLEMING

For municipal officials, managing the all-important and multifaceted relationships with the province or territory is key. In this chapter, John E. Fleming offers insights into the workings of those governments, as seen from both sides. His subsequent success as a deputy minister and community leader was built on his city management experience in Metro Toronto and British Columbia, and later as CAO in Halton Region, Ontario, and the City of London. Fleming offers the kind of practical tips that any city manager can employ when trying to persuade the provincial and federal governments to respond positively to the needs of your municipality.

Municipalities are "creatures of the provinces." This chapter looks at what lies behind that simple statement. How can senior municipal officials work with their counterparts at the other levels (or orders) of government? What are the critical relationship issues for practitioners of municipal government in Canada?

This chapter is dedicated to providing city managers with a collection of strategies and practical tips for successfully building and maintaining strong and effective relationships with senior officials in the federal/provincial/territorial (F/P/T) orders of government. For those in leadership positions in local government, such as city managers, it is important to understand your "counterparties." If you are going to have an influential relationship with officials in the provincial/territorial capital or in Ottawa, you need to understand the lens through which they see their municipal counterparts. Or, as the Scottish Bard wrote, "O wad some Pow'r the giftie gie us; To see oursels as ithers see us!" The first part of this chapter lays that groundwork. The final section uses that foundation to provide strategies and practical measures for building a stronger intergovernmental relationship.

That word "relationship" is key. Effective intergovernmental relationships rely on understanding your governmental counterparties.

Their institutional and political realities might interfere with their ability or willingness to respond positively to your advocacy or to understand your political and operational circumstances. For purposes of the discussion that follows, the four key "differentiating factors" are: (1) structures and systems; (2) roles and authorities; (3) methods of decision making; and, of course, (4) the political context.

Structures and Systems

Municipalities might be the government "closest to the people" in terms of both democratic accountability and service delivery, but every municipal official learns early that Canada's Constitution Act makes municipal governments "creatures of the provinces and territories," regardless of their size or status.

The structures and styles of each order of government have changed with the evolution of government generally in Canada and have become more intertwined. Solid municipal/federal/provincial/territorial working relationships have never been more important. Nothing has highlighted the existential importance of these relationships more than the need for effective coordination and collaboration among all orders of government in Canada in response to the COVID-19 pandemic.

Historically, municipalities have tended to focus on local regulations and the effective delivery of a broad range of services to individuals and communities. Over time, other orders of government have focused more on broad policy and fiscal issues. The challenge of this evolution is that other orders of government increasingly need to employ or direct municipalities to deliver their policy and program goals. When developing policies, programs, and delivery mandates, however, officials in other orders of government might lack the first-hand experience, community connections, and practical knowledge enjoyed by municipalities. If both sides collaborate, municipalities can play a larger role in policy development and program design, thereby making them more effective.

There is growing interdependence among all levels of government on that broad policy thinking. This is manifest in the increasingly common use of the relatively new term "multilevel governance." Martin Horak and Robert Young have made a significant contribution to this literature in Canada with a series of publications focused on "multigovernance" (Horak & Young, 2012), while Lucas and Smith illustrate how municipalities have exercised their increasing strength (Lucas & Smith, 2019). Canadian municipal politicians have the capacity to leverage media profiles, electoral mandates, implementation responsibilities, and even infrastructure ownership (Sayers & Alcantara, 2018) into a level of involvement in public policy issues that goes well beyond what one would expect from a "creature of the province."

Readers of this book certainly do not need a civics lesson, but for purposes of developing solid intergovernmental relations, we need to remind ourselves of important differences in the decision-making context between the municipal and other orders of government. We need to understand how the four "differentiating factors" mentioned earlier will play out. Again, it comes down to understanding your "counterparty."

Roles and Authorities

Increasingly in parliamentary government, the premier or prime minister commands the unquestioned loyalty of the governing majority in the legislature. In contrast, provincial officials – both civil servants and political staff – might be puzzled that a mayor cannot make firm commitments on behalf of council or restrain council members from criticizing the provincial government. Those same officials might be surprised that a mayor who supports the provincial government on a matter of mutual interest might feel at liberty to oppose that government on some unrelated issue later in the month. Provincial and federal officials might expect more from a mayor than a mayor is in a position to promise or guarantee.

This situation is further complicated by the fact that some mayors take the view that they can win over council or commit the municipality – and in some cases, they can. In 2001, Ontario's new Municipal Act redefined the role of a mayor as the "chief executive officer" of the municipality, although there was concern by some that this had the potential to conflict with the role of the city manager or chief administrative officer. Subsequently, many Ontario mayors and other heads of council began to identify themselves as the CEO of their municipal corporation. The same statutory change that bestowed that title on the head of council, however, immediately went on to circumscribe this role by describing the limited powers the title actually conferred on the head of council. Ultimately, a judicial inquiry into an abuse of office in one Ontario municipality resulted in the unheeded recommendation by Associate Chief Justice Frank Marrocco that the provision be removed (Marrocco, 2020).

A proactive city manager can help provincial and federal officials understand these realities and anticipate their consequences.

Methods of Decision Making

Other orders of government are guided by the parliamentary principles of "cabinet solidarity" and maintaining the "confidence of the legislature." Despite their profile, ministers and deputy ministers rarely act in isolation. Most major issues are decided by cabinet, closely managed by the premier or prime minister and their political staff. Unlike in the fishbowl world of municipal decision making, those cabinet decisions are also debated in secret and the views of participants in cabinet deliberations are not known outside the cabinet process. Government members of the legislature or parliament may provide political "soundings" for ministers and for the party in power, but they do not have the autonomy of individual municipal councillors.

Provincial and federal officials might not understand the fact of "shifting majorities" on a municipal council and the effort that must be invested by municipal political leadership to achieve majority support on council for a set of policy objectives. Although governed by provincial rules on openness and transparency, provincial and federal officials might not understand that city managers and their staffs make policy recommendations in an open forum, prior to receiving political direction. If they fail to appreciate these municipal realities, there is a risk that provincial and federal officials might see municipal governments and their senior staff as unpredictable, inconsistent, or "fair weather friends."

Like the municipal council, cabinet is sensitive to both electoral cycles and annual planning and budget cycles. Conventional wisdom is that governments will introduce restraint measures and eliminate programs shortly after the election so the pain will be forgotten by the next election, and save the introduction of new programs and other "goodies" for the period immediately before an election. For city managers and municipal leaders generally, timing can be as important as the merits of their case.

Shorter-term budget and planning cycles also have an impact on decision making. There is a feeling that treasury departments underestimate expected revenue early in the annual budget cycle. Then, when more revenue than was budgeted arrives during the year, it creates an unexpected surplus that becomes available for expenditure.

In sum, this means that the decision-making process in parliamentary forms of government is centralized in cabinet and hidden from public view, although there are times and places where some outside influence can seep through. Municipal leaders asking other orders of government to make legislative or budgetary changes need to be aware of these governments' electoral, planning, and budgeting cycles and the importance of timing and the potential impact of both public and private lobbying. Of equal importance, municipal leaders, including city managers, must ensure that a weak understanding of municipal political and legal basics does not impede the ability of their provincial and federal counterparts to respond to municipal requests and needs.

The real decision-making process in Westminster-style governments begins in cabinet. Different first ministers lead their cabinets in different ways, but the first minister clearly has a great deal of power stemming from her or his position as party leader and the ability to hand out rewards such as cabinet and other positions. Ministers present and defend their views, and one can imagine some vigorous and spirited debates within the sound-proofed walls of the cabinet meeting room. But once a decision is made, the principle of cabinet collectivity requires all ministers (and, to a certain extent, all elected members of the party) to accept and defend it. Iron discipline prevails. This is integral to maintaining party unity and the confidence of the legislature.

Since all major policy decisions must come to cabinet, the competition among ministers for the time and attention of cabinet can be challenging. Not all ministers will be granted cabinet time to consider their issues, regardless of how important some ministers might feel their issue is. Ministers and their public servants on occasion might be open to or actively seek input into the government's policy and planning work. Ministers could feel that a strong groundswell of public opinion would be very helpful in making their case in cabinet.

When amendments to or introduction of legislation or regulation are required to implement a decision of cabinet, formal processes are followed. Changes to government regulations and some policies require only cabinet or ministerial approval. Changes in *legislation* (statutes) or the introduction of new legislation are matters for the full legislature, where members of all parties and independents can hold full debate. In practice, governments find that the regulation process (including minister's orders) under existing statutes is more under their control, since enacting legislation subjects their actions to more protracted public debate, opposition scrutiny, and, often, unwelcome criticism. City managers and other municipal leaders should give consideration to the easiest route to "yes" when making requests of other governments and their officials.

Good Governance Observations

It is worthy of note that, in Canada's F/P/T governments, a significant part of programming is delivered through a broad range of outsourcing arrangements. The Institute on Governance (2011) estimates, for example, that, in Canada, 65 to 90 per cent of government budgets are delivered by organizations outside the formal public service As one of the many bodies that deliver provincial programs, municipalities should keep this important fact in mind as they work to build relationships and influence policy. The Institute on Governance's work on the concept of the governance continuum, describing how Westminster governments have evolved to this distributed model of both service delivery and accountability, is worthy of exploration. Although there are some parallels in the outsourcing of municipal programs across the country, this model has taken on prominence in the F/P/T orders of government. The Institute on Governance's research on the implications for autonomy in such systems adds depth to the city manager's understanding of its relevance to relationship building.

One tool that some first ministers now use to communicate their desires to ministers is a "mandate letter" specifying the expectations the first minister has of each cabinet minister. At one point, these were confidential, but the practice of making them public is becoming more common. They are *essential reading* for anyone with an interest in understanding ministerial mandates. When city managers are looking for support from a ministry or department on an issue, finding it in a mandate letter greatly improves its prospect of acceptance.

Ministers are responsible politically for their portfolio and their department or ministry. The deputy minister is the professional public servant who functions as the administrative head and chief operating officer of the department. Her or his role is to oversee the work of the public servants under her or his direct management, while providing impartial professional advice, information, and recommendations to the minister and the government.

Ministers are also supported by publicly funded political staff. They are often young, relatively new graduates from university, well versed in the work and the ideology of the party. They are often without a great deal of workplace experience, however, especially in the highly specialized environment that characterizes the workplace of the public servants with whom they will interact on behalf of the minister. Some move from assignment to assignment, in different parts of government. They are appointed by party officials in the first minister's office, and their job is to provide partisan political advice to their minister. They do not necessarily know very much about the department in which they are currently lodged.

The Political Context

As noted earlier, unlike most governments in the municipal world, Westminster governments are built around party politics. Once elected, the platform of a political party will form that government's agenda, business plans, communications, and priorities, at least until exigencies arise. Unlike the individual municipal councillor, there is little room for individual members of a Westminster-style legislature to set policy, vote freely in the legislative body, or speak their mind openly and independently on matters of interest to the government.

City managers should also distinguish between government and opposition members of the legislature. On matters of policy, government members might be in a position to influence government decisions in relation to local issues. If the local member is a member of cabinet or, better still, the relevant minister, that influence could be crucial. Even if the local member is not in cabinet, keeping her or him informed and aware of constituency information and attitudes can be helpful. Similarly, representatives of opposition parties should not be excluded from efforts to share locally relevant data, trends, and concerns. Criticism or simple nudging on a policy issue by an opposition member might encourage the government to take the desired action.

Strategies and Practical Advice

Now that we have identified the ways in which city managers can overcome and even leverage the distinctions between municipal decision making and that of other orders of government, we are in a much better position to develop strategies that will lead to success in intergovernmental relations.

Strategy #1: Map Your Relationships

To "map" the relationship between a municipal government and other orders of government – that is, to *structure* an intergovernmental relationship – some basic questions need to be considered. Who is doing the talking and with whom is the relationship being established? That is, to whom exactly is the municipality "speaking"? Above all, what is the message? Are "we" all on the same page on that message at the municipal level?

Taking into account these foundational conditions, there are several tips for success as city managers work to build relationships and communicate with their counterparts in the other orders of government.

Begin by thinking of this entire process as one of building a successful and effective "communications protocol." Such a protocol will serve you well, if done carefully and thoughtfully. Summed up, think of this as "the right people focused on the right relationships."

In developing the protocol with the municipal council, determine very carefully the purpose of the relationship to be established or the nature of the message to be delivered to colleagues in the other orders of government. There are, of course, protocols to be observed. The generally accepted principle is that *elected* municipal officials will relate and speak to their elected counterparts in the other orders of government, while *appointed* municipal officials will do likewise. As discussed below, city managers should also cultivate relationships with key political staff.

Strategy is crucial. At the municipal level, there should be a clear and agreed strategy, designating who will speak for the municipality, where that message will be addressed, and a clear delineation of what the message is. Optimal advantage should also be taken of any pre-existing relationships: if an appointed official has an existing relationship with an elected member, or better yet, with a minister, it is logical and expedient to take advantage of that. Such contact is faster, easier, closer, and more likely to lead to positive results.

As noted above, individual councillors are used to having a lot of political autonomy, so resolve with them any differences in how they see the intended message or purpose. If differences remain, consider and agree how to present them as transparently as possible rather than ignore them. The goal is to avoid a reaction by the minister or other senior elected officials such as "I'm ignoring them until they get their act together."

Strategy #2: Focus the Message

Focusing the municipality's intergovernmental strategy, while seemingly similar to the concepts of mapping relationships, deserves separate mention.

The policy and legislative agendas of the other orders of government are more complex and far reaching than those of a municipal government. At the same time, the traditional municipal focus on local service delivery raises a complex set of challenges in the modern context. Climate change, growth, development planning, transit, and, in many cases, the full range of human service delivery issues are now on the municipal agenda, along with the confounding matter of efficiency and effectiveness in the use of scarce tax dollars. So how should the city manager "focus the message"?

Review very carefully all you can locate about the government's agenda. Place emphasis on "mandate letter" references pertaining to your issue. Gear your message and your relationships as closely as possible to align with your understanding of the government's position. The municipality needs to consider what it knows about the government's interests, its agenda, its priorities, and indeed its capacity to respond, as well as to understand the minister's mandate. Tying the municipality's needs or concerns to the current priorities of the government, however tenuously, will increase the likelihood that the issue will catch the attention of those who might be able to help.

When you have the opportunity to meet with a minister, respect the considerable demands on a minister's time; stay focused, stay on point, be as succinct as possible.

Pay careful attention to the calendar: is the government at the beginning of its mandate? In the middle? Nearing the end, and headed to the polls again soon? Other "calendars" also require attention. As noted, other orders of government work in tightly controlled cycles of planning and budgeting, the timing of which might not always align well with the needs of the municipality. The timing of those cycles will not change, so the municipality must work to focus its message to align with the opportunities as they present themselves.

Often the primary issues of concern are financial, whether it be a matter of costs imposed by other orders of government or their apparent unwillingness to share revenue. In this respect, the concerns of one municipality are often the concern of many others, leading over time to the formation of the many associations and federations of municipal leaders, both political and administrative. Active membership and participation in these bodies can be useful, for all the obvious reasons. Never assume, though, that engagement in these broader organizations should replace the time and effort you invest in forming focused relationships between the municipality and whatever other orders or parts of government might be able to assist.

Strategy #3: Government versus Opposition and Confidentiality in the Relationship

It is important to maintain a good relationship with local elected members of the legislature. Government members can help make your case to the government, but keep opposition members in the loop as well.

In your discussions with government officials, you might be trusted with some confidential information. Never breach that trust, especially in any dealings with members other than those in government.

It is in the best interests of city managers to work with their councils on establishing those all-important relationships with both key elected and public service leaders. In particular, they must take steps to ensure, directly, that information and advice that might be shared with either elected or public service leaders should be communicated to the other side as well. Although good communication between ministers and their deputies and staff is the goal, it does not always happen as it should. During my time as a provincial public servant, I was on occasion frustrated to learn that the political side of the house had learned of stakeholder views on a matter on which public servants were working hard and of which we were not aware. Taking steps to avoid that communication misfire, whether deliberate or accidental, goes a long way to "making it all work" and avoiding wasted time.

Respect, also, the right of elected members who are *not* on the government side to be kept abreast of local issues. They represent the constituency, and should have access to publicly available information on these issues. In fact, opposition members' pressure on your issue might prove beneficial in both securing and refocusing the government's attention. *However* ... offending the government or a government member with ill-chosen words or timing is rarely a helpful strategy.

Strategy #4: Be Solution Oriented

Just as in the business world, public servants are often told: "Don't bring me problems; bring me solutions!" This thinking is relevant to working with the other orders of government, even though it might not always be practical or even possible to present easy solutions.

First and foremost, always tie the municipal issue to the government's agenda and priorities as closely as possible. In doing so, avoid the temptation to lay the problem at the feet of the government, even if the problem arises as a result of the government's action or inaction.

Aim to identify workable solutions to a problem by bringing forward steps or actions the municipality can take and by working with the involved other order of government. Wherever possible, establish win-win approaches, whether pragmatic or political, whereby both levels of government will be seen to benefit.

Strategy #5: Political Staff

As challenging as it might seem on occasion, the political staff of the minister who is relevant to your issue could be the city manager's best, if not only, means of access to the government's political decision making. Hence, it is worth the investment of time and effort to cultivate good working relationships with that staff. Take the opportunity to help them learn the issues and the solutions. Where necessary, start all over again when some morning you learn that there is someone new on the file.

Municipalities need to understand that political staff are not analogous to executive or administrative assistants to municipal councillors.

Provincial staff are assigned to the minister by the first minister's office. They are partisan appointments whose first loyalty is to the party. Municipal political staffers are generally chosen by the councillor, loyal to the councillor, and usually charged with addressing the myriad complaints and requests of constituents to the councillor about service delivery.

In dealing with political staff, accept them for what they are: a key means of access to the government in power. Recognize the opportunity for a relationship built on the premise of a two-way street: they gain access to an important constituency point of view, as well as advice and information, and you gain the opportunity to listen, educate, and inform, all of which works to the advantage of the municipality.

Understand that political staff might not always be in the same posting in the government. Do not be frustrated when reassignment occurs after time and effort have been invested in building a good working relationship with a particular individual. Start over again with the successor, and build from there. Appreciate, as well, that political staffers might not always tell the city manager the whole story about what is going on, even if they are in information-gathering mode, for two key reasons: they simply are not privy to the full picture or they might have been told explicitly, perhaps because of cabinet confidentiality, the limits of what they can share.

Conclusion: The Road Ahead

The road that stretches ahead of city managers in Canada will no doubt be festooned with signs indicating sharp and twisting turns, limits on speed, and the inevitable CAUTION and YIELD warnings.

Astute city managers will pay careful attention to building, maintaining, and sustaining strong and effective intergovernmental working relationships, and support to the best of their ability the work of their councils to do likewise.

May the road ahead be a smooth one!

REFERENCES

Horak, M., & Young, R. (Eds.). (2012). *Sites of governance: Multilevel governance and policy making in Canada*. McGill-Queen's University Press.

Institute on Governance. (2011, March). The governance continuum: Origins & conceptual construct. Public Governance Exchange Working Paper. Retrieved from https://iog.ca/docs/the_governance_continuum_a_pgex_working_paper_pd_18577.pdf

Lucas, J., & Smith, A. (2019). Multilevel policy from the municipal perspective: A pan-Canadian survey. *Canadian Public Administration*, *62*(2), 270–93. https://doi.org/10.1111/capa.12316

Marrocco, F. A. (2020, 2 November). *Transparency and the public trust: Report of the Collingwood Judicial Inquiry*. Retrieved from http://www.collingwoodinquiry.ca/report/index.html

Sayers, A., & Alcantara, C. (2018). Repowering the state: Linking physical assets to state power. Unpublished manuscript. Western University.

15 Leading Beyond: Building Relationships for Intergovernmental Collaboration

GAIL STEPHENS WITH ZACK TAYLOR

Gail Stephens has been city manager of two of Canada's provincial capitals, Winnipeg and Victoria. That "fishbowl" environment, coupled with her leadership experience with federal Crown corporations and large regulated organizations, gives Stephens particular insights into the dynamics of intergovernmental relations. Working with co-author and municipal government scholar Professor Zack Taylor, Stephens explains how intergovernmental negotiations can yield agreements that overcome the often brittle and conflicting mandates of governments and their agencies. As they point out with examples, real success often depends on developing ongoing relationships among officials and identifying shared objectives, rather than simply advocating for a policy or a program outcome through political channels.

The past two decades have witnessed a major expansion of policy collaboration between municipalities and the federal and provincial governments. Politicians and senior administrators in municipalities large and small, often working with their counterparts in neighbouring jurisdictions, are in constant dialogue with provincial and federal officials. These policy-making and delivery collaborations cover the full range of public programs and projects: infrastructure, housing and homelessness, economic development, and environmental protection, to name only a few.

As the chief administrative officer and city manager, respectively, of two Canadian provincial capital cities – Winnipeg, Manitoba, and Victoria, British Columbia – I saw first hand how much cross-level relationships between administrators matter, although these are often overshadowed by the more visible cross-level relationships between politicians. Before serving as a CAO, I had also served as a deputy minister in both provincial governments. I was a well-known figure in government circles, which helped me build relationships across administrative silos and levels of government.

In this chapter, I discuss and draw lessons from my experience with multilevel policy collaboration in the domain of housing and homelessness in these two very different provincial and municipal contexts. First, however, I briefly discuss the constraints municipal administrative leaders face as they confront complex policy dilemmas, and how relationship building can overcome them.

Cities in Multilevel Governance

The legal powers and fiscal resources of Canadian municipalities are often characterized as limited. Although there is evidence that the scope of municipalities' autonomous statutory authority has expanded in recent decades (Taylor & Dobson, 2019) and that municipalities raise and spend more money per capita than ever before (Taylor & Bradford, 2020), they remain constitutional "creatures of the provinces" (Cooper, 1996; Hirschl, 2020) and dependent on provincial and federal governments to fund a substantial portion of operating and capital expenditures (Slack, 2009; Tindal et al., 2017, pp. 179–86).

Although compared to other levels of government, municipalities are necessarily constrained by their smaller population, fiscal capacity, and territorial jurisdiction, municipalities and their community partners possess something that provinces and the federal government do not: detailed knowledge of local needs and conditions. Municipalities are not simply administrative conveniences of the provinces – policy "takers" rather than policy "makers." Rather, they are institutions through which local residents democratically set policy priorities and local policy professionals bring their local knowledge to bear on important problems. They are the level of government that is most in touch with the concerns of people and businesses as residents, taxpayers, and employers. The combining of local knowledge, regulatory and other authority, and resources, but perhaps especially local knowledge, with provincial and federal fiscal resources enables the tailoring of programs to local conditions and is the essence of today's multilevel policy collaborations (Bradford, 2018; Leo, 2006). At best, municipalities are laboratories of policy innovation and the proving grounds of ideas that can be applied elsewhere. Local governments can be more flexible, and take more risks, than provincial and federal governments, which have larger sunk costs and must balance a wider range of interests in the delivery of universal programs.

In parallel with Canadians' traditional understanding of *federalism*, which views governing authority as entirely contained within the constitutional division of powers between the federal and provincial governments, we now see numerous instances of *multilevel governance*: partnerships of governments and non-governmental organizations at all levels to deliver specific projects and programs (Hooghe & Marks, 2003; Horak, 2013; Horak & Young, 2012). From coast to coast to coast, there has been a dramatic acceleration in recent years of federal-municipal and federal-provincial-municipal initiatives, often involving community organizations and customized to local needs and conditions, focusing on local economic development, housing and homelessness, urban Indigenous peoples, infrastructure, and "smart cities" (Taylor & Bradford, 2020).

Relationship Building Is a Key Task of Local Leadership

Long-term collaborations, especially between different agencies and levels of government, depend on good relationships. With careful nurturing, strong relationships enable give-and-take (Axelrod, 1984). Small "wins" can unlock the development of larger projects. Research on metropolitan governance shows that municipalities are more likely to engage in joint policy-making ventures when their political and administrative leaders come to know and trust each other (Feiock, 2013), which is more likely if they have similar professional and personal backgrounds (Foster, 2000). Building effective long-term relationships requires entrepreneurial behaviour on the part of local leaders. Agranoff (2005) has documented the proliferation of economic development partnerships between local governments and the private sector, emphasizing the central role "public executives" can play in bridging divides, convening stakeholders, building networks, and brokering agreements. Outside government, Wolfe and Nelles (2008) see a role for community leaders to deploy their "civic capital" to promote intergovernmental relationships and partnerships.

These findings are relevant to Canada's new multilevel collaborations, which have created new lines of communication among governments and between government officials and leaders of community organizations. Compared to the old days, when intergovernmental relations were more hierarchical and municipalities were generally on the receiving end of decisions made by "higher powers," today's policy tables are round and feature two-way dialogue about priorities. In such an environment, relationships matter more than ever. Building relationships across levels of government is now a key task of local administrative leaders, supplementing their other roles, as described by David Siegel (2015): "leading up" (engaging with political leadership), "leading out" (engaging with the public and community and business organizations), and "leading down" (managing the public service). We might characterize this as "leading beyond."

The media tend to focus on elected officials – how mayors and municipal associations represent city interests on Parliament Hill and at provincial legislatures. Less visible are relationships between senior administrators. Having been a provincial deputy minister, a federal Crown agency CEO, and a municipal chief administrative officer, I have sat on both sides of the table and have a particular perspective on how strong relationships can mobilize institutions and resources to move projects forward. Having worked over the years at all levels of government, I was fortunate in being able to build trust, respect, and support through those relationships.

Selling Winnipeg Hydro

One example that stands out in my mind is the sale of Winnipeg Hydro to Manitoba Hydro. The City of Winnipeg and several surrounding municipalities were amalgamated on 1 January 1972, creating a new single-tier municipal government. Thirty years later, however, some services remained unconsolidated. Electricity distribution, welfare, and public health, for example, were municipally provided to residents of the pre-amalgamation City of Winnipeg area – only one-third of the city – while everyone else received services from the provincial utility, Manitoba Hydro. This came to be seen as inefficient and inequitable.

When I became the chief administrative officer of Winnipeg, the aging infrastructure for the city-owned electricity distribution asset, Winnipeg Hydro, was of particular concern to the municipal management team. Winnipeg Hydro produced less energy than required due to outdated infrastructure. The gap was made up by purchasing electricity from Manitoba Hydro. As in many other Canadian municipalities heavily reliant on property taxes, there was never enough funding to close the infrastructure deficit. Winnipeg Hydro's electricity rates matched those of Manitoba Hydro, which meant that additional capital could be raised only by increasing property taxes – a practical impossibility at the time. As Winnipeg Hydro had a positive reputation among residents, selling it was a sensitive issue for several municipal politicians, including the mayor, who had campaigned on a promise to keep Winnipeg Hydro in municipal hands.

The administration at the City of Winnipeg had done its homework by bringing in a team of experts to determine the current value of the asset and the discounted value of a stream of future earnings in present dollars. We also knew what kind of capital and operational investment the city would need to keep Winnipeg Hydro economically viable. Going into negotiations with the province, the city had all it needed to bargain in its best interests. At the time, there was significant public pressure to release the work of the experts; however, we knew that we would be at a commercial disadvantage if we made this information public. A publicly known appraised value likely would become the price ceiling. Due to the potential financial harm to the city with its release, the information was not subject to freedom of information requests. I led the conversation with the politicians behind closed doors to help them understand the risks and accept my advice and that of my chief financial officer. Eventually, we released a report that stated the reasons the City of Winnipeg could not make public the work of the expert appraisers.

Having worked with many of the provincial deputy ministers in key departments, including Treasury Board, Finance, and what is now called Crown Services, I was able to have meaningful discussions on the merits of the sale for both parties, the communication strategy, and how negotiations between the parties might work.

The union leadership was on board. They realized that, if Winnipeg Hydro continued to deteriorate, jobs and benefits would be lost. A crucial element of the agreement, critical to union support, was the guaranteed transfer of all Winnipeg Hydro workers, and their significant current and future pension and benefit liabilities, to the provincial utility. We had learned from the earlier transfer of responsibility for social services to the province. Under that arrangement, over 100 workers were guaranteed positions within the municipal government even though there were few appropriate roles available. From the city's perspective, the best option was to transfer the entire employee complement of Winnipeg Hydro to the province with a job guarantee – an option we were pleased to secure.

In the end, Winnipeg Hydro was fully absorbed into the provincial utility. As CAO of Winnipeg, I worked with the administrative team and the mayor to look at ways to help the politicians achieve public policy objectives through the sale, and my provincial counterparts did the same. Benefits flowed to both parties. Winnipeg advanced its downtown revitalization strategy when Manitoba Hydro constructed a new, LEED-certified head office downtown. The city also achieved a measure of financial sustainability, receiving annual payments in perpetuity. As noted, all employees and associated costs were transferred to Manitoba Hydro. At the same time, Manitoba Hydro achieved economies of scale, opportunities to increase energy production, and the addition of highly skilled Winnipeg Hydro employees. Every step of the process was carefully planned and executed by administrators at both levels of government, who worked closely with the political leadership. The mayor and the premier played a key role in communicating the plan to the public.

Years later, a Manitoba Hydro board member confessed confidentially to me that Winnipeg's negotiated transfer agreement "really did well for the city." I took this as a sign of the effectiveness of our relationship-building strategy.

Institutional Context Matters for Building Intergovernmental Relationships

Although new policy collaborations promise to overcome traditional "one size fits all" approaches and to mobilize resources in more creative and effective ways, we should not forget that existing institutions and systems remain in place. As my very different experiences in Winnipeg and Victoria taught me, a municipality's ability to participate in and insert its priorities into new intergovernmental projects and programs continues to depends on its relative "heft" within the province and how it is embedded in regional institutions.

Winnipeg and Victoria are both provincial capitals, but the similarity ends there. Well over half of Manitobans – 58 per cent – live in the City of Winnipeg, and the city accounts for 91 per cent of the population of the census metropolitan area (CMA). Winnipeg is a juggernaut that dominates the province; no provincial government can ignore the city and its voters. Victoria, by contrast, accounts for only 1.8 per cent of British Columbia's population, and less than a quarter of the population of the Victoria CMA. As BC's second largest population centre after Metro Vancouver, Victoria and its region must always compete for policy attention from the provincial government. Moreover, Manitoba's federal representatives must always keep Winnipeg in mind; the same is not true of British Columbia's, who are more likely attuned to the needs of the Lower Mainland.

Their institutions also differ. With a single-tier system of local government, no intermediate layer of government or administration sits between Winnipeg and the provincial government. In contrast, since the 1960s, British Columbia's municipalities and unincorporated areas have been organized into federations called regional districts. Victoria is but one of thirteen municipalities (along with three unincorporated electoral districts and ten First Nations Reserves) that make up the Capital Regional District. It is also not the largest. Suburban Saanich, with 114,000 residents compared with Victoria's 86,000, has greater representation on the regional district board under the district's weighted voting system.

By virtue of its "heft" within the province and the absence of intermediary institutions, the City of Winnipeg was almost always at the table for discussions with the other levels of government. Public servants and the politicians frequently worked together to host major events, such as the 1999 Pan Am Games, the 2002 North American Indigenous Games, and the World Junior Hockey Championships, and they have hosted dignitaries jointly, including the Queen in 2002 and 2010, Princess Anne in 1999, and the Duke of Edinburgh in 1997. They have also worked together on emergency preparedness, including flooding events, power outages, blizzards, and the West Nile Virus. There have been long-term, tri-level infrastructure agreements and other partnerships. With origins dating back to a federal-provincial-municipal Memorandum of Understanding (MOU) signed in 1980, successive Urban Development Agreements (UDAs) for Winnipeg have leveraged public and private funds across levels of government to pursue multiple place-based policy goals: economic development, neighbourhood renewal, and Indigenous engagement in Winnipeg's inner city (Bradford, 2020, pp. 7–9). (Victoria was on track to negotiate a UDA in 2005, but tri-level agreements were curtailed when the Conservatives took power in 2006.)

Victoria, on the other hand, has had to work very hard to be at the table with the other levels of government. We often competed with the other municipalities in the region for capital money to build critical infrastructure projects. For example, Victoria was unable to secure the one-third share of provincial funding for the largest infrastructure project ever undertaken by the city – the replacement of the Johnson Street Bridge – despite having lined up a one-third share from the federal government and an additional share of Canada's Gas Tax Fund. At the same time, the province did choose to support the McKenzie Interchange in Saanich – a significant regional priority. With the spotlight often on British Columbia's larger municipalities, particularly Vancouver, Richmond, and Surrey, it was difficult to get the attention of provincial officials, especially at a political level.

Nevertheless, as provincial capitals, Winnipeg and Victoria both have large municipal, provincial, and federal government footprints. As local residents, provincial and municipal public servants might share an emotional investment in the community and understanding of what makes the city tick. Proximity lowered the cost of making informal or formal connections with public servants at other levels of government and enabled us to put city issues on the public agenda. This was particularly acute during Winnipeg's "Flood of the Century" in 1997 and subsequent recovery and mitigation investments, including expanding the floodway. All the decision makers could connect face-to-face when time was of the essence, and critical support personnel such as the Canadian Armed Forces provided flood protection relief and emergency management expertise to both the city and the rest of Manitoba. This factor is idiosyncratic, however, existing in only a few Canadian cities.

Building Multilevel Relationships to Address Homelessness

Despite their differences, the two cities share a common experience of how intergovernmental relationships have helped improve significant issues facing their communities. Their stories are about how a variety of participants came together to help the most vulnerable people in their community: the homeless. Both communities, like many cities in Canada, struggle to find housing for individuals and families who cannot secure safe, appropriate housing because of financial, mental, behavioural, physical, and other challenges.

An important impetus for multilevel action on homelessness was the federal government's 1999 National Homelessness Initiative (later renamed the Homelessness Partnering Strategy), which invested $753 million over three years and has since been renewed several times. Rather than pursuing a top-down, command-and-control approach, the federal government devised a multilevel collaborative model, whereby federal fiscal resources are directed towards priorities set by local tables that bring together community-based stakeholders with officials from all levels of government (Taylor & Bradford, 2015, pp. 205–6). Federal funds are directed towards the communities with the greatest need, and local partners have considerable flexibility in the design of local programs within general guidelines. Since fiscal year 2014/15, the program has emphasized a housing-first approach to homelessness.

Winnipeg

In 2000, Winnipeg had a large number of homeless or near homeless people living in short-term or crisis shelters and on the street. The city's long, cold winters pose significant dangers to this vulnerable sector. Winnipeg also has the largest Indigenous population of all Canadian cities, and Indigenous people are disproportionately represented among the homeless: the Homeless Hub reported that, in 2018, the share of respondents to a Winnipeg street survey identifying as Indigenous was 65.9 per cent (Homeless Hub, 2019). The homeless population was also growing as newcomers to Winnipeg from rural Manitoba failed to secure adequate housing or culturally appropriate support upon arrival. Complicating the situation were low vacancy rates for rental properties and rental assistance programs that provided less than the average rental cost. The situation could not continue. The community looked to its political leaders to find solutions.

The governments of Canada, Manitoba, and the City of Winnipeg strategized about how best to revitalize Winnipeg's inner city and address homelessness. The initiative was led by political leaders of the day and sustained over thirteen years by administrators at all three levels of government. Lloyd Axworthy, Minister of Foreign Affairs and Member of Parliament for Winnipeg South Centre, was keenly interested in urban renewal; Winnipeg mayor Glen Murray was passionate about revitalizing the downtown; and Premier Gary Doer recognized the challenges facing Winnipeg's inner city and wanted to help solve them.

When I became Winnipeg's CAO in 1998, I led a far-reaching reorganization of city government. I was the first CAO, taking over from a board of commissioners. An implicit part of my new job was to prove – to City Council, senior staff, and the community – the merit of the council-manager model of civic administration, in contrast to the arrangements that preceded me. A key part of my work in those years was bringing about positive culture change while at the same time making deep changes to institutional structures. In this context, I sought to focus the city's attention on profound challenges facing the city, including inner-city revitalization and homelessness. I actively supported the mayor's push for federal-provincial-municipal action by mobilizing our team's knowledge and resources.

In 2000, the three levels of government signed an MOU to establish the Winnipeg Housing and Homelessness Initiative (WHHI). The MOU was renewed in 2003 and again in 2008 to extend the mandate until 2013. The essence of the initiative was to provide a one-stop service for individuals and community organizations to access needed information on housing and homelessness programs. After numerous discussions, housing staff involved from all three levels of government decided to co-locate relevant government offices into a Single Window Office located in downtown Winnipeg. The co-location was intended to streamline processes, improve information sharing between government offices, and make it easier for individuals and the community to access services. This was recognized as an important innovation at the time, and it was unlocked by careful relationship building across government levels and silos.

The MOU also enabled the pooling of funding across levels of government to build, repair or rehabilitate housing units in Winnipeg's inner city, along with enhanced programs and services for the homeless. Funding was provided by Canada Mortgage and Housing Corporation, Manitoba Family Services and Housing, and the City of Winnipeg. Hundreds of units were built, repaired, and rehabilitated during the term of the MOU.

The WHHI evolved into a collaborative network connecting governments to neighbourhood organizations, non-profit housing groups, community service providers, financial institutions, and other industry professionals. Funding priorities were determined by the Community Plan developed by representatives of the private and voluntary sectors. A concerned group of community leaders working with managers in Winnipeg's Community Services and Planning and Development departments played keys roles in getting the WHHI launched. They were on the front line and experienced first-hand the inefficiencies of having the most vulnerable people try to navigate their way through three levels of bureaucracy. The WHHI exemplifies how multilevel governance can be place based, hitching the resources of all levels of governments to objectives determined by those who best understand community needs.

The MOU expired in 2013, but its work is continued by the Doorways initiative, which administers intake, assessment, and referral to housing support programs. The motto of Housing First Doorways says it all: *Opening doors to the resources that are right for you … community collaboration, banding together to end homelessness.*

Victoria

Much as in Winnipeg (but with a more welcoming climate), Victoria faced a growing homeless population with large numbers of people living in shelters and on the street. Victoria as a whole and its downtown in particular are geographically much smaller than Winnipeg. Shelter space is limited in the core. High property values and low vacancy rates have made rental options extremely unaffordable for a growing proportion of the population, not only in Victoria but also across the Capital Region. To compound this, in 2008, the BC Supreme Court struck down a Victoria by-law, ruling that it was unconstitutional for Victoria to restrict overnight camping in its parks if all shelter beds in the city were full. Being a small city with very limited resources that is embedded in an institutionally complex metropolitan area, Victoria could not address the crisis on its own. But, as in Winnipeg, the situation could not continue, and the community looked to its political leaders to find solutions.

In 2007, Victoria's then-mayor Alan Lowe commissioned a task force of community and business leaders to examine the challenges faced by residents – mental illness, addictions, and homelessness – and recommend actions to address them. As a result of the task force's recommendations, the Greater Victoria Coalition to End Homelessness was formed in 2008. The Coalition was much more than an intergovernmental initiative, although each level of government contributed resources to it. The Coalition also involved service providers, non-profit organizations, business, post-secondary institutions, faith organizations, people with lived experience of being homeless, and community volunteers. Groups included the Boys and Girls Club of Victoria, the Victoria Foundation, Binkadi Community Services (a social enterprise catering to people who fall through the cracks between established programs), the YMCA-YWCA, and the Aboriginal Coalition to End Homelessness.

At the City of Victoria, both the politicians and we in the administration worked hard to support the Coalition's advocacy for new funding from all levels of government for housing and operating dollars to keep the work of the Coalition going. We committed funding in our annual budgets (both capital and operating), ensured that municipal expertise (including police, fire, and planning) was there to help, and by serving as Coalition Board and Committee members. We also engaged with the community to raise awareness and support for the cause. Although homelessness remains a problem in the Capital Region, the Coalition has made significant strides in creating housing and housing supports.

From Local Advocacy to Multilevel Action

These stories show how important local alignment of advocacy is to building relationships across levels of government. As a municipal administrator, I worked closely with the mayor, community organizations, unions, and so on to create a local consensus on issues that we could bring to other levels of government. A key challenge for dealing with other levels of government is identifying your interlocutor. At the provincial level, the municipal affairs ministry is the logical contact point for many legal and regulatory questions concerning municipalities; however, for many issues we had to make other connections. This can be especially difficult at the federal level, where there is no minister responsible for municipal affairs, and experiments with an urban affairs ministry have been fleeting. Linking social welfare, public health, housing, and downtown revitalization, homelessness illustrates the complex interweaving of policy sectors and government jurisdictions.

One of the virtues of Winnipeg's urban development agreements is that they formalized communication pathways between sectoral leads at the local, provincial, and federal levels, cross-cutting silos and constitutional jurisdiction. The strategy of bundling sectoral issues to address place-based problems meant that we did not have to rely on a single interlocutor at other levels of government. Nevertheless, we – the local administrative and political leadership – had to work hard to make and maintain relationships with counterparts at other levels.

Gender and Leadership

These experiences illustrate the importance of collaboration in city leadership and highlight the importance of intergovernmental relationship building. A key aspect that must be considered is gender: I was the first CAO of Winnipeg, having replaced an all-male Board of Commissioners. In meeting after meeting, I was often the only woman in the room. I remember attending my first North American Big City Caucus in 1998. While getting a glass of wine at a reception for the delegates and their partners, the woman next to me in line asked, "which city does your husband manage?"

At the beginning, there was a significant fear of the unknown within the organization. Could this woman really lead the city? Will she be too emotional? Does she know what she is doing? At my first meeting with the leadership team, no one said a word as they wrote down everything I said. At a time when few women were in leadership positions, I was surprised that some women were less than supportive. To be sure, I was mentored by the first female mayor of Winnipeg, Susan Thompson, who wholeheartedly believed in what I could accomplish for the city. But this was not always the case. During a strategic planning session with the senior leadership team, for example, I overheard a female executive on the phone telling someone that the session was an enormous waste of her time.

In my experience, men and women have different leadership styles and approach relationship building differently. Women tend to communicate more openly through words, while men seem to prefer action to words. Women tend to look for connection and support in relationships. For example, women tend to ask a lot of questions before projects begin, while men tend to dive in. Most women work in a naturally collaborative way, while men routinely challenge others and expect to be challenged as well. Women tend to be more compassionate and willing to spend time in building relationships, while men are anxious to get down to brass tacks. Ultimately, I think being a woman helped in intergovernmental relations. The sale of Winnipeg Hydro showed how seeing both sides of an argument and demonstrating empathy and understanding can lead to "win-win" compromises despite significant obstacles. As governing has become more complex and interconnected, the capacity for empathetic collaboration has become an essential skill.

Much has changed in twenty-five years. When I was first appointed CAO in 1998, you could count the number of women leaders of major North American cities on one hand. There are now many more women serving in government leadership positions across Canada, not only at the municipal level, but also provincially and federally. Mentorship by women leaders in my generation, who had overcome these barriers, cleared the way for those who followed.

Lessons Learned

My experiences in Winnipeg and Victoria taught me how important relationships between governments are to tackling important community problems. I will conclude with four lessons I have learned about relationship building: be proactive, inclusive, clear about shared goals, and transparent.

Be proactive: To build effective relationships, you cannot wait for other people to come to you; you need to go to them. This requires respecting other people's turf and giving a little before making demands on other people's time and resources. Meeting in person signals dedication and respect, as does showing gratitude and giving public credit to people for their contributions. You need to invest the time and energy in fostering trust and respect. It also means developing some of the key relationships well in advance of an emerging issue or crisis. Established relationships and already being a "trusted advisor" work better than "cold calls" to people who might not even know what a "city manager" is and does.

Be inclusive: An effective policy collaboration must have all the key players around the table. Identifying who they are requires keeping your ear to the ground and being out in the community. Not everyone might trust local government; you need to remain humble and earn the trust of community stakeholders and your counterparts in other governments. This was especially important in the homelessness initiatives in both cities, where we had to nurture relationships with a wide range of organizations with differing interests.

Be clear about shared goals: If the parties around the table agree on and are committed to the objectives of the program or project, disagreements on other issues can be managed and overcome. You need to assign your most creative and innovative people to the collaboration. Front-line employees need to be deeply involved from the onset and they need to see the benefits of the collaboration and work together as a team in solving issues that arise.

Be transparent: Always make sure that no meetings end with unanswered questions, and make sure the politicians and community leaders are kept fully informed of decisions made. This means taking a "no surprises" approach. If something is about to hit the media – good or bad – make sure the other party is aware. In that vein, be aware that the municipal political environment is not the same as a legislature or Parliament Hill, where "loyalty" and consistent support are prized. In the municipal world, today's critic on one issue frequently can be tomorrow's supporter on another – and civil servants are quoted in the media. At the provincial and federal level, however, criticism, complaints, or demands on other issues by city officials (whether political or management) might confuse or undermine the confidence of key provincial or federal officials. This is exemplified by the Winnipeg Hydro case, where we had to walk a fine line between being highly transparent in negotiations, but also carefully manage the expectations of the public and politicians.

Conclusion

To conclude, city managers work in an increasingly challenging and multidimensional environment that requires them to make new kinds of relationships. As Siegel (2015) writes, they not only lead *up* by informing and presenting options to elected officials, lead *down* as heads of the local public service, and lead *out* by communicating with the public. They also lead *beyond* local institutions by building and nurturing relationships with their counterparts in other levels of government.

The impetus for multilevel relationship building starts with a significant community issue that the local municipality cannot address on its own. Recent decades have seen the emergence of new models of intergovernmental collaboration to address place-based problems. Constructing multilevel relationships takes political leadership from the mayor, as well as from provincial and federal elected officials. It also takes strong community input and support. Nevertheless, senior administrators, often working behind the scenes, play an essential role by mobilizing their cross-level professional relationships, expertise, and resources to create and sustain multilevel partnerships. These roles and skills will only become more important as such arrangements become more common.

REFERENCES

Agranoff, R. (2005). Managing collaborative performance: Changing the boundaries of the state? *Public Performance & Management Review 29*(1), 18–45. http://doi.org/10.1080/15309576.2005.11051856

Axelrod, R. (1984). *The evolution of cooperation*. Basic Books.

Bradford, N. (2018, 15 November). A national urban policy for Canada? The implicit federal agenda. *IRPP Insight* 24.

Bradford, N. (2020). Policy in place: Revisiting Canada's tri-level agreements. IMFG Papers on Municipal Finance and Governance 50. Institute on Municipal Finance & Governance. https://tspace.library.utoronto.ca/bitstream/1807/124753/1/imfgpaper_no60_inclusivegovernance.pdf

Cooper, R. (1996). Municipal law, delegated legislation and democracy. *Canadian Public Administration 39*(3), 290–313. http://doi.org/10.1111/j.1754-7121.1996.tb00134.x

Feiock, R. C. (2013). The institutional collective action framework. *Policy Studies Journal 41*(3), 397–425. https://doi.org/10.1111/psj.12023

Foster, K. A. (2000). Regional capital. In R. Greenstein and W. Wiewel (Eds.), *Urban-suburban dependencies* (pp. 83–118). Lincoln Institute of Land Policy.

Hirschl, R. (2020). *City, state: Constitutionalism and the megacity*. Oxford University Press.

Homeless Hub. (2019). Community profile: Winnipeg. Retrieved 5 October 2019 from https://www.homelesshub.ca/community-profile/winnipeg

Hooghe, L., & Marks, G. (2003). Unraveling the central state, but how? Types of multi-level governance. *American Political Science Review 97*(2), 233–43. https://doi.org/10.1017/S0003055403000649

Horak, M. (2013). "State rescaling in practice: Urban governance reform in Toronto." *Urban Research & Practice 6*(3), 311–28. http://doi.org/10.1080/17535069.2013.846005

Horak, M., & Young, R. (Eds.). (2012). *Sites of governance: Multilevel governance and policy making in Canada's big cities*. McGill-Queen's University Press.

Leo, C. (2006). Deep federalism: Respecting community difference in national policy." *Canadian Journal of Political Science 39*(3), 481–506. http://doi.org/10.1017/S0008423906060240

Siegel, D. (2015.) *Leaders in the shadows: The leadership qualities of municipal chief administrative officers*. University of Toronto Press.

Slack, N. E. (2009, 17–18 September). Provincial-local fiscal transfers in Canada: Provincial control trumps local accountability. Conference on General Grants vs. Earmarked Grants: Theory and Practice, Copenhagen.

Taylor, Z., & Bradford, N. (2015). The new localism: Canadian urban governance in the twenty-first century. In P. Filion, M. Moos, T. Vinodrai, &

R. Walker (Eds.), *Canadian cities in transition: Perspectives for an urban age* (pp. 194–208). Oxford University Press.

Taylor, Z., & Bradford, N. (2020). Governing Canadian cities. In M. Moos, T. Vinodrai, & R. Walker (Eds.), *Canadian cities in transition* (pp. 33–50). Oxford University Press.

Taylor, Z., & Dobson, A. (2019). Power and purpose: Canadian municipal law in transition. IMFG Papers on Municipal Finance and Governance 47. Institute on Municipal Finance & Governance. https://tspace.library.utoronto.ca/bitstream/1807/99780/1/IMFG_Paper_No47_Power_and_Purpose_Taylor_Dobson.pdf

Tindal, C. R., Nobes Tindal, S., Stewart, K., & Smith, P. J. (2017). *Local government in Canada* (9th ed.). Nelson.

Wolfe, D. A., & Nelles, J. (2008). The role of civic capital and civic associations in cluster policy." In C. Karlsson (Ed.), *Handbook of research on innovation and clusters: Cases and policies* (pp. 374–92). Edward Elgar.

16 More than Resilience: Towards an "Antifragile" Organization – The Case of Gatineau

MARIE-HÉLÈNE LAJOIE AND PIERRE PRÉVOST

The City of Gatineau is one of Quebec's largest cities; most of Canada knows it as the "other half" of Canada's National Capital Region. Gatineau's award-winning former city manager, Marie-Hélène Lajoie, also has the unhappy distinction of knowing more about managing civic crises than any city manager would want to, following a succession of floods, a major tornado, and COVID-19. With her co-author, Université du Québec à Montréal associate professor and municipal expert Pierre Prévost, Lajoie provides an extensive, experience-enriched analysis of the best ways to prepare, mobilize, and restore your community in the face of the disastrous events that can strike any municipality. They conclude that a municipality needs to be more than just "robust" in its response: the goal is to attain "antifragility."

The purpose of this chapter is to describe how the City of Gatineau, Quebec, has dealt with a series of crises in the past few years and to develop some lessons learned that will be valuable to other municipalities. Gatineau is a particularly good candidate to tell this story because it has been visited with a tornado, several floods, and, of course, the COVID-19 pandemic, and it has learned some important lessons in dealing with those crises.

We begin with a short description of the city and the context surrounding its approach to crises. The following section discusses the challenges facing the municipal organization before, during, and after emergency situations. The next section focuses on the effects of crises on the municipal organization and its stakeholders in the short, medium, and long term. The final section provides advice to other municipalities in the form of lessons learned, before the conclusion ties this story together.

The City of Gatineau and Its Experience of Emergency Situations

The City of Gatineau (Ville de Gatineau) is the product of an amalgamation of five former cities and a regional government in 2002. It has almost 300,000 residents, which makes it the fourth-largest city in Quebec and the eighteenth-largest city in Canada, and it is continuing to grow. Gatineau forms most of the Quebec portion of the National Capital Region of Canada, which it shares with Ottawa on the Ontario side. In 2020, the city had more than 3,500 employees and a budget of $650 million.

The city manages all public security (police, fire, 911) and civil security services. Its territory covers 342 square kilometres, and has an urban area mainly located in the south and a rural area farther north. It is bordered by the Ottawa River and crossed by three major rivers that flow into it: the Gatineau, the Lièvre, and the Blanche. This hydrography is important, as it occasionally creates a very serious risk of flooding.

Of course, we do not intend to compare our experiences to disasters of a much greater magnitude such as those faced by Lac-Mégantic, Quebec (a 2013 rail derailment that destroyed the entire downtown area and claimed forty-seven direct victims) or Fort McMurray, Alberta (the 2017 forest fires that razed entire neighbourhoods and a major flood in the city centre in the spring of 2020, during the pandemic). Fortunately, our experience with emergencies does not compare to these dire situations, but our lived experience has common elements that might give many of our municipal peers fresh insights, particularly in the following two ways.

First, for the five years during which the events unfolded, the same two incumbents occupied the positions of mayor and city manager. This "continuity in misfortune" offers an interesting example of the adaptation of roles (and people) as events unfold.

Second, all these emergency measures episodes happened in parallel while we were continuing to deliver municipal services elsewhere in our municipality in an almost normal fashion. Although they were significant disasters, they never affected the entire municipality (except, though on a different scale, for the COVID-19 pandemic).

Although it has suffered various natural disasters before, Gatineau now seems resigned to the realities that have generated emergency preparation and/or interventions for four years in a row. Our serial woes began in the spring of 2017 with major flooding, followed in September 2018 by a category 3 (F-3) tornado, a landmark event that razed a significant portion of a neighbourhood in seconds. In the spring of 2019, another series of flooding events occurred, even more severe than those of 2017. We naively believed that the year 2020 would allow us to breathe a bit and get back on track with our professional and personal lives. In March, however, the COVID-19 pandemic forced us to modify fundamentally the deployment of our services in response to directives issued by Quebec Public Health. Luckily there were no floods in the spring of 2020; however, the emergency response plan had had to be adapted to make it functional in times of a pandemic, especially since the pandemic was expected to last until late 2021.

Adequate preparation is an essential obligation for municipal organizations, but it is insufficient to ensure the success of the response. Because this was a priority for the then-city manager and council, the newly amalgamated City of Gatineau got itself prepared. It had complied with the obligations prescribed for municipalities by Quebec's Civil Protection Act. It had carried out various vulnerability studies in a timely fashion and it had adopted a Civil Security Plan, along with seventeen "sectoral" plans flowing from it. From this point of view, it can be said that we were quite well prepared to live through disruptive events, such as those we later endured. But over four consecutive years of such events, it was the repetition that proved to be an unprecedented test for the organization.

Usually, an organization can put a climatic event or a disaster behind it after a recovery period, but the recurring events experienced by the City of Gatineau have probably marked our organization for a generation. We have lost the equivalent of three months each year in which to carry out our normal municipal operations and our usual planning. We explain this in more detail in the following pages because this is a source of "added value," drawn from our varied and cumulative experience. And as the title of the chapter suggests, beyond simple resilience, we believe that municipal organizations should learn the basics of what Nassim Nicholas Taleb (2012) has called "antifragility": "Antifragility is beyond resilience or robustness. The resilient resists shocks and stays the same; the antifragile gets better" or, ultimately, tends to learn during each episode of crisis and to improve over time.

The Challenges Facing the Municipal Organization Before, During, and After Emergency Situations

The daily life of a municipality is turned upside down in several ways when an emergency arises. Obviously, the magnitude of the challenge matches the severity of the situation, but we must maintain the services that the majority of residents expect to receive – because it is rare that the entire municipality is affected in the same way – while intervening

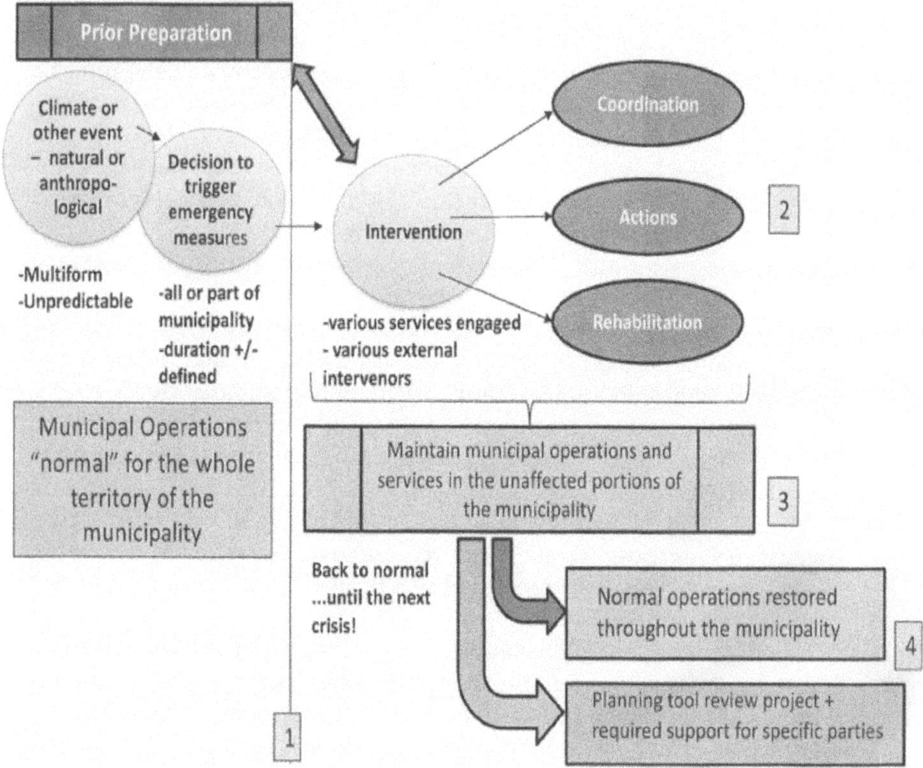

Figure 16.1 Sequence and Consequences of an Emergency Situation

in the affected area(s) in an emergency operational mode. Finally, we need to draw lessons and collect information that will allow us to adapt the municipality or organization to enable it to get through a similar situation better in the future.

Figure 16.1 reflects the reality that the municipal organization faces with such a problem. It illustrates the three phases of the emergency life cycle: preparation, intervention, and return to normal. Some authors propose four stages: preparation, mitigation, intervention, and return to normal (Henstra, 2010). Mitigation refers to the preparatory efforts of the municipal administration to minimize the possible effects of an apprehended situation, through preventive planning, the availability of special equipment, adequate regulations, and so forth. For our part, we integrate the mitigation aspect into the preparation phase.

Preparing for Emergency Situations (The "Before")

In figure 16.1 the intervention in an emergency situation is to the right of the vertical line. It is part of advance planning that is incorporated into the sectoral intervention plans. The quality of sectoral plans (floods, major disasters, earthquakes, etc.) is measured by the completeness of their inventories of risk and resources, among other things. The level of detail in the plans varies (French, 2011). The plans are adopted by the city and put into practice during simulations that allow everyone in the organization to better understand their own role, the roles of others, and their interactions, which allows them to identify areas of weakness, difficulties in the field, and so forth. As Henstra rightly points out, "[t]he quality of a Local Government's emergency planning largely determines the effectiveness of its response efforts when disaster strikes" (Henstra, 2010, p. 236).

Everything to the left of the vertical line refers to the operations and services that a municipality delivers on a daily basis. This normal operation includes prior preparation for emergency situations, as well as preparing emergency plans and adapting regulations to reduce the impacts of an emergency situation. It also includes a civil security watch activity, which ensures not only that the administrative processes related to emergency preparedness have an owner, but also that the leaders of the organization are able to make the necessary arrangements to initiate emergency measures. Anticipation is a decisive factor in emergency-related decision making. It is better to put the organization on an unnecessary alert for a few hours than to delay and risk more serious problems. The consequences of a delay in intervening are significant. For example, we lose crucial hours if managers are difficult to reach or if maintenance teams are reduced during the weekend.

It is difficult to maintain the interest of the city council and the municipal administration in preparedness (Prévost, 2018, p. 133). Making this an important part of the organizational culture will focus the attention of managers on the need to ensure that the organization is ready and that the emergency intervention process will be successful.

The "culture of emergency" that permeates the municipal organization ensures that senior managers are attuned to the importance of preparedness. For example, annual emergency-situation simulations have always been carried out in the City of Gatineau to ensure that all managers are able to understand the scope of their role and the nature of their interactions with other managers.

In 2015, the City of Gatineau invested in the establishment of a permanent, well-equipped Emergency Measures Coordination Centre (known by its French acronym, the CCMU), as well as an emergency operations centre (French acronym COUS), in the same location. In the same year, working jointly with a private firm,[1] we also set up an emergency application ("Urgento") for smartphones. This capacity gave us the flexibility to operate more efficiently, especially at the crucial moment of triggering the emergency declaration. Getting a head start in emergency response interventions provides valuable time.

Back in 2002, the new City of Gatineau had created an administrative division responsible for civil security (which later became the "Civil Security Office"), with specific responsibility for preparation tasks, monitoring, and coordinating post-event recovery. The city council of the day saw the need to undertake four measures to deal with potential emergencies: (a) prepare intervention plans; (b) establish an adequate training and implementation regime; (c) put in place adequate infrastructure and equipment; and (d) create a specialized administrative division for the task. Each of these initiatives had been recommended by the city manager and the administration. While not perfect, Gatineau's anticipatory measures meant that the city was not caught off guard when a large-scale emergency hit in the form of the spring floods of 2017.

Intervention in Emergency Situations (The "During")

Intervention is the second phase identified in figure 16.1. It can be broken down into coordination, field operations, and rehabilitation, with a cross-cutting emphasis on good communication.

COORDINATION

In an emergency, coordination is the key to success! Even more than in a normal situation, it is a question of properly coordinating the actions of different departments, transmitting new information in real time, and allocating resources quickly. It shakes up conventions and habits.

The intervention phase of an emergency response always begins with communications to our employees by the Urgento app (when an emergency is anticipated) and to the general population (if it becomes a

1 The private firm collaborated in the development of a software tool called RBSoft. Urgento's specific ringtone sounds even if the phone is in silent mode. Using Urgento saves precious minutes calling out members of the Emergency Measures Coordination Centre in the event of an alert.

crisis). The message must be effective and concise, and it must convey our concerns "in clear language, not alarmist, empathetic and reassuring" (Dancause, 2017). Communication must be fast, to prevent social media from distorting the problem, and multimodal, because residents now have a choice among several channels of communication.

Emergency situations stimulate the flow of adrenaline: emergencies mean long hours on the job even if some people are not used to this kind of schedule; decisions must be made immediately despite incomplete information; and emergencies require interdepartmental teamwork and a flattening of administrative organization charts. In the events from 2017 through 2019, this coordination function was carried out mainly through the CCMU and, at a more local or tactical level, by the municipal COUS. The regular feedback of information from the field to the control centre made it possible to better coordinate all operations and prioritize certain actions.

The city manager has a multipronged role in coordinating emergency measures. First, there is the responsibility for ongoing operations of the municipality. This is the primary daily concern of the majority of residents, local businesses, and city council members, even if there is an emergency situation somewhere in the municipality. Second, there is the coordination of emergency measures being carried out on a continuous schedule and requiring a special presence and focus at the operational level. Third is coordination with elected representatives, including the mayor's office. During an emergency, this expands to include officials of other governments. Fourth, there is planning for changes that will result from the emergency situation which can affect the municipal organization and future municipal planning. In other words, preparing for the post-crisis period.

Since this is an inordinately heavy burden for one person, the City of Gatineau has entrusted a deputy city manager with the job of ensuring the continuity of regular services and operations, while coordination of emergency measures is assigned to another deputy city manager, thus leaving the city manager more time to devote to other tasks – in particular, liaison with political leaders and officials of other governments. From our hard-learned experience, these latter responsibilities are to be considered critical in terms of scope, and require a link with political stakeholders and other organizations, beyond the operational aspects managed by the CCMU that only the city manager can fulfil.

FIELD OPERATIONS

The City of Gatineau's actions have focused on the evacuation and reception of disaster victims who can no longer reside in their homes, the mitigation of effects of floods, and aid and support for victims trying to preserve their properties against storm damage. During the floods, a significant part of the operations focused on securing places and people, particularly with the help of nautical patrols and calls to residents. Another significant part of the operations involved delivering and filling sandbags or raising access routes, in order to keep as many properties as possible from the effects of water and from being physically cut off.

During all these activities, communications must be efficient 24/7 between city services, coordinated either by the CCMU (when more strategic or on a bigger scale) or the COUS (if more local and/or operational). The city must also be effective in communicating with other intervenors (e.g., to convene on specific operations) and the population in general (to inform and, when necessary, direct the help).

As part of these operations, the city has sometimes departed from its normal procurement policies for goods and services in order to speed up the response. Since the Charter of the City of Gatineau grants it extraordinary powers in the event of a crisis, including spending power, there was no need for a declaration of a state of emergency, as normally would be the case for the majority of Quebec municipalities.

REHABILITATION

The rehabilitation phase involves bringing affected people, affected sites, and operations or services back to something resembling normal conditions. It involves cleaning the sites used to fill sandbags, helping disaster victims get rid of the thousands of stacked sandbags, and rehabilitating parks, signage, and other properties that were damaged during the emergency.

Recovery is difficult to define. It goes beyond the usual mandates of a municipality and often resembles social services more than community services. Experience teaches us, however, that disasters produce many jurisdictional "grey areas," and by default the municipality often inherits them. Luckily for disaster victims who continue to need support ranging from housing rehabilitation to dealing with mental health issues, our municipal workforce has developed a range of skills to assist with these issues.

Restoration remains poorly defined. We can establish the moment when it *begins* (generally when the operational dimension of municipal activities returns to normal), but it remains difficult to declare its *end,* since support for disaster victims continues to engage the city for some time. The municipality often remains the only organization that maintains a presence on the ground in direct contact with the disaster victims, even for activities that should not, at first blush, be seen as the responsibility of the city. Although city staff might be in the community after the emergency, they and staff of other agencies inevitably return to their normal day-to-day duties and become less involved in the resolution of difficult post-disaster issues.

Experience teaches us that a sense of urgency must continue to ensure that the various bureaucracies, whether city services or external agencies, do not lose sight of the goal of a successful conclusion. For example, recent immigrants affected by the disasters had difficulty expressing themselves in French and were unfamiliar with our practices and customs, making it even harder for them to get by on their own. On a human level, such situations proved to be more difficult to cope with than the floods.

The Peculiarities of a Pandemic

A pandemic like the one that has affected the world's population since the start of 2020 is a health emergency rather than a civil security emergency. However, like all organizations and employers providing essential services, municipalities had a duty to adapt quickly to support the health effort and to assume various other related responsibilities. The effects of a pandemic on municipal activities and facilities produce the challenges of staff reassignments in the many essential tasks (water production, snow removal, police, fire, and so forth) and the redesign of both workplaces and public spaces. Of course, such a context will cruelly underline the various fragilities pre-existing in the organization, such as a lack of necessary redundancy in key personnel and strategic activities. Our experience shows that the human resources department and the technology department are truly on the front line in this type of crisis.

Here is a brief overview of Gatineau's municipal activities cancelled or postponed, facilities temporarily closed, and changes to certain uses and operational procedures:

- most planned public consultations;
- public performances in municipal facilities;
- the city-wide "spring cleaning" program (a residents' voluntary program supervised by city staff);
- compost distribution;
- sports and aquatic centres, arenas;
- service counters and reception centres for residents;
- administrative offices, the municipal court, the community police station;
- settling remote work arrangements for nearly 900 employees, which implies purchasing bandwidth, increasing cybersecurity, purchasing personal IT equipment, and so forth; and
- revised disinfection protocols for facilities, sites, and equipment.

Return to Normal: Continuity for Some and a Return to Normal for Others (The "After")

In parallel with the intervention mentioned in figure 16.1, the municipal organization must maintain the usual services across the municipality, while minimizing disruption. When an emergency affects 20 per cent of the population, the remaining 80 per cent believe that the city should continue to do its regular job. However, a situation that affects only a minority of residents can consume up to 80 per cent of a city's effort and resources.

Maintaining services elsewhere in the municipality during an emergency response depends very much on the duration of the event. If it lasts beyond a few days, a plan "B" is required to deal with overtime, staff reallocations, or modified service contracts with suppliers. To properly pace the additional effort required of our employees, the private sector is also called upon to carry out certain routine municipal operations (roadway crack filling, cleaning streets, and so forth). Good labour relations can facilitate setting aside certain provisions of collective agreements (e.g., callback lists, schedules).

Every councillor should be kept in the loop from the beginning so they understand that the exigencies of the emergency situation will sometimes interfere with the normal expectations of service delivery. Council members will also come to understand that the emergency event could mean important changes for the future, whether by postponing or cancelling certain activities or projects, or by requiring regulatory changes. The city manager should devote considerable time to this task, because when the emergency vanishes, everybody has a natural tendency to get back to where they stood before the interruption.

The final step envisioned in figure 16.1 is the return to normal, but this is often a new normal. Indeed, an emergency has many effects on a municipal organization – to say nothing of when emergencies recur almost without interruption. As stated before, some of the residue of the recovery phase can drag on for months or years. An impressive amount of administrative work most certainly will be required to receive the financial compensation promised by other levels of government during the event. And that is without counting the effort devoted to the post-event evaluation, to learn lessons for any future similar event.

In addition, the information drawn from lived experience can lead to adjustments in the internal organization and land-use planning principles – notably, to respond to and take into account the multiple impacts of climate change. This new context means that yesterday's answers (e.g., preparation) probably will not be sufficient to cope with tomorrow's situations. We will have to adapt constantly the level of our preparedness.

Emergencies undeniably create an additional workload for managers and staff. This can be alleviated, however, by adequate prior preparation, including developing a strong culture of emergency, which might be best defined as the integration in normal municipal operations of the inevitable "hijacking" of resources that an emergency event will mean. To put it briefly, a municipal organization does not substitute an emergency response for its usual work; it *superimposes* it. This is true before, during, and after an emergency situation. It is important to instil a "culture of urgency" that permeates every level of the organization. The role of the city manager as the promoter of this culture is, of course, irreplaceable.

Effects on the Municipal Organization and Stakeholders in the Short, Medium, and Long Term

The Organizational Effects

In crisis situations, emergency responses frequently need to be coordinated between the municipality and other organizations with legitimate roles, operating in the same geographic area – mainly public utility companies and provincial authorities in public health or civil security, and sometimes even the military. A review of the handling of Hurricane Katrina argued that it was important to employ "collaborative management" and to recognize the areas of strength of individual organizations. This allowed the organizations "to become aware of the skills and knowledge needed to build trusting and lasting relationships with fellow collaborators" (Koliba et al., 2011, p. 218).

Gatineau accepted this idea of collaborative management, which is likely one reason it fared better than other regions where there was a great deal of "editorial noise" emitted by political actors and the media.[2] Our hypothesis is that a city like Gatineau, both by its size and by the seriousness of its preparation, turns out to be generally better equipped and, above all, better informed on the evolution of

2 We are referring here to debates that have taken place between municipalities and ministries on the subject of reciprocal responsibilities during emergency situations, including the aspects of restoration, financing, and modifications to flood zone maps. While not without problems, the City of Gatineau's issues have not proved to be insurmountable. A certain amount of duplication exists, however, between two civil security coordination "tables" operating in the same territory (the city and the regional civil security department). For example, this could be resolved easily enough, in order to avoid wasting time, if each table dealt exclusively with its own portion of territory.

emergency situations. This gives the municipality de facto authority that is not called into question by external stakeholders such as the military, provincial health and social service authorities, and so forth. These stakeholders are then more willing to place themselves in a collaborative mode.[3] Some of these organizations even participate in simulations organized by the City of Gatineau to improve our common response in case of emergency. The simple fact that it is familiar ground for the municipality allows it to capitalize on this advantage.

Trust between organizations is crucial to avoiding unwanted slippages, as the following example will illustrate. During the 2017 flood, the local gas distributor wanted to shut off its gas supply to a particular street to avoid sending its staff into flooded conditions. The city, however, did not want to evacuate hundreds of additional victims. At the city's request, the distributor immediately changed its mind.

In an emergency, organizational leadership is essential because there is no time to explain everything or to justify some decisions. The City of Gatineau has positioned itself as a leader in each of the emergency situations it experienced between 2017 and 2019, counting on – and appreciating – the collaboration of many stakeholders of all kinds. The city has never hesitated to exercise leadership in any situation, even if this occasionally has created discomfort within the hierarchies of partner organizations. This leadership role has allowed it to avoid the situation where "coordination may suffer from 'underlap' in the exercise of authority" (Christensen et al., 2016, p. 892). For example, the military normally would take control of operations, but this is not what happened in Gatineau. This is also the reason the city manager had to prioritize her tasks, giving her a more effective coordinating role with the city council, the mayor's office, and the higher echelons of other organizations.

In the face of dealing with this serious crisis, the city also hosted several impromptu visits by senior officials and other dignitaries who came to share the victims' distress. The photo-ops and security obligations required in connection with visits by these distinguished visitors can be a burden on already overwhelmed teams, especially when the dignitaries want to visit the operations centre. However, it is simply a question of making necessary adjustments, because in return we have

3 Of course, there were a few "hiccups" over several weeks of parallel intervention by many stakeholders. Most of the time, these were initiatives that had not been announced or discussed at the CCMU, but this is more anecdote than a deliberate disregard of the opinions of other stakeholders.

seen first-hand the positive effects that these short visits can have on the victims and on the population in general.

These situations highlight the need to improve some critical operations, by making them more resistant to any emergency situation that can – and will probably – occur. Operators and equipment at the water plants are the most obvious examples of this need. Better and more frequent training and more equipment readily available in some key locations are other improvements that we are trying to implement in Gatineau. Thus, the task is more than just replacing equipment or having people rested, which would compare to "resilience." We try to make the whole organization "antifragile," as this concept was already described earlier in this chapter. We want to go beyond restoring operations to their previous level; antifragility means that we are making these operations more robust so that they will be able to withstand future emergencies better.

The whole idea is to attain a capacity to learn from our experiences that goes far beyond simple debriefings and subsequent adjustments; the "antifragile" nature of our organization must therefore be independent from the person that leads it (the city manager). As the first level of public management, always close to the residents and what affects them in their daily life, we must respond more appropriately in the future to events that take root in emergency episodes. This will also require a continued commitment by council to get the necessary budgets approved. There is a serious challenge ahead of us.

This objective will become evident to any city manager in the coming years. Those who still have not been overwhelmed by recurring emergency situations will need to learn resilience, which already presents some difficulties, and budgetary issues. Emergency management at the municipal level gradually will be accepted as a new "line of business." Natural disasters and emergency situations, combined with the expectations of the public, will produce a change in the type of experience and training that will be deemed indispensable for various positions in our organizations. This will be a challenge as well as an opportunity since many people who would never have hoped to work in our field of activity might find a place and enrich our organization. This eventually will come out in the recruitment of human resources, procurement decisions, and labour contracts – for example, making room for adjustments in job description in times of emergency.

Employees

Intervening in an emergency situation generates human effects that can be weighty and will remain significant for many people. Each situation is different, taking into account the training and expectations of individuals, their professional practices, and what they might do under normal circumstances. Municipalities bring together many types of employees, some of whom are more familiar with emergency interventions than others.

Distinctions can be made among different situations ranging from crisis to disaster to tragedy. The City of Gatineau uses this operational definition: Disaster situations involve *performing unfamiliar tasks* and *setting up new response and mobilization structures*, as well as *coordinating people and teams not accustomed to working together* (social workers from various CSSSs [Centres de santé et de services sociaux du Québec], Red Cross volunteers, police officers, firefighters, municipal employees, etc.) (Maltais et al., 2015, p. 52, emphasis added).

For many municipal employees, responding to a disaster requires thinking outside the box, performing unaccustomed tasks, and possibly accompanying and supporting vulnerable people (the victims) or people seeking to help (volunteers). And most of the time, this must be done on an improvised basis, without much support and while making decisions quickly. Weeks and months after an event, some employees have told us, "I didn't expect this!" Other employees rather appreciated the open-ended environment that existed during the emergency situation, despite the fatigue. Some liked the atmosphere of solidarity and excitement that prevailed during these stressful times. Emergency situations, however, should remain a bracketed situation, after which one recovers and things return to normal.

The succession of events spread over four years (floods, tornadoes, floods, pandemic), however, caused cumulative fatigue among employees of our organization, which notably resulted in an increase in sick leaves and to difficult personal and family situations for some of them. As Maltais et al., 2015, p. 61) note: "Workers experience both negative and positive consequences when dealing with people in pain. Thus, some workers dealing with the distress of victims may be led to develop compassion fatigue, vicarious trauma and secondary traumatic stress or, at least, to present some of the symptoms associated with these disorders. The negative consequences most often mentioned in the context of this study remain *fatigue and stress. Feelings of helplessness* towards the victims were also highlighted by some respondents, a finding that agrees with what other researchers have said" (emphasis added). Comments collected during a debriefing session organized by the city sounded like this lament from a manager involved in emergency measures since 2017: "You run on adrenaline for weeks and then you fall back into a routine with a built-up backlog of tasks that is hard to catch up. This year [2019], I noticed that the accumulated fatigue remained for weeks and that even the annual vacation did not make it go away. The next year is going to be long!" And this was before the 2020 pandemic, which called for other types of adaptation from everyone – among other things, the absence of personal interaction with colleagues due to months of teleworking.

Throughout an emergency, the best advice we can give to city managers is never to neglect human resources. Even more than in normal times, it is our employees who make the difference in an emergency situation, because that is when we must count on the involvement, creativity, and resourcefulness of everyone. Many of these people are in contact with disoriented or vulnerable residents. They must be able to go about their task with a "free spirit." How does a city manager promote this attitude? By taking care of logistical details, such as making sure their families are safe, or that certain needs are met by other municipal colleagues, in order to free them from everyday worries. Sometimes these are little things, but they can make a world of difference in employee engagement.

After a crisis, returning to all the work that has been put aside and built up for weeks can be stressful for some employees or can generate disinterest because these mundane tasks seem less meaningful than emergency tasks.

The first duty of city managers is to ensure that all employees who have contributed to the recovery of the city and its residents have themselves recovered and that their stress levels have returned to normal.

Formal recognition by the city is very important to employees. In Gatineau we held several recognition events to highlight the remarkable work of employees during the difficult times we went through. For example, a dinner at the arena recognized the contribution of all city employees and the pride the city derived from it; this included employees who were not directly involved in a crisis, to emphasize that teamwork is the key to success. In addition, an artwork was dedicated to city employees to mark the "duty of remembrance" in the face of disturbing events. Once again, we are talking about the human factor as a priority since the municipal corporation is first and foremost, even in normal times, in the business of serving its people.

Municipal managers should use the crisis as an opportunity to review policies to determine if changes can be made to reduce the impact of future events. For example, should land development policy be made more restrictive in flood plains? It is difficult to forego future development, but a post-disaster reassessment is an opportunity for some geographical areas to return to their natural condition, allowing them to buffer the impact of development. This is of the utmost importance in a context of rapid climate change, since natural disasters and disruptions will happen more often.

Municipal managers, too, have to digest these events, even if they have to keep a stiff upper lip in many situations where their own reaction is appraised by many. They sometimes experience emotional strain and fatigue, although they are still expected to be effective and to resume their normal, demanding responsibilities. It can be a taxing situation for any city manager.

The Expectations of Elected Officials and Municipal Residents

Municipal managers know from experience that, in urban areas, people are more dependent on public authorities than are those living in rural areas. Although a rural municipality can encourage its population to become self-reliant in an emergency, such an expectation of an urban population is less realistic. Beyond encouraging each household to have an emergency kit, it is difficult to ask individuals and neighbourhoods in an urban setting to take charge of their own destiny in the event of an emergency.

A recent study examining the concept of responsibility in flood prevention and management concludes: "These findings suggest two policy priorities for Canadian governments as part of the broader implementation of FRM (Flood Risk Management), which include: (a) strengthening the sense of personal responsibility for flood mitigation to further reduce dependence on public disaster assistance, and (b) translating the willingness to pay for PLFP [property-level flood protection] measures into their actual implementation" (Henstra et al., 2019, p. 8). Society seems to be developing a great reliance on public authorities, and this has particular implications for municipalities. When an emergency is over, most stakeholders other than the municipality are quick to flee and return to their normal practices, leaving the municipality to manage the consequences of these situations. This includes upgrading the sites used, cleaning up, and providing longer-term support for victims. Some elected officials are sensitive to concerns of local residents and are reluctant to end the emergency intervention, so the phases of operation on the ground and recovery can become more burdensome.

Urban life can lead to loneliness and social isolation, causing the municipality to be seen as the de facto "close caregiver," to paraphrase the term used in social work. Almost two years after the floods of 2017, a few people still remained under the responsibility of the city, while all the other stakeholders had withdrawn. One council member summed up the dilemma this way: "Sometimes we have the impression that we are replacing the family in supporting victims. Is this our role? At the same time, we can't take chances when faced with the distress being experienced by some people."

Unless something is done to define the scope of municipal intervention in emergencies, these expanding expectations will place increasing burdens on the municipality. One remedy would be to draw on civil society for support. We have been blessed with a flood of volunteers wishing to make a contribution, and the presence of social media is perhaps an accelerator of this tendency to want to do something. This, combined with a better capacity of individuals to take care of themselves in emergency situations, might be considered as part of the "anti-fragile" organization that we want to promote.

These are the elements that set the municipal sector apart. We do not leave after a disaster – we take responsibility for the rest, whatever it is. This reality will have to be integrated into the optimal sharing of resources and responsibilities for the future, because unfortunately there will always be episodes requiring emergency interventions. On each occasion, we will have to live up to those expectations.

Lessons Learned

Crisis management can be compared to project management in the sense that there is a beginning, a middle, and an end. An important part of project management is that the organization learns and integrates as much information as possible to improve its performance for next time. If we borrow an "analysis grid" specific to project management (Quigley & Lauck, 2020), we can use a few of its headings to draw important lessons:

- What were the strengths of the municipal response and those of other responders during the emergency?
- What were the weak points?
- What impacts have been significant for the normal functioning of our organization?
- What processes were found to be appropriate/inappropriate for carrying out the emergency intervention?
- What "vulnerabilities" were exposed by this intervention?

Asking ourselves these questions led us to identify several lessons learned from our interventions in emergency situations. The following five lessons apply particularly to the municipal organization and to the role of the city manager.

Lesson 1: Preparation and practice are the building blocks of a "culture of emergency" where the example must come from the top (senior management and elected officials)

In a nutshell, to be good you have to prepare yourself, practice often, and intervene quickly and efficiently. This passes inevitably through the identification of the risks, the preparation of sectoral plans, and extensive practice to make sure you will react adequately in an emergency situation. Said like that, it sounds obvious, but it is a truth that cannot be overstated. Teams must be formed to ensure maximum redundancy, improve protocols with other organizations, and execute contracts for goods and services that will allow us to operate smoothly during an emergency. The participation of senior managers in the annual exercise and their presence in the various teams validates the importance of adequate preparation. In short, as city manager, you must show you believe in the importance of that preparation, otherwise the rest of the team will not adhere to the idea.

For city council, emergency preparedness must be considered just as important as day-to-day operations; it cannot be postponed under the pretext of budget cuts. The essence of emergency preparedness is acquiring sound reflexes, based on a mastery of our role and an awareness of the resources at our disposal, including the development of informal networks with organizations such as community groups.

Lesson 2: Communication is multimodal and at the heart of emergency response

Managing an emergency means managing communication and recognizing that residents now obtain their information almost instantly through many sources. Since disasters unsettle many residents, delivering the most precise, mobilizing messages possible in real time is essential. This can involve correcting false messages sent on social media and streaming media. Social media can be a great way to spread accurate, timely news, to connect with potential volunteers, to form self-help groups, and to provide support. City councillors should be kept informed constantly of developments – if necessary, through daily two-way briefings during which they can also provide information and their impressions of the situation on the ground.

Lesson 3: Municipal employees must become responsible for an emergency situation while retaining their normal duties

Emergencies remind us that our people are the foundation of our success as a service organization. Their well-being and their preparation must be at the centre of our concerns and we, as an organization, must ensure proper supervision, training, and working conditions before an emergency, proper support and leadership during an emergency, and finally proper relief and recognition after an emergency.

Lesson 4: Residents are an important support; we must know how to manage their expectations and channel their energy constructively

Perhaps the biggest lesson learned during these events is the leveraging effect of a community wanting to help and willing to support those affected. Unless the influx of volunteers is managed well, however, it could make matters worse. Whether deployed for repetitive tasks (filling sandbags) or specific tasks (supporting disaster victims, taking care of their pets), volunteers must have effective supervision and support from the municipality so that they are not at risk. A logistical plan must be mastered in advance because, in the heat of the moment, you will not have time to worry about such things.

Lesson 5: With climate change effects and other trends, past patterns are not a sufficient guide to future planning of emergency interventions

The work carried out in municipal organizations must be reassessed in the light of climate change impacts that will affect our urbanized environments, from waterworks planning to the schedules of swimming pools and playgrounds in heat waves, and, of course, planning for emergency response interventions due to climate change incidents (floods, wind storms, droughts, and brush fires). In eastern Canada, the summer of 2020 saw the most days on record with temperatures above 30° C (Météo Média, 2020). Our experience in Gatineau taught us that we need to invest in improving weather forecasting and understanding regional hydrology. We also need to modify our land-use planning to minimize the consequences of recurring emergency situations.

Conclusion

In conclusion, we wish to highlight two phenomena as key factors leading to more emergency interventions in the face of disasters (forest fires, floods, ice storms) or difficult situations for certain categories of residents, such as the elderly (longer and more frequent heat waves). They are (1) changes in the public's expectations of municipal intervention; and (2) the various impacts of climate change.

Cumulatively, these two developments tend to reduce the sphere of private responsibility and widen that of public authorities. As a result, municipalities will have to intervene more and more often in emergency situations. This is almost a new "line of business" for municipalities, to be performed alongside those for which our current organizational charts are designed.

These expectations will have two predictable effects. The first effect is to help redefine the profile of people who want to pursue a career in the municipal sector – in particular, at the highest levels of management. The second effect is to bolster the capacity of municipal organizations that have been weakened by years of budget and staffing cuts or reductions in resource levels. How many essential positions are not covered adequately by "redundancy" in our cities? How much equipment and infrastructure (including technological equipment and networks) are no longer at the level required to ensure that they remain invulnerable in the face of disasters of all kinds?

We believe that the present situation takes us beyond a search for robustness or even resilience to reach a level of excellence where the organization learns to intervene better from time to time, without loss of individual competence or collective memory, and by allocating sufficient resources to replace and upgrade equipment. This is why the title of this chapter refers to the concept of "antifragility": we think that every municipal organization should strive to become stronger when it is exposed to stressors.

Municipalities will constantly face uncertainties from various directions: natural causes (those we already know, amplified by climate change), anthropological causes (pandemics), technological causes (cyberattacks), and financial causes (more abrupt or more protracted recessions). These threats will define a much more uncertain environment than the one in which we have developed our municipal organizations. The many weaknesses that we can all currently see in our municipal organizations will have to be corrected, redundancy will have to be re-established everywhere, the renewal of aging staff cohorts will have to be ensured, and so forth. This is a renewal that is worth pursuing, because cities are more than ever the essential pillars of the quality of life that defines our society.

In this chapter, we also gave several examples where cities must show leadership in emergency situations. The other side of the coin for municipal organizations, however, is that exercising leadership usually comes with more responsibility, including managing any fallout. But do we really have a choice? Can we afford to hesitate? We could explore defining and limiting the areas over which municipal leadership can be exercised, by defining the services that the community should expect from its municipal government during these crises. This is clearly a political decision, as it is about setting limits in advance on what the municipality can provide in any effort to support people in need. But it can help our organizations become "antifragile," by better delineating the scope of our responsibility.

On another note, the experiences of the City of Gatineau show a very clear feeling that, to better manage the learning curve of emergency management, it is important to share our experiences and to "move on to the next," building on the observations made from these multiple emergency interventions. Emergency situations (to which we can now all add "life during a pandemic") are unique in that months or years can pass between emergencies. Many positions in our organization might be filled with new people, if and when a major new tornado or pandemic hits. We must never forget the lessons learned through hardship.

These reasons, among others, allow us to reflect on what we have learned and to highlight what could still be improved in the future. We hope that our descriptions and analysis will help our fellow city managers to better prepare their organizations to deal with the various emergency situations that could be just around the corner.

REFERENCES

Christensen, T., Laegreid, P., & Rykkja, L. H. (2016). Organizing for crisis management: Building governance capacity and legitimacy. *Public Administration Review*, *76*(6), 887–97. https://doi.org/10.1111/puar.12558

Dancause, D. (2017, December). L'alerte et la communication de masse en situation de sinistre. *Le sablier*, pp. 39–46.

French, P. E. (2011). Enhancing the legitimacy of local government pandemic influenza planning through transparency and public engagement. *Public Administration Review*, *71*(2), 253–65. https://doi.org/10.1111/j.1540-6210.2011.02336.x

Henstra, D. (2010). Evaluating local government emergency management programs: What framework should public managers adopt? *Public*

Administration Review, *70*(2), 236–46. https://doi.org/10.1111/j.1540-6210.2010.02130.x

Henstra, D., Thistlethwaite, J., Brown, C., & Scott, D. (2019). Flood risk management and shared responsibility: Exploring Canadian public attitudes and expectations. *Journal of Flood Risk Management*, *12*(1), 1–10. https://doi.org/10.1111/jfr3.12346

Koliba, C. J., Zia, A., & Mills, R. (2011). Accountability in governance networks: An assessment of public, private, and nonprofit emergency management practices following Hurricane Katrina. *Public Administration Review*, *71*(2), 210–20. http://doi.org/10.1111/j.1540-6210.2011.02332.x

Maltais, D., Bolduc, V., Gauthier, V., & Gauthier, S. (2015). Les retombées de l'intervention en situation de crise, de tragédie ou de sinistre sur la vie professionnelle et personnelle des intervenants sociaux des CSSS du Québec. *Revue intervention* (142), 51–64. https://constellation.uqac.ca/id/eprint/5880/1/C.Sintervention_142_6_les-retombees-de-l-intervention.pdf

Météo Média. (2020, 19 June). Nos experts le confirment : l'été 2020 passera à l'histoire. Retrieved from https://www.meteomedia.com/ca/nouvelles/article/apercu-de-lete-2020-quelle-region-sera-la-grande-gagnante

Prévost, P. (2018). *Le gouvernement municipal en questions*. JFD Éditions.

Quigley, J., & Lauck, S. (2020, 6 April). The importance of documenting lessons learned. *PMTips*. Retrieved from https://pmtips.net/article/the-importance-of-documenting-lessons-learned

Taleb, N. N. (2012). *Antifragile: Things that gain from disorder*. Random House.

17 Managing during a Crisis: Lessons from Fort McMurray

JAMIE DOYLE AND DON LIDSTONE

Dealing with a crisis requires careful navigation of situations, capacity, and obligations, as well as meeting public expectations. For lessons learned from the floods and wildfires that have devasted Fort McMurray, Alberta, it is insightful to hear the first-person reflections of the municipality's CAO Jamie Doyle and the perspective of municipal legal expert Don Lidstone. In addition to describing their experiences, they offer practical suggestions for crisis readiness, response, and resilience.

Throughout Canadian history, local governments have faced imminent and prospective crises – wildfires, floods, tsunamis, derailments, economic busts, pandemics, sinkholes, debris torrents, rockslides – that have placed considerable pressure on both elected officials and city staff. Crisis response is important for local governments: they are on the front lines of crises as the order of government closest to the people affected, closest to the ground, and in control of the nearest resources for response.

Fort McMurray is the urban service hub for Alberta's Regional Municipality of Wood Buffalo (RMWB). Wood Buffalo is one of the largest municipal areas in Canada, running from Conklin in the south to the Northwest Territory border in the north, and with a population of 112,000, encompassing several urban settlements in addition to the Fort McMurray townsite. It is home to the Athabasca oil sands and one of the fastest-growing industrial areas in the country. Within the geographic limits of Wood Buffalo there are five self-governing First Nations communities, with which the municipality works collaboratively.

Fort McMurray suffered massive flooding destruction and evacuation in 2012 and 2020, widespread wildfire destruction and evacuation in 2016, the effects of the COVID-19 pandemic in the community and the outlying work camps in 2020, the disruptive decline in the price of oil in 2020, several train derailments, and ongoing political turmoil from exogenous sources regarding the oil sands extraction industry.

I have been the Wood Buffalo chief administrative officer (CAO) or head of planning and development during most of these crises, to the present day. I have participated in emergency planning and response for most of my career, starting with the recovery operation for Swissair Flight 111 in 1998 (off the coast of Nova Scotia) and most recently with the COVID-19 pandemic. As CAO and as the senior administrator reporting directly to council, I have had the responsibility of facilitating policy and strategic elements to deal with uncertainties and demonstrate stable leadership during a crisis. Emergency readiness and response require budgetary and fiscal analysis and preparation, networking with other governments, establishing clear legal and risk management pathways, managing staffing and volunteer resources in line with labour agreements, providing for insurance and indemnity, and advising council on immediate response and future policies.

In this chapter, with the help of municipal solicitor Don Lidstone, QC, I address the need to prepare for and respond to crises, and to balance the political dynamic, fiscal and resource constraints, public expectations, and the obligation to save lives and protect property. I discuss financial and jurisdictional constraints of local government, emergency preparedness, crisis management, intergovernmental cooperation, stakeholder engagement, the command centre and chain of command, mitigation, recovery, damage assessment, and lessons learned. Importantly, I also discuss the personal impacts of a crisis and how I have managed personally.

Personal Background

My first experience with a crisis was as a member of the Canadian Armed Forces responsible for dealing with the debris and human remains from Swissair Flight 111, which crashed off Nova Scotia in 1998 with the loss of 229 lives. As in the case of all crises or emergencies, one did not know what one was getting into. In this regard, it is my sense that every city manager must be as prepared as a student who is expecting a fight after school to be ready for whatever is coming when the bell rings at the end of classes that day.

My military training started with a sergeant saying soldiers are most effective when they realize that they are already dead; only then can they act in an objective and effective manner, not based on emotion or politics. In the military, we were trained to deal with pressure, intensity, and the unexpected, and in that regard every soldier in wartime, as well as every city manager in anticipation of a crisis, needs to have in place a process, logistics, a team, appreciation of the power of a decision, advance preparation and training, a chain of command, and an innate appreciation of the need for creativity and an understanding that time is of the essence.

Wood Buffalo Events

Flooding

Wood Buffalo experienced major flooding in 2012 and 2013. In June 2013, a local state of emergency was declared in the municipality. Approximately 150 people were evacuated from low-lying communities along the Hangingstone River. The situation dramatically worsened during the 2020 flooding of the Athabasca River, when 13,000 people were evacuated; insured flood damages exceeded $228 million.

The 2012, 2013, and 2020 flood events raised questions about flood risk management. Instead of continually responding to increasing risks of catastrophic flooding, the municipality was advised to engage the full spectrum of stakeholders to coordinate and pay for risk reduction and emergency response (Henstra et al., 2018). This included educating and encouraging or requiring owners and occupiers who locate in flood-prone areas to buy recently available overland flood insurance, while at the same time coordinating prevention and response with the federal and provincial governments.

Alberta municipalities have always faced risks of flooding, but more extreme weather and population growth have increased risks to public safety and property loss. In response, Wood Buffalo and other communities prevailed upon the provincial government to amend the Municipal Government Act (MGA) in 2013 to create regulations for controlling development in floodways. To date, the regulations have not been finalized. Meanwhile, municipalities continue to have common law and other obligations to incorporate sound planning measures into their land-use bylaw and statutory plans with respect to development that might be subject to flooding.

As a former director of planning and now CAO of Wood Buffalo, I have encouraged development of regional and municipal development plans under the Alberta Land Stewardship Act to support development of municipal flood mitigation plans and the expansion of flood hazard mapping under the MGA.

Municipalities have several tools to regulate land and buildings in flood hazard areas. The role of a city manager is to help elected officials weigh the costs and benefits of policy alternatives, including:

(a) establishing other locations for rebuilding; (b) requiring insurance; (c) requiring living areas and equipment to be located above prescribed flood levels; (d) forcing permanent evacuations or relocations; and (e) paying a substantial portion of the capital cost of flood prevention.

Wildfires

During the 2016 wildfires, 88,000 people were evacuated. The estimated cost of the impact of the fire on improvements and infrastructure was $8.9 billion (KPMG, 2017). The wildfires burned from 1 May 2016 to 2 August 2016, with a state of emergency in effect from 4 May to 1 July 2016. The Wood Buffalo experience with wildfires underlined the necessity for emergency planning, management, and response.

Up to this point in my non-military career, I had not seen such a level of disaster. This was not the straightforward hierarchy of command experienced by the military. Involvement in crisis with the military was much easier: one showed up, received orders, and went off to perform in a conditioned manner. In the 2016 wildfire, however, we had no established policy or plan to lean on, and the senior leadership team effort without a recovery policy and plan framework proved to be debilitating.

As the Director, Planning and Development at the time, I found the response/recovery chaotic, unpredictable, and relentless. There was an uncoordinated assembly of people and resources. As I entered the Regional Operations Centre, I was unable to secure the smallest of things, like an access card to be in the building. There were no printers, ink, or individuals assigned to handle an influx of people and resources. I would describe it as one massive emergency vacuum. Everyone worked sixteen to eighteen hours a day under immense pressure with very little direction. Early on, it was clear that help was needed – serious, professional help. Accordingly, external subject matter experts were retained to help the team design, implement, and utilize recovery policies, plans, and business/operational continuity plans.

Prior to the wildfire and before I became Deputy CAO and later CAO, Wood Buffalo was undergoing restructuring of its municipal operations, with changes made to departments, functions, and positions across the organization. Therefore, recovery structures were established parallel to regular municipal operations. The level of organizational change occurring at the time of the 2016 wildfire was a hinderance to recovery.

The Wildfire Governance Model (figure 17.1), an example of proper governance, was created subsequently to help establish a stable base from which to plan and implement recovery activities in future emergencies. The model had two streams overseen by the RMWB: Municipal

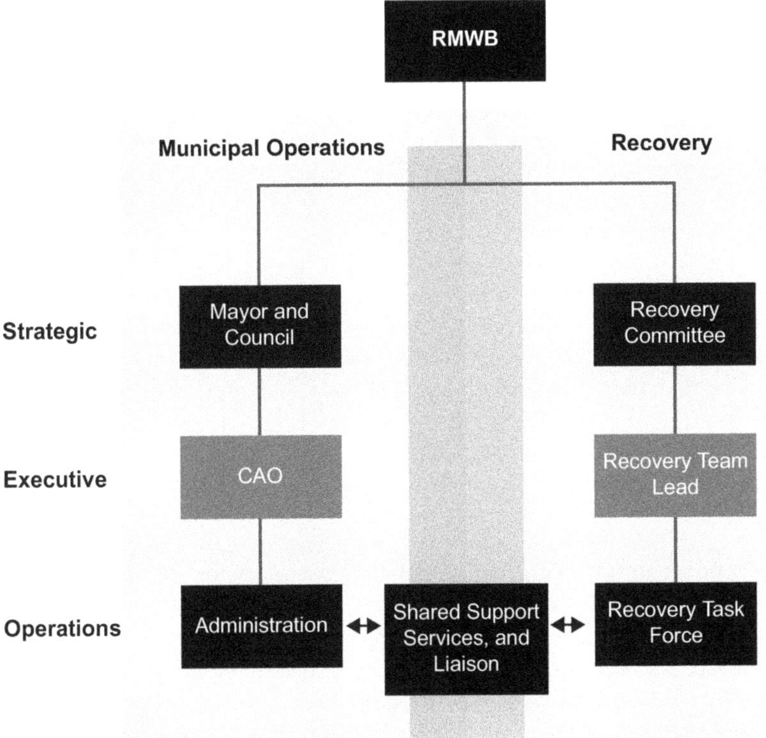

Figure 17.1 The Wildfire Governance Model

Operations and Recovery. During the 2020 flood event, except for the formal committee, we employed a similar model to deal with the issue.

Constraints

Municipalities in Canada operate under statutory and budgetary constraints. Under the MGA, for example, municipalities in Alberta are not allowed to budget for a deficit, and total actual revenues ultimately must be equal to or greater than total actual expenditures. Accordingly, a municipality cannot operate outside these constraints even to spend money on disaster response, relief, recovery, or prevention.

A constraint is the need for the local government to put all decisions and communications on the public record, subject to protection of privacy and confidentiality rules, so a city manager must be familiar with this requirement during the time of crisis.

Another major constraint is the political will of elected officials. In my respectful submission, elected officials should ensure that legislation is in place to support the emergency plan they have adopted before any emergency occurs. Council, for example, needs to have the political will to engage in coercive actions such as preventing reconstruction in a flood plain, ordering evacuation, or requiring face masks in facilities during a pandemic.

Emergency Management

Based on the Wood Buffalo experiences with flooding, wildfires, and COVID-19, I believe that best practices in emergency management include: (a) preparedness, (b) stakeholder engagement, (c) an advance response plan, (d) advance training, (e) intergovernmental cooperation, (f) mitigation plans, (g) education of residents, (h) warning systems, and (i) a wildfire governance model.

Preparedness

Every community should prepare for emergencies by identifying potential crisis events and preparing for them with plans and policies. Preparedness includes stakeholder agreements, emergency response plans, advance training, mutual aid agreements with other governments, mitigation planning, public education, warning systems, and an emergency governance model (Boin et al., 2013). These matters are discussed in the ensuing paragraphs.

Stakeholder Engagement

When developing an emergency plan, the local government should enlist and communicate with the unions, volunteer search and rescue organizations, the media, the business community, surrounding communities, Indigenous partners, and the provincial or territorial government. An emergency such as the COVID-19 pandemic can crush otherwise robust businesses, which in turn affects tax assessment and jobs. This means early and ongoing involvement of the business community in the development and evolution of the emergency plan, including recovery (Institute for Business and Home Safety, 1999, p. 1).

An Advance Response Plan

The emergency response plan should be in writing and developed and endorsed by the emergency participatory stakeholders. It should be adopted by the elected council so that it is a policy decision and not an operational decision, to deflect liability (*Just v. British Columbia*, [1989] 2 SCR 1228), and to validate emergency actions of the parties covered by the policy (Kuban, 1996, p. 24). Liability in negligence might arise, however, if loss occurs because of the negligent implementation of policy decisions at an operational level (*Kamloops v. Neilson*, [1984] 2 SCR 2). In the *Kamloops* case, a homeowner sued the city for damages arising from the city's failure to enforce its bylaw even though the bylaw contained an express duty to enforce. The court in the *Kamloops* and *Just* cases stated among other things that the city could protect itself from liability by adopting a policy in good faith at the council level to enforce or not to enforce in accordance with the policy.

The basic elements required to establish liability in negligence are:

1. the municipality must owe the plaintiff a duty of care;
2. there must be a breach of that duty (i.e., the municipality's conduct must fall below the standard of care); and
3. the breach of the duty must cause damage to the plaintiff.

The court uses a two-step test to determine whether a duty of care is owed:

1. Is there a sufficiently close relationship between the parties (the municipality and the person who has suffered damage) so that, in the reasonable contemplation of the municipality, carelessness on its part might cause damage to that person? If so,
2. Are there any considerations which ought to negate or limit (a) the scope of the duty and (b) the class of persons to whom it is owed or (c) the damages to which a breach of it may give rise? (*Kamloops v. Neilson*).

The first step of the test presents a relatively low threshold. It will generally be met if it can be shown that there is a relationship of proximity between the municipality and the other party, such that it is reasonably foreseeable that carelessness on the part of the municipality would result in injury to the other party (*Ryan v. Victoria (City)*, [1999] 1 SCR 201).

The second step requires a determination of whether any factors exist that should eliminate or limit the duty found under the first branch of the test. With respect to government bodies, a distinction is drawn between policy and operational decisions. In general, a municipality does not owe a duty of care for "true policy decisions" – that is, decisions made at a high level (e.g., council) that balance financial, economic, social, and other political factors (*Just v. British Columbia*). It is important to note that policy decisions must be reasonable and made in good faith to negate the duty of care.

In contrast, a municipality owes a private law duty of care for both operational decisions and the implementation of policy decisions. For example, if a municipality adopts a policy regarding dredging a creek, it must ensure that it implements that policy in a manner that meets the standard of care required in the circumstances.

It is important to note also that a municipality may be held to owe a duty of care when it has knowledge of a potential hazard and fails to take reasonable actions in the circumstances, such as giving notice or mitigating the hazard (if it is reasonable for it to do so).

Once it is determined that a duty of care is owed, to avoid liability a municipality must "exercise the standard of care … that would be expected of an ordinary, reasonable and prudent person in the same circumstances" (*Brown v. British Columbia (Minister of Transportation and Highways)*, [1994] 1 SCR 420). The measure of what is reasonable in any given circumstance will depend on a variety of factors, including the likelihood of a known or foreseeable harm, the gravity of that harm, and the burden or cost which would be incurred to prevent injury (*Ryan v. Victoria [City]*).

Advance Training

The training of personnel is critical to an emergency response plan. Basic and subsequent technical and routine training will prepare responders, including fire/rescue, police, ambulance, public works personnel, and volunteers for their respective responsibilities under the plan. It is also essential to prepare elected officials for dealing with transparency and accountability issues that arise in the aftermath of a crisis (Perry & Lindell, 2003, p. 345).

Intergovernmental Cooperation

Intergovernmental cooperation is critical because of the limited resources and statutory budget constraints affecting local governments. Formal relations with the provincial emergency program are necessary because, as a creature of the provincial government, a local government must depend on financial assistance and other resources. For municipalities that are near First Nations or other municipalities, mutual aid agreements are valuable for the party that needs to call upon aid. Such legal agreements can cover personnel, equipment, transportation, shelter, and other services, and address issues of liability and compensation (Waugh, 2007) .

Mitigation Plans

Mitigation planning requires identification of effective means of relieving persons and property of some of the effects of the emergency. Most mitigation involves capital expenditures (e.g., dykes, berms, debris-torrent catchers, fire breaks), so engagement of the resources (such as grants and co-funding programs) of the provincial and federal governments is necessary.

Education of Residents and Warning Systems

Education of potentially affected residents and effective warning systems to alert the public are required components of an emergency plan. Education involves both inculcation of community values and explicit training so that affected persons know what to do in the event of an emergency (Hall, 2007, p. 35). A warning mechanism is essential for communities concerned about risks of tsunami hazards, debris torrents, or other matters where people might have time to get to safety. The education program can include the warning system. Equally important is a communications plan and system for public advisories and mobilization during a crisis (Bullock et al., 2004).

A Wildfire Governance Model

In Fort McMurray, the Wildfire Governance Model was created based on the experience of the 2016 wildfire. I recommend that every local government create an emergency governance model to address with precision the roles of elected officials, staff, emergency and works personnel, other local and provincial/federal agencies, volunteers, and the community. This should happen as part of an emergency response plan, not as a result of a crisis or emergency (Kelly et al., 2019).

An Emergency Operations Centre

The establishment of an emergency operations centre is critical to the successful implementation of an emergency plan. The location and logistical nerves must be established in advance as part of the emergency plan. During a crisis, the chain of command under the emergency plan takes over. Typically, it is not the city manager, but an operational commander designated in advance under the plan, such as the mayor or the fire chief, who is at the top of the chain.

Decisions in consultation with the city manager and, if necessary, council must often be made in relation to evacuations, sanctuaries, emergency shelters, explosives, hazardous materials, and so forth. The emergency operations centre carries out the requisite leadership and mobilization of the incident management system. The centre also disseminates information to the public, including the media. The mayor should be actively involved, given the need for authoritative communications with the public, declarations of states of local emergency, networking with other orders of government, and engaging other elected officials. It is not in my view advisable, however, for the mayor to be the head of the chain of command absent from deep emergency training and experience, and this should be reflected in the emergency plan.

When the crisis passes, recovery is critical to the fabric of the community. This entails recovery policies, a recovery plan, continuity of operations, damage assessment, insurance and indemnity, and financial reconciliation with the municipal budget (Henstra, 2010).

Recovery Policy and Plan

Our municipality did not have a robust, well-understood, organizationally supported recovery policy and plan to address the effects of wildfires. Having experienced the disaster of the 2016 wildfire, I believe municipalities must create recovery governance and organization structures. They must recognize in advance the pros and cons of each model before committing. As an example, would governance reside outside the organizational and executionary process, and to what extent would council have representation? How would communication happen within the organization? These decisions can also have implications for potential disaster recovery program funding from the other orders of government – who pays for what? One of the most important decisions to understand is balancing the need to focus on recovery, separate from municipal operations. This also involves knowing what internal resources fit with external subject matter experts.

The recovery framework/plan Wood Buffalo used to recover from the wildfire included legislation, governance, budget, task force, planning, and all activities related to recovery. The recovery planning document has two elements: the campaign plan and the recovery plan itself. The campaign plan was established as a high-level, one-page guide to recovery for all stakeholders. Its purpose was to simplify the complexity of recovery and provide an easily understandable guide to create a standard operating picture for all as to what recovery from the wildfire within the region would entail. As stated, prior to this recovery plan, most organizational staff had no understanding of response and recovery.

The campaign plan outlined the principal challenges to be addressed during the Wood Buffalo recovery phase. It included best practices and five key action areas, referred to as pillars: *People, Economy, Reconstruction, Environment, and Mitigation*. The best practices were related to associated objectives and desired outcomes for each key action area, risks, performance indicators, an overarching narrative, and a desired end state. The elements of the plan are as follows.

People: Ensure the right resources are available to support the overall physical, mental, and social well-being of Albertans; mental health supports; temporary housing; support to local authorities.
Economy: Encourage job creation and economic diversification while building stronger relationships with industry and small businesses; small business support; hire and buy local.
Reconstruction: Encourage innovative solutions and responsible development and involve local companies and workers wherever possible; rebuilding; consumer protection and public safety standards.
Environment: Monitor long-term environmental impacts and mitigate risks, if required; environmental testing and monitoring.
Mitigation: Invest in disaster reduction by supporting mitigation of wildfire and other public safety risks; disaster preparedness; FireSmart; flood mitigation.

The recovery plan elaborated on the campaign plan and described who has responsibility for implementing recovery-related activities and how they would be managed. It acted as the bridge between the strategic campaign plan and day-to-day recovery activities, which were documented in detailed plans for each of the pillars, including roles and responsibilities to implement. The ability to easily understand and communicate the policy and plan is vitally important. The campaign plan was that vehicle.

Damage Assessment

The Rapid Damage Assessment tool and process was an efficient and effective means to assess damaged properties and communicate to residents the extent of damage before they returned to the community (Ali Farazmand, 2001). Fortunately, the municipality had completed geospatial information system (GIS) mapping not long before the wildfire, and these data enabled the team to quickly understand the damage to structures across the region. Within a week all structures had been assessed and information provided to residents through a dedicated platform on the municipal website to help them plan for their return or other actions. Although the tool was effective, having better definitions of the building typology (e.g., residential versus commercial, industrial) would have been beneficial. This also would have allowed for more accurate counting (e.g., a duplex versus a single-family dwelling). This tool was considered successful by residents and stakeholders.

Finally, consistent damage assessment criteria were needed for safety code officers to maintain consistency in their assessments and support of the data-collection process. Safety code officers were armed with technology to inspect and report from the field, which allowed them to provide real-time updates for evacuated residents.

A "sifting" program, which allowed homeowners to re-enter and go through the remains of their properties to look for valuables or heirlooms, was implemented, based on lessons learned following the 2010 Slave Lake Wildfire. Staff had been in continuous contact with the Town of Slave Lake and had learned much from their staff and elected officials. One of the most prevalent insights was the idea of closure for residents. The Wood Buffalo program saw 1,100 properties experience the sifting program.

Insurance, Financial Reconciliation, and Indemnity

It is critical to have experts to help navigate your organization through the Disaster Recovery Program. Resources included the non-profit Disaster Recovery Institute, the Mount Royal University Centre for Community Disaster Research, the Canadian Red Cross, Province of Alberta Disaster Recovery, and several private providers.

As a result of the wildfire, Wood Buffalo lost 1,595 buildings and structures, containing 2,579 dwelling units, according to Wood Buffalo GIS data updated as of 1 June 2020. The Insurance Bureau of Canada reported that the wildfire was by far the costliest insured natural disaster in Canadian history, at an estimated $3.6 billion in insured property damage (KPMG, 2017). The total impact of the wildfire – including reduced oil sands revenue, losses to public infrastructure and private property, the effects on the environment and on the physical and mental health of residents and first responders – was estimated at almost $8.9 billion. Many properties affected by the various crises in Fort McMurray were partially insured, underinsured, or uninsured. Many members of the public felt it was unfair that they had paid high insurance premiums while others were simply bailed out by government. Private property losses were estimated at $3.98 billion and businesses lost estimated net revenue of $54.7 million, infrastructure losses totalled $4.54 billion, insurers paid over $3.77 billion in claims, non-insured costs were over $615 million, the federal government committed $452 million plus $90 million to match donations to the Red Cross, and the Province of Alberta ran up costs of over $195 million, including $7 million for owners' property tax relief, distributed based on criteria established by the municipality (KPMG, 2017). The federal government also paid for damages on First Nations reserves.

Our wildfire experience was so profound that we needed to capture what happened and when. Council and staff believed a report was needed to summarize the lessons learned and engaged KPMG to help piece that together (KPMG, 2017). It has become the foundation of information many of us turn to when trying to recapture and refresh memories of 2016.

Conclusion

A crisis will engage the deepest experience and greatest skills and test the moral and pragmatic fibre of the city manager. There will be a time in any major crisis when the city manager must frame his or her professional advice, including on health and safety issues, in a way that reflects the political and the community environment in which decisions must be made and implemented.

Fort McMurray has been visited by more natural disasters in the past ten years than most places would see in centuries, including massive flooding destruction and evacuation in 2012 and 2020, widespread wildfire destruction and evacuation in 2016, the effects of the COVID-19 pandemic in the work camps in 2020, the disruptive decline in the price of oil on the local economy in 2020, train derailments, and more. The cost to the residents and the municipality has been huge: 88,000 people were evacuated during the 2016 fires and the estimated cost of improvements and infrastructure was $8.9 billion; in 2020, 13,000 people were evacuated from flooded areas and insured damages exceeded $228 million. Our residents, however, are resilient, and the municipality is coming through this stronger than we ever have been.

We have learned a great deal. In the context of an emergency plan, including an emergency governance plan, the city manager must facilitate planning and response to deal with future events and demonstrate stable leadership during a crisis. Emergency readiness and response require budgetary and fiscal analysis and preparation, networking with other governments, clear legal and risk management pathways, staffing and volunteer management, responsible insurance and indemnity programs, and guidance of the mayor and council on immediate response and future policies.

REFERENCES

Ali Farazmand, E. (2001). *Handbook of crisis and emergency management*. Marcel Dekker.

Boin, A., Ekengren, M., & Rhinard, M. (2013). *The European Union as crisis manager: Patterns and prospects*. Cambridge University Press.

Bullock, J. A., Haddow, G. D., & Bell, R. (2004). Communicating during emergencies in the United States. *Australian Journal of Emergency Management*, *19*(2), 3–7.

Hall, P. (2007). Early warning systems: Reframing the discussion. *Australian Journal of Emergency Management*, *22*(2), 32–6.

Henstra, D. (2010). Evaluating local government emergency management programs: What framework should public managers adopt? *Public Administration Review*, *70*(2), 236–46. https://doi.org/10.1111/j.1540-6210.2010.02130.x

Henstra, D., Thistlethwaite, J., Brown, C., & Scott, D. (2018). Flood risk management and shared responsibility: Exploring Canadian attitudes and expectations. *Journal of Flood Risk Management*. https://doi.org/10.1111/jfr3.12346

Institute for Business and Home Safety. (1999). *Open for business: A disaster planning toolkit for the small business owner*. Institute for Business and Home Safety.

Kelly, E. C., Charnley, S., & Pixley, J. (2019, December). Polycentric systems for wildlife governance in the western United States. *Land Use Policy*, *89*, 104214. https://www.sciencedirect.com/science/article/abs/pii/S0264837719305198

KPMG. (2017). *Wood Buffalo wildfire: Post-incident assessment report*. Prepared for Alberta Emergency Management Agency. https://www.alberta.ca/assets/documents/Wildfire-KPMG-Report.pdf?platform=hootsuite

Kuban, R. (1996). The role of government in emergency preparedness. *Canadian Public Administration*, *39*(2), 239–44. https://doi.org/10.1111/j.1754-7121.1996.tb00130.x

Perry, R. W., & Lindell, M. K. (2003). Preparedness for emergency response: Guidelines for the emergency planning process. *Disasters*, *27*(4), 336–50. http://doi.org/10.1111/j.0361-3666.2003.00237.x. Medline:14725091

Waugh, W. L. (2007). EMAC, Katrina, and the governors of Louisiana and Mississippi. *Public Administration Review*, *67*(s1), 107–13. https://doi.org/10.1111/j.1540-6210.2007.00819.x

18 Building Partnerships: Hard Work, Patience, Commitment, Adaptation, and Opportunities

JAG SHARMA

Partnerships have become an important part of municipal governance, and they provide great opportunities. Building those partnerships is not easy, however; it requires hard work, patience, commitment, and adaptation. Jag Sharma is currently President and CEO of the Toronto Community Housing Corporation, but he has extensive experience as a city manager. When he was in Oshawa, Ontario, he was instrumental in developing a very active partnership with several educational institutions. When he moved to Newmarket, Ontario, he became involved in a partnership of area municipalities that had been in existence for some time, but was continuing to grow and develop.

In my career as a city manager, I have had the opportunity to be involved in two very interesting partnerships. Both of them have been exceptionally productive and rewarding to the partners and to me personally. As the subtitle of this chapter indicates, however, they did not always come about easily. They required hard work, patience, commitment, and adaptation, but they resulted in a great opportunity to improve the quality of life for residents. The purpose of this chapter is to analyse the various ways that governments can use partnerships in such areas as co-production and co-governance, and to share my experiences working with two partnerships that have functioned very well.

I begin with a discussion of some of the reasons governments use partnerships and why they are becoming more attractive. In the main portion of the chapter, I then consider four different types of partnerships: public-private (P3s), public/not-for-profit (NFP), public-educational, and intermunicipal. The latter two types get special attention because I have had some interesting personal experiences with them. I conclude with some lessons I learned in working with these two partnerships.

The Purpose of Partnerships

Governments have used partnerships for many years for many different purposes. When the word became fashionable in the 1980s and 1990s during the heyday of New Public Management (NPM), it was overused, so it is important to have a clear definition. Kernaghan defines a partnership as "a relationship involving *the sharing of power, work, support and/or information* with others for the achievement of joint goals and/or mutual benefits" (Kernaghan, 1993, p. 61, emphasis in original). The key word in the definition is sharing; this sets a real partnership apart from other tools popularized by NPM such as contracting out or joined-up government.

The first wave of P3s sought to access private capital for major infrastructure projects or program outsourcing ventures, citing the presumed ability of P3s to produce results that were more consistently on-time, on-budget, without scope creep and potentially more innovative when contrasted with conventional public tenders and program delivery. Typical projects were the Confederation Bridge between New Brunswick and Prince Edward Island, highway 407 in southern Ontario, and numerous health care facilities and transit projects (Siemiatycki, 2015).

Over time, partnerships have been used in a variety of ways, but they generally have been seen as a way of improving service to the public and providing increased value for money (Canada, 2020). Not only can they produce financial benefits; they can also promote best practices, mitigate resource requirements, and, ultimately, deliver projects with a high level of excellence. Collaborative partnerships will continue to be a growing area of opportunity for municipalities looking to be efficient and progressive.

The potential benefits of partnerships that have been identified include:

- *cost savings* – for example, by using private sector expertise in project management and specialized construction techniques;
- *perceived mutual benefit* – for example, by advancing a First Nations wellness centre that will enhance the lives of Indigenous people;
- *filling a shared need* – for example, by constructing a recreation facility that benefits both a recreation club and the local government;
- *provision of public support* – for example, to an initiative by a not-for-profit organization in the social sector;
- *leverage of external resources* – for example, by drawing on private funds for upfront financing of expensive projects;

- *shared expertise or resources* – for example, by taking advantage of specialized expertise or resources in areas such as project management; and
- *extending the partners' respective mandates and capacities* – for example, by supporting a worthy project that might not be directly within the mandate of a local government to provide.

Partnerships are not easy to develop, they have risks, and they often fail or fade. Still, for all the hardships that come with them, partnerships are here to stay because the benefits are worth it.

During these unprecedented times, the need for partnerships is strongly underscored. Well before COVID-19, there was a growing sentiment of tax fatigue: according to the Fraser Institute (2020), the average Ontario family "will pay 43.3 per cent of its income in federal, provincial and municipal taxes this year." When the current Progressive Conservative government came to power in Ontario in 2018, it was facing a significant annual deficit and an equally daunting accumulated debt. It wanted to deal with the situation without either increasing taxes or reducing service levels, which meant that the main avenue available was increasing efficiency.

It quickly became clear that this discipline would apply not only to the provincial government, but it would also extend to the entire MUSH sector (municipalities, universities, schools, health care) funded by the provincial government. The Ontario government launched an Audit and Accountability Fund in 2019 that provided funding to municipalities to undertake reviews to modernize service delivery and find improved governance mechanisms

In January 2019, headlines indicated "Ontario reviewing regional governments, raising prospect of future amalgamations" (Boisvert, 2019). This reminded municipalities of an initiative undertaken twenty years previously by the Harris Progressive Conservative government, which involved restructurings and amalgamations that resulted in reducing the number of municipalities in the province by about half.

These two initiatives caused municipalities to start thinking preemptively about how they could demonstrate their devotion to efficiency in order to head off forced or traditional amalgamation, which would be very difficult, especially considering the time required, varying levels of commitment, logistics, aligning collective agreements, and many other considerations. Voluntary shared service delivery in the form of partnerships was clearly preferable to another round of forced amalgamations.

Types of Partnerships

Public-Private Partnerships

As the name suggests, P3s are partnership between private sector companies and any of the three orders of government or Indigenous groups. There are many different types of P3s, but most are some combination of design, build, finance, operate, maintain, transfer, and own. In October 2020, the website of the Canadian Council for Public-Private Partnerships identified fifty-nine municipal projects in progress totalling almost $12 billion. (Canadian Council for Public-Private Partnerships, 2020) These included roads and bridges, transit expansion projects, water and wastewater facilities, recreation complexes, and many others.

Although there are many indisputable benefits of P3s, there are also challenges. P3s can yield financial efficiencies, but the traditional project size puts many municipalities at a disadvantage – the lowest-cost project on the Canadian Council for Public-Private Partnerships' website was for $2.5 million. P3s can be costly for all partners to manage and coordinate, making them unattractive for smaller projects. The municipality must employ fairly sophisticated staff resources to manage the project, which would also place this beyond the grasp of many municipalities without increasing their staff expertise, particularly in the areas of engineering, procurement, and finance. Then, the next obstacle is that "there is more scrutiny of P3s at the local level, not least because projects must be approved by council in full public view (federal and provincial deals are approved by treasury boards behind closed doors)" (Hanniman, 2013).

There can also be problems with the operation of the partnership. Contract failure occurs when one or both sides are unable to comply with the terms of the contract or they are in conflict about their mutual obligations under the contract. This can happen easily where the project is very large, complex, and extends over a significant period of time. There can also be political problems when the public sector values of transparency and accountability clash with the private sector organization's desire to protect proprietary business information (Berardi, 2008).

P3s are becoming quite common because they can provide funding and specialized expertise that many governments do not have. Governments must exercise care, however, to ensure that the project is financially beneficial, that proper accountability is maintained, and that the municipality is not exposing itself to excessive risk. If those conditions are met, public-private partnerships can be win-win situations for everyone involved.

Public/Not-for-Profit Partnerships

Public/NFP partnerships are a growing area of interest because they allow the public to be more involved in the delivery of government services. By the numbers, these are probably the most common type of partnership. NFP client-facing groups such as the John Howard Society, United Way, faith groups, local sports clubs, and many others are often considered to be more trusted and closer to segments of the community than are governments. "Nonprofits can also serve as a coordinator, facilitator, community builder, or mission steward in government-nonprofit partnerships" (Cheng, 2019, p. 190).

Partnerships between governments and NFP organizations frequently are geared to co-production and co-governance. When governments deliver services on their own, there is an idea that they know the "one best way" to provide the services and that they should have a monopoly on the provision of those services (Davis & Ostrom, 1991). Yet there are other ways to provide services. For example, "[c]o-production means delivering public services in an equal and reciprocal relationship between professionals, people using services, their families and their neighbours. Where activities are co-produced in this way, both services and neighbourhoods become far more effective agents of change" (Boyle & Harris, 2009).

Co-governance refers to recognition that civil society is composed of a network of individuals and groups, all of whom have a stake in the services provided and, therefore, they should all have a role in making decisions about the service. Co-governance involves developing a mechanism to ensure that shared decision making occurs. This is more complicated than co-production because it requires governments to give up their traditional monopoly on the control of certain services, leaving the CAO to explain to council that it will not have complete control over a service for which it provides a significant amount of the funding. This poses a problem because municipalities struggle to let go of control even when the NFP group has greater knowledge and understanding of the challenge or opportunity.

Public-Educational Partnerships

Many municipalities that have post-secondary institutions within their boundaries have taken advantage of the expertise found in these institutions. This can be a mix of informal and formal agreements (so-called town-and-gown agreements are common in university towns). Niagara, Hamilton, Guelph, Kingston, and Oshawa all have formally established partnerships in place. From economic development to innovation to healthy neighbourhoods, they all play key roles in their communities.

TeachingCity Oshawa

During my time as city manager in Oshawa, the city developed TeachingCity Oshawa. The concept was born at a key lunch meeting of Professor Daniel Hoornweg from the University of Ontario Institute of Technology (UOIT), known as Ontario Tech University; then-councillor, later mayor Dan Carter; and me as the city manager. Professor Hoornweg led us through discussions of collaboration and the need to mimic something similar to a teaching hospital and create post-secondary opportunities to experience municipal business. Teaching hospitals straddle the university and the community; they provide an important service to the community while serving a research and teaching function for the university. Could this be replicated in fields other than health care?

From a municipal vantage point, there was interest in creating a talent pool that would have a greater understanding of municipal activities and could engage current municipal employees to give them a new experience. Silos can be a challenge for municipal administration. TeachingCity Oshawa was an opportunity to transcend silos through youthful enthusiasm and remove traditional municipal blinders.

BUILDING SUPPORT

I was sold on the idea, but then the hard work began. I needed to build support in both the Corporate Leadership Team and council.

The corporate leadership team consisted of seven members: the CAO, commissioners of corporate services, development services, financial services, and community services, the executive director of human resources, and the city solicitor. My team was accustomed to my bringing forward thoughts, ideas, or curve balls for us to think through. The TeachingCity idea had to have a "hook" (Fraser Institute, 2020), and I landed on human resources. Most municipalities are experiencing a war for talent. Although there were a few different hooks available such as financial, relationship building, and others, the main angle I used was that this would help us in our war for talent. Familiarizing post-secondary students with the complexities of municipal government and developing a talent pool that is knowledgeable about the city would increase interest in working for the city.

With the main hook firmly in place, it took about a month to discuss other challenges identified by the team. Team members needed to be reassured about where the resources would come from, how this would affect their staff, and how it would be embedded in work plans. Financially we outlined an initial cost of less than $100,000 for the first year. The human resource issue was more challenging. With the fiscal challenges we had in the city, there were not many new positions, and the vast majority of them were for frontline staff. After a detailed team review of vacant positions and emerging leaders (more on emerging leaders later), we outlined a strategy to redeploy an emerging leader and delete a position that had virtually net zero impact. I had built up a great deal of credit with my team, so they permitted me to make a significant withdrawal in asking them to trust me on this one. Two down and third to go.

Embedding TeachingCity in work plans caused me to draw on an approach I insist on for continuous improvement. All projects undertaken must align with annual department deliverables. This will not be perfect on day one, but over a year or two the alignment between projects will improve significantly. When they were satisfied that their concerns had been addressed, team members supported the idea. At this point, I went back to Professor Hoornweg to let him know that I had cleared one hurdle.

Getting council on side was more complicated. I did not want to spring a new idea on councillors suddenly, so I undertook what I refer to as "socializing" the idea with council. Since some of them might see this as a radical, risky adventure, I decided to introduce the concept to them slowly and in a way that would not seem threatening. This involved finding a councillor who would introduce the idea to his fellow councillors. I was fortunate to enlist Councillor Dan Carter as a champion. He helped in many strategic ways. First, an idea coming from a fellow councillor would be viewed differently from something coming purely from staff. Councillor Carter was also chair of the finance committee, which meant that finding the required financial room was not a significant challenge as he was already supportive. Most important, he had a great relationship with other councillors, which made it much easier to socialize the idea. He also had great connections with post-secondary institutions in Oshawa. Together, we slowly seeded the idea through different meetings, and after the mayor and councillors had heard about it for approximately two months, we formalized the opportunity.

While socializing the idea with council, I worked with the Corporate Leadership Team and we drew on a group of emerging leaders. These were city staff members who had been identified through a rigorous process for strategic investment. They ended up being our go-to people for special assignments and development opportunities. Together, we developed an outline of how this initiative would be structured: who would be involved, what it might cost, how it would be managed, why it would be a great opportunity for the city, what sort of headlines it would create, how it would fit council priorities, and so forth. I was conscious that presenting a new idea to council that had gaping holes would be a recipe for failure.

The goal is to get the right heads nodding up and down with you during council's consideration of the opportunity. The meeting with council included senior officials from Ontario Tech to underscore their interest. It is one thing for the CAO to recommend support; it is another when council can scan the room and get those unofficial nods of approval that give them further confidence.

As we moved towards an agreement with Ontario Tech, we realized that we were not including some other local educational institutions (Durham College, Trent University, institutions in the Greater Toronto Area) so we slowed down to circulate the idea and assess their interest. Our patience paid off when they joined the project. The idea then crossed borders with the inclusion of the University of Toronto and the Canadian Urban Institute (CUI) as a result of Professor Hoornweg's initiatives. This meant that we needed to reconsider what an agreement would look like. The fortunate part was that the new partners considerably enhanced our pitch to council. What council would not want to support a collaboration between the city and four post-secondary institutions as well as CUI?

The next step was to move the post-secondary institutions from being interested to making a firm commitment. Ontario Tech was first to the table, and this prompted the others to move forward.

The fact that we had proceeded by way of a Memorandum of Agreement (MOA), rather than a formal agreement, proved to be a very wise decision. The informality associated with the MOA format made everyone more comfortable. This was still somewhat complicated, however, as everyone had to agree on governance and terms. I went back to council to update it on progress, and discovered that it was still excited over the idea. We were now about eight months in, however, and I was aware that time kills great projects.

We rushed to complete an MOA, but this required legal staff from each institution to clear it. Municipalities are not the only ones with time-consuming and risk-averse internal processes; our post-secondary partners had approval processes as well.

As we approached the ten-month mark, we needed to push it over the goal line. From the city's perspective, we were in the midst of budget discussions and needed the funds approved to allow the project to start. So, it was important to consolidate the support of our post-secondary partners.

We used several methods to cement our relationship. One of the most important was simply effective listening. We were comfortable with engaging in active listening, then breaking out in smaller groups for brainstorming, then regrouping to continue talking There was also significant peer pressure as a result of who was at the table and the threat of "not being part of it."

The prospective partners had many of the same concerns as had the management team earlier. The city played the important roles of leader and mediator, but each participant had one vote in the decision-making process. A key to keeping everyone on side was flexibility. It was understood that the basic financial commitment expected from everyone was fairly minimal. Beyond that basic commitment, partners could choose the projects in which they wanted to participate, and they negotiated the contribution of human and financial resources they would make to those projects. Thus, they could ensure that they would contribute only to projects that aligned with their own objectives. Everyone accepted that this meant that all partners would not necessarily be involved in, and make a financial contribution to, every project. This made joining the partnership much easier.

Reports were generated and the important council meeting was scheduled. Senior staff from the post-secondary institutions attended the meeting to demonstrate support and answer any questions. Council approved the idea unanimously and with great enthusiasm.

A key aspect of my reports to council was ensuring that the governance model was well understood. The partnership was governed by a steering committee composed of one senior staff member from each organization. This committee would consider opportunities with a goal of providing value to each party, meaning that the project was not controlled by council even though it was partially funded through the city. The senior staff on the steering committee not only brought forward priorities from their respective organizations' current strategic plans; they also laid the foundation for future strategic plans that would consider the interests of each participating organization. In theory, over time, each organization's strategic plan would become complementary, allowing for even more collaboration.

The city provides some support through the rental of a downtown property and the occasional time of city employees. With the municipality, several educational institutions, and a municipal think tank on side, it became possible to leverage funds from other sources. For example, one project received a substantial grant from the RBC Foundation. A number of other initiatives have been undertaken since inception. The two examples described below provide a flavour of what the partners are doing.

The Diversity and Inclusion Plan

"The City of Oshawa's Diversity and Inclusion Plan is a five to ten year framework for ensuring all people feel welcome and involved in our community. The goal is [to] make sure community members have fair access to programs, services and employment opportunities in Oshawa. It also outlines internal recommendations to enhance diversity, equity and inclusion within the staff" (City of Oshawa, n.d.).

THE DIVERSITY AND INCLUSION PLAN

Research conducted by faculty and students of Ontario Tech allowed the city to draw on the best practices from other countries and industries in developing its diversity and inclusion plan. It cost us nothing when a study of this nature would have easily cost $100,000–$200,000 with the traditional approach. The strength of the partners paid dividends as it engendered much more goodwill than the traditional approach because the community was truly part of this project. It was recognized by other municipalities as an approach to replicate.

City Idea Lab

"City Idea Lab allows post-secondary students to work directly with faculty and city staff to co-design solutions to local issues through knowledge transfer, dialogue, and experimentation. Each semester, students work on unique city-identified challenge questions" (City Idea Lab, 2021).

CITY IDEA LAB

The city purchased some repurposed retail units on the ground floor of a parking garage to create City Idea Lab in downtown Oshawa. Ontario Tech and Durham College provided furniture and technology. This brought more students to our downtown core, which was part of our downtown strategy. Classes were taught related to social challenges in Oshawa, with tours and exposure to city data, staff, and problems. Solutions were developed and brought back to the city. Engagement was huge from post-secondary students, city staff, and NFP groups. This partnership continues to grow and develop new ideas. It has been beneficial to all partners and to the local community.

This partnership clearly meets Kernaghan's definition of "a relationship involving *the sharing of power, work, support and/or information* with others for the achievement of joint goals and/or mutual benefits" (Kernaghan, 1993, p. 61, emphasis in original). It also provides examples of the concepts of co-production and co-governance discussed earlier in the chapter. The diversity and inclusion plan is a classic example of co-production. The city needed a plan and had some ideas about what the plan should include; the post-secondary institutions had the research expertise to draw on experience in other places. The result was a plan that satisfied the needs of the city at a cost considerably lower than it would have paid consultants for such a plan.

Co-governance is modelled in the steering committee consisting of representatives of all the member organizations. The decision that members could opt into specific initiatives and pass up on the opportunity for others simplified decision making while keeping all members involved in the overall structure. The loose nature of the governance and funding arrangement has been a strength of the partnership.

The N6: A Municipal Collaboration

The N6 collaboration comprises the Northern Six local municipalities in the Regional Municipality of York (or York Region), immediately north of Toronto. The N6 municipalities are the Township of King, and the towns of Whitchurch-Stouffville, Georgina, East Gwillimbury, Aurora, and Newmarket. These six local municipalities form a natural combination because they are contiguous and comparatively small with a total population of almost 280,000, representing 25 per cent of York Region's population (as of 2016).

Many smaller municipalities outside the Greater Toronto-Hamilton Area are unable to benefit from the economies of scale and the resources generated by larger municipalities. This situation is likely to become worse if Ken Coates's prediction holds true: "[F]or countless smaller centres across Canada, these are worrying times, to be sure. Economic growth has slowed or reversed in most communities, particularly in rural areas and resource-dependent towns" (Coates, 2019).

Partnerships such as the N6 are difficult to achieve, as municipalities are always concerned with how they are identified. Each has a rich and storied history that make it passionate about how it is represented. Although this might seem trivial, it is an important factor that can make or break a successful partnership. There can also be some concern that any form of collaboration could be a precursor to consolidation, which they all fear.

The N6 collaboration was formed in 2006 by the mayors and CAOs of the Northern Six municipalities as a way to share services and sometimes take a shared position on issues. The mayors and CAOs generally meet quarterly to discuss progress and brainstorm new opportunities. The mayors share ideas of where they might like us to focus, but CAOs bring forward opportunities as well. Ultimately, when the priorities are identified, it is over to the CAOs to make them happen and to update on progress. The group has developed shared services in many functions, such as internal audit, solid waste and recycling collection, insurance and risk management, and animal control.

N6 has no employees, although someone usually steps forward to take minutes of meetings and handle similar clerical tasks. When the group decides on an initiative, such as a joint-purchasing arrangement that requires a request for proposals, a task group of middle managers from the affected municipalities will meet to organize that initiative.

One of the N6 partnership's first initiatives was internal audit. None of the N6 had an internal auditor and none of them could justify this as a full-time position, so they entered into an MOU with York Region to provide this service. A side benefit is that the regional auditors could, with permission, provide comparative data for the six to assist in benchmarking best practices.

The N6 collaboration has been highly beneficial to its members. It has resulted in significant savings and improved the quality of services, and it has done this while allowing each of the six to maintain its separate identity, which is a very important value for them. Because of their size and location, the spectre of amalgamation comes up occasionally (Latchford, 2019), and there was concern that this could have been on the agenda during the review of regional governments mentioned earlier. This partnership allowed the six to argue that they were already obtaining all of the financial benefits of combined service delivery without the political and logistical baggage of a forced amalgamation (Town of Aurora, 2020). Of course, this argument is a double-edged sword in that it could be turned around to say that these municipalities effectively already have merged several of their services in such a way that full amalgamation is just the next incremental step. At this point, however, the partners see this arrangement as an efficient way of dealing with the provision of certain services. The only potential obstacles to the N6 partnership's continued existence are the usual pressures of time, other priorities, risk aversion, and motivating people to participate.

Lessons Learned: Hard Work, Patience, Commitment, Adaptation, and Opportunities

The purpose of this chapter was to analyse the various ways that governments can use partnerships and to share my experiences working with two partnerships that have been very successful. The subtitle of the chapter warned that partnerships involve hard work, patience, commitment, and adaptation, at the same time that they promise significant opportunity.

Hard work. Creating a partnership begins with doing exploratory work to attract a partner and socializing decision makers and others in your own organization to accept an idea that will be foreign to them. That is just the beginning of the hard work, because now you need to figure out how the co-production and co-governance will work and sell these ideas to all partners. And all of this needs to be handled delicately because it is a very fragile package at this point.

The TeachingCity initiative required a great deal of hard work on my part to keep all the actors in the city in place while simultaneously ensuring that the increasing number of community partners was still on side. A false step at any point could have brought the whole package crashing down.

Patience. Maintaining some level of speed in moving forward is essential because time can kill even the best project. Patience, however, is a virtue as well. You will be selling an idea that will be foreign to many of the decision makers. Partnerships are still a relatively new idea to municipal governments, and there are stories of governments that were burned by partnerships that went bad. You should expect your councillors to begin discussion in a somewhat risk-averse mode. You need to increase their comfort level by providing them the hard information they need to make their decision, but you need to respect the fact that they will need time to digest the information.

TeachingCity could have been completed much more quickly, but we slowed down at one point to take on more partners. Still, the inclusion of additional partners made the expanded partnership much more attractive to council. We also had to take the time to work out the co-production and co-governance aspects of the partnership. Handling these improperly could have scuttled the entire project.

Commitment. Persevering through the inevitable hard work and delays can make it difficult to maintain your commitment to a partnership, but that level of commitment is important in selling the project to those around you. They will be sceptical about whether this will work, and they are wise to have a healthy level of scepticism. Staff might be worried that a new initiative will take resources that they need to do their job. Risk-averse councillors will be worried that this could fail and be both a money pit and an embarrassment for the municipality. Your level of commitment will help you endure in the face of these obstacles and your confidence will help those around you develop the courage they need to pursue a risky project.

In the years since the N6 partnership began, most of the mayors and CAOs who have driven the project have changed several times. It is, however, a good project that provides significant value to the public. I had no difficulty developing a strong commitment to the partnership, even though I arrived after it had been in existence for many years. It helps me do my job.

Adaptation. Probably the most important and also the most difficult characteristic that you will need to develop is adaptation. By definition, entering into a partnership means that you and your organization will not be calling all the shots. You should begin the process with a clear understanding of what you want from the partnership and about the lines you will not able to cross. For example, accountability and transparency are core values of municipal governments, while some private sector companies need to preserve trade secrets or other competitive information. It is unlikely that these two types of organizations can undertake a successful partnership unless these values can be reconciled.

You must be flexible in dealing with partners, but you must also ensure that your organization is receiving value from the partnership. Partnerships only work when all partners are receiving some value from them.

Not all parties will want to participate in all projects. When we discovered this in TeachingCity, we turned it into a strength by giving partners the flexibility to carve out their own projects. This also allowed partners to initiate their own projects and find the funding for them.

Not every project will go flawlessly; plan on adjustments. Of the projects the N6 partnership has considered, some fell together quickly and easily, others required much more tugging and hauling to get them moving, and some just never moved forward.

Conclusion: Realizing the Opportunities

The partnerships described in this chapter have definitely produced value. TeachingCity is an innovative partnership that provides valuable learning opportunities to students and faculty who in turn have produced research of significant value to the city. The N6 partnership has allowed the partner municipalities to engage in activities, such as internal audit, that none of them could do on its own.

My experiences with these partnerships have taught me how valuable they can be. I also learned that they require hard work, patience, commitment, and adaptation to realize the tremendous opportunity they represent to work with private sector partners, other governments, and the local community to improve the quality of services in an economic and efficient manner. As the resources available to government become more strained, we should look to partnerships as a way for governments to make an impact without increasing the resources devoted to governments in the form of taxation.

REFERENCES

Berardi, J. (2008). The Niagara casinos partnership: A game of chance? In K. Rasmussen & D. Siegel (Eds.), *Professionalism and public service: Essays in honour of Kenneth Kernaghan* (pp. 207–35). University of Toronto Press.

Boisvert, N. (2019, 19 January). Ontario reviewing regional governments, raising prospect of future amalgamations. *CBC News*. https://www.cbc.ca/news/canada/toronto/ontario-regional-government-review-1.4978949

Boyle, D., & Harris, M. (2009, December). The challenge of co-production: How equal partnerships between professionals and the public are crucial to improving public services. Discussion paper. Retrieved from https://media.nesta.org.uk/documents/the_challenge_of_co-production.pdf

Canada. (2020, 25 October). Guideline to implementing Budget 2011 directions on public-private partnerships. https://www.tbs-sct.gc.ca/pol/doc-eng.aspx?id=25576§ion=html

Canadian Council for Public-Private Partnerships. (2020, 24 October). Projects. http://www.p3spectrum.ca/project/

Cheng, Y. (2019). Governing government-nonprofit partnerships: Linking governance mechanisms to collaboration stages. *Public Performance & Management Review*, *42*(1), 190–212. https://doi.org/10.1080/15309576.2018.1489294

City of Oshawa. (n.d.). Diversity and inclusion plan. Retrieved from https://www.oshawa.ca/en/city-hall/diversity-and-inclusion-plan.aspx?_mid_=3676

City Idea Lab. (2021). Spring 2021. Retrieved from https://oshawacityidealab.squarespace.com/spring-2021

Coates, K. (2019, September). City states and the future of Canada's smaller communities. *Municipal World*. https://www.municipalworld.com/articles/city-states-and-the-future-of-canadas-smaller-communities/

Davis, G., & Ostrom, E. (1991). A political economy approach to education: Choice and co-production. *International Political Science Review*, *12*(4), 313–35. https://doi.org/10.1177/019251219101200405

Fraser Institute. (2020, 19 August). Tax relief should be top priority for Doug Ford. https://www.fraserinstitute.org/article/tax-relief-should-be-top-priority-for-doug-ford

Hanniman, K. (2013). Borrowing today for the city of tomorrow? Municipal debt & alternative financing. Institute on Municipal Finance & Governance.

Kernaghan, K. (1993). Partnerships and public administration: Conceptual and practical considerations. *Canadian Public Administration*, *36*(1), 57–76. https://doi.org/10.1111/j.1754-7121.1993.tb02166.x

Latchford, T. (2019, 31 January). Analysis: Should the York Region northern six municipalities amalgamate? https://www.yorkregion.com/news-story/9151131-analysis-should-the-york-region-northern-six-municipalities-amalgamate

Siemiatycki, M. (2015). Public-private partnerships in Canada: Some reflections on twenty years of practice. *Canadian Public Administration*, *58*(3), 343–62. http://doi.org/10.1111/capa.12119

Town of Aurora. (2020, 26 October). N6 municipalities in York Region respond to provincial announcement on regional governance review. https://www.aurora.ca/en/news/n6-municipalities-in-york-region-respond-to-provincial-announcement-on-regional-governance-review.aspx

19 Nurturing the Community's Soul Source

LINDA RAPP

Local government has relied on collaboration with volunteers, businesses, and community groups to enhance quality of life opportunities beyond municipal services. The late Linda Rapp's extensive recreation career provides key insights for working with groups to undertake community development efforts such as projects, programs, and events. This cooperative spirit is evident in her leadership approach as Whitehorse's city manager to public engagement and hosting the Arctic Games.

My family owned a country general store that served surrounding farming communities. It was an amazing childhood, and I always felt a strong sense of community even though it was never discussed. We were not wealthy, and thinking back I don't know how we managed to stock the store adequately. Families would pick up supplies that were entered into a ledger to be paid for after harvest. While we carried that debt, we were supported by the whole community and our home freezer was never empty. Community effort also went into developing an outdoor skating rink, maintaining the school, and organizing special community events. These childhood experiences gave me a strong appreciation of how a community works and develops.

People have told me community is in my DNA. I've always been interested in community leadership and my early career was in recreation. Thirty years ago, when I was starting my recreation career with the City of Whitehorse, the focus was on public works and building the infrastructure. Parks and recreation services were important to address the social needs of the community, but they were heavily dependent on volunteer organizations and individuals.

Here is my story – what I believe and what I have learned – and a model I present to describe key considerations for local government's collaborative efforts with community stakeholders. My personal experience through five case studies for the City of Whitehorse reveals lessons learned for organizational and CAO readiness to tap a community's soul source through community development efforts.

What Is Community Development?

Community development and community engagement are co-dependent. In my mind, community development refers to people and a local government coming together to achieve common aims. The result is collective action that produces desired outputs: programs and projects. Community engagement might focus on inputs: ideas and feedback to local government decisions and actions. It involves people having a voice on matters that will affect their lives, neighbourhood, or the community. In my experience, meaningful community development is difficult to achieve without well-intentioned community engagement as the starting point.

Often, community development resides in the planning department for the process of physically developing a community. Public engagement processes such as charrettes and world cafés (Rowe et al., 2013; World Cafe, 2020) can be helpful in co-creating a vision for a new neighbourhood. Meaningful engagement can lead to successful place making: transforming a public physical space to reflect community values and aspirations and to connect people to place.

Community development is more than developing local physical elements and land uses. It is only through community engagement for a wider range of local government activities that you truly develop the soul of the community culture and grow community-minded people. My experiences support what Harvard Business School's Peter Drucker coined: "culture eats strategy for breakfast" (Drucker, 1959, p. 28). The culture of a community improves when it employs a community development lens throughout all its diverse strategic and operational activities.

As a lens for strategic activities, community development works best as an upfront consideration – who else would have a vested interest in the project or initiative and what might they bring to the table? It also functions as a lens for operational activities in considering additional insights and finding options to address issues of service delivery.

Considerations

Based on my experience, here are some key considerations for involving residents and businesses in community development efforts.

Resource mobilization: There will be times when you will need to leverage community involvement to deliver projects or events. Having positive stakeholder relationships helps local governments to access resources when needed. I am continuously meeting new groups and sustaining relationships with local businesses and volunteer groups even when there is no pending need for help for a city initiative. As well, people will bring forth ideas seeking local government support if there is a foundation of trust.

Implementation success: Empowering the community means the community has some ownership of the plan or project and consequently its implementation. Community organizations have networks of individuals that can support both start-up implementation and ongoing operations. I have learned that seeking stakeholder support of a city project at the eleventh hour requires selling it rather than sharing it.

Expertise development: Building stakeholder teamwork and expertise into the project supports community and organizational capacity building. There have been many times when uncertainty among city staff waned when local expertise filled internal knowledge gaps. At the same time, mutual training and knowledge sharing among staff and stakeholders have bolstered local group organizational and planning skills. Well-organized groups require less city intervention to ensure their continuity to provide a needed services.

In-kind contribution: Many volunteer organizations do not have the administrative support or infrastructure required to achieve their aims. The city, however, can provide funds, facilities, and/or equipment. I remind elected officials that eligible groups provide services to meet specific needs that otherwise would be expected as city services. Focusing on the "investment in community" and "subsidizing" a service or program or project are really the same thing, with a value judgment. It is often easier to support community investment over subsidizing a particular interest group. The key is identifying how the investment adds value to the community.

Community network: Building relationships requires building organization linkages that will serve the municipality beyond a specific initiative. The community development network is not only available to the municipality; it also enables collaboration among community organizations. Ongoing city support of volunteers and groups takes effort, so do not engage or activate until you are ready to commit to your part in the relationship. Be sincere and do not bring individuals or groups into the process if there is no real role or benefit to them or the project.

Councils are increasingly interested in performance metrics as competition increases for taxpayers' dollars. This makes supporting community development initiatives financially challenging because the outcome is less tangible than allocations to directly provided municipal services such as roads, utilities, and facilities. Requests for funding contributions for a community development initiative need to focus on identifying the community benefit and value-added outcomes. Municipal leaders need to be mindful of what William Bruce Cameron (1963, p. 13) advised: "Not everything that counts can be counted; not everything that can be counted counts."

A community development initiative is successful only when it achieves a community benefit. This does not mean the initial goal is always achieved, but rather that the process has been a positive experience creating learning, understanding, skill development, empathy, and relationship/network building. Hard outputs matter, but so do soft outputs such as trust and ongoing relationships.

Community Development in Action

I found that the Relationship Formulation Process Model from the City of Richmond, British Columbia, provided a framework to examine a few of my community development experiences (City of Richmond, 2004). The model is based on encouraging community involvement and engagement through four initial steps and two implementation steps:

1) clarifying who has initiated the project – is the champion for the initiative a person, single group, or number of interests?
2) determining if the city is involved – does the program or project fall within its service menu or strategic agenda?
3) determining how the city is involved – what role or resources must the city provide to aid the project sponsors to move forward?
4) establishing who will be the other partners in the relationship – how will the city ensure effective communication from and accountability by the other party(s)?
5) determining the type of relationship – will it be informal with casual liaison expectations, or formal by way of a contract or agreement?
6) ascertaining the support needed for the relationship – does the other party require additional assistance, such as training, administrative support, or external expertise to be an effective partner?

The following four case studies demonstrate these steps in action in the City of Whitehorse. There are elements of success as well as failure, all with key learnings that highlight why incorporating a community development model is in the interest of residents and the municipal governments that serve them.

Millennium Trail: Empowering Individuals towards a Goal

Father Jean-Marie Mouchet was a senior citizen well known in the community for his passion for walking and skiing. He had an idea for an accessible paved five-kilometre loop along the downtown waterfront. The city took on administration of the group process, including completing funding applications, arranging meeting set-up and notes, and preparing council reports and communication. With the focus on accessibility key to the project, a representative from the Council on Disabilities was recruited. There was also representation from the Riverdale Community Association (the neighbourhood the trail would affect) and the Rotary Service Club, which gave the project community credibility.

Meetings were often held by walking on-site, where the area was studied and challenges identified. Of course, there were some initial challenges, as some people did not want to see a natural trail paved, but the principle of "accessible to all" was a solid response and empathy was created. This is a good example of steps 5 and 6 of the Relationship Formulation Process Model (exploring the type of relationship and what is needed to support it), where a clear understanding of the desired outcomes provided a solid foundation for collaboration.

In the end it was a successful community development project because residents and government shared a common vision. Community members embraced the project and quickly incorporated it into their daily active lifestyle experiences.

Never underestimate the power of passionate people. I have found that it is important to give voice to community interests. When they are positive, it is advantageous to collaborate and meet the diverse needs of the community. I have also found that actively listening to concerns with an open mind can result in constructive and positive outcomes.

Skateboard Park: Mixing Generations and Different Community Members

In the early 1990s, a by-law banned skateboarding from downtown sidewalks and business parking lots. Neighbourhood streets were starting to see a collection of handmade apparatus that were not built to any safety standard. A group of young people approached the city requesting a skateboard park because there was really nowhere else for them to go. They had no interest in becoming a "formal non-profit group" or understanding the steps that would be involved, but they were passionate about their sport. A few meetings were held (with pizza; food brings people together) to understand the request and the group's vision.

A volunteer landscape architect came forward to work with the group, which was encouraged to bring pictures from magazines or videos highlighting the features they liked. This formed the basis of the park design. The recreation department worked with the Yukon government to get permission to use a small piece of land near two schools, with good bus access and visibility. It was not in a residential area and would not be considered a disturbance.

Funding opportunities required a not-for-profit organization to apply. Staff met with a few service clubs to pitch the idea of supporting the project, and the Grey Mountain Lions agreed. They brought their networks and community credibility to the project. The young people learned about municipal process and attended the required city council meetings to present their plan, including a video they had put together. The visual of the partnership and the creativity was not lost on city council or the community.

The youth actively fundraised by collecting items and services from the community. The timing was also good in that there was significant funding available federally to address youth-at-risk. In the end, approximately $900,000 was raised and the project became a reality. Throughout the project, the youth were acknowledged as the experts. Their vision was accepted and they were on-site regularly during construction to approve the work under way.

The project was a success and served the community well for over twenty years. It was a success because of the process of working with the target group that would use the facility. Mutual respect was achieved through different generations and different skill sets working together. This story demonstrates steps 3 and 4 of the Relationship Formulation Process Model (how the city is involved and with whom the city is developing a relationship), where the city's role was to facilitate the process and to secure the land from the Yukon government, and the relationship being developed was with the youth in the community.

CAOs should not fear bringing diverse interests together. Having a wide range of facilitation skills helps you to enable conflicting views to be heard respectfully, with the potential for collaborative solutions. Community development initiatives can provide an antidote to polarization within the community. In this digital world, it is important to provide experiences that keep people connected to something bigger than their personal perspective.

Canada Winter Games: Having a Common Purpose

Hosting the 2007 Canada Winter Games, the first Games hosted north of the sixtieth parallel, was a huge undertaking for the Yukon. With the City of Whitehorse as a lead, we knew we would need to mobilize the entire community. As much as we wanted to deliver a uniquely northern event and set a new standard, we also wanted to be smart and leverage every opportunity to see a legacy for the community after the Games. We knew we could deliver the sport competitions, but the legacy of sport facilities, housing, volunteer capacity building, and marketing the North were considered legacy items that would remain as benefits to the community after the Games. Some approaches were innovative and proved to be successful:

- *The Canada Games Centre.* A sport multiplex facility was planned and constructed with significant community engagement. The goal was to build a facility that addressed gaps in the community while meeting the technical specifications for national-level sport competitions – for example, badminton required a 30-foot ceiling for competition, which allowed for a running and walking track that the community needed. To this day, 10 per cent of the population uses the Canada Games Centre every day. It is the centre of community.
- *The Athletes Village.* The Games required special quarters for the athletes' accommodation. To fill this requirement, the Yukon government financed a housing project at the local college that could be transformed after the Games to much-needed seniors' residences.
- *A Pan-North approach.* This strategy was used to market the Games as a celebration of Canada's North as host of people from the "South," and allowed the showcasing of uniquely northern elements of sport and culture. This aspect prompted local pride in being a "Northerner" while enhancing worldwide tourism opportunities.
- *Additional training for local coaches and officials.* Local coaches and officials received additional training to contribute to the numbers that would be required for the Games. It reduced the number of outside officials who needed to be flown in and enhanced diverse sport development capacity in Yukon Territory
- *A Venue Management Model.* This model, used for planning, involved training the whole volunteer sector in a new process. Volunteer planning skills that were developed still benefit the community today.
- *The fostering of community pride.* The community's pride as host was evident throughout the Games and especially at the wrap-up

volunteer event at the conclusion of the Games. It was three solid years of planning but delivered community benefits that will never be forgotten.

For this initiative, every step of the Relationship Formulation Process Model and every tool listed in step 6 (the tools needed to support the relationship) was used to support the relationship, including agreements, MOUs, a communications strategy, and risk assessment. Today, Whitehorse continues to benefit from the legacy of well-planned Games amenities. Equally important, the community groups and networks remain strong enough to offer diverse services to residents well beyond the city's capacity.

It is easy to get excited about significant events, but these can quickly become negative legacies without due diligence. I have learned that solid documentation of expectations and commitments must accompany the good intentions of stakeholders in any project. Some perseverance is required as volunteers often resist such bureaucratic requirements.

Bus-Wrap Initiative: Considering Inclusion, Culture, and Patience

Most Canadians have seen transit vehicles wrapped in a plastic skin carrying a commercial or public service message, commonly known as a bus-wrap. The request to create a transit bus-wrap came to the city from two First Nations governments within the Whitehorse city boundary: the councils of Kwanlin Dun and Ta'an Kwachan. The request's timing was good, as the Truth and Reconciliation Commission of Canada's Final Report, outlining the calls to action for reconciliation for local government consideration, had recently been released.

A group was established to move the project forward. Funding was not a challenge, as contributions came from all three parties (the two First Nations and the city government). The process established that Indigenous Elders would select the artwork to be converted to a bus-wrap, but the project stalled at this point because the Elders initially were unable to agree on the representative artwork.

The project might have ended there and then, or the city might have intervened to push the project to completion at the risk of eroding the relationship. Participants eventually realized, however, that compromise and collaboration were needed – that the project would not happen if they could not focus on the artwork rather than on the membership of the artist. All participants exercised patience, and it took almost two years to bring this project to the finish line. In the end, the process was as meaningful as the final result.

The unveiling of the bus-wrap became a celebration of the relationship and trust that had developed through the project. On the morning of the unveiling, the Elders were picked up by the bus with the bus-wrap and taken to the unveiling site. The celebration included the signing of a Declaration of Commitment by the mayor of Whitehorse and both chiefs of the First Nations governments. The declaration indicated that they agreed to continue to work together on reconciliation. The public was invited to participate in the celebration and share tea and bannock. A ninety-year-old Elder who participated had never been on public transit before, but indicated she would now feel comfortable accessing the service.

In this example, steps 4 and 5 of the Relationship Formulation Process Model (with whom the city is developing a relationship and the type of relationship) are clearly exemplified by the relationship building that occurred with the two First Nations governments through a specific project of mutual interest. Although it was a partnership approach to addressing reconciliation, the more significant aspect is the ongoing communication and efforts by all three parties to collaborate in serving the interests of the greater community of communities.

As a CAO with many irons in the fire, you will find it is often easier to be transactional in dealing with specific projects. Get it done and move on to the next initiative. It takes patience to allow some processes to unfold to achieve the greatest community benefits. A meaningful community development effort results in enduring relationships for future opportunities – that is the essence of transformational leadership!

Trail Plan: Learning that a Good Process Can Fade

In 1997, mostly in response to the emergence of trail use conflicts, the city developed a Trail Plan. Terms of reference were developed and a committee struck representing a variety of trail users. The initial work of the community representation was very successful. The members of the group listened to all the different perspectives on trail development and designation (multi-use, motorized, non-motorized). They developed understanding and empathy and were able to work together to develop principles and a vision as well as standards for trail development and maintenance. The work of the community members – other than a role with ongoing trail stewardship – should have concluded at that point. But by keeping the community involved in the process through implementation in various neighbourhoods, the process began to deteriorate and be manipulated by special interests, and the committee was dissolved.

When engaging in community development initiatives, it is important to think about the timing of involving the community. In this case, step 6 of the Relationship Formulation Process Model (the support needed for the relationship) was missed, resulting in a lack of clarity for participants' understanding of their ongoing role. Since then, the city has ensured that a terms of reference or project charter is developed for community partnerships. In addition to stating purpose, roles, expectations, and process, a "sunset" clause is inserted as a prompt for the city to decide whether or not to extend the arrangement.

Conclusion

I believe a strong community requires many contributors. Residents and local groups are fundamental through their unique abilities to lead or help municipal government initiatives such as policy development, place making, service delivery, and special events. Consequently, there are core competencies that need attention and development for CAOs to facilitate and participate in community-led community initiatives.

Engagement is key initially to mobilizing people, organizations, and partners in developing goals, executing plans, and delivering results. Actively listening to different viewpoints to convey genuine interest in others' ideas and concerns nurtures open dialogue. Being receptive to possibilities and aligning city and potential partners' interests lays the relationship groundwork before any partnership can be pursued and ultimately sustained.

Alignment of city and third-party interests requires the CAO's clear and consistent communication regarding the city's aims and conditions. Any agreements built on false understanding by either party will render the initiative vulnerable. More significantly, the expected longer-term relationship will also be damaged. The CAO needs negotiation and perhaps mediation skills to reach solid partnership arrangements that council can support and that do not put the city at risk. At the same time, the CAO needs to have conviction for the project to convince council to give up an element of control and certainty.

The collaborative CAO needs to be adaptive to changing conditions. Projects can encounter difficulties that might require the city to adjust its role in the face of potential abandonment. Patience is required to realize that other people or organizations do not have the same competencies as you or the city to implement a project.

Employing the steps in the Relationship Formulation Process Model will lead many projects and community initiatives to successful outcomes for your community. Collaborating for community development is more than just project management with other stakeholders. The CAO needs well-developed people skills to build and maintain effective working relationships or networks of groups and people who are, or might someday be, instrumental in achieving community goals. If you as the CAO do not have all the required collaborative competencies, develop them or seek them out in others on your leadership team. As a civic leader, you play a critical community development role in fostering conditions for a healthier, more vibrant, and inclusive community.

REFERENCES

Cameron, W. B. (1963). *Informal sociology: A casual introduction to sociological thinking*. Random House.

City of Richmond. (2004). A framework to encourage community involvement and establish/maintain effective relationships. City of Richmond Parks, Recreation and Cultural Services. https://www.richmond.ca/__shared/assets/community_involve8053.pdf

Drucker, P. (1959). Work and tools. *Technology and Culture*, 1(1), 28–37. https://doi.org/10.2307/3100785

Rowe, W. E., Graf, M., Agger-Gupta, N., Piggot-Irvine, E., & Harris, B. (2013). *Action research engagement: Creating the foundations for organizational change.* Action Learning, Action Research Association (ALARA), monograph series 5. Royal Roads University, School of Leadership Studies. https://www.researchgate.net/publication/259932785_Action_Research_Engagement_Creating_the_Foundations_for_Organizational_Change

World Cafe. (2020). About us. https://theworldcafe.com/about-us/history/

20 Community Development: Navigating the Rocky Shoals of Community Change

ROBERT BUCHAN

The aspiration to effect changes in local government relies on developing and maintaining relevant stakeholder group support over the long term as strategic efforts are incrementally implemented. Robert Buchan, former CAO of North Saanich, British Columbia, shares insights on real-world community development practices based on his development of a theory of "transformational incrementalism." His insights offer considerations for how city managers and their staff can develop strategic approaches to achieve change incrementally in our urban systems.

City managers hold differing opinions on their role grounded in the wide variety of their professional backgrounds and experience. My own professional background is in the planning field, and this has influenced how I perceived and conducted myself in ten years of working as a city manager. I saw my role as being in the business of community development.

When I engaged with staff in food system planning, neighbourhood planning, parks planning, and revitalization, for example, I was aspiring to bring about a better, more sustainable, healthier, and resilient community. Late in my career, I became interested in local food systems because of their potential role in making communities more sustainable and resilient. This interest led me to undertake a PhD program in 2012 at the University of Victoria, where my research focused on planning processes intended to effect change. The product of this effort is a theory based on what actually occurs in planning processes: a change theory called Transformative Incrementalism (TI), acknowledged by "change masters" with experience in a variety of urban planning focuses (Buchan, 2019) as being highly relevant to their change efforts. I have introduced TI and explored its relevance to other urban system topics in previous writings; this chapter furthers those works by exploring the implications of TI for community development in local government settings and for the city manager in particular.

I begin with a discussion of the concept of community development. I then examine change processes generally before explaining the theory of TI. I discuss the practice of TI, its implications for community development, and process considerations.

Community Development

The International Association for Community Development (2020) defines community development as "a practice-based profession and an academic discipline that promotes participative democracy, sustainable development, rights, economic opportunity, equality, and social justice, through the organization, education, and empowerment of people within their communities, whether these be of locality, identity, or interest, in urban and rural settings." This definition might not resonate perfectly with local governments that sometimes label their planning and development functions as community development. Local governments commonly focus on public engagement and sustainable development, although matters of social justice, equality, and rights are perhaps much less of a local government service function, especially in smaller and more rural local governments. The planning and development functions are often more focused on the planned allocation and development of land resources than they are in organizing and empowering communities to take on community development initiatives. Having said this, there is certainly local government activity in community education, engagement, and enabling public voice and influence through planning processes. These activities, however, might create some discomfort for those civil servants who see the appropriate role of staff as being in line with the Westminster model, where staff are expected to be neutral and relatively invisible compared to the public profile of elected officials.

When local government staff engage in public processes to promote sustainability, they are often very visible and acting in the clear light of day, rather than from the "shadows" (Siegel, 2015). This is not unusual or inappropriate behaviour; in fact, it is implicitly sanctioned by the Canadian Institute of Planners in its definition of "planning": "the scientific, aesthetic, and orderly disposition of land, resources, facilities and services *with* a view to securing the physical, economic and social efficiency, health and well-being of urban and rural communities" (Canadian Institute of Planners, 2020, emphasis added). The goal of securing the social efficiency, health, and well-being of communities necessarily involves making changes to urban systems.

Some city managers take the position that social and cultural matters, or even the challenge of sustainable development, are not the core focus of local governments. In Canada, the jurisdiction and objects of municipal action are derived from the provinces as a result of the division of powers in the Constitution Act. In British Columbia, the province has set out the broad purpose of municipalities in section 7 of the Community Charter (SBC 2003, chapter 26), which establishes that, in addition to providing governance and services, municipalities are also charged with fostering the economic, social, and environmental well-being of their community.

This broad mandate clearly sets matters of community development within the purview of local governments, at least in British Columbia. It then follows that, if social, environmental, or economic conditions are not good, local government actions to change those conditions for the better would be appropriate. In other words, local government is legitimately in the business of effecting change. This business, however, is challenging and risky since there are often vested interests in the status quo. Those interests are found in civil society, industry, and political and public service spheres of stakeholders. Efforts to effect change might present threats to those vested interests and can create conflict and controversy. This is often evident in land-use planning and development approval work.

Efforts to effect change through community development can be seen as radical behaviour – not politically radical, but in terms of promoting systems change. Indeed, this is the point of becoming a more sustainable world. We are seeking to change behaviour and systems that are not sustainable. In other words, the goal of effecting systems and behavioural change is at the heart of community development in all its forms. This, though, can present serious challenges for city managers and their staff, who can be placed in the position of having to interpret the public interest and attempt to build its understanding of and support for change. How does the city manager administer such efforts in a way that protects staff from becoming targets of interests that would oppose the change goals? City managers must be able to navigate the rocky shoals of community change management.

Successful navigation requires a deep understanding of the values and goals found in each group of stakeholders and laying out a path (e.g., a set of strategic actions) that results in sufficiently broad support from all groups of stakeholders. Seasoned city managers know from experience that, without such support, any initiative that aspires to effect change typically takes a long time and is achieved by maintaining support while a series of progressive actions is implemented, with results incrementally bringing about the change goal. Change is seldom achieved by a single action.

Causes of Change (Change Processes in the Wheelhouse of Local Government)

As a former city manager with a city planning background, and having recently completed a dissertation on the process for effecting change, I am surprised by the general lack of attention given to understanding how change actually occurs at the community level. There are volumes of professional and academic writing on how we plan and what the end goals of such planning might look like, but there is limited material that focuses specifically on how change occurs at the community level. A good understanding of the process by which change occurs would be critical knowledge for developing effective change strategies.

Change can occur in a number of ways, including revolution, reform movements such as the racial protests in United States (and globally) resulting from George Floyd's murder on 25 May 2020, the civil rights movements in the 1960s, and technology, which is perhaps the most powerful source of change. An early example of technological change is found in how agriculture changed human kind 10,000 years ago (Roberts, 2008; Van de Ryn & Calthorpe, 1986). As an early technology, agriculture enabled humans to remain in one place rather than constantly moving to find new food sources. Agriculture enabled human kind to become a people *in situ* (Buchan, 2019).

More recent history shows how transportation technologies (first the train and then automobiles) enabled our cities to grow and expand outward to the countryside (Angottie, 2009). The impact of those technologies caused profound changes in our urban systems and collectively on the planet. Each of these powerful waves of change affected our values, norms, behaviours, and environment, with dramatic human and environmental impacts. In the face of these major changes, local public servants have been more reactive that proactive.

What of proactive action (enlightened management) as an alternative way of change? Community development and planning efforts are intended to effect change before the occurrence of unintentional and dramatic results from revolution, reform, or technological change with unintentional consequences. Enlightened management is based on Karl Mannheim's view of planning as a way to guide social change (Friedman, 1973) and Habermas's view of people having the capacity to reflect and reason (Allen, 2007). This is about informed, forward thinking that attempts to move us from unsustainable behaviour to increasingly more sustainable and resilient behaviour and systems (Buchan, 2017).

To engage effectively in enlightened management through community development actions, however, requires a good understanding of how change actually occurs on the ground. Transformative incrementalism was developed with the goal of acquiring that understanding. Early in my career, I was disappointed that plans and strategies could be adopted but then languish on the shelf. Even those documents that did receive some implementation effort could run into barriers from stakeholder groups. I learned that successful change aspirations were not likely to be realized in singular actions but required ongoing support and resources.

Transformative Incrementalism

Transformational Incrementalism describes the process for achieving change during times when we are not responding to crisis. It is grounded in the experiences of effective local government staff, elected officials, and public stakeholders. TI describes the timeframe and variables of the deeply social process involved in effecting change in urban systems. The timeframe is long, with small changes occurring incrementally until conditions allow for more ambitious changes. These conditions are characterized by a broad alignment of values (and therefore support for change) across the populations of elected officials, staff, the public, and industry. Getting to that alignment takes time as values might have to evolve and as the status quo presents challenges to change efforts. One elected official in my research summarized the need for a broad alignment of values nicely: if a good idea is held by only one or two people, it will remain just a good idea; however, if the idea resonates with enough people in the local government bureaucracy, among elected officials, within the public, and within industry, it has the potential for successful and sustained implementation. Accordingly, the goal of achieving broad alignment is the main social process identified by TI.

The core variable in TI is influence. As a soft form of power, influence is the ability to secure outcomes that depend on the actions of other participants. TI sees influence as the most important variable, as it directs change towards specific outcomes. Talking about influence and power makes local government professionals uneasy. It is the that-which-shall-not-be-named topic in local government (Buchan, 2017), in part because it places staff in the role of influencing others, which would seem to be in conflict with the Westminster model of government. This is not an inappropriate role for staff, but it is one that has significant ethical considerations. Siegel (2015), for example, implicitly acknowledges the role of the CAO in influencing others through leading up (influencing politicians) and leading out (influencing people and organizations outside of local government). Similarly, when professional staff give policy advice to elected officials, they have considerable influence. They choose the

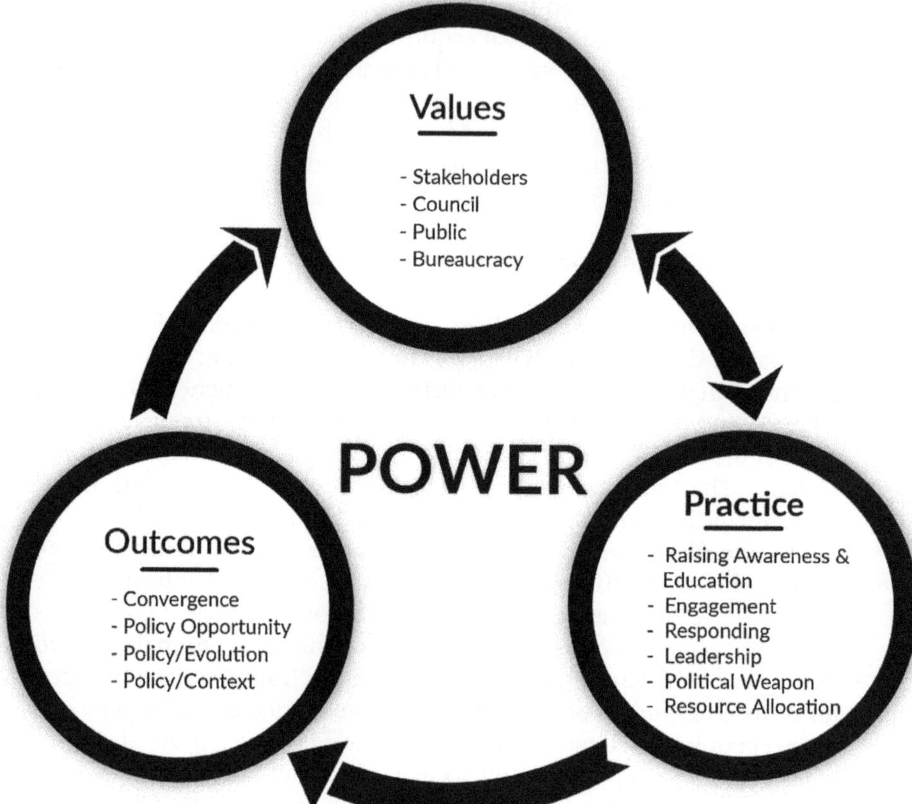

Figure 20.1 The Change Process
Adapted from Buchan et al., 2018.

information and arguments that go into their reports, and they occupy a privileged position in having an audience with the elected officials.

The prospect of having more influence over community development goals was one of the reasons for my shifting from city planner to city manager; however, I was soon to realize that, although there was indeed more influence in the city manager role, successful change still required initial and ongoing support from staff, council, the public, and industry.

In addition to influence, the other variables in the change process are values, practice, and outcomes. Figure 20.1 illustrates a process where values affect practice and practice can be directed at changing values. Practice also affects outcomes, which, in turn, affect values.

Values are important because they motivate and guide behaviour, and when sufficiently widely held they provide support for change-oriented actions. When they are not widely held, efforts to shift values through education, awareness building, and other engagement efforts have to occur. This takes time, and lots of it.

Practice is equally important, and can take the form of leadership, engagement, and education as well as projects and programs. Successful practice is critical for advancing a change goal. It is hard to build support and change values when an initiative fails. Outcomes can be a growing shift and alignment in values. They can produce opportunities for further initiatives. A good TI practitioner is always looking for opportunities to advance a change goal ethically. This is called principled opportunism (Buchan et al., 2018). Over time, and as a result of many incremental changes in policy and advances, the policy environment/context changes and supports more ambitious changes. This change in the policy environment, however, requires an associated change in values among all those involved.

TI in Practice

The process involved in applying TI has been covered in other writing (Buchan & Holland, 2021), as have examples of TI in practice in *Transformative Incrementalism: A Journey to Sustainability* (Buchan, 2019). In the latter, a number of change masters explain the change process through the lens of TI. For example, Andrea Reimer (former councillor, City of Vancouver), describes Vancouver's experience in moving towards its goal of becoming a sustainable city. In her experience, values and culture are critical parts of the social process. She describes values as the roots of a tree. With deep roots of supportive values comes a broad array of people who contribute to and accelerate the pace of change.

Former Vancouver city planning director Larry Beasley (2019) chronicles a purposeful transformative change guided by the City of Vancouver from the 1980s through the early 2000s to develop a high-quality urban environment. Although the changes resulted from many factors, influence, practice, values, and leadership were critical in the transformative process.

Dave Witty (2019) describes the transformation of the City of Langford, British Columbia, as being the result of a mayor who had great influence in combination with an aligned council and staff, as well as a public that was not just open to change but broadly supportive. This rare alignment of values and goals enabled a relatively fast transformation of the community. This case study highlights the fact that, once the alignment of values is achieved, the pace of change quickens. I served as city planner and city manager for twelve years in Langford, and was impressed by the degree of agreement within the city for change. There was a broad alignment of values across stakeholder groups that enabled rapid, albeit incremental, steps towards a community transformation.

In addition to these change stories, Buchan (2019) includes other case studies of transformative change from the perspective of a real estate developer and a local food system activist. Each change master describes the role of influence, values, practice, and outcomes in their case studies. The result of change efforts worked incrementally over time to create the conditions for accelerated change. In all cases, it is clear that local government staff play an important role in the change process and act as leaders, principled opportunists, and partners working with other participants in bringing about transformative community development.

Implications of TI for Community Development in Local Government Environments

A number of challenges and risks are involved in undertaking community development goals aimed at effecting transformative change. The first is the resistance and opposition that can come from those who benefit from the status quo and who might see change as negatively affecting their interests. Certainly, this is obvious when the development industry sees planning and resulting regulation intended to encourage more sustainable patterns of development and building standards. To protect their economic interests, such opponents might be pointed and critical of staff and elected officials advocating for the changes. This places the city manager in a place where he or she must navigate through potentially dangerous conflicts that can negatively impact staff, elected officials, the city manager, and the change initiative itself. In such cases, it is important to have political leadership that openly owns the initiative and provides support for staff.

Opposition can come from members of the public if they feel that their activities could be affected as a result of implementing new plans and regulations. This is demonstrated when residents oppose high-density, mixed-use developments in or near their neighbourhoods or when roads are modified to make space for bicycle lanes. It is also seen in the response of private interests to policies that prioritize urban redevelopment over greenfield development. The risk to staff and elected officials has often played out, resulting in opposition that sees staff replaced (including the city manager) and elected officials not re-elected. It is risky to be a change agent. As TI suggests, however, when values are broadly held, opposition and conflict should diminish. This illustrates the critical importance of having processes that educate, build support, and shift community values when they are not aligned, and then of maintaining them once aligned so change efforts can proceed more rapidly and effectively.

Process Considerations

It is beyond the scope of this chapter to discuss in detail the role of TI in community development (see Buchan & Holland, 2021), but it is worthwhile to provide a brief summary. In using TI in community development, it is necessary to assess the policy environment and to know the community's values and where it is situated in the incremental evolution towards a change goal. For example, are there any existing programs or policies that relate positively to the goal? If the issue at the heart of the change goal is not known as an issue by council, the public, or even other city departments, initial efforts need to focus on raising awareness and developing understanding of the issue. This then creates an environment where more ambitious actions can be proposed, approved, and implemented.

The analysis of community values needs to take into account those of each of the participant groups (the public, elected officials, municipal departments, industry). This will determine where education, engagement, and value-shifting dialogue must occur to build the broad alignment of values needed to support change. In addition to understanding community and subgroup values, it is important to find out who are the community leaders and influencers. These people will be important partners in the necessary community development work.

Once these assessments are complete, a long-term advocacy strategy can be developed that focuses on the sequence of initiatives needed and the nature of the engagement. Key elements of the strategy would be to build relationships and trust, build credibility through "quick win" projects, support leaders and champions, and provide ongoing advocacy and education as values shift and support and momentum build.

As values align and converge, more ambitious initiatives can be undertaken and will likely be expected. Beasley (2019) observes that transformation is never actually complete. There can be significant change but society is not a static thing. The next version of the community subsequently becomes the next status quo, which in turn might need to be challenged, rethought, and have its shortcomings addressed. In this view, change is a complex and ongoing social process, not a final outcome. In other words, the foundational process in community development involves understanding community values, building relationships, and having dialogues that shift values so that a convergence of values and support develops.

Conclusion

The Westminster model proposes a myth – that of the value-neutral, impartial, and invisible public servant. This is mythological because our professions are trained in and imbedded with values: public safety for engineers, sustainable development for planners, healthy communities for parks and recreation professionals, and so forth. Transformational Incrementalism exposes this myth by showing how local government staff engage in community development processes designed to shift values and build support for initiatives that work towards better public safety and healthier, more sustainable and resilient communities.

TI also presents some questions about how local government civil servants should go about their job professionally. Because the current Westminster model is arguably a problematic fit with how local government staff actually operate, what is needed is either a modified version of that model or a wholly new model of local government decision making – one that addresses appropriate professional conduct as staff work with the public, elected officials, industry, and non-government organizations on initiatives that foster social, environmental, and economic community well-being. A new model of local government service could address important questions such as:

- What are the ethical questions and parameters for the practice of advocacy by staff?
- What guidance can be given to staff leaders who engage in principled opportunism?
- What is expected of staff in representing professional principles when faced with contrary views from management or elected officials?
- How involved should staff be when working with community partners and interest groups towards change goals?

It is not within the scope of this chapter to address these questions, but it is important to acknowledge and assert that, although while local government staff legitimately have, and advance, values based on professional principles, a boundary remains that separates political behaviour from professional behaviour. The ability to help define that boundary, while enabling staff to undertake their duties and appropriately respond to and follow political direction, is an important skill of the contemporary city manager. The city manager understands the influence that staff can have, and sees it as a privilege given to staff provided they do not abuse their advisory role but remain deferential to and respectful of the governing role of elected officials. The city manager who understands the role that local government staff – along with civil society, elected officials, and industry – can play in effecting change is positioned to be an effective change agent.

It is also important to recognize that there are ethical imperatives for staff behaviour. For example, the Canadian Institute of Planners (2020) code of conduct stipulates that professional planners provide full, clear, and accurate information on planning matters to decision makers and the public. This means that planning staff must present all material information on a matter before the elected officials and public, not just information that might support staff's preferred position. The city manager needs to be vigilant in overseeing reports and other documents to ensure this aspect of ethical behaviour is adhered to.

Further, the city manager must ensure that there is an appropriate balance between advocacy for change, deference to the ultimate decision-making role of elected officials, and respect for public and stakeholder values. When staff engage in advocacy and dialogue intended to promote education and awareness and, ultimately, shifts in values and behaviour, the engagement should be based on professional principles and knowledge that are clear and transparently shared with all participants. With such an approach, it is more likely that debate will be seen as driven by principles rather than personal agendas. This will enable the city manager to defend staff should an engagement become controversial.

The city manager who understands the change process as articulated by TI is more effective in guiding change. Rather than just undertaking projects and programs with aspirations for change, that city manager can ensure there is evidence that stakeholder values and awareness are aligned and supportive of change initiatives. If the alignment of values is not there, efforts to raise awareness and shift values should be pursued first. The strategic planning process is one way of planning actions that aspire to affect change incrementally. If used with TI as a guide, those actions will have a greater prospect of success.

Finally, it is useful to differentiate Transformational Incrementalism from Lindblom's incrementalism (Lindblom 1959), discussed by Macgregor and Szwarc (in this volume). Lindblom described incrementalism as a branch method where the public servant looks at previous policies and develops new policy approaches that stem from those past approaches. This contrasts with the root method of policy development, which is a more intensive, rigorous analysis of all the factors and variables involved in a policy problem to develop an entirely new approach. Many practitioners fail to understand Lindblom's incrementalism and simply see it as making small steps, rather than the small differences between policy options. To this end, TI offers a very different view of incrementalism. It describes change as occurring in small, incremental steps in a complex social environment in which city managers and staff work hard to develop and maintain sufficient support from all stakeholder groups to enable a succession of actions to be implemented over a significant period of time. Change results from the successful implementation of such efforts, which include value-shifting dialogues with stakeholders along with other programs, projects, and initiatives that aspire to bring about community and systems change. In this context, aspirational incrementalism is one description of Transformational Incrementalism in practice.

REFERENCES

Allen, A. (2007). Systematically distorted subjectivity? Habermas and the critique of power. *Philosophy and Social Criticism, 33*(5), 641–50. http://doi.org/10.1177/0191453707078926

Angottie, T. (2009). Urban planning for food security: Reinventing city and countryside with Jane Jacobs. *Plan Canada, 49*(2), 55–7. https://www.cip-icu.ca/Files/Plan-Canada/plan-canada-issues/Plan-Canada-Vol-49-No-2-Summer-ete-2009.aspx

Beasley, L. (2019). A case study of Downtown Vancouver. In L. Buchan (Ed.), *Transformative incrementalism: A journey to sustainable* (pp. 53–82). Municipal World.

Buchan, R. (2017). Power: That-which-must-not-be-named. *Plan Canada, 57*(4), 44–7. https://www.kelmanonline.com/httpdocs/files/CIP/plancanadawinter2017/index.html

Buchan, R. (Ed.). (2019). *Transformative incrementalism: A journey to sustainability.* Municipal World.

Buchan, R., Cloutier, D., & Friedman, A. (2018). "Transformative incrementalism: Planning for transformative change in local food systems." *Progress in Planning, 134*, 100424. https://doi.org/10.1016/j.progress.2018.07.002

Buchan, R., & Holland, M. (2021). *Transformative incrementalism: Implications for transformative planning practice.* Routledge.

Canadian Institute of Planners. (2020, 11 August). Statement of values. https://www.cip-icu.ca/Files/Statement-of-Values/Statement-of-Values.aspx

Friedman, J. (1973). *Retracking America: A theory of transactive planning*. Anchor Press/Doubleday.

International Association for Community Development. (2020, 11 August). Our history. https://www.iacdglobal.org/about/brief-history/

Lindblom, C. E. (1959). The science of 'muddling through.' *Public Administration Review*, *19*(2), 79–88. https://doi.org/10.2307/973677

Roberts, P. (2008). *The end of food*. First Mariner Books.

Siegel, D. (2015). *Leaders in the shadows: The leadership qualities of municipal chief administrative officers*. University of Toronto Press.

Van de Ryn, S., & Calthorpe, P. (1986). *Sustainable communities: A new design synthesis for cities, suburbs, and towns*. Sierra Club Books.

Witty, D. (2019). A case study of Langford, B.C. In L. Buchan (Ed.), *Transformative incrementalism: A journey to sustainable* (pp. 83–100). Municipal World.

21 From Dreams of Being a Rock-and-Roll Drummer to City Manager

DAVID CALDER

As Kenny Rogers advised, "you got to know when to hold 'em, know when to fold 'em." Cambridge, Ontario, city manager David Calder provides an entertaining but thoughtful examination of career progression, with lessons for any current or aspiring city manager. Sometimes city managers are recruited from within the ranks of senior officials of the municipality; other times someone with city management experience elsewhere promises the leadership the mayor and council seek. As Calder points out, those realities can force hard decisions about staying with a current employer or seeking a new opportunity. Those decisions certainly have career, reputational, and family implications, and Calder uses his own experience to offer advice on those uncertain choices.

The Early Years

A question often asked of me is, "how did you become a city manager?" The answer is not simple, but I made conscious career decisions on my journey to the city manager's office. I also had to obtain certain skills in order to serve in the role. In this chapter, I identify some key career decisions, learnings, and core competencies obtained leading to my role as a chief administrative officer or city manager, a term I generally use in this chapter. But first, it is helpful to start at the beginning.

In my mid-teens, it became apparent that I was not going to achieve my dream of becoming a rock-and-roll drummer and that another pathway to a more realistic career would need to be found. Interesting enough, one of my childhood band members did become a well-known baroque lutenist, but even this achievement was secondary to a career in education. It would be a number of years before I found my career direction with the encouragement and assistance of family.

I grew up in a household where political activism and volunteerism were practised in the local community. Both my parents were passionate about community and became directly involved in local community agencies and eventually local government. Their activism was initiated when their neighbourhood was going to be affected by the reconstruction by the local municipality of a beautiful old street in Woodstock, Ontario, that would require the removal of a large number of mature trees for the purposes of a road widening. They and others appeared before the local council of the day and advocated for a change in the construction design, which they eventually achieved with the support of the local council. This was my introduction to the workings of municipal government.

My father was involved in the local Chamber of Commerce to advocate for local business. He went on to be a director of the Ontario Chamber of Commerce and the Canadian Chamber of Commerce. My mother was encouraged to run for local office, and was first an alderman (the terminology of the day) and eventually ran successfully for the office of mayor of Woodstock, a position she held for three two-year terms. She also became the first female to serve on the Oxford County Council. After her time in municipal government, she was appointed chair of the Criminal Injuries Compensation Board and then acting chair of what was then known as the Ontario Police Commission.

As much of the conversation at family get-togethers was about local and municipal issues, it was suggested that, as I contemplated going to university, I should consider a career in municipal administration. I subsequently went to university to study both political science and public administration. While attending university, I began to obtain practical experience in the field of public administration to enhance my formal education. Working part time for a municipality was a valuable addition to my formal education. Admittedly, obtaining such opportunities is easier said than done, but I watched the job board in the political science department of the university for job opportunities directly related to municipal work.

I recognize that, due to my particular socio-economic background, I had certain advantages and opportunities that might not be afforded to others. My experience is, however, that anyone can leverage the experiences and advice of others in order to help them set their direction towards a career in municipal leadership. Aspiring young people can identify mentors and seek the advice and guidance of others. Throughout the municipal world, there is a desire and a willingness to support hard-working and capable professionals on their journey of continuous self-improvement.

I made the decision early that I was not interested in working at the provincial or federal level but would focus on the municipal sector. Later in my career, I would use my network of sector contacts to identify positions that might be coming available and took advantage of a provincial program supporting intern programs in municipalities. Also, one of my mentors suggested getting involved in a professional association, which was an invaluable pipeline to municipal sector opportunities. As well, being able to show future employers that I was participating in professional associations by being on standing committees or involved with their governance boards showed strong interest in professional development.

Mentorship

A valuable tool for developing skills for future leadership opportunities is identifying mentors to provide career guidance and advice. I was fortunate to have a number of mentors early in my career, and I continue to identify mentors to this day. Mentors have helped guide me in obtaining the skills and knowledge that later would become important aspects of leadership development, leading to the role of city manager or chief administrative officer. Mentors are a great source of advice, as they understand the leadership issues that a new or aspiring city manager might encounter. Some issues, due to the sensitive nature of the topic, cannot be discussed with colleagues within the organization, so having some outside support is crucial for good decision making.

Mentorship is defined as "a relationship in which a more experienced or more knowledgeable person helps to guide a less experienced and less knowledgeable person" (Roche, 1979). It is a learning and development partnership between someone with vast experience and someone who wants to learn. The important aspect of mentorship is that the one looking to be mentored has to want to learn. There must be a realization that, as careers develop, the notion of lifelong learning is an important reality and that, in order to excel, training and development never end. The municipal sector is ever-changing due to the introduction of new legislation, changing municipal policies, new strategic direction, and innovation. Learning from those who have gone before us and have gained a wealth of experiences can help to define a career path for those just beginning their municipal career and for those aspiring to leadership roles within municipal organizations.

Mentors are a valuable resource that I did not think of leveraging as an individual just entering employment in the municipal sector. The concept of mentorship was introduced to me after I entered the workplace. As a result, having mentors provided me with the "psychosocial" support (e.g., role modelling, friendship, emotional support, and encouragement) and career-related support (e.g., providing advice, discussing goals) (Kram, 1983). These supports are now sought out from me by others who are identifying career development opportunities in order to advance to leadership roles.

A number of municipal professional associations also support mentoring programs through the provision of mentors to interested members. For example, the Association of Municipal Managers, Clerks and Treasurers of Ontario has a mentorship program that "formally connects the individual to build productive relationships that are development oriented by facilitating the opportunity to learn and connect with others outside their respective organizations" (AMCTO, n.d.). The Ontario Municipal Administrators' Association (OMAA) has a similar mentorship program that can provide support for aspiring city managers as well as for those currently in the position of city manager. In fact, the membership structure of the OMAA promotes membership for aspiring city managers.

The Long and Winding Road: The Path to the City Manager's Office

As previously noted, my educational choices reflected my goal to work in local government. When I started looking for career opportunities in the municipal sector, there were programs available to municipalities to help hire students who were studying public administration or political science as it relates to municipal government. I obtained a part-time job with the Township of Anderdon, in southwestern Ontario, as a student attending the University of Windsor, and worked in the clerk/administrator's department of this small rural municipal organization. Subsequently, upon graduation, I applied under the Ontario Municipal Internship Program for a position with the City of York, a mid-sized urban municipality. The program provided the opportunity to work in the clerk's office, assisting with preparations for the upcoming municipal election. This was a great opportunity to gain practical experience following graduation from university. My experience with the City of York provided me an opportunity to learn about the functions of an urban municipality, with a large municipal council and a more complex organizational structure. Unfortunately, the province no longer supports such internship programs financially.

When mapping out my career path, I believed that it was important to continue working in a municipal clerk's office due to the diversity of functions and responsibilities available there. In addition, exposure to elected officials as municipal clerk serving the mayor and council would prove invaluable for building leadership competencies such as political acuity, which is beneficial in my role as city manager. The municipal clerk is the secretariat for the corporation, so all governance reporting flows through the clerk's office.

At the beginning of my career, I had set my sights on eventually becoming a municipal clerk. I applied for a position with the Regional Municipality of Peel – a very large region taking in the municipalities of Mississauga, Brampton, and Caledon, Ontario – as a committee coordinator. I was interested in learning about and gaining experience in an upper-tier municipality. I felt that working for a regional municipality would add to my experience and knowledge previously gained in a small rural township and a mid-sized urban municipal government. It did not occur to me at the time that this experience would also be beneficial when I decided to extend my career path towards becoming a city manager.

A career plan is necessary, but there is danger in moving too quickly or not staying in positions very long: it might look as though you are hopping from job to job. Chatzky (2018) defines job hopping as "spending less than two years in a position [and] can be an easy path to a higher salary – but experts caution that bouncing from position to position can be a serious red flag to prospective employers." The municipal sector is relatively small and the network is active, so having a reputation of job hopping will not help with future career progression. A two-to-five-year commitment to a position is reasonable before advancing to other opportunities.

Internal progression should also be considered if there is opportunity in the organization and the work environment is positive. "Overall, the more years people stayed with a company the faster they made it to the top" (Hamori, 2010, p. 154). Moving quickly up the ranks of one organization is not always possible but it can happen, so it should not be discounted as a way to progress into a leadership position. Although some individuals might desire a variety of different work challenges, municipal organizations are modelled on a hierarchical structure that sometimes requires time and experience in order to advance.

Cambridge, Ontario

After two years' gaining experience with the Regional Municipality of Peel, there was no opportunity for movement into the clerk's role, so I had to look outside that organization for advancement. I was fortunate to obtain the position of deputy city clerk with the City of Cambridge, Ontario. This position brought me closer to my young family, which had stayed in Kitchener-Waterloo while I commuted to Brampton. At the time, my spouse was travelling in the opposite direction to teach school in Oxford County.

Around the same time as I obtained my new position, my spouse was hired by the local school board in Kitchener-Waterloo. Working in the same community we lived in was a huge benefit to our lifestyle and also provided a sense of belonging to the local community. My career growth was no more important than my spouse's: she was dedicated to the teaching profession and was a very impactful educator. She was well recognized within the school board for taking on a variety of roles that might not have been available had we moved around the province to accommodate my career. As a result, the plan was always to work around the Regional Municipality of Waterloo, as there are a number of urban municipalities within a short drive. This became increasingly important as our careers progressed and we raised a family.

The City of Cambridge is one of seven municipalities in Waterloo Region. Cambridge was my first full-time position in a lower-tier urban municipality. The deputy clerk position provided many new opportunities to learn in such areas of service delivery as urban planning, licensing, economic development, and finance. I also worked with a number of experienced municipal clerks and learned to supervise union and non-union staff and to interact with the mayor and other elected officials. I wanted to work in a lower-tier municipality, as I found there is more opportunity to interact with and directly serve the ratepayer. My experience in a regional municipality was one of focusing on the operational aspect of service delivery, rather than direct interaction with the public.

Over the years, I moved up in the organization, becoming city clerk and commissioner of public access and council services. My skills were developing in terms of administrative leadership and my ability to serve council. The city manager of the day promoted me because of the value I was bringing to the organization through hard work, my political acuity, professional development, and public service skills.

During my tenure with the city, I felt it would be a good time to improve my leadership skills and, with the support of the city, I enrolled in "Leadership Waterloo Region," a community leadership development program for those wanting to improve their knowledge of the community. This experience provided broader community knowledge related to community building and an opportunity to expand my professional network. My years of service with Cambridge and continuous development of my executive level skills through professional designations and certifications provided opportunities to move up the ranks early in my career, but my progression eventually did plateau due to the inability to move to the top echelon of the organization. Once again, looking outside the organization as part of my career path would be necessary in order to advance.

Another consideration when mapping out a career path is, when should one move on? In retrospect, I might have stayed with the City of Cambridge too long before making the next career move and might have lost some valuable time to gain additional experience and potential income by not seeking out further advancement at an important point in my career. By the time I decided I wanted to take on a larger leadership role, such as city manager, it was clear that the current city manager at Cambridge was not likely to move on in the short term. Little did I know at the time that an opportunity at the City of Cambridge would come my way a decade later.

Waterloo, Ontario

In order to get more leadership experience at the executive level, I applied for the position of general manager of corporate services with the City of Waterloo. This position had a broader range of responsibilities such as asset management, economic development, and legal services, larger budget responsibilities, and more staff to manage than I had previously experienced. I wanted the opportunity to provide leadership and gain knowledge in these areas. I also wanted the experience of working for the city manager of the City of Waterloo, whom I respected as a leader and innovator. Although the position with Waterloo was not the city manager position, I was now part of the senior leadership team of decision makers and department heads.

I was with the City of Waterloo for about six years, but my tenure was not exactly as planned. Again, I might have stayed there a little too long, but I developed some core competencies required of a city manager, such as strategic planning, managerial skills, and community building, which would be key when transitioning into the role of a city manager.

When the city manager moved on to another opportunity, I applied for the position, but another internal candidate was the preferred choice. I should have started looking for a position outside of the organization at that point. This was a lesson learned. I did not leave, however, and I thought I could continue to excel in the position of general manager. Unfortunately, that was not the view of the new leader, who wanted to make organizational changes in a few areas of the administration. I was terminated from my position about six months later. I should have stepped out of the way before being terminated, but I had become too comfortable in my role rather than looking for new challenges. As well, I sense that the new city manager did not want the runner-up candidate scrutinizing the new leader. It might also have been convenient to let me go, thinking I would have good prospects for finding another position due to my experience. This was certainly a case of not knowing when to leave and not being aware of the need to branch out to another municipality in order to seek new opportunities. Although termination is a blow to the ego, I decided my new job was to find another job and take the opportunity to set my sights higher and compete for other city manager positions.

One of the tools I developed during my municipal career was a network of colleagues. Networks can be powerful tools, and I used mine to seek out career opportunities that would continue to advance my career path. I met with people whom I respected to obtain advice and to confirm that I had the necessary skill set to be a city manager, and then actively sought such a position. In addition, the network knew I was looking for a new opportunity and would provide information on upcoming leadership positions and information about specific municipal organizations, which helped determine if an organization was a good fit for me.

Good Times: The CAO's Office

My first experience as a CAO was with the Town of Tillsonburg, Ontario. With a population of 16,000, it was smaller than most of the other municipal organizations where I had worked, but it was an excellent starting point for my city manager career.

Often, deciding on a location to work is one of the constraining realities of a city manager, as the number of positions is limited by the number of municipal jurisdictions in your preferred geographic region. One of my realities was that, while other members of my family were supportive of my desire to advance to a city manager position, they preferred to stay in Kitchener-Waterloo. I commuted approximately 200 kilometres a day for five years in order to gain experience as a city manager. In my case, the extra investment in time and travel was the trade-off to gain experience as a city manager.

The opportunities for a CAO in a smaller municipality are amazing. As a leader in the community, you are front and centre and it is truly like working in a fish bowl, as residents are quite tuned in to their local political scene and the workings of the civic administration. Your every action can be scrutinized for praise or criticism. Your personality has to allow you to be comfortable with interacting with local leaders and residents. It is important to be able to identify with community leaders and understand the challenges they face. Community leaders are often associated with such organizations as the Chamber of Commerce, hospital board, service groups, and local businesses. All are part of the broader community that a city manager will have to embrace to establish positive partnerships and collaboration.

A core competency of a CAO in a smaller municipality is community building, which involves building relationships and inspiring people to work collaboratively. Often, a job description for a CAO will have wording such as, "you are highly regarded as an inclusion relationship builder who places great value on earning the confidence of others through leveraging diversity, team building, community engagement, and nurturing strong external partnerships with stakeholders." But what does this mean? You have to have a presence in the community and be comfortable getting out and meeting people, obtaining diverse opinions, gathering input, and listening to stakeholders. This is all part of the core competency of community building.

Being a CAO of a smaller municipality provides the opportunity to make change and accomplish objectives relatively quickly because the organizational structure is not overly bureaucratic. The downside is that the financial resources are limited and necessary staff expertise is frequently not available. A term often used in smaller municipalities is a "hands-on CAO," meaning that you will be involved in day-to-day service delivery and might have limited ability to concentrate on strategic planning, which has been identified as a core competency for a city manager.

City Manager of Cambridge

I am currently the city manager with the City of Cambridge, so my career path has come full circle in terms of geography. I had moved to other positions to gain experience, and when the opportunity with Cambridge was presented, I knew I had the competencies and experience to compete for the position. I am now back where I was once the city clerk, providing administrative leadership, guiding the organization with a team of dedicated staff through a pandemic, and ensuring council has the best information in order to make good decisions for the benefit of the community. Along the way, I have developed a set of competencies that have allowed me to obtain and hold the position that I began to dream of when I decided that I did not want to be a rock-and-roll drummer and settled for second best.

Core Competencies for a Successful City Manager

A 2020 survey of OMAA members found that 50 per cent of then-current CAOs had fewer than five years' experience, 40 per cent of their predecessors were terminated, and 45 per cent had retired (Ontario

Municipal Administrators' Association, 2020). Turnover, in fact, is relatively high among CAOs, especially when an election results in a new head of council or council members whose platforms revolved around the need for change. The CAO, as council's only employee, can be the first change that elected officials initiate. This high turnover could also be a result of the incumbent CAO's lacking certain competencies that elected officials expect. If you identify the competencies you lack early in your career, you can plan a pathway to developing them.

Situational leadership is the idea that an organization seeks a leader who has certain specific skills that fit the needs of that organization at that point in time. In other words, there is no "one-size-fits-all" CAO. "The notion of situational leadership is that a CAO must employ appropriate leadership to suit the prevailing context, expectations or imperatives" (McIntosh, 2020a). Leadership must be adaptable to the particular political environment and organizational culture of the municipality. This requires the prospective candidate for a CAO position to research the municipal organization and its political environment to identify the current leadership challenges and determine what core competencies are required to be successful. This might require changing the focus from one competency to another, depending on the strengths required to lead in a given municipality. For example, community building was a competency I required as CAO in Tillsonburg, but my next position, which would be a return to Cambridge, required me to develop political acuity.

A CAO Competency Framework

Everyone's municipal administration career journey is different, but developing a set of core competencies is common to every city manager or CAO. Working with Gordon McIntosh, the OMAA has been developing a *CAO Competency Framework*, a list of core competencies that every city manager or CAO should acquire and that can be used "as a basis for customization of a personalized CAO profile" (McIntosh, 2020b). Municipal administrators are keenly aware that leadership requirements are changing and aspiring city managers are looking for development guidance in order to help map a pathway to city manager engagements. In addition, current city managers are interested in planning and developing their careers in order to take on other city manager assignments, whether with a larger municipality, or moving from a rural to an urban municipality or from a lower-tier to an upper-tier municipality. It is also anticipated that the *CAO Competency Framework* will be a tool that can increase job stability.

As part of the early work to build a *CAO Competency Framework*, the OMAA surveyed and held a workshop to identify competencies required for CAO success. The survey data show that the majority of then-current CAOs were coming to the end of their careers. As a result, opportunities in Ontario will appear in the near future and aspiring CAOs need to be prepared for those opportunities in a time of changing leadership competencies. The data also indicate that CAOs are well educated in the academic sense, but how does one obtain identified core competencies in order to ensure successful leadership? Once core competencies are identified, the ability to obtain core competency skills through training and development opportunities is important not only to achieve the position of city manager but also to ensure success in the role.

The ability to be a strategic thinker is often identified as a core competency for anyone desiring to become a city manager and is needed to develop the community's vision, mission, and values, identifying long-term goals and objectives, and identifying short-term priorities through the development of corporate business plans and strategic plans. Many city managers are of the opinion that at least 50 per cent of their focus should be on setting strategic direction; in reality, only between 5 per cent and 20 per cent of their time is spent on strategic initiatives. (Ontario Municipal Administrators' Association, 2020). Through findings from survey work, the authors of the *CAO Competency Framework* state: "there is no 'correct, one size fits all,' 'if you don't do it this way you got it wrong' strategic plan style or horizon for local government. The important thing is to strive for a plan that builds the capacity of the municipality it is meant to serve. Authenticity to the community and customization to the capacity of the organization are key" (StrategyCorp, Inc., 2019).

The point is that a city manager must make the time to focus on strategic planning, which, in turn, will define the strategic direction of the municipal organization and help council set its goals and objectives. A city manager who is not a strategic thinker or does not embrace strategic planning will not be able to provide council with such assistance.

Another core competency often identified as a skill for a city manager is political acuity, identified as the "elusive competency" (Constantinou, 2015). Political acuity has been defined as "a way of thinking and behaviour; putting information and skills together to better guide choices and behaviour in a given context, to accomplish your goals and objectives" (Constantinou, n.d.). As a core competency, the aspect of political acuity in my mind is really being perceptive to what the governors (employer) want to achieve and helping elected officials to achieve desired outcomes. It is the ability to understand the political environment one is working in and to be aware of shifting priorities over time.

The difficulty in the past has been how an aspiring city manager develops political acuity as a core competency. Since city managers are recruited, hired, and evaluated by elected officials, political acuity might be one of the most important but most difficult core competencies for a city manager to develop. The city manager needs to view the political landscape to understand what council might or might not support. Council is the final decision maker, and the city manager and staff are tasked with the implementation of council's decisions. It serves no one any value by having the city manager battle council on a direction or initiative.

I have observed a number of failings of executive leadership due to resistance to a specific position of a mayor or council. The successful city manager is not a "yes" person to council, but a provider of advice and administrative expertise. For example, city staff in Cambridge recommended that a couple of outdoor swimming pools be closed due to age and cost, but knowing that certain councillors were concerned that the community would be losing an asset, staff recommended a splash pad be installed to replace the pool. A water feature remained, costs were lowered, and a certain service level was preserved: a win-win.

Five Core Competencies

As work continues by the OMAA in Ontario, the objective is to create a contemporary CAO leader profile. The question to be answered is what are the core competencies required to lead increasingly complex municipal organizations that continue to challenge CAO leadership? A number of capabilities have been identified by incumbents for five CAO roles:

- *Trusted advisor* to council's governance role by adapting to its expectations while retaining professional values with speaking truth to power that instils political confidence in the position. In my view, this is a core competency associated with political acuity that any aspiring candidate requires to move from a professional or even managerial role to that of a city manager.
- *Strategic thinker*, to facilitate council vision for the community and move from corporate goals to operational activities with attention to setting realistic priorities and proactively managing dynamic change. I think that being strategic applies not only to corporate direction, but also to the ability to simplify and seek innovative solutions to complex civic challenges.

- *Community builder*, to create partnerships among various community and external interests by nurturing mutual aims and shared resources for community-wide benefit. I found this to be an area that requires personal confidence over time to align diverse interests while generating enthusiasm towards the city's goals or objectives.
- *Performance manager*, to oversee civic service delivery and internal services with a view to maximizing efficiency and ensuring performance accountability. As a manager this is what I did, but as a CAO my challenge was to let go – to delegate responsibility and then hold managers accountable.
- *Role model*, to display exemplary leadership practices and safeguard the values of a respectful workplace by mentoring the potential in others and being self-aware of their impact on organizational culture. This is core: all the other capabilities are for naught if the city manager does not have respect as an authentic person and personal leadership mastery.

As Gordon McIntosh has observed: "The professional background of CAOs does not guarantee success in their leadership role. The need for CAO leadership competency insights is critical for succession planning and successful tenures" (McIntosh, 2020a). As the OMAA work progresses, the intent is to provide aspiring city managers with a framework to assess their leadership competence within each of these capabilities. Success indicators and development needs for forty competencies will enable them to self-assess their city manager readiness. Incumbent CAOs will also use this CAO professional development continuum to enhance their adaptive leadership approach to different situations. I am personally looking to add the *Contemporary CAO Profile* to my toolkit to coach my senior managers to help them be better leaders – and, who knows, maybe future city managers.

In conclusion, to build a successful city manager career in today's municipal environment, it is advantageous to have a variety of experiences in the municipal sector, develop a good professional network for support and knowledge sharing, leverage opportunities with professional associations, and be aware of the core competencies required of a CAO. Through the work of creating a CAO professional development continuum, municipal executive professional associations can then begin to focus on creating learning opportunities through the provision of training modules specific to core competencies. The development of executive leadership focusing on identified CAO competencies will enhance the provision of good municipal governance and will contribute to the success of city manager leadership excellence across Canada.

REFERENCES

Association of Municipal Managers, Clerks and Treasurers of Ontario. (n.d.). *Mentorship program*. www.amcto.com

Chatzky, J. (2018, 24 April). Job-hopping is on the rise: Should you consider switching roles to make more money? *NBC News, Better By Today*. https://www.nbcnews.com/better/business/job-hopping-rise-should-you-consider-switching-roles-make-more-ncna868641

Constantinou, P. P. (2015, June). Political acuity: The elusive competency. *Canadian Government Executive*, pp. 14–15.

Constantinou, P. P. (n.d.). He just doesn't get it. https://www.omaa.on.ca/en/workshops-and-events/resources/2018-Fall-Workshop/Political-Acuity-in-Municipal-AdministrationFINAL-DECK.pdf

Hamori, M. (2010). Managing yourself: Job-hopping to the top and other career fallacies. *Harvard Business Review*, July–August, 154–7. https://hbr.org/2010/07/managing-yourself-job-hopping-to-the-top-and-other-career-fallacies

Kram, K. E. (1983). Phases of mentor relationships. *Academy of Management Journal*, *26*(4), 608–25. https://doi.org/10.5465/255910

McIntosh, G. (2020a, April). OMAA contemporary CAO leader profile. Ontario Municipal Administrators' Association. https://www.omaa.on.ca/en/index.asp

McIntosh, G. (2020b, April). OMAA contemporary CAO leader profile, Executive summary. Ontario Municipal Administrators' Association. https://www.omaa.on.ca/en/index.asp

Ontario Municipal Administrators' Association. (2020). CAO skills survey. https://www.omaa.on.ca/en/index.asp

Roche, G. R. (1979). Much ado about mentors. *Harvard Business Review*, 14–28. https://hbr.org/1979/01/much-ado-about-mentors

StrategyCorp, Inc. (2019). Ontario municipal chief administrative officer survey, 2019: A candid look at the issues on the minds of Ontario CAOs. https://strategycorp.com/wp-content/uploads/2019/08/StrategyCorp_CAO_Report_2019.pdf

22 A City Manager's Career Journey

JOHN BURKE

A career of interest and variety as a city manager often requires periodic relocation to new municipalities. But a bemused, veteran city manager once warned that a poorly planned career can leave city managers with more equity in their car than in their house! Career planning is part of being a successful city manager. Former Ontario deputy minister John Burke maps out a career path shared by many successful city managers. In Burke's case, beginning with a county in Cape Breton, he progressed to manage a succession of larger cities in Nova Scotia, Alberta, and Ontario, including the City of Ottawa. He offers experience-based advice on making the difficult professional and family decisions that constitute the career path of city managers.

During my final year of university completing my Bachelor of Commerce degree, I accepted an offer of employment with a professional accounting firm as an articling student accountant. This was very much aligned with my career plan to become a professional chartered accountant. My career goal at the time was someday to become a partner in the firm. If that career path did not work out, it would prepare me for a career in finance with another company. All businesses require financial support, so it seemed both a desired opportunity in the first instance and alternatively a backup plan should I leave the professional accounting world.

My first year as a student accountant exposed me to a variety of accounting and auditing challenges in the private, public, and non-profit sectors. These different experiences broadened my knowledge base beyond what I had originally imagined. Towards the end of my first year, I was asked to consider a position as a clerk-treasurer in a small municipality. Although that type of opportunity was not on my radar screen, I did speak to both the warden and the CAO of the municipality, and in the end decided it might be an exciting opportunity and one that could lead to quick advancement.

It was a difficult decision, as I had to abandon my career aspiration of becoming a professional accountant. However, I had participated in a couple of municipal audits/projects, and was somewhat intrigued by the scope and responsibility of local government. I was offered and accepted the position. The job title was formally Clerk-Treasurer, but it was really a director of finance position and second-in-command to the CAO. After I had been in that position for a year, the CAO left to pursue another opportunity elsewhere in local government, and I was appointed acting CAO at the tender age of twenty-five. Following further discussions with the warden and council, I was formally appointed CAO. This launched my career in local government, which spanned a total of twenty-nine years.

From a small rural community in Cape Breton to a variety of municipalities in different parts of Canada, I was able to manage my career in a way that gave me a wide array of experiences, different challenges, exposure to rural and urban issues, and the opportunity to work with many different elected officials, staff, and residents. Following my municipal government experience, I was again most fortunate to be given the opportunity to be a provincial deputy minister for almost another twelve years. My skills and experience at the local level were clearly transferable to the provincial scene, and I was able to work with very capable public servants and serve our elected leadership, as well as gain substantial experience at another order of government.

Career Lessons Learned

When you set a career path, be sure to leave sufficient flexibility to make changes on-the-fly, as opportunities do not always present themselves in the orderly fashion you have imagined them in your mind. Life is full of surprises, and you should remain open to the many possibilities you might encounter. By all means, follow your dreams, but try not to get so fixated on your plan that you miss out on what could be other exciting prospects.

When I look at the beginning of my public service career, I am reminded how vital and important were my initial conversations with the warden and the CAO in describing the job, their expectations, and their willingness to assist me in negotiating the requirements and public policy nuances of government. Their guidance and support helped me on a career path that lasted over forty years.

While still a student, the most important thing is to consider where you want to go and then attempt to align your courses and programs to meet the basic requirements of that career path. Some positions tend to be generalist (manager, supervisor, and so forth) in nature; others are quite specialist oriented (lawyer, accountant, engineer, and so forth). Either type of background will serve you well in government and prepare you for advancement should that be your choice. If your career plan includes a desire to work for government, jobs in the private or non-profit sectors can lead you there as well – many of the skill sets needed to perform in those sectors are easily transferable to the public sector.

Assuming that you have accepted a position in government, you need to think about how to manage your current assignment and at the same time consider what additional skills you need to acquire in order to advance your career. Look at professional development choices, core competency enrichment, involvement in peer organizations, and so forth. Also, develop informal relationships both inside and outside the organization to broaden your contacts as well as to find new ways of adding value to your work. Working with a "mentor" sometimes can provide guidance in developing your career path and identifying what you need to do to position yourself for success. There is often a great benefit to having someone who can act as an objective guide to assist you in your career goals.

If you entered government as a specialist and you are looking to move to a more generalist position, you will need to manage the transition from one role to the other. This does not mean completely abandoning your specialist skills, but simply adding to your competencies so that you can become an effective generalist. The other aspect of advancement and career progression is that job scope will change as you morph from one role to another. You will encounter different work content along with additional responsibilities, as well as new people with different attitudes and expectations. You need to be sufficiently prepared for the challenges that come with those changes.

As you progress through the organization or as external opportunities unfold and as your upwardly mobile aspirations grow, you will continually need to examine whether your current professional credentials match the changing requirements for new opportunities. In saying this, I have found it important to identify ways in which I could enhance my professional credentials. When I saw that I could benefit from more professional education, I joined other aspiring city managers from across Canada in completing an in-residence university program focused on municipal management and local government.

Do you want your career path to be managed through unsolicited opportunities, or do you want to be proactive in selecting the types of career choices that are available to you or those you wish to seek out?

Municipal employers are understandably uneasy about losing their CAO, but it is important to stay connected to the employment marketplace. That means maintaining networks, monitoring employment sites, and, on occasion, confidentially applying for positions that might represent a career advancement or to round out your experience.

In making these career-enhancing choices, it is important to look at the current and changing role of a CAO/city manager and try to align your current skill set with the demanding needs of such a dynamic position. What will become clear is that your hard credentials, background, and experience make you an attractive candidate, but the soft skills will keep you in the game.

A CAO's Leadership Style

Your leadership style plays a significant role in both qualifying and maintaining your job. Examine and be aware of the various leadership styles that work best for you. Do not focus on having one style in particular; rather, have a style that is flexible enough to deal with a variety of changing conditions. Interpersonal skills are vital to a successful local government career.

During my very early years as CAO, one of my first lessons was to speak and question before you act. A good example involved a contract we had entered into with a local agency called a village commission to maintain its water and sewer system. An issue arose when a commission member, who was also on my local council, decided to give direction to contract staff doing commission work. Our works superintendent complained to me that this was interfering with our contract obligations and asked that I address the issue. Instead of speaking to the local councillor, I sent a strongly worded letter to the commission warning that our contractual work was at risk because of interference of the local councillor. This of course set off a contentious round of discussions, which put me at odds with the local councillor. Clearly this could have been much better handled by simply speaking to the councillor and explaining the complications that can ensue. I never again repeated that error of judgment and chalked it up to a "teachable moment."

You need to be adept at exhibiting a style that, simultaneously, builds confidence with elected officials and staff, demonstrates knowledge of how to address issues, shows empathy with the needs of stakeholders, and earns respect as a professional.

Gaining and retaining the confidence of the mayor and council, staff, and the community at large are vital to your effectiveness as a manager. You are the lynchpin between the political decisions of council and the leadership decisions that implement those decisions. Developing a sound relationship with the media is also vital, as they are one way the public is informed of what is happening at city hall. You will also need to be familiar with the use of social media. Because local government is so open and accessible, you need to be able to adjust quickly to changing conditions and circumstances.

How do you keep the job fresh and stimulating? After all, councils change and their priorities often change to reflect community needs or meet external challenges. Your leadership style must be able to adapt and be situational in nature. If you accept that local government provides the services that matter most to your residents and businesses on a daily basis, the need to be light on your feet is imperative. The issues for which you are responsible range from animal care to zoning, but there is an expectation that you will react quickly to attend to the needs of the public.

Agility and Intelligence

Although the day-to-day requirements of the job will keep you busy, you must not get stale or complacent. Always keep an eye on what the future might hold and be prepared to make adjustments. Keeping current with changing situations – including senior government initiatives with local impacts – is vital to your effectiveness as a CAO. Council expects to be kept abreast of changing circumstances and how they might affect current policies and service delivery – no one likes surprises. This means developing relationships with officials of other orders of government or their agencies, so that you get an early start on issues that will appear at the municipal council table and might have dramatic effects on your current plans and the political dynamics in council.

Although your credentials and interpersonal skills will, it is hoped, serve you well, it is important to remember that your experience is one of the most significant aspects of your effectiveness as a CAO. Being able to draw on the many situations you have faced along the way will allow you to bring added value to most issues and how they might be resolved.

Staying up-to-date on changing political priorities both within your community and beyond will be of great assistance to you. Understanding the context of what is leading to new issues arising, or being able to anticipate the causal nature of such issues, will allow you to be ready with suggested options, which elected officials will surely seek. Anticipating the effects of new or adjusted service delivery programs on resources and how they will be carried out will assist council in making well-informed decisions that will produce the desired outcomes.

In my case, I found this happened when we completed a review of the previous five years of a major sports facility whose operation had been buried in a city departmental budget. We discovered that the facility, which supported, among other things, a pro football team and a major junior hockey team, had required an annual taxpayer subsidy as high as $6 million. Although pro football had left town a couple of years earlier, junior hockey, an annual exhibition, and various major entertainment events had become the main source of revenue. Over the course of two years, with a complete focused core service review, establishing the facility as a stand-alone cost centre and tracking its total operations, we were able to reduce the annual taxpayer subsidy to $750,000 without materially affecting the main purpose of the facility. We also examined very closely the possibly of redeveloping the site for continued use for entertainment as well as for some residential development. This was overtaken by a decision to amalgamate the city along with many other local municipalities into a new, single-tier local government.

Developing a keen sense of political acuity – which means to be clear on how the elected leadership might want to move ahead – will boost councillors' confidence in you. It is equally important to "speak truth to power" when you are concerned, for example, about unwelcome effects on the financial stability of the organization. Maintaining your independence in a firm but diplomatic way might expose you to some risk, but you will be seen as prudent and as helping to protect the political leadership should things go wrong. Saying nothing while knowing that a council decision might come back to haunt them will not improve your stock value. Ultimately, it is important that you be seen as reliable, trustworthy, and effective in delivering on the things that councillors and the general public see as having the highest priority for the community.

Transparency, Democratic Accountability, and Clarity

You must remind yourself regularly that your work and recommendations to council are mostly in the public domain and subject to full disclosure. You must be ready to do your homework in a professional fashion and to defend your recommendations in a public forum, often on local TV, with social media ready to critique your options – the general public will make its views known. Some of the discussion and debate might even attract provincial or national attention, which raises the bar of being prepared to justify or modify your professional advice.

You are indeed in a fishbowl, which means instant accountability, and you need to be prepared for that.

All these factors weigh on how your career will move forward, make a sharp U-turn, or come to a grinding halt. Many a fine CAO has experienced the rigours of public scrutiny and suffered the indignity of a public flogging because of the style and content of their advice to council.

Having strong council-staff relationships can often mitigate the potential impacts of contentious items debated in council and in the community. As professionals, we must continue to remind ourselves that we are there to provide our best advice based on defensible research of issues or possible new policy initiatives, to offer reasonable options to address the subject at hand, and to make our best recommendation.

Matters that are before council are there for a decision. That decision is not yours to make. You must respect council's final decision and do your absolute best to deliver it in the most efficient, effective, and economical manner. If council does not follow your advice on a regular basis, it might be an early sign that it has lost confidence in your ability to serve its needs and those of the community. At that point, you would be wise to have a heart-to-heart private (*in camera*) talk with the mayor and council. Try to determine what needs to change to make the relationship work for all parties. It is also a good opportunity to determine what you are failing to see and a chance for them to be more explicit about their expectations of you and staff and to "clear the air."

Public service has its special set of challenges that distinguishes it from either the non-profit or private sectors. The business of running a municipality is largely done in an open and transparent fashion, with many legal rules governing its conduct. These rules, laws, and regulations are mostly set by the province in which the municipality operates, augmented by local by-laws passed by council. The legislative framework usually consists of how the structure is established, the election of local representatives, operating scope, enabling mandates, fiscal parameters, designation of boundaries for both wards and the municipality, and so forth.

In Canada, municipalities are not a formal level of government, but a "creature of the province," mostly subject to provincial direction and oversight. Land-use planning is one of the most important functions of local government, and yet the vast majority of the rules are set out in provincial legislation. All of this affects how you manage your career and your operating style given the inherent constraints. In other words, you are often not free to decide on your own what you believe to be the best course of action on any given major issue or mandate.

The Impact of Professional Relationships on a CAO's Career

Your primary initial consideration as CAO is to establish a sound and solid working relationship with the mayor and council. I do not mean making them your lifelong friends, but rather setting up a respectful and professional relationship built on trust and confidence. You will need to develop an independent roster of things that best reflect the collective priorities of council. You can do this by having a strategic plan that sets out a clear, agreed-upon mission, as well as complementary goals and objectives.

As staff leader, you need to have a relationship with the mayor that is a bit different from that with council. After all, most mayors will be full time at the office, while councillors might be either full time or part time depending on the size of the municipality. The mayor will tend to be your main contact with the elected leadership. Establishing a solid relationship with the mayor will often provide you with a reliable sounding board for how council might want to see certain issues come forward for its consideration. I say this, with the caution that you not automatically take direct instruction from the mayor, but rather get a sense of scope and urgency on matters as they make their way to council for a decision.

As CAO, you also need to keep the mayor informed of major issues that are coming down the pike before you have an opportunity to advise the entire council. Councils expect the mayor to lead, so seeing the city manager working closely with the mayor will be accepted and also useful to the mayor and the city manager, as long as the focus is on policy development and execution and not on electoral politics. Another caution is to make sure that you treat the mayor's office respectfully but not exclusively: do not become the mayor's chief of staff, so to speak. Remember that the council – as a whole – is the primary decision maker, not the mayor alone nor any other individual member of council, no matter how influential or persistent. CAOs who do not recognize this fine distinction can experience negative outcomes to their career.

The CAO has line authority over municipal staff, but the openness of municipal government can allow either individual staff members or unions to have access to the political leadership in ways that can complicate your life. Councils and council members are subject to various interests putting pressure on them to make decisions that in your view might not be in the long-term interest of the municipality. This pressure can be mitigated by relying on policy, such as strategic plan priorities, or by insisting that council members seek "council direction" from their peers on council to bolster problematic requests.

Another major part of the CAO's role is your relationship with the media. You will often be approached by the media when an important item is coming before council for consideration and decision. Knowing when and how to engage the media can be beneficial if done in a way that does not interfere with the role of elected officials in communicating with the public. Stick to the facts and stay away from whatever politics might be involved. In the age of social media, with its accelerated "cycle time" for advancing issues, this will require you to offer perspectives that are evidence based and carefully considered, including insisting on the time to develop an informed recommendation. But it also means recognizing that staff are no longer the exclusive source of information and policy advice on items on the council's agenda.

Last, but not least, as CAO you must manage your relationship with the general public and its many faces. People will want to engage in a way that allows them to influence your advice to council. While being accessible to all interested parties, trying to be popular with everyone is usually not a terribly effective strategy. Listen politely, but do not prefer one opinion over another until you have examined fully the issues at hand. In the end, you and only you will be accountable for your professional advice to council, invariably in a public forum with TV cameras rolling.

When to Move on: Considerations for the Next Step in Your CAO Career

Finally, keep in mind that CAOs tend to have a "shelf life" that cannot be ignored. Whether you are approached by head-hunters or actively seeking new opportunities, be sure to determine how well any new challenge would fit your overall career goals. How you tend to your career objectives will determine if you can transition successfully from your current job to another. How do you select the right opportunity? Is it a progressive move? Is it the right fit? What about compensation? Will the new job be maintenance or one that involves considerable change? Recognize when to fish and when to cut bait.

How long is long enough? Do not overstay your welcome. What about family considerations? Spouses might have career demands and aspirations that might make it difficult to accommodate your career ambitions or to accelerate them. In particular, school-age children make friends and establish their own relationships; these would be materially disrupted. Try to ensure that decisions affecting the family are aired out before a final relocation decision is made. Being mindful and sensitive to their needs is paramount to helping mitigate the effects of any disruptions on all family members. This takes on a new meaning as children age, make friends, and deepen their roots in their community. Spouses establish social connections with friends and community relationships such as volunteering and belonging to groups or organizations. All these ties must be addressed before a final decision is made about pursuing your career aspirations. Going to a new community can be stressful for everyone and create family tensions. Most times, you will rely on your own intelligence regarding the new challenge and speak to people you trust professionally to give you guidance on what to expect.

Conclusion

In the end, many issues and concerns will affect what you decide to do. Doing your homework well in advance will prepare you for change and set you up for a successful career outcome. Managing your career will mainly be your own responsibility, and the decisions you make along the way will determine if your experience matches your expectations.

Above all, enjoy what you do. Serving the public is a privilege and an honour. Always bring your "A" game. In a recent convocation address to the graduating class at Notre Dame, Dr Anthony Fauci, Director of the National Institute of Allergy and Infectious Diseases in the United States, said, "be a perpetual student, expect the unexpected, embrace public service, lead by example and finally, pursue happiness" (della Cava, 2020) – good advice indeed for any aspiring city manager.

REFERENCE

della Cava, M. (2020, 24 May). Straight-talking Anthony Fauci has been the nation's voice on the coronavirus. Who is he? *USAToday*. https://www.usatoday.com/story/news/nation/2020/05/03/coronavirus-white-house-expert-dr-anthony-fauci-americans-trust/3042991001/

23 Mentoring: Building the Next Generation of Municipal Professionals

TONY HADDAD, GERARD LEWIS, AND JIM PINE

Developing the next generation of professionals is one of the most important tasks of the current generation of professionals, and mentoring is a valuable tool for developing that new talent. Gerard Lewis of Newfoundland and Labrador and Tony Haddad and Jim Pine of Ontario all have extensive municipal experience and significant involvement with professional associations. In this chapter, they draw on their experience to provide practical advice about mentoring that next generation.

The *Cambridge Dictionary* defines *mentoring* as: "the act or process of helping and giving advice to a younger or less experienced person, especially in a job or at school."

In this chapter, we focus on mentoring and providing advice to less experienced people, both younger and older, as they develop their careers in the Canadian municipal sector, as seen through the eyes and experience of three seasoned chief administrative officers, drawing on experience with municipalities in Newfoundland and Labrador and in Ontario.

You can decide when the time is right to explore the positive impact that mentoring can have on your professional career. As the mentor or the "mentee," the mentoring relationship can accelerate your career to new heights. The benefits of mentoring are countless. For individuals, personal experience suggests that quality mentoring can lead to greater career success, including promotions, enhanced compensation, and increased upward advancement. Organizations that embrace mentoring are rewarded with higher levels of employee engagement, retention, and knowledge sharing. Terri A. Scandura has found that most Fortune 500 companies see mentoring as an important employee development tool, with 71 per cent of them having mentoring programs (*Knowledge at Wharton*, 2007). Various academic studies since the 1980s have demonstrated the many benefits of mentoring. "Clearly, employees who have mentors earn more money, are better socialized into the organization and are more productive," Scandura says. "They experience less stress and get promoted more rapidly. Because of the positive benefits shown to mentors, companies are still very interested in this process" (*Knowledge at Wharton*, 2007).

Although these findings are encouraging, mentoring is not a magic wand that automatically creates success. The truth is that effective mentoring takes effort, and creating successful mentoring relationships requires specific skills, sensibilities, and structure from *both* the mentor and the mentee.

Did you know? January is National Mentoring Month!

What Makes a Good Mentor?

A good mentor needs to be more than just a successful individual. It requires a willingness to reflect on and share your own experiences, including your failures. Great mentors must be able to both "talk the talk" and "walk the walk."

There are specific qualities that you should seek in a mentor. A good mentor should have the desire to develop and help others without any "official" reward because the mentor genuinely wants to see others succeed. This requires having the ability and availability to commit real time and energy to the mentoring relationship. Good intentions are not enough: mentoring takes time!

A good mentor also must have current and relevant industry or organizational knowledge, expertise, and/or skills. The best mentors have deep knowledge in an area that the mentee wishes to develop and want to share both their stories about "how I did it right" *and* "how I did it wrong." Both experiences provide valuable opportunities for learning.

Mentors should also have a growth mindset and a learning attitude. The best teachers have always been those who remain curious learners themselves. Would you rather be advised by someone whose mind is shut because he or she knows it all or by someone whose mind is open and always looking to deepen his or her knowledge?

Finally, a good mentor must have the skills to develop others, including active listening, asking powerful, open-ended questions, self-reflection, providing feedback, and being able to share stories that include personal anecdotes, case examples, and honest insight.

What Makes a Good Mentee?

Just as there are specific characteristics of a successful mentor, so there are attributes and sensibilities that make for a good mentee. This is important, because mentees must remember that mentors are doing this from the goodness of their heart, so being a good mentee is the best way to ensure the relationship enjoys a healthy purposeful existence.

Mentees need to be:

- *committed to expanding their capabilities and focused on achieving professional results.*
- *clear about their career goals, needs, and wants.* Mentoring is not therapy where one just rambles aimlessly; mentees are responsible for creating the mentoring agenda, so they must be clear about what they hope to get from mentoring.
- *willing to ask for help, show vulnerability, and explore different paths and perspectives.* Mentees must be open and receptive to learning and trying new ideas.
- *able to seek and accept feedback, even the "constructive" kind, and act upon it.*
- *personally responsible and accountable.* Mentors want to see movement and growth; if you say you are going to do something, then do it – sitting on the sidelines in a mentoring relationship will not work.
- *ready, willing, and able to meet on a regular basis.* Relationships take time to develop, so mentees must also be committed to upholding their end of the bargain.

The Mentoring Relationship

A mentoring relationship must be managed and nurtured. It is a joint venture that requires both parties to attend actively to its care and feeding. The chances of creating and sustaining a successful mentoring relationship are enhanced by adopting a few simple best practices. The first step is to design the alliance (see box 1).

Box 1. Designing the Mentor/Mentee Alliance

Take time to discuss the structure of the relationship. Both parties need to have a shared understanding of the relationship process. This means discussing and articulating things such as:

- *contact and response times*: who contacts whom? how? what are acceptable response times?
- *meetings*: where, when, how often? are you meeting in person, on the phone, or virtually?

- *confidentiality*: what is shareable and what is not?
- *focus*: what are the parameters of the mentoring – what is in and out of bounds?
- *feedback*: what are the expectations around giving and receiving feedback?
- *goals and accountability*: what does each party want from this experience? how does the mentee want the mentor to hold him or her accountable? how does the mentor want the mentee to hold him or her accountable?

Get to know each other: A mentoring relationship is like any other relationship: it takes time to develop. And like other relationships, it will grow faster and stronger if both parties take the time to get to know each other as *people*. Resist the temptation to dive headfirst into career problem solving and advising. Build trust by learning about each other.

Set the agenda: Both parties need to be clear about the purpose and focus of the mentoring. Additionally, the mentor and mentee should articulate what they hope to get out of the experience.

Reflect and evaluate: Every few meetings, one (or both) of the parties should ask, how is this going for you? what has been helpful? what has not? what could I do differently to make this a more rewarding experience? As awkward as it might feel, initiating evaluative conversations will keep the relationship working for both of you.

Set boundaries: Both parties need to have a comfortable relationship with each other, but they need to have an understanding about boundaries. Supervisors and subordinates have an arm's-length relationship; a mentor and mentee do not have to be this distanced from each other. It is best, however, to avoid becoming good friends; a good mentor cannot always be a loyal cheerleader. There could well be times when the mentor will need to criticize, show impatience, or say things the mentee would rather not hear. It is awkward to do that from a position of friendship. The mentor and mentee need to determine how to negotiate this arrangement.

Create cross-cultural or cross-gender relationships: The increasing emphasis on diversity in the workplace has led to questions about mentoring members of equity-seeking groups. Being mentored by a member from the majority group might give the mentee an entrée into the inner circle, but it might be difficult for the privileged mentor to identify with the issues faced by a member of an equity-seeking group. There is some useful material (Crutcher, 2014; DeWaard & Chavhan, 2020; Kuhl, 2019), but the main guidance involves having a frank conversation about issues that are difficult to discuss. Likewise, mentoring relationships between men and women need to have clear boundaries and sensitivity to workplace perceptions.

Effective mentoring is all about effective communication and the building of a trusted relationship. It is focused on building a two-way relationship where both parties learn and develop personally and professionally. In any mentoring relationship, it is essential to establish trust, communicate openly and often, and see each other as individuals.

Close out: If you are part of a formal mentoring relationship or have negotiated a specific number of mentoring meetings, take the time to close out. This is when each party should reflect and appreciate: what was most rewarding? what did you find the most valuable? what are you most grateful for? Mentees *and* mentors should clearly articulate their appreciation for the other. Be specific about what you learned and gained from the experience.

Mentoring is a great opportunity to deliver a rewarding and potentially life-changing experience for both the mentor and the mentee. It is one of the most important activities that a person can engage in to enhance career and professional life. It takes time and commitment, but it is well worth the effort. Whether you are the mentor or the mentee, it is a win-win for your career. Box 2 discusses some different types of mentoring.

Box 2. Types of Mentoring

Some examples of key mentoring models to consider:

- *One-on-one mentoring*: the traditional model of mentoring, where one mentor and one mentee agree to enter a mentoring relationship to help develop, improve, and achieve agreed-upon objectives; here, the mentor has more experience in an area that the mentee is interested in, and so can act as an advisor and guide.
- *Peer mentoring*: involves colleagues of a similar age and experience level mentoring each other; they might take turns acting as mentor and mentee, but peer mentoring is about creating a formal support system, learning together, and holding each other accountable.

- *Group mentoring*: involves one mentor working with several mentees in a group; this type helps reach and impact more mentees in a short time and helps improve everybody's teamwork skills by informally mentoring one another.
- *Team mentoring*: involves a group of mentors and mentees who carry out mentoring sessions as a team, which helps to promote diversity and inclusion, as it creates a space for several different people, with different opinions and perspectives, to come together and learn from one another.; this is good for teamwork, and eliminates any potential favouritism or elitism that can exist with one-on-one mentoring.
- *Virtual mentoring*: involves mentoring sessions taking place not in person, but over a phone or video call. During the current COVID-19 pandemic, video calls, meetings, and training have become the only option, and so there is no reason mentoring should not be the same. Mentoring is a highly effective way of supporting remote teams in this time, creating community, and tackling stress and isolation. It can be just as impactful if it is well planned, managed, and both mentor and mentee are on the same page.

Ten Characteristics of a Good Mentoring Relationship

Conversation: Have a meaningful conversation that will impact areas of your life or business that matter most to you. Such a conversation makes the most of your strengths, factoring in your current constraints and creates a set of possibilities that will show you how to make meaningful progress in a reasonable amount of time.

Commitment: A good mentor goes beyond normal expectations and changes his or her agenda and strives to make you a better YOU. Such a mentor is committed to your growth journey through the ups and downs you experience, and entering and navigating you out of your comfort zone to make something extraordinary happen. You can measure the commitment of a mentor by the tough questions you are asked with the intention of getting you to see things that you have not seen and getting you unstuck.

Curiosity: There is a reason you continue to do what you are doing even when it might not be producing the results you are expecting in your life or business. Whatever the reason, it is not too late to change course. You need to generate the curiosity to look at things you are exposed to today with a different set of eyes. A good mentor opens the doors to curiosity so that you get back that childlike enthusiasm to learn and grow.

Clarity: Clarity is the side-effect of a good mentoring relationship. Think about it: you are so close to your life and business that it is hard for you to get a "helicopter view" of them. In a good mentoring relationship, this comes automatically, as your mentor is someone who cares about life and business and, by default, has a "helicopter view" of both. The conversations automatically help you bring clarity to your goals and actions.

Capacity: Power is "the capacity to secure the dominance of one's values or goals" (Pfiffner & Sherwood, 1960, p. 77). If you increase your capacity, you can produce better and bigger results in the same amount of time. Sometimes it is a small shift in the way you are thinking that will put your capacity into high gear. Your mentor can unlock that untapped capacity, which you can put to work to accelerate your success rate. A good way to know this is if, at the end of a conversation with your mentor, you begin to find some things that seemed impossible have become totally possible.

Confidence: Confidence will empower you and give you the motivation to take the right actions. Sometimes, what might be preventing you from taking those right actions (even when you know you should) are the limiting beliefs you have about yourself and the lack of confidence in pulling something off. A good mentor might not give you strength, but will help you discover your hidden strengths and help you move beyond your limiting beliefs. "A good mentor believes in you a lot more than you believe in yourself and becomes your champion" (Ravi Gundlapalli, quoted in Banerjee, 2017).

Connections: The right connections at the right time can open new doors, expand your capacity, and give you credibility by association. A good mentor thoughtfully connects you to the right people via his or her network. It is important that you grow and earn to deserve such introductions.

Choreography: Navigating out of your comfort zone is never easy or fun. Logically, there is discomfort on the path that generally creates resistance, tempting you to go back to "tried and tested" approaches. A good mentor not only can help you choose among the available options at hand, but can also teach you how to choregraph the sequence of steps so that you get maximum leverage.

Celebration: In a good mentoring relationship, the mentor and mentee celebrate their relationship and the mini, micro, and macro victories they co-create as they build a relationship that steers your life journey in a compelling way. A good mentoring relationship is a two-way street and both of you are co-creating your future. The mentor benefits by being there and watching you grow in your journey. "Teach someone if you want to know how much you have learned. Mentor someone if you want to know how valuable you are to those around you" (Setty, 2015). Good mentors are those who enjoy being of immense value to others and seeing good things happen to those they care about.

Candour: The mentee should be able to depend on the mentor to provide an honest assessment of where he or she stands and his or her chances of progressing. Some people would like to move into a position they simply are not capable of attaining, for reasons of intellect, temperament, or some other basic characteristic. This will certainly be a difficult conversation, but you owe it to your mentee to ensure that he or she is aware of the obstacles on his or her chosen path. This could be leavened by a discussion of an alternative path for which the person is more suited.

A similar problem can arise if the mentee is capable of achieving the desired position but is unrealistically impatient or not motivated to take the intermediate steps necessary to achieve the goal. This could require a "tough love" kind of discussion in which you make clear the consequences of not pursuing the necessary pathway. As with all such conversations, the person's initial reaction might be to push back in anger, but the longer-run outcome could be beneficial.

Benefits of Mentoring

The benefits of mentoring go way beyond the mentee's self-development, positively affecting the mentors themselves as well as their organizations (box 3).

Box 3. Benefits of Mentoring

For personal development:

- *Increased confidence*: People with mentors generally benefit from higher confidence in themselves, whether it is the ability to share ideas comfortably in meetings or stand up for yourself in a challenging situation. Mentors also might experience an increase in self-confidence, as their mentee's success reaffirms their abilities and coaching techniques.
- *Higher self-awareness*: Working out your goals with someone you look up to requires serious self-analysis around strengths, weaknesses, and values. As a result, those who mentor might be more self-aware than those who do not – and self-awareness is highly beneficial when it comes to career development.

- *Exposure to new ways of thinking*: For both mentee and mentor, the mentoring process exposes new ideas and revelatory ways of thinking or problem solving. This can have long-lasting effects on both people in the partnership, encouraging innovation.
- *Giving and receiving feedback*: Feedback is something we should all want in order to improve, but probably do not ask for enough. Similarly, managers everywhere struggle with delivering feedback honestly and effectively. Mentorship helps people develop their relationship with feedback in a productive way.

For career development:

- *Job satisfaction*: Reaching your goals makes you feel fulfilled and successful. With the help of mentors, mentees can achieve their career goals and job satisfaction naturally increases. Similarly, those who mentor often consider their job more meaningful and therefore experience higher job satisfaction and fulfillment than those who do not.
- *Personal network*: Those with mentors benefit from growing their personal network outside of their colleagues. Mentors can introduce mentees to a whole range of inspirational and important people that might have an impact on mentees' careers later.

For an organization:

- *Positive company culture*: A successful mentoring program fosters a culture of leaning, nurturing, and growth. This will filter through the entire organization and create teams of people who feel satisfied and happy at work.
- *Diversity in leadership*: Mentoring can help increase considerably the representation of members in equity-seeking groups at the management level; many organizations use mentoring to increase gender and ethnic diversity in leadership roles.
- *Knowledge sharing*: Mentoring is an effective and low-cost way for senior employees to pass on knowledge of the industry and organization to younger staff.
- *Employee engagement and retention*: With mentees and mentors generally feeling more satisfied and fulfilled, mentoring has a positive effect on employee engagement and retention.
- *Recruitment*: Mentoring programs are an attractive work perk for many people, particularly millennials, who have come to expect mentoring and development opportunities from companies.

The Keys to a Successful Mentorship

Mentoring can be an incredible method for acquiring insights into your own goals and business practices, establishing personal accountability, building your professional network, and gaining invaluable experience (box 4).

Box 4. Optimizing Outcomes

To maximize the impact of the mentorship relationship and its outcome, focus on the following key factors:

- *Consider compatibility*: The most successful pairings are based on an honest assessment of the strengths and weaknesses of both the mentor and mentee.
- *Prioritize quality over quantity*: The quality of the relationship should matter as much as the quantity of mentorships, if not more. The focus of any mentorship program should be on the value gained from the pairings rather than the total number of pairings.
- *Match supply with demand*: If you are considering joining a mentorship program, make sure there are enough mentors to fulfil the demand from prospective mentees.
- *Communicate candidly*: Regular communications in any mentorship relationship are necessary to keep the connection healthy and fulfilling.
- *Remember that mentorship is a two-way street*: There is an assumption that the mentee gains value and the mentor offers that value, but the value of giving can often outweigh the value of receiving. Mentors and mentees develop strong bonds that often extend into lifelong friendships; moreover, mentorship is an advanced form of leadership that will improve this skill set (Pattani, n.d.).

Mentoring at the Municipal Level

Part of professionalism is understanding that the current generation of professionals has an obligation to develop the next generation. Several associations of municipal managers have mentoring programs. The Professional Municipal Association of Newfoundland and Labrador facilitates new administrators looking to be mentored by matching them with mentors available in their region. The Association of Municipal

Administrators of New Brunswick provides a Mentorship Program and Handbook to offer support and guidance to new municipal managers.

The Canadian Association of Municipal Administrators (CAMA), the national association for municipal managers in Canada, has created a Political Acumen Toolkit dealing with mentorship and established a Mentorship Forum. CAMA's website contains significant and beneficial information on mentoring and is a great resource to potential mentors and mentees in the municipal arena (CAMA, n.d.).

In Ontario, municipal leaders, working with staff in the Ministry of Municipal Affairs, have developed ONWARD, a broad-scope initiative directed at recruiting, mentoring, developing, and retaining the next generation of municipal leaders. Elements of the program provide advice about mentoring, succession planning, and leadership development. ONWARD initially focused on raising awareness of career opportunities in the municipal sector, the need for succession planning, and the promotion of current leaders to mentor their colleagues and subordinates to help prepare them to be the next generation of municipal leaders (Dyke, 2016).

The best mentors of the next generation are the current generation of municipal leaders. It is important for all professional associations throughout the country to continue to play the important role of encouraging their members to be mentors.

Mentoring in Our Careers: Reflections

Reflections of CAO Jim Pine

As I reflect over my thirty-two years as a CAO and nine as a provincial public servant, there is no question that I owe the successes in my career to the early mentoring I received.

I was fortunate to begin my career as a municipal advisor trainee with the province of Ontario in a small field office in London. I was taken under the wings of three seasoned colleagues who were committed to the principle of mentoring new talent. Chuck, Nigel, and Peter immediately made me feel part of the team and offered their wisdom and guidance willingly and fully. All three imparted to me the basic "operating principle" they shared, which has guided my approach over the decades. That principle is simple: Always remember that you work for the public, that it is a privilege, and that the actions you take will have a bearing on how civil servants are viewed. Treat them with respect, and you will help the organization be successful. I have tried to live by those words of advice throughout my career at both the provincial and local government levels.

Early in my municipal career, I sought out several seasoned CAOs for their insights on being successful. Two pieces of advice in particular have stuck with me over the years. First, remember that you serve elected officials, who have been chosen to represent their constituents' interests. Your job as CAO is to listen carefully to their concerns and ideas and determine how best to support council. Every councillor I have worked with over the years has been interested in some form of change – most of the time, change that moves the municipality forward. Second, a CAO who embraces this supporting role professionally and ethically has the opportunity for a long and successful career.

Being a public servant is a privilege and an honourable profession. Listen to your elected officials, try to respond to their concerns and their aspirations. And do not be afraid to lead and promote innovation. I believe these basic approaches will serve you well whether in a big municipality or in a rural setting.

Reflections of former CAO Tony Haddad

My career in municipal administration began as a community college graduate at the age of nineteen. Uncertain about what exactly I wanted to do, an opportunity for summer employment was offered to me at the City of Windsor. The treasurer hired me for a job processing parking revenue – sorting, wrapping, banking, and recording journal entries. Hence the launch of my municipal career. The treasurer also became my mentor, treating me as the son he did not have, encouraging me to consider furthering my education, to take municipal courses to learn more about the municipal business, and how to enjoy myself while doing so.

Developing a career in the public sector means that you have the privilege of serving the public, your community, and the broader public sector, where many professionals serve in a similar capacity every day, improving the life of residents and businesses through program and service delivery.

My first mentor said something that has stuck with me: take a position and defend it. Right or wrong, it is a position you have taken based on your research and knowledge. If right, it will be acknowledged; if not, admit your error, make amends, and learn a valuable lesson so you do not make the same error again. Another piece of advice that has made a lasting impression is: surround yourself with good people; they will make you look better as a leader. Although we might not have all the answers, knowing where or from whom to get the answers is critical to success. There is always someone smarter than you – have that person on your team. Lastly, seek out and accept critical assessment of your efforts; peer reviews are valuable.

Giving back or paying it forward in your profession is a rewarding opportunity to help influence the professional development of a colleague. Learning from your experience helps overcome hurdles that are avoidable, if recognized. No need to relive a negative experience. If it is shared, positive outcomes can be achieved, thus becoming a learning experience instead of an error.

We all have had mentors who influenced our careers. These lessons, if applied, can be valuable tools in the development of our own careers as well as those with whom we share them. As leaders, we are always being observed. Our actions can provide a positive influence on a mentee.

Reflections of CAO Gerard Lewis

My municipal career started in 1985 with the Town of Gander, Newfoundland and Labrador, where the town manager helped me transition from the private sector to the municipal sector while providing advice and guidance and serving as my mentor. He encouraged my participation in the Professional Municipal Association (PMA), which provided opportunities to meet other municipal administrators and local government officials. One of these was Harvey Hodder, mayor of Mount Pearl, who encouraged me to apply for the position of town clerk/assistant city manager in 1989. He shared invaluable advice on my position that was beneficial in my twenty-two-year career with the City of Mount Pearl, where I retired as chief administrative officer in 2011.

While serving on the board of directors of the PMA, I met two respected officials with the provincial Department of Municipal Affairs, John Moore and Keith Warren. I consider both to be mentors who have had a positive impact on my career. In 1997, we provided training to other administrators on behalf of the department. This relationship turned into a lifelong friendship and was of immense benefit in my full development as a more well-rounded municipal administrator.

As president of our association, I assisted in the recruitment of a new town clerk/manager for another municipality and served as her mentor as she commenced working in the municipal field. She later advised me that I became "an important mentor and provided the tools, guidance, support, and feedback needed while dealing with the multiple unique aspects of municipal government" (Marie Pretty, Chief of Staff, City of Lloydminster).

As CAO I met other CAOs and town managers of the municipalities in our region for networking meetings.

"What is a mentor? Someone you look up to and hold in high regard. Someone you seek advice from and will give you honest feedback.

Someone that will not judge. Someone that will give you perspective and something to think about. Someone that will support you yet challenge you in the same breath. If you follow their advice, you will soar and flourish. Someone that you respect, trust, and admire. A mentor will also leave the world a better place, than they originally found it" (Dawn Chaplin, CAO, Town of Torbay).

I worked closely with the executive director of our municipal association, and over the years developed a great deal of respect for her. "I have had the pleasure of knowing Gerard for approximately fifteen years now. As I began my career in municipal government, he was immediately seen as a mentor and guiding force. His in-depth knowledge of the municipal sector and his willingness to share that knowledge, makes him a tremendous resource. Sector associations seek him out to speak at conferences and regional meetings, while municipalities utilize his expertise in policy development and HR matters" (Krista Parsons, former executive director of Professional Municipal Administrators of Newfoundland and Labrador).

Conclusion: Mentoring and the Positive Effects on the Next Generation of Municipal Leaders

No one has all the answers, especially so as we start our careers. So taking the time to listen as a mentee and being prepared to share experiences as a mentor will always bring positive results. Those who are receptive to hearing from people with experience will chart a course that weathers some of the ups and downs of a career. The next generation of municipal leaders will be critical to communities everywhere. Those who learn from others will be the best of the best.

Continuing learning allows us to develop and adapt our thinking on many topics. Experiential learning is even more valuable, as we can apply these lessons to everyday actions and decisions we are called upon to make. Communication is also a critical element in the public sector as we share information internally and externally with stakeholders, the community, customers, colleagues, senior management, and council. As we help to develop the next generation of municipal leaders, our mentoring will give them a view of best practices, lessons learned, pitfalls to avoid, and a basis for plotting their own course towards advancement. Mentoring is an ongoing element of our education and professional development efforts.

Mentoring is more important in the municipal sector than in the private sector. Private sector decisions are made based on what is best for the bottom line; decisions at the municipal level are based on the provision of municipal services that have a positive impact on the quality of life for residents of your municipality.

No specific college or university program is designed to produce a CAO as there is for an accountant, engineer, or planner. A significant number of CAOs obtain their positions with other qualifications and learn what makes a great CAO through networking with and mentoring from other senior experienced CAOs.

The future of the municipal management profession requires the dedication and willingness of senior CAOs to share their knowledge and assist other aspiring CAOs. Most senior CAOs who make great mentors are those who are truly knowledgeable and respected in their field. They are often seen in volunteer positions in their provincial municipal associations or provincial civil service. Aspiring CAOs want to be in senior CAOs' company because of their reputation as knowledgeable and respected administrators and because of the aspirants' desire to emulate them and become better in their chosen field.

Mentoring is even more critical as the next generation of municipal leaders takes over and senior municipal leaders take their well-deserved retirement. Their years of experience and knowledge can be of great assistance to those who take their place to continue the tradition of the provision of superior municipal service.

Our mentoring efforts have shared knowledge, experience, and advice with our mentees in the hope that this coaching will enhance their views and approaches to managing their municipal careers over time. This advice has generally been well accepted, particularly by younger professionals who have not yet developed a broad base of municipal experience. Intrigue and attentiveness to how situations were handled created a level of amazement on the part of mentees to the open-mindedness of their mentor in addressing a challenge. Providing tools to support outside-the-box thinking and creativity is a key mentoring objective in supporting the professional development of mentees.

REFERENCES

Banerjee, B. (2017, 13 January). Good mentoring relationship. https://www.linkedin.com/pulse/good-mentoring-relationship-reproduced-from-article-written-banerjee/

CAMA. (n.d.). Political acumen toolkit: Mentorship. Canadian Association of Municipal Administrators. https://politicalacumen.camacam.ca/toolkit/mentorship/

Crutcher, B. N. (2014). Cross-cultural mentoring: A pathway to making excellence inclusive. *Liberal Education*, 100(2). http://dx.doi.org/10.22329/jtl.v14i1.6255

DeWaard, H., & Chavhan, R. (2020). Cross-cultural mentoring. *Journal of Teaching and Learning*, *14*(1), pp. 43–58.https://doi.org/10.22329/jtl.v14i1.6255

Dyke, G. (2016). A message from the president. *OMAA Annual Report 2016*. Ontario Municipal Administrators' Association. https://www.omaa.on.ca/en/about-omaa/resources/2016-OMAA-Annual-Report---04-26-17.pdf

Knowledge at Wharton. (2007, 16 May). Workplace loyalties change, but the value of mentoring doesn't. https://knowledge.wharton.upenn.edu/article/worklace-loyalties-change-but-the-value-of-mentoring-doesnt/#:~:text=Various%20academic%20studies%20since%20the,and%20get%20promoted%20more%20rapidly

Kuhl, J. (2019). *Dig your heels in*. Penguin Random House.

Pattani, A. (n.d.). 4 key facets of successful mentoring relationships. *Inc. com*. https://www.inc.com/entrepreneurs-organization/4-key-facets-of-successful-mentoring-relationships.html

Pfiffner, J. F., & Sherwood, F. P. (1960). *Administrativeorganization*. Prentice-Hall.

Setty, R. (2015, 12 February). *9* characteristics of a good mentoring relationship. *HuffPost*. https://www.huffpost.com/entry/9-characteristics-of-a-good-mentoring-relationship_b_6674602

24 The Canadian City Manager Looks to the Future

MICHAEL FENN, GORDON MCINTOSH, AND DAVID SIEGEL

As editors we have been given a wonderful gift in the form of twenty-three papers written by thirty-one city managers and allied local government experts. This chapter uses that wealth of personal insights to chart the future of local government, the city manager role, and the city management profession. Drawing on the information in these twenty-four chapters, we identify ten issues and opportunities that local governments and city managers will face in the future.

The purpose of this chapter is to examine these themes from the wisdom provided by our contributors *"in their own words"* to offer considerations for aspiring and current city managers, councils, professional associations, and training institutions.

Future Opportunities: Reconciliation, Diversity, and Inclusion

Most Canadians now see accommodating diversity and fostering inclusion, including reconciliation with Indigenous Canadians, as a shared responsibility, especially in light of history. Several of our authors go further, identifying diversity, inclusion and reconciliation as enriching and strengthening the quality of municipal decision making and improving the quality and effectiveness of the programs, policies, and services delivered in our communities.

On reconciliation, we recall the challenging words of a First Nations leader, cited by the Truth and Reconciliation Commission of Canada (TRC):

> Speaking to local community leaders at the Union of British Columbia Municipalities convention in September 2014, Tsilhqot'in Chief Percy Guichon said,
>
> We do live side-by-side and we need to work on a relationship to create or promote a common understanding among all our constituents ... we need

> to find the best way forward to consult with each other, regardless of what legal obligations might exist. I mean, that's just neighbourly, right? ... We share a lot of common interests in areas like resource development. We need to find ways to work together, to support one another on these difficult topics. (Truth and Reconciliation Commission of Canada, 2015, p. 301, reference omitted)

The TRC's Call to Action #57 lays out the challenges, from embracing reconciliation as a municipality to equipping municipal staff to understand the roles they can play in respecting rights, recognizing history, resolving conflicts, and fighting racism (Truth and Reconciliation Commission of Canada, 2015, pp. 329–30). The TRC applauds the proclamations by the cities of Toronto, Edmonton, and Calgary, as well as Vancouver's 2014 "City of Reconciliation" framework with the Musqueam, Squamish, and Tsleil-Waututh First Nations and urban Indigenous people initiative (Report from City Manager to Vancouver City Council 2014; Truth and Reconciliation Commission of Canada, 2015, p. 309). As our authors demonstrate, city managers in municipalities large and small can contribute to reconciliation in a variety of ways, from modest but symbolic breakthroughs through to more formal, comprehensive and long-lasting initiatives.

On the broader diversity and inclusion issues, especially in relation to advancing gender equity, city managers must continue to press forward. As some of our authors demonstrate from their own pioneering careers as women in city management, Canada's municipalities will benefit from having managerial leadership and workforces that more closely resemble the communities they serve and to accommodate new talent and skills. Leveraging the stimulating advantages of diversity and inclusion, in processes ranging from public engagement to innovative strategic decision making, will be key to future success for Canada's municipalities and their city managers.

Future Crises: We Can't Foresee Them, but We Can Prepare for Them

When city managers put their experience with disasters "in their own words," everyone hears their passion for their communities. Our contributors are unique, both in the harrowing experiences of their municipalities, but also with backgrounds equipping them for agile and creative responses. They also have experienced not just one but a series of disasters and emergencies, distilling widely applicable lessons for all city managers. As city managers anticipate the impacts of climate change and health emergencies, we are reminded that – in the words of Yogi Berra – "the future ain't what it used to be!"

We have learned the importance of preparation and anticipation before an emergency arrives, as well as its inherent unpredictability, the challenges of marshalling resources, including those over which you have limited control, trying to communicate effectively to a variety of audiences in real time despite the "fog of war," the need to maintain essential municipal services, including to those less directly affected, and, how to move forward after the worst has passed without failing to learn hard-won recent lessons.

A cautionary tale, after our experience with the COVID-19 pandemic, is the challenge of building organizational capacity to deal with emergencies, particularly when things are quiet and the political and budgetary priority is low. Will future infrastructure budgets incorporate potentially expensive or disruptive mitigation measures, from engineering to land use, as well as funding emergency management centres and staff training? As city managers look to the future, will they rise to the challenge of Marie-Hélène Lajoie and Pierre Prévost to build a "culture of emergency" and go beyond mere robustness or resilience to achieve municipal "antifragility"?

As Jamie Doyle and Donald Lidstone highlight from their Fort McMurray experience, there is a need for an appropriate governance model for emergencies, often the first casualty of disaster management. What is the proper role for the mayor? How does the city manager coordinate across a range of key actors, many of whom have accountabilities that lie elsewhere, whether politically, operationally, legally, or financially? How does the city manager delegate in an emergency?

Once the disaster is upon the municipality, effective communications are essential. This goes beyond the crucial task of informing residents and businesses during a period of crisis. It extends to demonstrating political oversight without inviting inappropriate political involvement in operational response. It means anticipating unscheduled visits by officials and the media, upon whom you might have to rely for support now or in the future. It means employing a range of media and languages, but respecting guardrails related to privacy, liability, and uncertain information.

The chapters by Lajoie and Prévost and Doyle and Lidstone remind us of something that we have all learned from the pandemic: the ability of a municipality and community to respond and recover depends on its people, both residents and municipal staff. Staff are expected to do their regular work while dealing with an emergency, even as they are concerned about their own families and property, affected by a disaster or health emergency. As Lajoie and Prévost observe, asking staff for heroic efforts several years in a row can lead some to say, "I never signed up for this!"

Although we cannot foresee the future, city managers know there will be more extreme weather events, recurring health emergencies, and other natural and human-made disasters.

City Managers Must Navigate the Political Arena

Our authors stress the importance of internal and external relationships, but it is paramount that the city manager, as council's direct employee responsible for civic operations, develop political trust. This dynamic interface requires three levels of attention: councillors, head of council, and council.

The attentive city manager takes time to understand councillors who come to office with different personalities, values, aims, and affiliations. The incumbent must nurture a distinct connection with each council member immediately after an election and through regular one-on-one sessions without becoming too political, as suggested by Jeff Fielding and Kate Graham, and by Tammy Crowder. Although the city manager does not serve each councillor, this relationship is important for two primary reasons: guidance and intervention.

It is not the city manager's role to help a councillor win a vote, but rather to help her or him to be an effective member of council. Councillors receiving objective guidance are often better proponents of their matters of interest and better participants at meetings. Both Carl Zehr and Bill Given suggest this is an overlapping role for the mayor and city manager. The prospect of respectful meetings and informed decisions enhances intracouncil relations with fewer dysfunctional consequences. Proactive councillor guidance enables the city manager to focus on her or his strategic leadership responsibilities, rather than on remedies for political dilemmas.

The mentoring city manager also must help administration understand the political realm, so that staff members do not become "political" by interpreting council's expectations. The city manager must ensure that the intent of an inquiry or directive is clear so that staff can assemble the necessary information for council to make an informed decision. Aside from civic governance training for staff, the successful city manager regularly engages management in debriefing the substance and tone of council decisions and directions, as John Leeburn states.

The protective city manager increasingly must guard staff from unwarranted political incursions into operations. Overzealous, frequent, or forensic councillor inquiries cause workload disruptions, morale issues, and sometimes safe workplace problems. One-on-one councillor conversations and standards of conduct might not be enough, and the pre-emptive city manager such as Crowder will employ regular council–city manager check-ins to ensure ongoing political attention to a healthy political-administrative interface. These may be closed or *in camera* meetings in accordance with council procedures, since staff performance might be discussed.

The politically astute city manager must have the confidence of the head of council and vice versa. Civic leadership at the apex is a vulnerable position for both these roles. Together, they must have the respect of councillors, administration, and the community to gain licence for their strategic role in moving the organization and community forward. The insightful city manager will ensure frequent, candid dialogue with the head of council, as advocated by former mayors Zehr and Given, to discuss both political and operational leadership challenges. The resulting mutual confidence avoids surprises and the stepping out of their respective roles.

The adaptive city manager must constantly "shape shift" his or her mayoral affiliation to exercise distinct but complementary roles. The mayor–city manager relationship is closely scrutinized, and if it is dysfunctional it taints both the internal culture and external regard. If it is too close or friendly, it can be perceived as manipulative by councillors, staff, and the public. It indeed requires a fine line for the city manager to nurture a "responsive" mayoral relationship while being professionally "responsible."

The savvy city manager must constantly navigate the "grey" aspects of council-staff relations. Crowder stresses that the dichotomous or "black and white" portrayal of the roles of council and administration is not helpful for contemporary civic leadership. Complex matters facing local governments require council and administration to play dual roles. The perceptive city manager must determine the right political-administrative interface fit to achieve the mutual confidence needed for role and strategic co-alignment to advance community and organizational goals, as advanced by Fielding and Graham.

Leadership-style misalignment with council expectations produces dire consequences for the city manager, the organization, and the community. If political confidence is diminished, the city manager loses the sentiment, or misreads the intentions, of the head of council, councillors, and council. Consequently, the city manager's effectiveness to guide staff in the preparation of decision-making information or strategy implementation is substantially reduced. Efforts to realign administration's approach, regain council confidence, or repair council-staff relations take away from the city manager's other organizational and strategic leadership responsibilities.

The political alignment imperative requires every city manager to reflect upon and enhance her or his political astuteness. This contemporary leadership competency requires councils to re-examine their recruitment and evaluation expectations beyond organizational and service managements skills. Likewise, municipal associations and training institutions must complement current curricula with knowledge, skill, and behavioural development associated with navigating the grey aspects of the political-administrative interface.

In the Future, Local Groups Will Be More Important

The city manager's closest and most important relationships are with the mayor and council, but he or she cannot forget the need to lead in three directions: "up" with political leadership, "out" with community partners, and "down" within the municipal organization. Of these, leading out and working with local community groups will be an increasingly important and complex relationship for the city manager.

Local groups are becoming more numerous and better organized, aided by the convenient, low-cost reach of social media. Some groups, such as recreation associations and heritage preservation groups, have been around for a long time. Others have come on the scene more recently around issues such as anti-racism and active transportation. Ad hoc groups come and go in response to issues such as traffic problems or development initiatives that involve high-density, multiuse projects or group homes.

At first, some local governments tended to resist these groups on the grounds that those with professional expertise in city hall knew best. Over time, however, it has become clear that the better strategy is to work with these groups to arrive at solutions that combine the professional expertise in city hall with the "street smarts" found in these groups. This not only produces better solutions to problems, but the involvement of residents increases the legitimacy of the actions government eventually takes.

Many municipalities now have organizational units that manage public engagement and that use dedicated web platforms and specialized software such as Have your Say, EngagementHQ, or Bang the Table. In many provinces, some form of engagement is now required by legislation as a part of the process of making planning decisions or changing municipal electoral systems. Most enlightened municipalities, however, have seen the value of working with community groups and simply build public engagement into almost every major decision that comes before council.

Sometimes the engagement results in win-win situations for both the municipality and the local group. Ann Mitchell describes how Sioux Lookout, Ontario, worked with local Indigenous groups to develop a community centre for local youths and to expand the airport terminal building to benefit both Indigenous groups and the municipality. Linda Rapp describes how Whitehorse, Yukon, relied on the expertise of local groups to develop a series of recreational trails in the community. It is possible that these ends could have been accomplished without the involvement of community groups, but working with the community made it easier and also helped to build trust between the partners involved in these projects.

Robert Buchan has pioneered the concept of transformational incrementalism (TI) to structure public engagement in community development. TI gives municipal staff members a key role in using their influence to develop "a broad alignment of values (and therefore support for change) across the populations of elected officials, staff, the public, and industry." This approach has been employed successfully in several situations.

In other cases, the engagement operates at a lower-profile level, but still provides important benefits for the municipality. Chris MacPherson describes how he builds support for his council's strategic plan by using a Power Wheel to identify the important actors in his community who need to be involved in particular initiatives. He then uses the Power Wheel to decide when and how to involve different people, recognizing that "Everyone on your Power Wheel will have their own agenda and perspective; to be successful, you must understand what those are."

Sometimes the engagement is more structured. One of the outcomes of New Public Management has been the greater use of partnerships to promote efficiency in the management of the municipality and greater involvement with the community.

Jag Sharma provides examples of two types of partnerships. The N6 is a partnership of six medium-size municipalities in the northern part of York Region, north of Toronto. The heads of council and CAOs meet quarterly to discuss sharing common services and taking a common position on issues. "The group has developed shared services in many functions, such as internal audit, solid waste and recycling collection, insurance and risk management, and animal control." The City of Oshawa, Ontario, developed a partnership with several local educational institutions to assist the city in researching opportunities for improving services and providing learning opportunities for both municipal staff and students. Initiatives like these improve the efficiency of the municipality while increasing the level of trust among partners, which smooths the way for the next project.

The future of local government almost certainly will see these local groups become better organized and more sophisticated in their knowledge. City managers need to find ways to make public engagement an integral part of the policy-making process, not a piece that reluctantly gets added on at the end. The good news about this is that, as these groups become more sophisticated, they will have a great deal to offer municipalities in terms of their local knowledge and the legitimacy they will lend to a project.

City managers will gain considerably if they can learn to work with these groups to accomplish joint goals that benefit the municipality. Contemporary city managers will see these benefits and mobilize resources to enhance local leadership capacity and group resilience. They will also be challenged by the degree to which local government simply provides information, gathers input, seeks feedback, or enables active involvement for various policies, decisions, programs, or services. However, these are not the only external actors that are important to city managers. Other governments also play an important role.

In the Future, Other Governments Will Still Be Important

Local, Indigenous, provincial-territorial, and federal governments are becoming more interwoven in both the development of policy and the delivery of services. This trend will become more pronounced in the future as the nature of services governments provide becomes more complex and transcends jurisdictional mandates and boundaries.

Urban transit systems involve the integration of municipal and provincial transit systems with a heavy infusion of capital investment from the federal government. Mitchell describes how Sioux Lookout, Ontario, worked with local Indigenous groups to obtain provincial funds to operate a shared-ride service. Affordable housing involves the interaction of municipal planning and zoning policies, development levies, on-reserve housing policies, provincial planning policies, and federal monetary policy that influences mortgage rates and terms.

In the future, individual governments will do very little in "splendid isolation."

A city manager needs to manage the internal aspects of her or his city conscientiously, but an astute manager also needs to understand where her or his city fits in the broader intergovernmental context. A distinction is sometimes made between "policy makers" who develop policies and impose them on others, and "policy takers" who receive policies developed elsewhere and must implement or abide by them. Traditionally, municipalities have been policy takers, but they are learning to develop influence that allows them to have a role in working with other governments to be policy makers. Gail Stephens and Zack Taylor argue that the detailed knowledge of local conditions that local governments possess is an important tool in exerting influence in the policy-making arena.

John E. Fleming draws on his experience working in several local governments and the Ontario provincial government to recommend five strategies that will help municipal managers exert more influence in dealing with other governments. His approach is geared to advising managers about how to build relationships and become policy makers rather than being purely policy takers.

Stephens and Taylor draw on Stephens's experience working in municipal, provincial, and federal governments to describe how her relationship building facilitated the sale of Winnipeg Hydro to Manitoba Hydro and how she dealt with a serious homelessness problem in Winnipeg and Victoria.

Historically, some municipalities have been satisfied to take the position of comfortable subordination (Siegel & Tindal, 2006) meaning that they have accepted the policies they were given by other governments and did what they could to implement them. This was comfortable in that the municipalities could complain about the policies they were given without taking any role in trying to influence their development.

As policies have become more interwoven, municipalities have developed "assertive maturity" and are demanding a role in making the policies they will implement. This has resulted in the development of the term multilevel governance, which recognizes that governance is now not a matter of different levels of government taking independent actions, but rather a function of the continuing interaction and intertwining of the various orders of government.

This means that it is now a part of the role of the city manager to look outside her or his municipality to find ways to influence policy makers in other orders of government. As governments continue to tackle more complex problems, the idea of multilevel government decisions, policies, and strategies will become more prevalent.

In the Future, City Managers Will Need a Strong Management Team

While relationships among governments are becoming more intertwined, interactions within individual governments are becoming more complex. Not only is the delivery of each service becoming more difficult, but the linkages among services that need to be seamless are also becoming more important. It is impossible for any one person to be knowledgeable about all these services. Therefore, one of the most important tasks facing the contemporary city manager does not have to do with any particular service, but with building a team to work collectively to manage the entire municipal corporation and to collaborate on policies and programs.

The team-building process has several steps. It is important to hire people who are proficient in managing their department and delivering their specific service, but that is just the beginning. Senior department heads really have two roles that can conflict with each other. One role is focused inward – being the leader of their department. This involves leading the people in their department and ensuring they have the resources they need to do their job. This can involve conflicts with other units in the never-ending battle for resources. The second role is working with the city manager and other department heads to manage the entire municipal corporation. This is what Leeburn refers to as "a 'one-city' view that put[s] the interests of the whole ahead of the interests of any one department." This requires the manager to look beyond departmental concerns and focus on making decisions that benefit the entire corporation, even if those decisions are contrary to the aims of the manager's own department. They must be "vice-presidents" of the municipal corporation. In the absence of this integration, both legislation and practice might lead to fragmentation of policy and politicization of the bureaucracy.

The city manager must also promote a diversity of views around the senior management table. A homogeneous group that agrees on everything will reduce tension around the table, but it will not necessarily produce decisions that consider the broad perspective or challenge the status quo. Diversity and inclusion are very important parts of the team-building process. The best decisions will be made when there are diverse inputs into the decision-making process. Sheila Bassi-Kellett and Shirley Hoy argue that encouraging diversity in teams is not a matter of fulfilling quotas or engaging in altruism; rather, a diverse workforce produces better decisions and increases the confidence that residents have in the quality of the municipal organization.

Building a team is not a one-time task. Municipalities work in a very unstable environment in which the needs of residents, provincial legislation, and the general work environment are constantly changing. The city manager must ensure that the team continues to work well as the environment around it changes, sometimes quite abruptly.

The city manager must build an organizational culture that nourishes these seemingly contradictory roles. Robert Earl created that culture by emphasizing clarity of purpose and freedom to innovate. Clarity of purpose ensures that everyone is on the same page and is pulling in the same direction. When a manager is confident that all the team members are motivated to go in the same direction, then the team leader can step back and allow the team members to innovate within their own spheres while ensuring that they contribute to the overall good of the municipality. Lajoie and Prévost counsel that effective delegation, particularly in emergency situations, leaves the city manager freer to focus on priorities, unplanned events, and overarching concerns.

A good team not only will work together in delivering the current services offered by the municipality; it will also function better at making decisions that affect the future of the municipality.

City Managers Need to Facilitate Strategic Alignment

Throughout this book, there is definitive acknowledgement that it is council that directs the administration. A shared sense of direction enables council to be effective in both developing strategy and making policy on behalf of the public. Its vision and goals must also be aligned with the community to leverage local resources and support to be viable stewards of the community's future. Fielding and Graham closely correlate political strategic alignment with staff members' ability to establish a clear line of sight to pursue their work.

The facilitative city manager must be creative to achieve a shared vision. MacPherson demonstrates that, if done well, it motivates everyone involved to overcome obstacles and harnesses resources beyond the local government's capacity. At the same time, widespread awareness of council's strategic direction holds it publicly accountable for the pursuit of stated goals. A clear strategic direction helps the city manager to align resources effectively with political expectations and remind council when it might be veering from its strategic agenda.

The community-minded city manager must move the organization beyond simply public awareness and consultation. Rapp stresses that meaningful stakeholder involvement in civic endeavours should not be treated as events, but as community development efforts to strengthen both local group capacity and sustainable services or programs. One of the lasting benefits of collaboration is a robust volunteer sector that offers programs beyond a local government's capacity. The city manager needs to ensure that staff are trained and equipped to engage the stakeholders in a creative and sustainable manner.

The transformational city manager recognizes that significant community change depends on enduring stakeholder relationships. "Wicked" challenges require disparate interests to align efforts and resources through a shared vision. Although the overall vision might not change, the pursuit of collective community-based action is a learning process gained from feedback, new information, failures, and successes. The city manager needs to prepare both council and staff to deal with the reality that community development requires giving up some element of control for problem definition, desired outcomes, and possible solutions.

The strategic city manager recognizes that role coalignment works best when elected officials focus on vision and goals, while staff focus on the implementation of strategies. On the one hand, when there is a vacuum in council's direction, staff will fill it, which creates a political and/or public sentiment that administration is running the show. On the other hand, if council does not have confidence in implementation efforts, it might venture into operations to correct the situation, given its oversight role. The city manager must develop practices that foster mutual staff and council confidence in strategic processes and direction. In fact, if the city manager fails this test, proposals for a "strong mayor" solution might be heard locally and provincially.

The adaptive city manager takes time to ask questions of council and ensure its political decisions and directions are clear. Being strategic is neither a linear process amid changing internal factors and external influences, nor the production of a plan that looks generic or sits on a shelf. Bruce Macgregor and David Szwarc portray strategic planning and managements as an incremental learning process. The responsive city manager will ensure that council's directions and operational strategies are the subject of continuous review, revision, and celebration.

Strategic thinking does not occur only at a corporate planning level. At every council meeting, requests for information and decisions are made that affect the present and future. Failing to meet council's information needs reduces political confidence in the advice administration provides. Conversely, frequent correct staff guesswork of political expectations again can produce a political sentiment that administration is running the show. The city manager must develop practices to ensure that the best information is available for council's decision making and direction setting.

Notwithstanding the city manager's best efforts to develop a clear sense of political strategic direction, it simply might not occur due to council dynamics. The city manager's role is to help council be the best it can be. The city manager must exercise her or his professionalism through persistence and patience in providing quality advice, facilitating a shared direction, and developing organizational capacity. He or she also has a professional obligation to advance strategies that further organizational and community sustainability. At the same time, the city manager must provide strategic leadership to align operational resources and effort to provide service excellence and respond to community needs.

For their part, councils need to embrace strategic functions as continuous community-based processes without immediate results for complex matters. This collective effort requires elected officials and management to recast the linear strategic approach to a more organic organizational learning process. Shifting from classic practices that produce an attractive strategic plan requires civic leadership training to include contemporary systems thinking, social innovation techniques, and strategic performance monitoring.

To Face the Future, the City Manager Must Exhibit Personal Mastery

Our authors vary greatly in their experience, professional backgrounds, and education. It is evident that there is no one best route to being a successful city manager. Certainly, there are various forms of city management certificates, but the authors' voices speak to the need for aspiring and incumbent city managers to rethink their personal development, councils to reconsider their recruitment and performance expectations, and associations and training institutions to refresh the prevailing managerial focus of training programs.

Many of the authors highlight the "alignment" imperative required to be successful. The city manager must facilitate goals embraced within the organization, throughout the community, and among external stakeholders. But it is not enough to be tactically astute; the city manager's leadership style must be compatible with all these interests to achieve requisite relations for strategic alignment.

This crucial alignment imperative emanating from our city managers' voices starts with the incumbent. Hoy exemplifies the self-confidence needed to advance in a traditionally male-dominated profession. David Calder notes the importance of actively learning from others. John Burke and Janice Baker propose self-reflection to fine-tune capabilities continually throughout one's career.

The implied personal mastery required of the city manager means learning from others in that role, peer counsel, personal reflection, and the advice of a mentor. Council, for its part, needs to articulate clearly the behavioural attributes that best suit organizational and political needs in order to guide its selection of a city manager and provide feedback. City management curricula should include topics such as physical and mental wellness, personality insights, leadership styles, giving and receiving feedback, active listening, and emotional intelligence.

The success of a city manager does not rest solely with the incumbent; it also requires the ability to motivate employees, as highlighted by the team-building experiences of Earl and Leeburn. Bassi-Kellett stresses the human resources skills needed to ensure an inclusive and healthy organizational culture. Tony Haddad, Gerard Lewis, and Jim Pine point out the significance of the city manager's leadership legacy to grow those around through mentoring efforts.

Pat Moyle and Hassaan Basit emphasize that associations and training institutions need to focus on emerging leadership capabilities beyond managerial skills. Some themes to consider from our authors' stories include coaching others, psychologically safe workplaces, inclusivity and diversity, cultural enhancement, team development, and employee engagement. Councils need to secure adequate support for leadership development that goes beyond technical and operational topics. City managers must take time to reflect on their capabilities to develop personal learning aims to model exemplary leadership.

The critical capability often labelled political astuteness leaps off the pages, but it is quite intangible to delineate. Fielding and Graham emphasize the sensitive navigation skills and behaviours needed for positive city manager–council relations. Former mayors Zehr and Given reinforce that political savvy is required to develop and sustain the respect of elected officials for both the person and the position. As Crowder observes, the dynamic political-administrative interface requires active listening and objectivity to be the trusted advisor.

Political astuteness is the cornerstone competency for success even if the city manager has exemplary leadership abilities. Many associations and recent articles on city management endeavour to unpack this critical capability. City managers would benefit from increased efforts, through research and training, to help them achieve a good fit in their political context through adaptive tactics, situational leadership strategies, and insights into the political realm, while maintaining a clear sense of personal and professional values.

The success of the city manager is not just an organizational matter. Every local government has different interests that require the city manager to champion creative community engagement efforts, as Rapp and Buchan illustrate. Of note is Mitchell's and Bassi-Kellett's focus on the emerging community leadership role to foster a welcoming and inclusive community. Advocacy and negotiation skills are the focus of Fleming and of Stephens and Taylor to help achieve favourable intergovernmental relations. Sharma underscores the collaboration talents required for shared services and positive relations with other organizations.

Councils must recognize the need to collaborate with an array of business, non-profit, and government organizations to enhance their capacity to meet community needs. City managers need to spend time on developing external relationships, shared services, and mutual strategic agendas. Beyond relationship building, agreement negotiation, reputation management, and inclusive community training programs, there must be a focus on how city managers can "get out of the kitchen." They need coaching, time management, and delegation capabilities to reduce their operational role and facilitate a shift to external relationships.

Positive internal and external relations are prerequisites to the second alignment imperative that many of our authors stress. MacPherson explains a creative approach to achieve a shared vision among relevant internal and external interests. The complex nature of community challenges necessitates incremental adjustments in response to changing conditions, as described by Buchan and by Macgregor and Szwarc. The emergency events recounted by Lajoie and Prévost and by Doyle and Lidstone remind us of the crisis management skills required of a city manager that are beyond typical strategic planning competencies.

In short, the strategic approach requires councils, city managers, and training programs to examine emerging practices to motivate elected officials and staff to get the "plan" off the shelf. Learning from successful (and failed) experiences of peers with innovative engagement, realistic priority setting, and community futures will enrich what we do. Councils and administrations that are not strategic have a problem with community stewardship. The city manager must have the toolkit and the confidence to help elected officials deal with complex matters beyond the delivery of services.

To Face the Future, the City Management Profession Must Be Strengthened

As philosopher George Santana observed, "those who cannot remember the past are condemned to repeat it." The hard-fought civic reforms of the twentieth century gave Canada the "council-manager plan" and the position of "city manager" or "chief administrative officer," which emphasized the importance of professional competence in municipal government. In an earlier era, when patronage and civic corruption were widespread, the council-manager plan aimed to distinguish the important legislative and policy-approving roles of politicians from practical and competent management of the policies, programs, public works, and community services delivered by municipal governments.

Those gains still can be eroded. Despite the advance of the council-manager plan, the position of city manager is never far from the political arena. City managers are conscious of the potential and recurring risks of political pressure, deviations from principle and approved policy, a lack of regard for expertise and public ethics, and, potentially, job security. On occasion, some mayors and councils might appoint or favour a city manager who can be relied upon to bend to political expediency – and dispense with those who are not.

Even the smallest municipal governments are complex organizations facing a daunting array of fiscal, political, societal, and managerial challenges. How can communities ensure that they benefit from the principled professionalism represented by the position of city manager? The first ingredient in any good relationship is a climate of mutual respect. That can be easier said than done, when public criticism of the city manager and staff by councillors is often popular with journalists and social media and seen by some as "part of the job."

Regardless of the relationship that exists between the city manager and the mayor and council, the core of that relationship must be respect for each other's intelligence and professionalism, for the challenges each "side" faces, and for the fact that both elected representatives and municipal staff are trying to serve the best interests of their communities (Fenn & Siegel, 2017, p. 21). The underlying principle is simple: policy decisions are council's business, management is management's business. To promote a good relationship, city managers and their staff must respect democracy, while councillors must respect professional management (Fenn & Siegel, 2017, p. 18).

In the future, the position of city manager also must be bolstered in the face of political, populist, and social media–driven efforts to diminish the value of expertise and experience. The future of our communities depends on municipalities insisting that the next generation of city managers has a strong commitment to professional city management. Ontario's recent embrace of a US-style political executive for major cities is an indication of the risk of failing to demonstrate to a wider public the advantages of non-political managerial leadership at the municipal level.

Too often in Canada, the city manager position is largely unknown or obscurely bureaucratic. Should that continue, the council-manager plan risks losing essential public support. The role and value of the city manager needs to be communicated more effectively to a broad audience, from politicians and community leaders to residents and businesses, and understood by everyone without the incumbent obtaining the media spotlight.

This message needs to be reinforced by practical supports such as adequate employment contracts and statutory recognition to protect the integrity of the city manager–CAO position. Correspondingly, there should be decisive action when an individual lowers professional standards or undermines the role; here, professional associations could have an important place. Likewise, there should be consequences when actions of council diminish the integrity of the city manager position.

Tomorrow's city managers must be able to demonstrate their professionalism and competence; to do so, they must be insulated from inappropriate pressures. Our legacy of good municipal government in Canada depends on encouraging a new generation of city managers through mentoring and progressive career opportunities, while promoting diversity, inclusion, public service ethics, and progressively earned professional competence.

Like physicians, accountants, and engineers, city managers and municipal CAOs often have wide authority, great responsibility, and a position of public trust. Bringing "professionalism" to the role of city manager will remain a key responsibility of current city managers and their professional associations, in order to sustain and enhance a position that Ontario's retired Associate Chief Justice Frank Marrocco has described as "a key pillar in the structure of the municipality" (Marrocco, 2020, vol. IV, p. 22).

In her chapter, Baker observes that there remains a debate about the status of the city manager in Canada. Should councils be obliged to have such a position? Should it be bolstered by statute and given clear roles and responsibilities? Most critically, being appointed by and responsible to politicians, should the city manager have a degree of statutory independence? In the inquiry report mentioned above, Justice Marrocco answered "yes" to all three of these questions. However, impatience with the perception of inadequate progress on key municipal issues such as housing can make provincial and local decision makers seek alternatives that appear to be more decisive, as we have seen with the Ontario government's embrace of the "strong mayor" at the potential expense of the position of city manager.

One area of focus is professional accountability, both for meeting organizational goals and for demonstrating values-based competencies. Reflecting the often-choppy waters through which city managers must navigate, Baker's call for principled professionalism is balanced with the experience-informed caution that "not every hill is a hill to die on." Her conclusion lifts the conversation about professionalism by observing that professions involve more than mere credentials – like other professionals, future city managers will be judged by their conduct, ethics, performance, and outputs.

How shall we develop the next generation of city managers? Certainly, city managers themselves must play a key role. They need to mentor aspiring city managers and encourage those with potential to consider it as a career choice. As several of our authors point out, there is no specific college or university program designed to produce city managers – in contrast with, say, accountants, engineers, or land-use planners. A significant number of CAOs obtain their positions with other qualifications and learn what makes a great city manager through networking and mentoring from senior, experienced CAOs with whom they work or interact, or merely observe.

Haddad, Lewis, and Pine urge current and aspiring city managers to leverage the tools of various municipal professional associations in making the mentorship process work – from developing political acuity and succession planning to recruiting and mentoring public servants with leadership potential. Another key feature of professionalism they cite is "continuous learning" to stay current with developments in a rapidly changing and incredibly multifaceted field.

Developing and improving communications skills likewise will be an essential attribute in a "profession" that demands more than an ability to explain clearly often complex or contentious issues to a variety of audiences and through a range of "platforms." It will require city managers to explain and demonstrate to a variety of constituencies the importance of impartial professional city management.

Professionalism and the City Manager: A Call to Action

The pre-eminent global association for city managers and CAOs, the International City/County Management Association, refers to "the Profession." Whether technically a profession or not, our conclusion is that the focus should be on enhancing the "professionalism" of the city manager position, in all its various aspects. Although much of the onus to be professional properly lies with the city manager, the Canadian Association of Municipal Administrators (CAMA) and professional associations in all provinces and territories have a role.

With professional authority should come professional responsibility. Should professional organizations consider the merit of a certification program or some similarly designated rite of passage for city managers? Globally, some jurisdictions impose on their city managers the obligation to make annual submissions of relevant professional development activities, much as lawyers, accountants, and physicians do. They also subject the city manager designation to peer review or a disciplinary process if there is a purported breach of professional behaviour.

As land-use planners, municipal clerks, and other local government professionals have demonstrated, "certification" needs to be rigorous and to provide proof of continuing mastery of required competencies, but need not be daunting, onerous, or time-consuming for people who stay on top of professional development on a continuing basis. The process employed by Canada's corporate directors might serve as a model: relevant experience, a core educational program, an examination of relevant knowledge, and a specified number of hours of annual professional development through conferences, seminars, or courses.

Looking to the future of the city manager profession, any requirements for certification will need to go beyond essential managerial skills. Many of our authors highlight the need for leadership capabilities such as strategic thinking, communications, community engagement, political acuity, emotional intelligence, and facilitation. At the same time, municipal associations must enhance political awareness of the advantages of having a certified city manager. This will require political associations and municipal affairs ministries to include this information in post-election orientation and ongoing conference sessions.

Complementing this effort should be a concerted drive by the various professional associations of city managers and CAOs to bolster legal support for the position of city manager – in ways that might not be realistic to expect from individual city managers or their mayors. Legislation that provides some tenure protection would help city managers to serve without fear of being fully professional: a balance between being responsive and responsible. An employment contract template, such as the one promoted by CAMA (2020), could assist both municipal councils and newly recruited city managers to strike the right balance. As recent experience in Ontario demonstrates, if the importance and efficacy of the city manager position is not fully appreciated, it is vulnerable to elimination.

As municipal government in Canada looks to an uncertain future, it depends upon efforts by individuals, councils, municipal associations, and provincial governments to listen to and act upon the voices of city managers in this book.

The City Manager as Place Shaper

Each chapter in this book focuses on an important slice of the role of the city manager – dealing with council, community development, team building, and so forth. Focusing only on slices, however, might obscure the central role of the city manager as the sole municipal employee with responsibility for the entire municipal corporation.

The city manager's role should go beyond simply administering existing legislation and responding to the desires of council and residents. Michael Lyons coined the phrase "place-shaping," which he defined as

> the creative use of powers and influence to promote the general well-being of a community and its citizens. It includes the following components:
>
> - building and shaping local identity;
>
> . . .
>
> - maintaining the cohesiveness of the community and supporting debate within it, ensuring smaller voices are heard;
> - helping to resolve disagreements;
> - working to make the local economy more successful while being sensitive to pressures on the environment;
>
> . . .
>
> - working with other bodies to response [*sic*] to complex challenges such as natural disasters and other emergencies. (Lyons Inquiry into Local Government, 2007, p. 3)

Lyons emphasizes that the role of the municipality goes beyond the spheres of responsibility enumerated in enabling legislation. He argues that the municipal corporation has an obligation to work with civil society to shape and improve the entire community.

Many city managers underestimate their own power and influence in their community. They sit atop the administrative hierarchy of the municipal government, which gives them considerable influence with council. They also have considerable status within the community that comes with their position as senior manager of one of the largest employers and economic drivers in the community. City managers should use this position wisely in helping to shape the broader community.

The city manager is not just the "manager" of a municipal bureaucracy, important as that role might be. Without encroaching on or supplanting the roles of mayor and council, the city manager can be a community leader – convening civil society leaders and business leaders to address the issues facing the broader local and regional community that they all serve.

In contemporary Canada, here are some of the questions the city manager should be addressing:

- What should my community be doing to address climate change?
- What should my community be doing to promote the inclusion of all marginalized groups and residents?

- What should my community be doing to address income inequality?
- How can I contribute to strengthening the evolving local economy?
- How can I work with civil society to improve the social and economic position of everyone in my community?
- What position should my community be occupying in the broader provincial, national, and international spheres?

These questions go considerably beyond the municipal corporation. They suggest that city managers should not only lead their own municipalities, but also play a leadership role to transform the municipal corporation and the broader community – to become a place shaper for the benefit of the well-being of the community.

REFERENCES

CAMA (2020, 5 November). CAMA launches CAO employment contract toolkit. Canadian Association of Municipal Administrators. Retrieved 9 October 2021 from https://www.camacam.ca/news/cama-launches-cao-employment-contract-toolkit

Fenn, M., & Siegel, D. (2017). *The evolving role of city managers and chief administrative officers*. University of Toronto, Institute on Municipal Finance and Governance.

Lyons Inquiry into Local Government. (2007). *Place-shaping: A shared ambition for the future of local govenment: Executive summary*. Her Majesty's Stationery Office.

Marrocco, F. A. (2020). *Transparency and the public trust: Report of the Collingwood Judicial Inquiry*. http://www.collingwoodinquiry.ca/report/index.html

Report from City Manager to Vancouver City Council. (2014, 28 October). *Framework for city of reconciliation*. http://former.vancouver.ca/ctyclerk/cclerk/20141028/documents/rr1.pdf

Siegel, D., & Tindal, C. R. (2006, March). Changing the municipal culture: From comfortable subordination to assertive maturity – Part I. *Municipal World*, pp. 37–40.

Truth and Reconciliation Commission of Canada. (2015). *Honouring the truth, reconciling for the future: Summary of the final report of the Truth and Reconciliation Commission of Canada*. https://publications.gc.ca/collections/collection_2015/trc/IR4-7-2015-eng.pdf

Contributors

Editors

Michael Fenn was city manager of Burlington, Ontario, and chief administrator of the regional municipality that became the amalgamated City of Hamilton. He later served as Ontario Deputy Minister of Municipal Affairs & Housing under three premiers. In 2019, he was Special Advisor to the Ontario government on municipal government reform. A board director with OMERS, the Ontario municipal employees' pension fund, Michael is a management consultant (primarily with StrategyCorp) and a policy research writer. Appointed to the Association of Municipalities of Ontario Honour Roll, Michael has also received the Ontario Lieutenant Governor's Medal of Distinction in Public Administration and the highest awards for career achievement from Ontario's two largest municipal administrators' associations, and his career has been profiled in the book, *Leaders in the Shadows: The Leadership Qualities of Municipal Chief Administrative Officers*.

Gordon McIntosh has forty years of executive, consultant, and educator roles in local government throughout Canada and overseas. He served as President of the Local Government Management Association of BC and received the Professional Award for Excellence as CAO for the 470 Gulf Islands in the Georgia Basin, British Columbia. He has conducted 1,400 sessions involving 130,000 elected and appointed civic leaders in Canada and elsewhere, including Palestine, Africa, the Philippines, and the Caribbean. Gordon delivers live and online leadership training, governance development, and strategic priority setting workshops for municipal associations and universities. His doctoral studies and current research focus on the CAO leadership role and the political/administrative interface.

David Siegel was a professor of political science and administrator at Brock University for over forty years before retiring recently. He taught and wrote extensively on local government and public administration. He has a PhD in political science from the University of Toronto and an MA in public administration from Carleton University, and is a Chartered Professional Accountant. He has consulted for municipalities, spoken at many conferences, and written or edited eight books and many articles. His most recent book is *Leaders in the Shadows: The Leadership Qualities of Municipal Chief Administrative Officers*. In retirement, he is also writing about baseball, particularly the minor-league Toronto Maple Leafs baseball team.

Contributors

Janice Baker is Chief Administrative Officer (CAO) for the Regional Municipality of Peel. After starting her career in the private sector, Janice discovered local government in 1987 and found her passion. Since then, she has spent her career helping to build communities, holding senior roles at both the City of St. John's, Newfoundland and Labrador and the City of Oshawa, Ontario, before joining the City of Mississauga, Ontario, as Commissioner of Corporate Services and Treasurer. From 2005 to 2020, she served as Mississauga's City Manager and CAO. Janice has received numerous awards during her career, including becoming in 2019 the first woman executive leader in local government to receive the Vanier Medal from the Institute of Public Administration of Canada.

Hassaan Basit started his career as an evolutionary biologist after graduating from the University of Toronto. He then completed a Masters in science communication from Queen's University, Belfast, and more recently an MBA in digital transformation from The DeGroote School of Business at McMaster University. Hassaan is the President and CEO of Conservation Halton. Holding progressively responsible leadership positions in the organization since joining in 2004, Hassaan has spent the past four years developing and implementing Conservation Halton's strategic plan. This plan successfully saw Conservation Halton's image and brand strengthened, budgets realigned, stakeholder communication refined, and the organization transformed into a leader in innovation and customer-centric service delivery.

Sheila Bassi-Kellett was born and raised in Toronto, and moved to the Northwest Territories in 1986. Over her more than thirty-five years in the territory, she has worked extensively in governance development and individual/organizational capacity building in the municipal, territorial, and private sectors. Living in both Yellowknife and Tulita, her career has taken her from Self Government Negotiator to CAO for a small community to Assistant Deputy Minister of Municipal and Community Affairs to Deputy Minister of Human Resources. After running her own management consultancy for three years, Sheila returned to public service when she joined the City of Yellowknife in March 2017 as City Manager. In 2020, she was recognized by *Municipal World* as a Woman of Influence in Local Government in Canada.

Rob Buchan, PhD, FCIP, is an adjunct professor at Simon Fraser University, an instructor at the University of Victoria, and the principal of iPlan Planning and Development Services. He was a city manager for eleven years and a city planner for thirty-two years. His professional work in official community plans, affordable housing, revitalization, trail planning, food system planning, and interface fire hazard planning has won nineteen awards of excellence, including induction into the Canadian Institute of Planners College of Fellows. In 2017, he developed the theory of Transformative Incrementalism in his dissertation at the University of Victoria.

John Burke is a retired public servant whose experience spanned more than forty years in municipal and provincial government in Canada. Much of his career was spent in the senior ranks of CAO/city manager and deputy minister. His first twenty-nine years of service started in Nova Scotia as a rural county CAO and ended as CAO in the City of Ottawa. During that time, he witnessed a remarkable change in both the function and structure of local government across the nation. He spent the next eleven years as a deputy minister in the province of Ontario. A native of Nova Scotia, he holds a Bachelor of Commerce degree from St Mary's University and a Diploma in Public Administration from Western University, and is a graduate of the Institute of Corporate Directors, Rotman School of Business at the University of Toronto.

David Calder is the City Manager, City of Cambridge, Ontario. He has also served as the CAO with the Town of Tillsonburg, Ontario, and president of Tillsonburg Hydro Inc. David was General Manager of Corporate Services, City of Waterloo and Director of Public Access and Council Services/City Clerk, City of Cambridge. David has also held positions with the former Township of Anderdon, the former City of York, the Region of Peel, and the City of Woodstock. David attended the University of Guelph, graduating with a BA and the University of Windsor, graduating with a Bachelor of Public Administration Degree.

David has been president of both the Association of Municipal Managers, Clerks and Treasurers of Ontario and the Ontario Municipal Administrators' Association (OMAA).

Tammy Crowder started her career as a city planner and has spent the past fifteen years working as a CAO in Nova Scotia. She has CAO experience in both rural and urban settings. She has a keen interest in council-CAO alignment through relationship building and strategic planning. She has a BA majoring in Geography from Mount Allision University and a graduate degree in Urban and Rural Planning from Dalhousie University. Tammy has taken numerous certificate programs in local government administration and leadership development.

Jamie Doyle currently serves as the CAO for the Town of Lunenburg, Nova Scotia, and previously served as the CAO of the Regional Municipality of Wood Buffalo (Fort McMurray), Alberta, where he was also the deputy CAO and director of planning and development. Jamie served as combat engineer with 45 Field Engineer Squadron of the Canadian Armed Forces in Sydney, Nova Scotia. He has a degree in Community Design from Dalhousie University, and a graduate diploma in Professional Project Management and a Municipal Executive Certificate from the University of Alberta. In all of Jamie's roles, he has experienced numerous crises. Most notable, however, was the 2016 wildfire in Fort McMurray.

Robert Earl has been a municipal leader for the past twenty-five years and is currently serving as CAO for the City of Colwood on Vancouver Island. Robert is a strategic and results-focused leader who has been recognized for his approach to municipal leadership. He was profiled in David Siegel's 2015 book *Leaders in the Shadows: The Leadership Qualities of Municipal Chief Administrative Officers*. He empowers his teams to take risks, be creative, and continually seek out ways to improve municipal programs and services.

Jeff Fielding is an award-winning local government leader. He has served as city manager of Calgary, Burlington, London, and Kitchener, and has held executive positions with Toronto and Winnipeg. He has taught in the University of Winnipeg's Geography Department, the University of Manitoba's City Planning program, and Western University's Ivey School of Business in the MBA and Executive MBA programs. Jeff is an Executive-in-Residence at the Ian O. Ihnatowycz Institute for Leadership at the Ivey School of Business, and currently works as a strategic advisor at Colliers Project Leaders.

John E. Fleming is especially qualified to write on the subject of the relationship between city managers and senior provincial and federal officials. He served four different municipalities in two different provinces over a twenty-three-year career in local government, ranging from single-tier municipalities to complex regional governments. For eleven of those municipal years, John was CAO/city administrator and prior to that in several senior departmental management positions. He capped off that long public service career serving as deputy minister in four different portfolios, where there were always contentious federal-provincial-territorial jurisdictional issues with which to contend, often with significance for local government. In his "retirement," John is heavily engaged in board governance: teaching, consulting, and sitting on numerous boards of directors. Keeping his municipal connections active, he continues to serve as a municipal integrity commissioner in the Greater Toronto Area.

Bill Given first joined the council of Grande Prairie, Alberta, in 2001 as an alderman, becoming at age twenty-four the youngest person ever elected to a seat on that council. He was re-elected in 2004 and 2007 and was successful in his bid for the mayor's seat in 2010, when he became the youngest mayor in the city's history. In December 2020, near the conclusion of his third term as mayor, Bill left elected office to take on the role of CAO for the Municipality of Jasper, in Alberta's Rocky Mountains. Bill has a Certificate in Local Authority Administration from the University of Alberta and a Master of Arts in Leadership from Royal Roads University.

Kate Graham researches, writes, speaks, and teaches about politics in Canada. She holds a PhD in Political Science (Local Government) from Western University, and now teaches at Western and Huron University College. Before entering academia, she spent ten years working in local government, most recently as Director, Community & Economic Innovation, at the City of London, Ontario. Kate is the creator and host of the Canada 2020 No Second Chances podcast, and has published two books. She continues to champion empowered local governments in her political and professional pursuits.

Tony Haddad is a senior advisor with StrategyCorp, a consulting and government relations firm. Retired in 2019 as the CAO for the Town of Tecumseh, Ontario, he has extensive, career-long experience in municipal finance and public administration. He has since been interim CAO for the Town of Amherstburg and the Municipality of Chatham-Kent, both in Ontario. Previously, he held executive positions with Regional Municipality of York, the Town of Oakville, the City of Windsor, and

Transit Windsor. He is a past president of AMCTO, was a director with the OMAA, is Chair of TransForm Shared Services Organization, Treasurer of Sun County AAA Minor Hockey Association, and President of the Circle of 7, and served as Secretary-Treasurer of the Tecumseh Police Services Board. He is also a member of the Advisory Committee at the School of Public Policy & Administration at York University. Tony holds a Master's degree in business and professional accreditations from public sector associations in Canada and the United States. He is the recipient of the St Clair College Alumni of Distinction Award, AMCTO's Prestige Award, and is an Honorary Member of OMAA.

Shirley Hoy's public service career spanned more than thirty years. She started her career in municipal government in 1980 in the former Metro Toronto. Between 1991 to 1996, she worked in the Ontario government as assistant deputy minister in three different ministries. She then returned to the City of Toronto as commissioner of community and neighbourhood services, and between 2001 to 2008 as city manager. From 2009 to 2014, she served as CEO of the Toronto Lands Corporation, a wholly owned subsidiary of the Toronto District School Board. Since 2014, she has been a senior advisor with StrategyCorp. With regard to volunteer activities, she has served as chair of the Governing Council of the University of Toronto and chair of the Board of Trustees of the United Way of Greater Toronto, and is currently a member of the Ontario Universities Council on Quality Assurance.

Marie-Hélène Lajoie was trained and worked as a lawyer before becoming head of the litigation department, first for the City of Aylmer, Quebec, then for the new amalgamated City of Gatineau, Quebec. In 2004, she was promoted to deputy CAO, and became CAO from 2013 to 2021. Since that day, on top of everyday business, she had to steer Gatineau's administration through a difficult period when many natural disasters happened one after the other. She was the first woman to head the administration of one of the big municipalities in Quebec. In 2016, after being involved for many years, she assumed the presidency of the Canadian Association of Municipal Administrators (CAMA), another first for a woman. Awarded the Order of Merit by the University of Ottawa's Faculty of Law in 2019, she now teaches in the Faculty's Civil Law section, as part of the Quebec Bar's Continuing Education Program. She is regularly invited to be a speaker by various associations.

John Leeburn established his human resources/organizational development consulting practice (https://driveod.ca/) in the summer of 2018 after thirty-one years in municipal government. He is also an instructor in the public administration division at Capilano University. He is a proud member of the small, but mighty group of municipal CAOs whose background and training was in human resources. John served in the City of New Westminster and the City of Maple Ridge, and retired after six years as the CAO in Port Coquitlam, all in British Columbia. John has a Batchelor of Commerce from the University of British Columbia, specializing in industrial relations, and an MBA from Simon Fraser University, where he wrote his provocatively titled thesis, "Does Size Matter: An Analysis of the Rationale for Municipal Amalgamation in Canada."

Gerard Lewis has over twenty-seven years of municipal leadership experience. He was the City Clerk and Chief Administrative Officer of the City of Mount Pearl, Newfoundland and Labrador, for twenty-two years, and prior to that was the Town Clerk for Gander, Newfoundland and Labrador. He has diplomas and certifications from the University of St Mary's, Alberta, Dalhousie University, and Memorial University of Newfoundland, and holds a Certified Municipal Clerk and Master Municipal Clerk designation from the International Institute of Municipal Clerks. He has served as President of Municipal Training and Development Corporation, Professional Municipal Administrators, and Newfoundland and Labrador Municipal Employee Benefits, Inc., and Director of the Canadian Association of Municipal Administrators. He has trained municipal government officials across Newfoundland and Labrador, Canada, and the Philippines. In 2012 he was awarded the Queen Elizabeth 11 Diamond Jubilee Medal. In 2012, Gerard co-founded LW Consulting, a leading Newfoundland and Labrador municipal consulting company. Today, he balances his time between LW Consulting, and his family.

Don Lidstone has practised municipal law since 1980. He is the founding partner of Lidstone & Company, a national law firm that acts for local governments. His focus is in the areas of local government governance, finance, land use, and bylaws. He has chaired numerous boards and commissions, published many papers and manuals, and consulted on the development of the BC *Community Charter* as well as other municipal statutes in several provinces and territories. He was designated Queen's Counsel in 2008.

Bruce Macgregor is a senior management executive with more than three decades of public service experience. Following early experience in the private sector, he served in senior roles in upper- and lower-tier municipalities. Through fifteen years as CAO for the Regional

Municipality of York, Ontario, he has overseen services to more than 1.2 million residents across nine local municipalities. Bruce has driven enduring changes in the delivery of critical infrastructure and programs, advancing longer-term perspectives and multiyear budgeting while fostering leadership strengths throughout the organization. He holds an undergraduate degree in engineering from the University of Toronto and has completed post-graduate studies (business) at the University of Toronto and Queen's University.

Chris MacPherson has worked in the City of Fredericton Office of the CAO for the past twenty years, the past ten as CAO. Prior to that, he held several senior positions within the City of Fredericton in a career that has spanned forty-five years. He is a graduate of the University of New Brunswick with degrees in Physical Education, Business Administration, and an MA. He is a graduate of the Senior Executives in State and Local Government certificate program from the JFK School of Government at Harvard University. He has a Lean 6 Sigma Green and Black Belt in process improvement. He is a past president and Honorary Life Member of CAMA, past president of the Institute of Public Administration of Canada (IPAC – Fredericton regional group), and the current International VP of the International City/County Management Association.

Ann Mitchell has more than twenty-six years' experience working in local government, and is passionate about her field. She has worked mainly in smaller municipalities, which she credits as fostering an environment of innovation and creativity. She is a firm believer in regional collaboration and has practised this in every one of her municipalities. Ann received her BA from Lakehead University and her Master of Municipal Leadership through the Schulich School of Business at York University. She completed her Diploma of Municipal Management and Certified Municipal Officer through AMCTO. A lifelong learner, Ann is currently completing a Master of Arts in Leadership at Royal Roads University, where her thesis is concentrating on the critical role of the CAO-council relationship.

Pat Moyle has over thirty-five years of leadership experience as CAO, city manager, and commissioner for a variety of Canadian municipalities. As CAO, he has successfully developed and implemented organizational change, launched comprehensive project management systems, developed practical and measurable strategic plans, created new budget systems, and improved the relationship between elected officials and the civic administration. He has also been active in municipal-provincial relations as the Executive Director of the Association of Municipalities of Ontario and has served on several intergovernmental panels. He currently has a consulting practice specializing in service and process reviews, mediation, executive compensation plans, interim CAO assignments, and managing executive recruiting.

Jim Pine has held a variety of leadership roles in both Ontario's public service and the municipal sector over the past forty-one years. For thirty-two of those years, he has served as a CAO in a number of municipalities, including his current employer, the County of Hastings, Ontario. He has been active throughout his career in provincial – municipal affairs. Jim, along with his colleague Tony Haddad, continue to lead *Onward*, an initiative to raise awareness of the demographic challenges facing municipal employers. Since 2010 Jim has been a senior member of the Eastern Ontario Regional Network, a municipal not-for-profit corporation committed to improving broadband and cellular connectivity across the region.

Pierre Prévost is an economist specializing in municipal affairs and a professional consultant with municipalities in Quebec. Throughout his career, he has occupied various positions in municipal management and acted as advisor for more than fifty municipalities, regional municipalities, and municipal transit services. Committed to the necessity of improving testimony and knowledge transfer at the municipal level, he has published three books on municipal management and politics. He also teaches at the Université du Québec à Montréal, where he is an associate professor in the Department of Political Science, mainly in the Municipal Services Management Program.

Linda Rapp acquired her first job with the City of Whitehorse, Yukon, as a recreation programmer in 1984. Linda's passion and commitment to community development led her to work closely on several significant community-led initiatives with local non-profit groups and organizations. Linda took advantage of many diverse corporate leadership development opportunities and eventually worked her way up to leisure services supervisor (1987), to manager, parks and recreation (2001), to director, community and recreation services (2012). In 2017 Linda accepted the position of interim city manager and was appointed permanently to this role in 2018.

Jag Sharma is a results-driven executive whose career has spanned private, Crown corporation, and public sectors in progressive leadership roles. He is currently President and CEO of Toronto Community Housing; previously, he was the city manager of the City of Oshawa and CAO for the Town of Newmarket, Ontario. Jag holds an MBA from Queen's University, and a BSc in Electrical Engineering, and is a practised Lean Six Sigma Black Belt professional. As well, he served on the board of OMAA for many years and supports the United Way, Greater Toronto Area, currently as a cabinet member representing Toronto Community Housing.

Gail Stephens was the City of Winnipeg's first CAO, replacing a board of commissioners; she also served as city manager for the City of Victoria. In those roles, she led many large initiatives, including the sale of Winnipeg Hydro, downtown revitalization projects, internal restructuring, and large capital infrastructure developments. She was CEO of the BC Pension Corporation and interim president and CEO of the Canadian Museum for Human Rights. She has worked in both the private and public sectors as a chief financial officer. She currently sits as a director on several public and not-for-profit boards, and provides management consulting services to a variety of clients. Gail has the professional accounting designation FCPA, FCGA. She has received numerous awards and recognition throughout her career.

David Szwarc is a senior advisor with StrategyCorp and a Distinguished Fellow with the School of Policy Studies at Queen's University. He is an experienced executive who has held positions as CAO, commissioner, and director with the Regional Municipality of Peel; community services manager with the province of Ontario; and director with the Regional Municipality of Halton. He is a guest lecturer in the MPA programs at the School of Public Policy, University of Toronto, and School of Policy Studies, Queen's University. David holds a Master's Degree in Public Administration from Queen's University, a BA from the University of Toronto, and an Executive Certificate in Public Leadership from Harvard University.

Zack Taylor is an associate professor of political science at Western University, where he teaches in the Local Government Program and is Director of the Centre for Urban Policy and Local Governance. He is also a fellow at the Institute on Municipal Finance and Governance at the University of Toronto and a non-practising Registered Professional Planner.

Carl Zehr is the former mayor of the City of Kitchener (1997–2014), a councillor for nine years prior to that, and a Region of Waterloo councillor for seven terms. He provided leadership in the creation of a transformative economic development strategy to broaden the economic base of the city and region. He played an active role on the Federation of Canadian Municipalities' Big City Mayors' Caucus and was its chair (2008–11). Upon his retirement in 2014, the square in front of Kitchener city hall was renamed Carl Zehr Square. Carl has the professional accounting designation FCPA, FCGA. He is a former governor and president of the Certified General Accountants Association of Ontario, as well as a former Director of CGA Canada.

Milton Keynes UK
Ingram Content Group UK Ltd.
UKHW012144210424
441411UK00002B/35